WHAT
Middletown
READ

A VOLUME IN THE SERIES

Studies in Print Culture and the History of the Book

EDITED BY

Greg Barnhisel

Robert A. Gross

Joan Shelley Rubin

Michael Winship

WHAT Middletown READ

PRINT CULTURE IN AN AMERICAN SMALL CITY

Frank Felsenstein
and
James J. Connolly

University of Massachusetts Press
Amherst and Boston

ISBN 978-1-62534-141-9 (paperback); 140-2 (hardcover)

Designed by Sally Nichols
Set in Adobe Minion Pro
Printed and bound by Sheridan Books, Inc.

Library of Congress Cataloging-in-Publication Data

Felsenstein, Frank.
What Middletown read : print culture in an American small city / Frank Felsenstein
and James J. Connolly.
pages cm. — (Studies in print culture and the history of the book)
Includes bibliographical references and index.
ISBN 978-1-62534-140-2 (hardcover : alk. paper) — ISBN 978-1-62534-141-9 (pbk. : alk. paper)
1. Books and reading—Indiana—Muncie—History—19th century. 2. Books and reading—
Indiana—Muncie—History—20th century. 3. Muncie Public Library—History—19th century.
4. Muncie Public Library—History—20th century. 5. Libraries and community—Indiana—
Muncie—History. I. Connolly, James J., 1962– II. Title.
Z1003.3.I6F45 2015
028´.909112650909034—dc23
2014050133

British Library Cataloguing-in-Publication Data
A catalogue record for this book is available from the British Library.

This publication is produced in part with support from
Ball State University, Muncie, Indiana.

For Carole, and for Beth

"The last thing one knows when writing a book
is what to put first."—Pascal

Contents

Acknowledgments

In one of America's best-loved musicals, *The Music Man* (1957), Meredith Willson depicted as his leading figure "Professor" Harold Hill, a traveling salesman and practiced con artist, who unlooses his charms on a small Midwestern city in 1912. Hill's well-rehearsed scam is thwarted only because he falls in love with Miss Marion Paroo, the town's librarian, and decides to stay on and face the consequences of his fraud. Implicitly, Willson, who grew up in the Midwest—Mason City, Iowa—during the early years of the twentieth century, confirms that, in more than one sense, the small town library is the unacknowledged (though in this case not unsung!) "heart" of the community.

As far as we are aware, Kate Wilson, the real-life librarian at the old Muncie Public Library during the period for which the What Middletown Read (WMR) archive survives, was never similarly courted and won. Her legacy is transcriptional rather than romantic, since, throughout her tenure as librarian, she assiduously recorded every single borrowing transaction for a period of more than ten years, covering most of the 1890s and into the opening years of the twentieth century. Although only rediscovered in 2003, most of these records are intact, giving us an unprecedented overview of the reading habits of the community that she served.

Cultural historians are beginning to appreciate the important place accorded to books and to reading in the lives of ordinary people across

America in the era following the Civil War. The shaping of the nation, the aspirations of an era that experienced inexorable change yet also clung to traditional values, and even the ethos of the Gilded Age are mirrored, albeit sometimes obliquely, in what people chose to read. The magnitude of the printed word in everyday lives, even before the founding of Muncie's library, can be illustrated by the will of a pioneering citizen, Samuel P. Wilson, Kate's own father, which was recorded by the clerk of the county court on August 5, 1873. In apparent descending order of substance, Samuel bequeathed to his wife "all of my books, household furniture, house furnishing goods, family wearing apparel, and family stores, for her use and support and the use and support of those members of my family who may reside with her after my decease." If the Wilson family was more than usually attached to the inherent value of books, the extensive borrowing records of the Muncie Public Library lead us to believe that their attachment was far from unique. Indeed, in terms of continuity, it could be argued that the library was to remain a habitually patronized location in the lives of everyday citizens through the century that followed. As a more recent manifestation of this continuity, it is perhaps significant that, throughout the period we spent constructing the WMR database and writing and researching this book, the director of the Muncie Public Library has been Virginia Nilles, who is a collateral descendant of Kate Wilson.

Ms. Nilles is but the first of many individuals without whose active cooperation and very real help neither the database nor this book would have been possible. Her colleagues at the Muncie Public Library, most particularly Mary Lou Gentis, Beth Kroehler, and Sara McKinley, guided us, backs bent double by necessity, up to the closed attic space of the newly renovated 1904 Carnegie building in which the archive was found, and alerted us to the existence of volumes of the manuscript diaries of Tom Ryan and Norene Hawk. Throughout, they and their staff were always enthusiastic, courteous, and expeditious in responding to our many otherwise unresolved questions. It was fitting that the public launch of the What Middletown Read database in March 2011 should have taken place before a packed audience in the Muncie Public Library.

Close cooperation with Archives and Special Collections in the Bracken Library at neighboring Ball State University, where we are both on the faculty, was instrumental in getting our project off the ground. Much of the manuscript material on which we based our research is in a fragile condition, and one of the first tasks was to digitize all of it, and make it globally accessible on the Web through the Bracken Library's Digital Media Repository. This was simultaneously an act of preservation that also allowed us to enhance and clarify often difficult to read documents. Central to this complex operation is our colleague John B. Straw, assistant dean for digital initiatives and special collections. Our thanks go to him and the team that worked under him, and to Arthur Hafner, dean of BSU's libraries.

A second overlapping team based in the Bracken Library took responsibility for designing and implementing the WMR database, from which so much of the statistical and other primary information in this book is culled. We were fortunate in being able to hire over a two-year period a capable web designer in Daniel J. Lakes. After many intensive meetings and much close discussion, our team came to a critical recognition that, rather than employing an off-the-shelf program, our database needed to be custom-designed in order to perform the quite complex tasks we expected of it. In making this decision and advancing the project, we received substantial help and benefited greatly from the expertise of Bradley D. Faust, Budi Wibowo, and Katharine Leigh. Cataloging staff working under Leigh were responsible for the precise identification (no small task!) and subsequent data entry of more than eleven thousand books that were inscribed in the manuscript catalog of the old Muncie Public Library between 1874 and 1903. Brad Hostetler also assisted us during the initial stages of developing the database.

BSU's English and history departments and, more particularly, the Honors College, were the wellsprings of our employment of several cohorts of undergraduate and graduate students, who, through the use of (among other sources) the U.S. census and local city directories, helped to profile many of the more than six thousand library patrons. The project staff, catalogers, and student researchers who were instrumental in compiling the database are separately listed on the WMR website at www.bsu.edu/libraries/wmr/project_staff.php. Among those who (among other tasks too numerous to list here) combed through contemporary local newspapers, looking to expand our knowledge of the place of books and reading in late nineteenth-century Muncie, we thank Jennifer Banning, Shannon Buchanan, Rebecca L. Jackson, Tricia Johnson, Kelly Hacker Jones, Tara Olivero, Meghan Reidy, Monica Robison, Michael Smith, and Rich Usdowski. Both Maria Staton and Abigail E. Comber, who in turn worked as WMR student project managers, later completed their doctorates in the English department. Our gratitude also extends to our two academic deans, James Ruebel, dean of the Honors College, and Michael A. Maggiotto, dean of the College of Sciences and Humanities, for their consistent enthusiasm and support of our efforts. Throughout, our work has been channeled through Ball State's Center for Middletown Studies.

Drawing from outside BSU, we were privileged to have a number of luminaries in the field of book history as honorary consultants for the project:

the late Robin Alston, Linda Connors, Robert Darnton, Christine Ferdinand, Christine Pawley, Jonathan Rose, and Wayne A. Wiegand. Most of these eminent leaders in their field visited Muncie to inspect the WMR archive, and all were generous with their advice and support. Christine Pawley's intelligent counsel has been especially valuable from the outset of the project. When Wayne Wiegand, widely known as the dean of American library historians, first scrutinized the records and was heard to mutter under his breath the word "Gold," we knew that there had to be value to our discovery!

We received specific assistance from a large number of individuals, and in acknowledging the following by name we are conscious that, by default rather than intention, we may be omitting others who contributed to the project. For their particular contribution, we acknowledge the very real help of Jane Aikin, Tom Glynn, Bruce Geelhoed, Mark Kanter, Robert Morris, Stephen Pentecost, John Plotz, James L. Pyle, Joel Shrock, Lynne Tatlock, Anne Trubek, Abigail Van Slyck, and Arthur P. Young. On a personal level, our largest debt is to our families, and particularly to Carole Felsenstein and Beth Hawke, for living with this project so patiently and for so long.

As well as the libraries already named, we are happy to express our gratitude to Jane Gorjevsky and the staff at the Butler Library at Columbia University in New York for making available to us through microfilm the archives of the Carnegie Foundation.

Without very generous institutional funding, the What Middletown Read project would be no more than a distant aspiration. Initial resources came as seed money from the office of Terry King, BSU's provost. That was followed with a progress grant from the Gladys Krieble Delmas Foundation. But by far the largest subvention we received was from the National Endowment for the Humanities as a Collaborative Research Grant. The NEH grant (reference number RZ-51013-09) supported both "the creation of a freely accessible digital database of library records from the Muncie, Indiana public library" and the preparation for publication of a complementary scholarly study. Publication of this book fulfills the second part of our commitment. It is our best way of thanking our funders, and also an acknowledgment of the good guidance we received from BSU's Sponsored Programs Office, whose staff greatly facilitated our efforts in pursuit of external support.

During the ten years and rising that we have been engaged in the WMR project, we have often been invited to share our findings at academic conferences and other presentations, both in the United States and abroad. Among these are an early offering at the Print Networks Conference on the History of the British Book Trade, which took place in England in 2005 at the University of Birmingham; papers at the annual conference of the Society for the History of Authorship, Reading and Publishing (SHARP), in Minneapolis in 2007, and at Trinity College, Dublin, in 2012; a team exposition of our findings at the Libraries History Seminar XII (Library History Round Table of the American Library Association), held at the University of Wisconsin–Madison in 2010; an at-home rendering of some of our findings at an international conference titled "Print Culture Histories Beyond the Metropolis," sponsored by the NEH and held at Ball State in 2013; and a full demonstration of the database and discussion of its genesis at the "Community Libraries: Connecting Readers in the Atlantic World" International Conference, in Chicago, which was sponsored by the U.K. Arts and Humanities Research Council and took place in 2014. We thank our various audiences at these and other presentations for their stimulating questions, which often extended our own thinking beyond the immediate parameters of our project. Versions of our talks at Birmingham and Madison were later published as separate essays in collected volumes, and have been considerably reworked and refined for the present book.

Our relations with our publisher, University of Massachusetts Press, have been never less than cordial, and for that we wish to thank in particular Brian Halley, senior editor with responsibility for the Studies in Print Culture and the History of the Book series, and Mary Bellino, our very capable manuscript editor. From the peer reading of our text through to publication, Brian's steady hand and good humor have only facilitated what might otherwise have been a complicated process. Mary's close reading of our text has proved particularly salutary, often making us rethink our postulations and correct where necessary. We also thank our referees for their careful reading of the initial manuscript and their valuable advice.

When, in one of the most memorable lyrics from *The Music Man*, Professor Harold Hill sings that "the civilized world accepts as unforgivable sin / Any talking out loud with any librarian," he echoes one of the first rules of a library, one that had to be invoked on the opening day of the reading room of the Muncie Public Library in 1875. It is our hope that an audible end result of the "What Middletown Read" project, now in concurrence both as a database and a book, will be a far greater comprehension of that "civilized world" within its broader context.

Introduction

We know very little about Maude Smith. Census records tell us she was born in Wayne County, Indiana, in 1880, the second of five children born to James Smith, an insurance agent, and his wife, Tina. She graduated from Muncie High School in 1899—an unusual achievement in a community where most children began working on a farm or in a factory before the age of eighteen—and took a job as a clerk at the Indiana Bridge Works. She married Cassius Allison, a carpenter's son who was also from Muncie, in 1908, and soon moved to Toledo, Ohio, where her husband took up work as an inspector in an auto parts factory. The couple had no children. Maude was widowed in 1934 and died in 1967, at the age of eighty-six.[1] Beyond these bare facts, her life remains mostly elusive. Vital statistics tell us nothing about the life of her mind, about her ambitions, her opinions, or her personality.

We can, however, recover one small but significant part of her intellectual life. Rediscovered circulation records from the Muncie Public Library permit us to ascertain which books Maude Smith borrowed over a period of more than three years. Smith joined the library on August 29, 1899, just two months after graduating from high school, and the library recorded exactly one hundred loans to her account between that date and December 3, 1902, when the extant circulation records end. The impression conveyed by her choices was of a person hungering to understand the world beyond her own small but growing eastern Indiana town. She quite often borrowed books that told stories of foreign lands, including fictional tales of travel, intrigue, and romance, and even otherworldly journeys. Her other selections included a healthy dose of conventional romantic fiction of the sort borrowed regularly by women from middle-class backgrounds and occasional children's books, presumably for her brother and sister Emmet and Emma, twins who turned ten just after she joined the library.

Smith appears in the historical record in at least one other place, and that reference, when joined with her borrowing records, reinforces our sense that she found in books a means to experience the world beyond her hometown. Smith was one of nine charter members of the Tourist Club of Muncie. The purpose of the club was to study "the life, literature, and peoples in other lands" and to report on them in epistolary form. Thus each meeting featured letters composed by club members, written as if they were corresponding while traveling abroad. The letters were "flights of fancy," derived from research into the customs and character of various locales.[2]

The borrowing records show that Smith, along with several other club members, used library holdings to help them prepare their letters. On three occasions in 1900 and 1901 Smith took home George Edward Raum's *Tour around the World,* with its sketches of the author's travels through four continents. Several of her letters likely described European destinations; she borrowed *A Tour around the World by General Grant,* the former president's account of his travels in the British Isles, Belgium, and Germany, and Curtis Guild's *Abroad Again,* which reported on a tour of Europe. Smith likely drew on Guild's discussion of France and Italy to prepare her invented correspondence, since she borrowed *Stories and Sights of France and Italy* just three days before taking out *Abroad Again.* Several months later she brought home Eliza Scidmore's *China: The Long-Lived Empire,* which in tandem with Raum's *Tour,* borrowed one day earlier, appears to have formed the basis of a letter to the club about the Middle Kingdom.

Even with this detail, the records at our disposal do not tell us everything we might wish to know about Maude Smith's reading experiences. No letters presented to the Tourist Club are known to survive. Nor do we have any other testimony from Smith or her fellow club members about the impressions they formed from their researches into foreign lands. We do not even know for certain that she read these travel books, although her borrowing patterns suggest strongly that she did at least consult them. Nevertheless, when we add a bit of social context we begin to get a sense of Smith's interests and aspirations from the list of books she borrowed over a period of roughly three years. She emerges from our inquiry as a curious young woman anxious to learn about the world beyond her hometown through print, a quality that cannot be derived from the skeletal information provided by census and burial records.

This glimpse into Smith's library records illustrates the value of the historical study of reading. Knowing something about the books that ordinary people read and how they put them to use in their lives opens up a dimension of historical experience that often eludes us. By tracing patterns of reading choices by individuals, groups, and communities, we gain some sense of their imaginative and emotional experiences. And for most of the industrial era, when print was the predominant medium of communication, we also gain a better sense of how ordinary people engaged with the wider world and situated themselves within it.

We have access to the borrowing choices made by Smith and several thousand of her neighbors through the discovery of the circulation records of the Muncie Public Library covering the years 1891 to 1902, with one two-and-a-half-year gap, from late May 1892 to early November 1894 (these records, we believe, were destroyed as a precautionary measure after a smallpox epidemic). Logs recording each circulation transaction, corresponding to numbered lists of patrons and books, permit us to determine who borrowed what during those years. These original records provide sufficient details for researchers to obtain demographic particulars about the majority of borrowers and bibliographic information about virtually all of the books and periodicals in the library's collection. These materials have been compiled and incorporated into a searchable resource, the What Middletown Read (WMR) database, which is freely accessible online (see the appendix for details about the database and original sources). The database includes approximately 175,000 individual loan records and constitutes the largest body of data about American library borrowing patterns during this historical period that we currently have available to us.[3]

We believe that the discovery of these circulation records and their digitization provide new ways to investigate print culture. With that in mind, our aims for this book are twofold. First, we seek to describe the evolving culture of print in a single, emblematic American community around the turn of the twentieth century. That period saw a dramatic increase in the circulation of books, magazines, and newspapers, a development integrally tied to broader social and economic transformations. Our second, complementary aim is to explain the origins and demonstrate the value of a digital resource such as the What Middletown Read database. We hope our study provides a guide for those interested in using the database in their own research, as well as an encouragement to scholars to seek out similar data.

While the WMR database cannot by itself provide access to the intimate details of individual or collective reading experiences, it helps us answer the question of who read what, or, more precisely, who borrowed what. The demographic details it supplies for many users allow inquiry into social patterns of borrowing, while the bibliographic details for each book permit examination of the sorts of borrowers attracted to particular titles, authors, or genres. More broadly, the database can also provide us with clues about why borrowers chose the books they did, about the relationship between readers in one community and their public library, about the nature of the public library as an institution of reading, and about the culture of print in a rapidly industrializing community.

There are of course limits to the evidence provided in the WMR database. Most obvious is the issue of whether a book borrowed was a book read. Clearly, such was not the case in every instance. Yet just as clearly, as Christine Pawley has argued, regular library use strongly suggests that the books taken out were read. It is difficult to imagine another explanation for repeated library visits.[4] The exact circumstances of the reading itself, if and when it occurred, can only be determined in a few cases, and from our sources we cannot know what a person made of what he or she read. Any study of library use must also acknowledge that even the most regular borrowers also had other sources of reading material, and circulation records give us evidence of only a fraction of their reading experiences. Finally, an important limitation of the Muncie library's records follows from the rather loose policy adopted by the staff with regard to the use of library cards. In a significant minority of circulation transactions, librarians permitted one person to use the card (and account) of another to borrow a book. Such cases are recorded in the circulation ledgers, where the account number tied to a given loan does not match the name entered as a borrower. These "borrowed card" transactions account for roughly 10 percent of all loans, and any analysis of the data must take this into account. Yet even with these caveats, the WMR database constitutes a fertile resource for understanding library usage and popular reading choices.

The database and this book take their name from Robert and Helen Lynd's *Middletown: A Study in American Culture* (1929), the first of a series of sociological studies examining Muncie over the course of the twentieth century. During that time the city has served as a barometer of American social trends, and it has been at the center of debates over what constitutes a typical American community.[5] It is almost certainly the most closely studied city of its size in the United States. Had extensive circulation records from a public library of this era been discovered in another community, they would have been of significant value for understanding reading patterns in the United States. That they were discovered in "Middletown," a community that has served as a laboratory for understanding modern American life, seems especially serendipitous.

One benefit of the discovery of these records is that they help us flesh out the cultural life in the period the Lynds employed as a baseline for their research. Their original Middletown book measured changes in various aspects of the community, comparing the industrialized city of the 1920s with its less fully developed predecessor of the 1890s. The Lynds even took note of library use as part of their measurement of the role of reading as a leisure-time activity, noting a decline in the intensity of reading as new activities and technologies gained in popularity. The evidence from the WMR database and other sources supports their contention that the social life of the 1890s was more print-centered (despite the comparative abundance of printed matter available during the 1920s), if only because competition from radio, films, and phonographs had not yet materialized. But our research also suggests a substantial engagement with the cultural currents of the day in a fashion that resembles what the Lynds found for the later period, especially among the group that the Lynds would later label the "business class."[6]

This book follows the example set by the Lynds in another respect as well. Just as they used Muncie as a microcosm from which to generalize about the evolution of modern American life, we draw on the circulation details provided by the WMR database, along with other sources, to explore broad trends in American print culture around the turn of the century. Our sources provide us with a good sense of how the library operated, about its development from a small-town institution into a cultural center in a rapidly growing industrial community, and about the role of ordinary users in shaping its character. The circulation data, which document precise borrowing choices spread over an eleven-year period, along with diaries, newspaper reports, and other archival materials, reveal something of the reading habits and popular tastes that prevailed in this community at this time, the demographic patterns tied to those habits and tastes, and the place of reading in the lives of ordinary people.

These records also afford us a glimpse of the way in which ordinary Americans such as Maude Smith pursued cosmopolitan ambitions through reading. As the case of Smith and the Tourist Club illustrates, other historical evidence, ranging from diaries to club records to government reports, allows us to set reading behavior in its historical context and gain a clearer sense of how texts were used. More broadly, we gain from these methods a fuller sense of how print culture developed, not in the metropolitan centers of American intellectual and cultural life but in a provincial outpost, albeit one destined to become an emblem of middle-American life in the modern era.

We do not contend that Muncie, in its role as "Middletown," fully represents a typical American community. But we do see its experience of rapid industrialization and population growth (from a small town of 5,000 people in 1880 to a bustling city of nearly 21,000 in 1900) as a common one. During that time, the northeastern and midwestern portions of the country experienced dramatic urban growth and substantial industrialization; Muncie's development certainly fits that pattern. The social questions arising out of these developments, including an intensifying process of class formation, were very much in evidence during these years, as was the movement toward a more integrated national economy and culture.

Readers and Their Library

The Muncie Public Library opened in 1875, and during its first twenty-eight years of operation it resided in two upstairs rooms of the City Building in downtown Muncie. As these humble accommodations suggest, it was a modest operation, funded initially by stock purchased by local citizens and small contributions from city coffers. The initial collection numbered fewer than two thousand books, most acquired by the purchase of a semiprivate library run by the local postmaster and contributions from a few residents. Until 1902 it was overseen by a succession of local women, none of them trained as librarians. The collection grew steadily, as did the number of patrons—that is, those who had registered for library cards—with both counts increasing markedly during the 1890s, following the discovery of a large supply of natural gas in the region that fueled a burst of industrialization and population growth in Muncie. By the beginning of the twentieth century Muncie had expanded to the point where a new, more up-to-date library was required in keeping with the city's expanded ambitions. The library board re-formed, hired a professionally trained librarian, and with the assistance of funds from Andrew Carnegie opened a suitably impressive building on the edge of the downtown district.

The scale of the investment in the new library suggests the importance accorded it by local residents. Throughout the 1890s, as the "gas boom" prompted rapid expansion, Muncie's boosters had cited the library as evidence of the city's cultural sophistication and described it as a means for the education and advancement of the citizenry. Usage increased steadily as the library grew. In 1900 the library recorded more than 23,000 loans of books and periodicals, a notable increase over previous years and a reflection of the growing demand for printed material in the city.

While boosters celebrated the library as a substantial cultural institution, day-to-day realities suggest it was also shaped by social patterns and cultural tensions. Institutional records make it clear that the library's leaders sought to influence the reading experiences of local patrons, though they were constrained by limited resources. The same records, along with circulation data, make it equally evident that patrons played a vital role in defining the character of the library, both by their presence there and by their borrowing choices. The majority of visitors were children, of almost every social description, and women from families headed by businessmen, professionals, and others with white-collar occupations. Their patronage, along with rules for decorum, marked the library as a respectable setting, and to some extent even a domestic space. (Organizers of a short-lived library for workingmen cited the public library's somewhat straitlaced social character as a principal reason for their undertaking.) The seemingly insatiable demand for popular, not especially edifying fiction also defined the library's function in ways its staff and directors did not necessarily intend.

By encouraging an examination of the role of a library in the life of its users, instead of the role of users in the life of the library, as Wayne Wiegand has phrased it, the WMR database helps reframe our understanding of the historical place of these institutions in their communities and in the wider society. The first historians of the public library movement cast it as a force for democracy and social mobility, echoing the claims advanced by professional librarians both then and now. Some subsequent scholarship took the opposite view: public libraries were tools for the social control of the lower classes. But Wiegand and other scholars have rejected both contentions and, more important, have dispensed with the core assumption they share: that there was a one-way flow of influence from library to patron. Reintroducing borrowers as active agents whose tastes and demands molded a library's catalog and operations, these scholars help us see public libraries in more complex, realistic terms, as entities that both shaped and were shaped by the communities they served. *What Middletown Read* affirms and amplifies their arguments.[7]

Borrowing Patterns and Reading Experiences

Considering library users as active agents draws our attention to the most elusive of historical phenomena, the reading experience. Although it was once seen as a passive process of reception, in which meanings produced by authors and conveyed by texts were received unchanged by readers, book historians now treat the interaction between text and reader as a dynamic process in which the reader plays an active role in creating meaning. Michel

De Certeau is among the scholars who have articulated the theoretical basis for such an approach, arguing that readers engage in "poaching," a process in which they construct their own idiosyncratic understandings of the meaning of any text, particularly as silent reading became the norm. If reading is approached in these terms, no two interpretations of a text are identical; each reader creates his or her own distinctive meanings, separate from what the text's author may have intended and separate from the meanings generated by other readers.[8]

Yet if every reader can construct her or his own interpretation of a text without limitations, common understandings of the same texts would be unlikely. Scholars have gotten past this difficulty by examining collectivities of readers. The impetus of this approach comes in large part from Stanley Fish's concept of interpretive communities. Fish argues that collections of readers, in his example literary scholars, did not operate in a vacuum but instead followed particular norms of interpretation that ensured that they at least approached a given text with a shared framework. Other scholars have broadened that insight and applied it to other groups, including sets of ordinary readers operating outside the academy. Roger Chartier has articulated a historical version of Fish's concept, in which groups of readers employed a common strategy of interpretation to make sense of texts through a process he calls "appropriation." This perspective has pushed historically oriented scholars of reading to consider how particular groups and settings have created meanings from books and other printed materials.[9]

The idea that the reading experience is not rooted simply in the text but also in the context is now a central element of print culture history. Few, if any, scholars in the field would argue that a reader is an entirely independent creator of purely idiosyncratic meaning. Instead, theorists have embarked on a search for "shared regularities," Chartier's phrase for the common interpretive approach adopted by historically situated groups of readers. These communities or audiences draw on a common fund of ideas, values, and perceptions as they interpret a text. That process is also constitutive, as the act of collective interpretation helps define the group, community, or nation.

The pursuit of contextualized reading experiences has taken many forms.[10] One cadre of scholars began to employ reader-response theory, a method that stresses the indeterminacy of textual meaning and seeks to situate readers in the historical and cultural contexts that define their reading experiences. Others have used ethnographic methods to focus on how specific groups developed reading practices in particular times and places.[11] More recently, the field has turned to developing a broadly gauged "social history of reading." This approach involves a wide range of research that draws on theories and techniques that consider a text in relationship to its authors, readers, and publishers and situates the act of reading in specific political, cultural, technological, and social contexts. Robert Darnton's idea of a "communication circuit" has been especially influential, if also controversial, in this regard. Still others seek an implied reader or audience in the text itself, or examine representations of readers for clues to the reading experience.[12]

A number of contemporary scholars have developed more concrete linkages between readers and text. Jonathan Rose's study *The Intellectual Life of the British Working Classes* is the foremost example of the use of autobiographies, diaries, and other primary evidence to recover the reading experiences and imaginative life of ordinary Britons during the nineteenth century. H. J. Jackson has examined reader annotations in her extensive studies of marginalia.[13] A team of English scholars created the Reading Experience Database, which aggregates comments about British texts for the period from 1450 to 1945, culled from diaries, marginalia, and other sources, offering opportunities to gauge individual and collective responses to texts. In Australia, researchers have compiled the Australian Common Reader, which (as of early 2015) makes available the circulation records and other historical records from seven small libraries.

In the United States, a handful of historians have used the records of private subscription libraries or other archival materials to document reading choices in the earlier periods of American history. David Hall's *Worlds of Wonder, Days of Judgment* employs library records as part of an effort to reconstruct less-than-orthodox religious ideas circulating among colonial New Englanders. Emily B. Todd's analysis of borrowing records from antebellum subscription libraries in Richmond and New Orleans uncovered an avid interest in popular fiction even in comparatively highbrow settings. Ronald Zboray's study *A Fictive People: Antebellum Economic Development and the American Reading Public* explored connections between economic patterns, the rise of a national culture, and individual reading choices. In each case, the introduction of historical readers and their borrowing choices into the broader field of cultural history revealed reading experiences less closely aligned to prevailing ideas of propriety and respectability.[14]

To date, the most thorough investigation of library circulation records is Christine Pawley's pathbreaking study of Osage, Iowa. Not only does her research go forward into the late nineteenth century, but it also examines the circulation records of a public library rather than a more exclusive subscription library. Pawley also succeeds in setting these records and the patterns they reveal into a richly drawn social portrait of a small midwestern town. She finds a reading public that gravitated toward popular fiction even when cultural authorities would prefer they stick to a more limited range of morally uplifting fare. But she also notes that these tastes generally did not challenge the Protestant-tinged, often nativist cultural ethos that prevailed in Osage and places like it. More provocatively, she finds an absence of sharp distinctions between the borrowing choices of men and women, even when books were devised for and marketed to one sex or the other. Pawley also moves beyond the library itself to explore the ways print culture helped define the community and how groups of women, Catholics, workers, and farmers organized their own alternative print cultures.

Pawley's work demonstrates the importance of contextualizing circulation records, both within the social patterns of a community and within its print culture. If, as Janice Radway has written, "meaning is defined socially rather than textually," it is necessary to situate reading choices and reading practices in concrete social contexts. Examining the circulation details of a busy library in Muncie, Indiana, a community that has already been richly documented, permits us to advance a number of arguments about historical reading experiences.[15]

The first of these connects reading with on-the-ground social change. Muncie, during the 1890s and early years of the twentieth century, was a city in the midst of a dramatic transformation. As the Lynds noted, the discovery of natural gas in the region not only fueled Muncie's industrial expansion and population growth but also set in motion a reconfiguration of the community's class structure. That process included a sorting of residents, both socioeconomically and geographically. The rise of industry produced a large jump in the number of wage-earning residents and a smaller increase in the city's middle class. By the middle of the 1890s Muncie had developed clearly demarcated residential districts for its rapidly growing population of workers and for members of a middle class that was also increasing in size, though not at the rate of the local working class. It should be noted, however, that this sorting was far from complete. The city still retained a substantial population of artisanal workers whose income and status paralleled that of the professional and managerial residents, and the boundaries between social classes remained permeable. Patterns of library use make it clear that the library's function within the community was shaped by these social dynamics. They also suggest that reading choices were related to social status in complex ways, as both reflections of social identities and a means of defining them.[16]

To a considerable extent, print also served to integrate the city with American society and culture. In a time and place in which the circulation of information and entertainment occurred chiefly through print, books, newspapers, and magazines were ubiquitous. By the end of 1902 the Muncie

Public Library held more than eleven thousand titles, but that was only a modest portion of the printed material available in the city. Muncie had three daily newspapers, with a fourth launched in 1899. Residents could now purchase books from a local bookstore, or from one of several drugstores; inexpensive books could be purchased through catalogs or through mail services that advertised in local newspapers.

While reading was most often undertaken as an individual endeavor, it also occurred in groups. During the 1870s and 1880s, the Woman's Club of Muncie, a small group of middle-class women, met regularly to discuss literature, and at least a half dozen similar organizations formed during the 1890s. Union locals established small lending libraries in these years, and several churches maintained reading rooms with modest collections. Both sets of institutions encouraged literary discussion among their members. There is also significant evidence of shared reading within families, including, in some instances, reading aloud. Although Muncie seems in certain respects a provincial place around the turn of the twentieth century, its residents had ready access to a range of printed material, encountered in a multiplicity of contexts, that offered means of experiencing the wider world.

Fiction was a key component of the printed material linking Muncie to life beyond the city limits. While locals read newspapers that often carried the latest reports from Washington, New York, and even Europe, as well as a growing number of national magazines, they also consumed fiction at a voracious rate. Even when borrowers are sorted demographically, whether by occupational standing, sex, or age, fiction constituted three-quarters (or more) of all books borrowed from the public library. Some of these selections were highbrow literature of the type that would have pleased the most discriminating librarians or teachers, but the vast majority of loans involved popular works that made only a modest literary mark in their day and are now long forgotten. There is ample evidence of the kind of intensive "binge reading" described by Emily Todd in antebellum Richmond and New Orleans, much of it in defiance of the prescriptions for good reading taking shape during the late nineteenth century, but tolerated and perhaps even promoted by the laissez-faire managerial style of the Muncie library's staff.[17]

The scale and detail of the What Middletown Read database allow us to make distinctions within this overall pattern. Perhaps most notable is the tendency among white-collar adult borrowers, most of whom were women, to take home newly published works of fiction, including in some instances stories serialized in popular magazines. In contrast, their blue-collar neighbors were less likely to borrow the newest material and a bit more likely to select older, more established titles. There are hints of this pattern among younger borrowers as well. It may be that users from more comfortable circumstances had access to home libraries that held classic titles, while those of lesser means relied on the public library for reading of every sort. Venturing further, we consider whether these choices signified greater attentiveness to the mass literary marketplace, a quality that might have served as a signifier of middle-class status as well as a characteristic of it.

Though rare, evidence gleaned from personal diaries provides us with a sharper sense of the central, if varied, role of reading and the library in everyday life. Such sources affirm that collective oral reading occurred within households, although individual silent reading was the norm. Seeking entertainment, formal and informal education, and a way of exploring the world beyond Muncie, ordinary residents turned to newspapers, magazines, and books, especially novels. As the diaries we explore in chapter 7 show, for a well-off, cosmopolitan young woman such as Sarah Heinsohn reading supplied a fund of cultural knowledge befitting her social status, though at times it took a back seat to social activities. For Norene Hawk, the daughter of a carriage maker, reading was a central part of daily life, a source of inspiration and escape. For a technically minded boy such as Tom Ryan, books and magazines offered a means of satisfying his curiosity about science and the physical world, even if hands-on tinkering more often captured his imagination. More generally, we know that children flocked to the library, where they borrowed and, it appears, often devoured books by popular authors such as Horatio Alger, Harry Castlemon (Charles Fosdick), Oliver Optic (William Taylor Adams), and Martha Finley.

Other source materials allow us to situate borrowing choices in the context of group activities that helped shape interpretive sensibilities. The library's collection supplemented school assignments, and we can at least occasionally see young pupils borrowing children's books as they learned to read, or older students selecting history, literature, and scientific works that augmented the high school curriculum. The records of the Woman's Club of Muncie, which evolved into a reform group during the 1890s, reveal that its members often turned to fiction as a means of exploring social questions. The club served as an interpretive community, encouraging its members to approach fiction in a manner similar to nonfiction: as evidence of how the world worked, as a stealthy means of venturing into the public arena at a time when women were supposed to remain in their feminine sphere, and perhaps even as a means of affirming that social problems could be resolved. Here, club records jibe with circulation data to suggest a particular approach to reading for a specific segment of the community.

In sum, set into its historical context, the information assembled in the

What Middletown Read database offers us a glimpse of the place of books and reading in the lives of ordinary Americans a little more than a century ago. There is not enough in it to reconstruct the whole of their mental worlds, nor even to trace all of their reading choices. The meanings they generated from the manifold texts they encountered often remain elusive. But we can gain a fuller sense of one community's print culture and a deeper appreciation of the ways in which library books and other printed material helped Maude Smith and several thousand of her neighbors explore the world.

What Middletown Read explores the culture of print in an industrializing American city in two parts. Part I traces the development of the city, its print culture, and its library. Chapter 1 offers a portrait of Muncie as a boomtown, a city experiencing growth through the final years of the nineteenth century brought on by the discovery of a large supply of natural gas in the region. The next chapter traces the origins and operations of the public library, as well as the campaign to construct a new, more modern library during the first years of the twentieth century. In chapter 3 we sketch the city's cosmopolitan ambitions, its print culture, and the significance accorded to the public library as a symbol and mechanism of cultural improvement.

In part II we approach the experience of reading in turn-of-the-century Muncie from several angles. In chapter 4 we analyze the borrowing patterns evident in the circulation data derived from the Muncie library's records. Chapter 5 investigates children's reading, as well as the relationship between the public library and the local educational system. Chapter 6 examines how women's literary clubs, most notably the Woman's Club of Muncie, encouraged reading, including the reading of fiction, as a means of better comprehending industrial society. Finally, the seventh chapter considers reading on an individual level, primarily by examining the diaries of several local residents. We close the book by considering what can and what cannot be learned from circulation records of the sort contained in the WMR database and by looking at evidence of reading in twentieth-century Middletown.

I

A City and Its Library

1

"Now We Are a City"

Portrait of a Boomtown

When Robert and Helen Lynd wrote *Middletown,* their famous account of life in Muncie, Indiana, during the 1920s, their aim was to document the impact of industrialization on an American community's values and behaviors. Anxious to draw a sharp contrast between the agrarian life of the nineteenth century and the modern urban environment of 1925, the Lynds chose the year 1890 as a baseline point for comparison. Middletown around that time, they wrote, was "a placid county seat" with "cows running through the streets" and local residents "drowsing about its courthouse square with its wooden pump." Acknowledging that "the thin wedge of industry" had arrived, they nevertheless insisted that a community where crop prices headlined the local paper and the inside pages featured a "farm and garden" column filled with "agricultural suggestions" was not yet a place infused with "an industrial culture."[1]

But Muncie in 1890, and during the decade that followed, was anything but a sleepy country town. The Lynds had crafted an image of a preindustrial town to suit their purposes. Heavily influenced by modernization theory and its emphasis on a sharp transition from an organic community to an impersonal modern society, they presented 1890s Muncie as a foil for the modern, manufacturing-driven society they were investigating. Their study contrasted the fractured, unstable city they claimed to have found in the 1920s with the supposedly more harmonious community of the past. In fact, Muncie in 1890 could hardly be called placid, even if it was not yet fully steeped in the regimented factory work, consumerism, and status anxiety that would be so evident a few decades later.

After the discovery in 1886 of a massive underground reservoir of natural gas in the region, as even the Lynds acknowledged, "the little town went wild." Forty new factories opened in Muncie between 1887 and 1890. Boosters reported that the population of the city more than doubled, from 7,000 to 15,000, between 1889 and 1892, and one estimate predicted more than 22,000 residents by 1895. As the *Muncie Daily News* noted as early as January 1888, "A few years ago we were a village, then a town, and now we are a city."[2] The rapid pace of change continued for most of the 1890s, slowing only as the gas supply sputtered and died soon after the turn of the century. Muncie during the final decade of the nineteenth century was neither a somnolent country town nor a fully realized industrial city. It was a boomtown.[3]

It is difficult to overstate the optimism and energy that pervaded the small eastern Indiana city in the years following the discovery of gas. Its residents, particularly the businessmen and boosters among them, confidently labeled Muncie "the city of eternal gas." Promising that the supply of the fuel was "practically inexhaustible," they anticipated steady, perhaps even spectacular growth for the foreseeable future. "It is not an idle prophecy to state that before five years, Muncie will be a city of 50,000 people," one promotional pamphlet declared in 1892, while another boasted of the city's "magnificent future." These ambitions were not limited to the realm of business. Even if the city lacked "wondrous scenery, lakes, cliffs, and mountains," it nevertheless possessed "advantages in the race of life" that made it an attractive place to live. It had "schools, churches, theatres, a street railroad, electric light, a perfect system of sewerage, and the very best of artesian water," boosters proclaimed, adding for good measure that "the entire city is dotted with palatial residences, filled with intelligent, educated and happy families." When a Congressional appropriation provided Muncie with federal funds for a new post office, representatives of Richmond, another eastern Indiana town, complained on the grounds that their community was substantially larger. The *Muncie Daily Times* reminded them that Richmond was not in the "Gas Belt" and "therefore not 'in it' when the choicest blessings of the nation come to be distributed."[4]

That sense of being "in it" came to define Muncie over the final decade of the nineteenth century. No longer an insignificant dot on the map, Muncie was now a substantial community, its citizens certain it was destined to become an important urban center. During the 1890s, residents came to view their city as, if not in the very center of things, then at least well connected to them. Those links were industrial, commercial, and, increasingly, cultural.

Living in Muncie did not mean living an isolated, provincial life. Rather, for those with the necessary resources, it was a place where one could, with relative ease, take advantage of the latest technological advances, buy the newest and most fashionable consumer goods, travel readily to any place in the civilized world, and take part in the predominant cultural and intellectual currents of the day.

Of course, these opportunities were open chiefly to the city's more fortunate citizens. Most residents, particularly newcomers, came in search of factory work. They labored long hours under harsh conditions and faced the prospect of layoff, injury, or even death with no social safety net. For workers and their families, life in Muncie did not mean access to the newest, choicest goods and services. Nor did it provide much time to consider the latest in literary or artistic trends. Yet their lives could hardly be called isolated. Through unions, churches, and the consumption of supposedly lowbrow or disreputable forms of cultural production during their leisure time, they were tied to wider developments in American life, and they took on identities and outlooks that transcended the locality in which they lived.

Cultural engagement was thus entangled with class formation. The emergence of an industrial proletariat spurred a smaller segment of the local community to distinguish itself from the laboring masses. To achieve this distinction, they mimicked metropolitan bourgeois behavior, forming clubs, staging elaborate parties, purchasing the latest consumer goods, and employing other forms of display that served to distinguish them from the city's ranks of industrial laborers. Increasingly aware of these differences, workers and their families fashioned their own cultural life that marked them off from their ostensibly more fashionable neighbors. These distinctions were still taking shape during the 1890s, and the boundary between them was blurry and permeable; families of skilled craftsmen and members of the petit bourgeoisie straddled or traversed the city's emerging social and cultural divide.

The Gas Boom

A tiny, obscure settlement on the western frontier of the United States through the first half of the nineteenth century, Muncie was very gradually becoming integrated into national transportation and communication networks when the gas boom radically accelerated its transformation into an urban place. The surge of economic activity and population growth that followed the discovery of gas produced the cultural institutions, diversity, vice, and social tensions we associate with city life.

There was little in the first century of human settlement along this bend
in the West Fork of the White River to suggest an urban future. The first to
arrive were Lenape Indians forced westward during the 1770s. Their village
served as a way station and trading post for fur trappers working the Old
Northwest Territory. White settlement began during the 1820s and increased
only slowly during what locals came to call the town's "pioneer days." Muncie
became the county seat of Delaware County when it was formed in 1827 and
officially became an incorporated city in 1865. Its population grew at a leisurely pace—to just 5,200 in 1880—and it only gradually engaged with the
main currents of American economic and cultural life (fig. 1).[5]

Transportation connections developed slowly over the nineteenth century.
The opening of the national road, which reached nearby Wayne County, thirty
miles south of Muncie, in 1827, offered the first links to the country's developing transportation network. Settlers carved a wagon path—later named
the "Old Pike"—to reach it, but it was a crude affair. It gradually improved as
travelers cut down trees, marked blazes, and laid logs over swampy stretches.
Roads got better through the middle decades of the nineteenth century, so
that by 1880 a Muncie editor could brag of the "eleven grand" turnpikes emanating out from the city in all directions.[6] These highways provided extensive, if not especially rapid, connections with the rest of the country.

Railroads proved to be more decisive linkages. Muncie's civic leaders
began agitating for the construction of lines that would connect their town
to the developing national rail system during the 1840s. The first line opened
along a twenty-five-mile route to Pendleton, Indiana, in 1850 and reached
Indianapolis, fifty miles to the southwest, two years later. Connections developed steadily from there, and by the end of the 1880s Muncie was linked not
only to Indianapolis but to Cleveland, Cincinnati, Chicago, and St. Louis (via
a rail system known locally as the "Big Four" route), and by extension to a
national rail network. The growth of railroads put Muncie and its neighbors
"immediately . . . on a new basis and started their development."[7]

Road and rail not only made it possible to move in and out of Muncie with
relative ease; they also facilitated communication with the wider world. Early
postal service was sporadic, but by midcentury a reliable transport system
ensured the regular delivery of mail, twice a week by coach from Richmond
and Peru, Indiana, and weekly from Indianapolis. Railroad connections
increased the delivery service to daily by the 1880s, while special postage
rates fostered the circulation of printed materials such as magazines and catalogs. The rail system also created corridors where telegraph and telephone
lines could be run. The first telephone exchange opened in Muncie in 1880,
and within a few years long-distance calling was possible. Quicker commu-

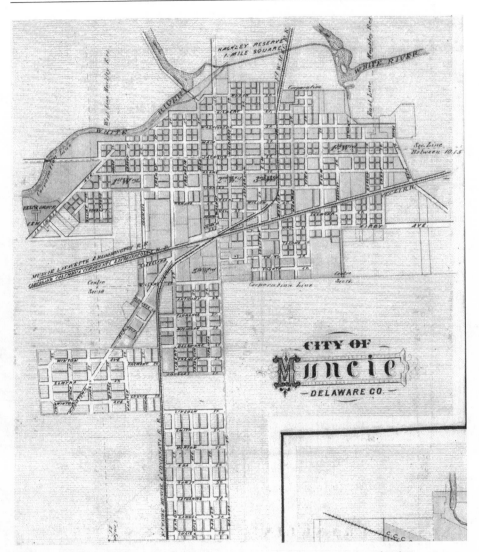

FIGURE 1. Muncie, 1876. From A. T. Andreas, *Illustrated Historical Atlas of Indiana* (Chicago: Baskin, Forster, and Co., 1876).

nication with the outside world made newspapers a viable proposition, and on the eve of the gas boom the city had three dailies (the *Times*, the *Herald*, and the *News*), all of which would continue to operate through the end of the century, along with a handful of weeklies.[8]

The pace of life began to quicken during the decade preceding the discovery of gas. Even before the advent of cheap fuel, Muncie was beginning to develop manufacturing. For a brief time during the middle 1880s it became

"the roller skating capital of the world," with several firms seeking to capitalize on the fad. A local businessman, Thad Neely, devised an improved means
of fastening wheels to shoes and began producing his product, called the
Muncie Roller Skate, during the early 1880s. Evidently inspired by Neely's
success—he had become a wealthy man by 1885—other local entrepreneurs
followed his example. Several claimed to have devised a new, or at least substantially improved, skate, and by the end of 1885 Muncie had five manufacturing operations producing roller skates. Enthusiasm for skating faded
within a few years and the firms shut down, but their sudden rise and fall
reflected a new dynamic at work in Muncie, as industrialization began to
gain traction and integrate the town into the national economy. Even before
the gas boom, Muncie featured an array of small manufacturing businesses
producing feather dusters, tiles and bricks, wheel spokes, and bedsprings,
among other products. Its largest factory was a plant that produced tool handles and bags for flax, run by the prominent local businessman James Boyce,
which employed a hundred people.[9]

Spurred on by modest industrial development, Muncie had begun taking
on the attributes of a city before the gas boom. Laid out in a grid fourteen
blocks long and seven blocks wide by the mid-1880s, the city featured a newly
opened four-story high school building, a large hotel, a new waterworks, and
several substantial office blocks at the city center. A few streets were paved,
and construction was under way on a huge, ornate county courthouse. A trip
to Chicago in 1885 introduced James Boyce to electric lights and inspired him
to build a generating plant for his factory, thus introducing another harbin-
ger of technological progress.[10]

The city was developing in a cultural sense as well. Described by one historian as a "cultural desert" during the 1870s, a decade later it featured an opera
house, an increasingly active club scene focused on culture and the arts, and,
not least, a small but growing public library. As one local historian put it,
Muncie by 1880 had advanced "in material development, in public spirit, in
civic improvement, in education and general culture and morality to a degree
that the general census tables would never indicate."[11]

If the spark of industrialization was present before the gas boom, the
unearthing of new fuel ignited an explosion of economic activity. Coal drillers working in Eaton, about eight miles north of Muncie, had encountered a
foul-smelling, flammable gas in 1876 but had simply covered the well because
they did not see any use for it. A decade later, after hearing about the discovery of a valuable reserve of natural gas in northwestern Ohio, a group
of entrepreneurs from Eaton and Fort Wayne returned to the same field to
drill again. They struck what appeared to be an enormous reserve of natu-

ral gas. Later in 1886, another set of investors formed the Muncie Exploring Company and built a second well about a mile east of the city. By November its flame was burning brightly, visible throughout the city.[12]

Tom Ryan, an excited fourteen-year-old, rode out to see the new well just as it was lit. "Steadily the flame was getting greater and more forcible," he wrote in his diary, and he added in capital letters an announcement of the event's date and time. Within days of the first flames from the new well, a group of Muncie businessmen, headed by Boyce, formed the Muncie Natural Gas Company. Quickly merging with the Muncie Exploring Company, the new firm began laying pipes into the city, and the first gas-fueled street lamps were in operation along Main Street by mid-December. On New Year's Day in 1887, gaslights were burning in a downtown jewelry store. Within a year, eight wells were producing within the city limits; by January 1889 there were twenty-five.[13]

Suddenly Muncie became one of the most desirable sites for industrial production in the United States and a national sensation. As one booster pamphlet put it, "The eyes of the world seem centered on the favored city." Almost daily, it seemed, trainloads of investors, job-seekers, reporters, and tourists arrived, and the American Association for the Advancement of Science sent three hundred representatives to investigate the wonders of natural gas. A front-page notice in the February 12, 1889, issue of the *New York Times,* headlined "Natural Gas the Attraction," reported on the arrival in Muncie of a "party of New York capitalists" headed by former New Jersey governor Leon Abbott. The group reportedly had $2 million at its disposal to invest in Muncie enterprises. Local businessmen were just as eager to attract new investment. They formed the Citizens' Enterprise Company in 1892 and created a $200,000 fund designed to help bring business to Muncie.[14]

A similar effort a few years earlier had lured what would become the city's signature business, the Ball Brothers Glass Manufacturing Company. After the Ball plant in Buffalo, New York, was destroyed by fire in 1886, the five Ball brothers began scouting for a new location. Frank Ball toured the Midwest to inspect potential sites and visited Muncie almost as an afterthought. He was impressed by his hosts' good manners, the local business atmosphere and— no doubt more significantly—the immediate offer, by a committee headed by Boyce, of $5,000, seven acres of land, and free access to a gas well. The Balls relocated their plant and began operations in Muncie in 1888. The business took off, becoming the leading maker of glass jars in the United States and the largest employer in Muncie through the early years of the twentieth century.[15]

It is difficult to overstate the optimism that pervaded Muncie after the discovery of gas. This was particularly the case among the businessmen seeking to promote the city, though it seemed true of the entire town. The New York–based Muncie Improvement Company (the group headed by Abbott) produced a promotional pamphlet that touted the city in glowing, almost poetic terms. Boasting that Muncie "possesses gas sufficient to supply the factories and firesides of a city of million people," the boosters envisioned a thriving, nearly idyllic urban future: "By its talismanic flame spire will be added to spire, block after block will radiate from the city's centre, whistle after whistle will add its shrill scream to the hum of industry, health-giving parks will spring up as if by fairy touch." The pamphlet promised that Muncie would become "a city in this centre of America whose fame shall flow forever onward." It was no wonder that Muncie soon came to be called (and to call itself) "the Magic City."[16]

The enthusiasm extended well beyond Delaware County and gave Muncie a national prominence as the place to be. A piece in the *Boston Herald* on March 6, 1889, less than three years after the advent of the gas boom, extolled the virtues of a city where "eighteen large factories have been located . . . within the last 18 months," and where "houses are furnished with heat, fuel, and light the year round for from $4 to $16 per year." Muncie, the headline proclaims, had become "THE NEW ELDORADO."[17] Other contemporary promotional literature issued by the city's Commercial Club or by its gas companies is no less brash in its hyperbole. Set in "the banner county of Indiana," boasts an anonymous author,

> one city at least in this growing state of golden groups of grain and great herds of cattle feeding upon luxuriant meadows, has caught the eye of the East, and the query comes, what new wonder has Nature's store house given to enrich, now fortunate, to be mighty, Muncie. . . . It is the flame that shoots from Nature's mighty reservoirs, lighting up the horizon of Muncie's future with untold benefits, bringing costless heat to the hearts of all, and setting the wheels of a thousand factories musically humming where once was heard only the popping of growing corn.[18]

The souvenir pamphlet lists the advantages of the city, including macadamized roadways, a central location within two hundred miles of major urban centers such as Detroit, Cincinnati, Indianapolis, Louisville, Columbus, and Cleveland, and railroad links "forming six outlets for its products to be shipped, and furnishing the same number of feeders for trade." Such a city of "splendid opportunities and boundless possibilities," divinely blessed by the recent discovery on its very doorstep of natural gas ("one of the choicest gifts of God"), can only continue to thrive. Muncie, it predicts, "possesses a location adapted to the building of a city of several hundred thousand inhabitants."[19]

Even after the initial optimism that was sparked by the gas boom, Muncie's proponents continued to magnify its potential as a major city well beyond its true size. "Its altitude above the banks of White River," runs one such endorsement from 1895, "impresses one with the especial fitness of the location for a large city."[20] In 1912, when the gas boom had long been consigned to history, a new city prospectus, while conceding that it would be in vain to look there for "cloud piercing 'sky-scrapers'" and acknowledging that Muncie is smaller than it appears, is adamant in its claim that a first-time visitor, "viewing the modern office buildings, the large stores, the heavy interurban traffic and sensing the metropolitan character of the people, might well conjecture that he was in a city of 75,000 or more inhabitants," rather than the 24,000 reported by the 1910 U.S. census. The prospectus anticipates the Lynds by more than a decade by declaring Muncie to be "a thoroughly representative American city." In its further recognition that "the population of Muncie is American by an overwhelming majority" (a statement that carried strong racial undertones), the prospectus also points to another factor that influenced Robert and Helen Lynd's crucial choice of Muncie as Middletown.[21]

If these ambitions were not quite realized in full, Muncie nevertheless experienced a dramatic transformation in its economy and social character. By 1900, 347 manufacturing establishments were operating within the city's limits, and their total capitalization exceeded $7 million. Census records for that year report 6,294 wage earners living in Muncie, the vast majority (5,703) of whom were males of sixteen and up. Six glass factories employed 1,810 people, and another 1,787 worked at one of the city's four iron and steel mills. The remainder were scattered across a variety of businesses, including furniture makers, carriage and wagon builders, foundries, and machine shops. There were 448 women working in local manufacturing operations, and 143 children. Most of those children, 136 in all, worked in glass factories, where their nimbleness was of value. If agricultural pursuits and their offshoots dominated local economic life fifteen years earlier, industry, with all of its consequences, now prevailed without question.[22]

As the industrial employment figures suggest, for every capitalist drawn to Muncie there were dozens who came seeking wage work. The 1900 census put the city's population at 20,942, nearly double the 1890 total and roughly four times larger than the population reported in the 1880 census. It appears that most of that growth took place during the first half of the 1890s. One estimate undertaken by local school authorities concluded that the city's population reached more than 22,000 in 1895, suggesting a slight decline over the ensuing five-year stretch.[23] That a decline took place in this period is not an unreasonable assumption. The flow of gas, despite assurances of centuries of abundance, began to slow during the late 1890s and would dwindle to nearly nothing by 1902. Its diminution prompted some businesses to depart for more promising locations. Others stayed, including most notably the Ball Brothers plant, and Muncie remained a prosperous industrial city, if no longer a boomtown, well into the twentieth century.

The overwhelming majority of newcomers were native-born whites: 19,707 (94%) of the city's 20,942 residents in 1900 were native-born, and of these just 739 were listed as "Negroes." The largest groups of immigrants came from England (450), Germany (353), and Ireland (344). Census takers did not compile statistics about the place of birth of those native to the United States, though records contained in the What Middletown Read database suggest that a majority came from other parts of Indiana and neighboring states (particularly Ohio), while a small but significant minority were born in the northeastern United States. As one would expect in a town with few immigrants, there were only small local populations of Catholics and Jews, while various Protestant denominations thrived, to judge by the number of Baptists, Episcopalians, Methodists, and Presbyterians.[24]

If the growth in population was impressive during the gas-boom years, the city's physical transformation was astonishing. One celebrated local story captured the pace of change. During the spring of 1887, James Boyce joined a group of local businessmen gathered in the Kirby House hotel. Hearing their complaints about a shortage of office space in the city's downtown to accommodate newly arrived businesses, Boyce asked one of the men what price he would pay to rent such rooms. The answer was $60 a month for offices in a lot at the northwest corner of Jefferson and Main Streets. "Gentleman," the enterprising Boyce supposedly declared, "if you will rent the rooms, I will have a brick building there in a week's time." Construction began the following Monday on a 96-by-24-foot building and continued through the days and nights that followed, aided by flaming gas lights set up around the property. Crowds gathered to watch the building go up. By Wednesday, young Tom Ryan recorded in his diary, the east half of the structure was almost complete and the west-side walls were erected. By Friday, the mesmerized Ryan reported, the building was finished and ready for occupancy.[25]

Not all of the changes took place quite so quickly, but the speed at which Muncie made the physical transition from town to city was nevertheless impressive. Within a decade the compact town of 1885 had given way to a segmented city with six wards. It included tony residential sections, work-

FIGURE 2. Courthouse Square (the intersection of Main and Walnut Streets), downtown Muncie, circa 1901. The city had developed significantly by the new century, with a thriving business district and an extensive streetcar network. Courtesy Ball State University Archives and Special Collections.

ing-class neighborhoods grouped around large factories, and a busy central commercial district (fig. 2). Tangles of telephone wires spanned city streets, which were paved throughout the downtown section. Sixteen miles of electrified streetcar lines ran on six routes emanating from the city center by 1895. The streetcar company built an amusement park at the end of its West Side line, along the banks of the White River. Thriving congregations of Baptists and United Methodists built impressive churches in the downtown area, while the edges of the city were dominated by large factories built by the Ball Brothers, Indiana Steel and Wire, the Whitely Malleable Castings Company, and the Indiana Bridge Company (fig. 3).[26]

Another indication of the urbanization of Muncie was the emergence of social problems associated with city life. The flood of newcomers in the city, known as the "gas-boom crowd," included more than a few opportunists with little interest in heeding local moral strictures. As one resident recalled a few years after the boom, Muncie quickly came to be known as a "free and easy town." Alcohol flowed readily from (in descending order of respectability) saloons, "quart shops," and "low dives." According to one report, employees at the Ball Glass works were so likely to spend their pay immediately on drink and entertainment that a local minister whose flock included many of

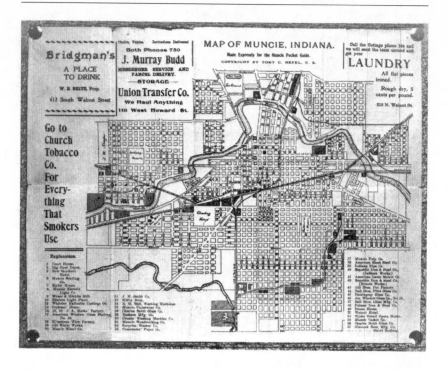

FIGURE 3. Muncie, 1901. Courtesy Ball State University Archives and Special Collections.

the plant's workers stood outside the plant each Friday (payday) to collect donations for fear that the money would disappear by Sunday. Prostitution, often based in saloons, flourished. The city soon had its own "Tenderloin District," populated by bawdy houses such as Mother Pierce's Ranch and well-known madams such as "Gas Well Minnie," Lulu Shoemaker, and "Little Flo" Blair. Gambling was pervasive as well, with most operations again located in saloons. Even chewing tobacco became a problem, and regulations soon emerged designed to reduce the amount of spittle polluting streets and sidewalks.[27]

The impulse to control behavior increased sharply in response to the new city's evident moral laxity, a reflection of increasing class tensions. Saloons, as the sites of so much of the activity deemed illicit, were the most frequent target of those seeking to reassert moral order. A local branch of the Woman's Christian Temperance Union was established and active by the early 1890s, and local churches organized the Citizens' League to Combat Vice in 1894. To inaugurate its campaign, the Citizens' League welcomed William Boole, a minister and prominent anti-saloon crusader from Brooklyn, New York, to the city. He delivered a series of lectures on the evils of drink and its connections to other forms of vice. Around the same time, the Woman's Club of Muncie began to take greater interest in local social and moral conditions, including honoring the Sabbath. Demands for closing taverns and saloons on Sundays became a major political and social issue, in large part because that was the only free day for the city's growing population of factory hands.[28]

Debates about Sunday closing laws point to sharp divisions on moral and religious matters that ran along class lines. The Lynds emphasized the shared sense of faith and community that cut across denominations in the Middletown of the 1890s, but this was largely a middle-class phenomenon. As the Lynds also noted, local workers took a dismissive attitude toward most Sunday closing measures. An 1893 fundraiser for the local Trades Council featured a skit titled "Enforcing the Sunday Law in Muncie, A Farce," and it was a common practice for unions to hold meetings on Sunday mornings. In 1900 a local paper even reported on a cockfight staged between ironworkers and glassworkers on a Sunday morning, an event sure to have ruffled the feathers of the city's bourgeois churchgoers. Religious leaders, as well as city boosters anxious to downplay Muncie's reputation as a wide-open town, stressed the Christian character of the city and campaigned constantly for moral improvement. But the working class evidently paid little heed.[29]

Disagreements of this sort underscored the city's increased social fragmentation. To fit their theoretical framework, the Lynds portrayed Middletown in 1890 as a largely harmonious community in which employers and employees lived, socialized, and worshiped, if not side by side, then at least in close proximity to each other. In fact the first signs of a sharper class divide and corresponding social segmentation were much in evidence in Muncie by the late nineteenth century. Poverty was increasingly noticeable in down-at-the-heels sections such as Shedtown, a neighborhood of ramshackle homes that arose on the south edge of town during the early 1890s. Other areas had a decidedly working-class character, such as the complex of workers' homes built by the proprietors of the Whitely iron and steel factory on the city's northeast side. To the west, investors established new middle-class suburbs such as Riverside, while the most "aristocratic" sections of the city lay immediately adjacent to downtown. Recreation took on class distinctions, as members of the city's middle class aped Gilded Age elites, joining cultural clubs, staging elaborate parties and dances, collecting "oriental" artifacts, and playing lawn tennis and croquet. Workers and their families were more likely to attend baseball games or boxing matches and to frequent saloons. Even churches divided along social lines, although the revivalists who came through town fairly often attracted a wide range of citizens.[30]

The depth and significance of these tensions grew evident in the response to a grave health crisis. An outbreak of smallpox struck the city during the summer of 1893, and the epidemic clearly had a socioeconomic dimension. Over several months, local health officials documented 150 infections, including 22 that led to death, in seventy households. All but seven of these households were in working-class sections of the city, and the bulk of them—more than fifty—were located in a "thickly settled, destitute neighborhood" on the south side that came to be known as the "infected district." The whole city all but shut down at the direction of public health officers seeking to contain the epidemic. Schools, government offices, and the public library were closed, as were many private businesses, most from late summer until early November. As part of an effort to quarantine the infected district, the newly established streetcar system stopped service to that area.[31]

Even more indicative of social tensions were the ways residents responded to public health measures, particularly the campaign to vaccinate the city. At a time when germ theory was not yet fully accepted as an explanation of the spread of disease, many greeted vaccination efforts with suspicion, and those doubts were most intense among workers. Reports pointed to the infected district as a center of "strong anti-vaccination sentiment" and cited indications that workers had ignored the requirement that they get the vaccine. One inspection found that only a few of the workers returning to the job at the Hemingray glass plant in November 1893 displayed the telltale scar produced by the vaccination. There were likely a number of reasons why working-class citizens were so resistant to vaccination. The city's doctors disagreed about what caused the epidemic, how best to prevent its spread, and even whether it was actually smallpox or chicken pox. There was a general suspicion of overly active government, a belief that vaccines could cause harm, a strong correlation between the meddling people campaigning against saloons and vice and those pushing vaccination, and a sense among some that business-men were demanding an unproven, perhaps risky, solution to the problem solely to ensure minimal interference with commerce and manufacturing.[32]

A Well-Connected City

The debate over the validity of vaccination was only one of many intellectual currents to flow through Muncie. When the installation of a new set of street-lights prompted one observer to suggest that they gave the city "a metropolitan air," the comment reflected a cultural self-understanding as much as it did a new built environment.[33] Residents of Muncie during the gas-boom days of the 1890s did not imagine themselves living on the fringes of civilization in the ways that their predecessors of a decade or two before might have.

Connections to the wider world created through roads, trains, telegraph, and telephone joined it to the main currents of American (and even European) cultural life. But as the smallpox controversy suggests, socioeconomic status influenced the character and content of these connections. Workers forged linkages and identities rooted in ties to labor organizations and an engagement with certain forms of popular culture. Others, particularly those with sufficient means, could imagine themselves as cultural sophisticates, even though they resided far from such cosmopolitan centers as New York, Boston, London, or Paris.

This sense of urbanity was of course a local perspective. Viewed from the outside, and especially from metropolitan areas, Muncie remained very much a provincial backwater. That point was brought home by a cartoon that appeared in the *New York Journal* in 1898. It was prompted by a remarkable display of pitching talent by Amos Rusie, the Indiana-born baseball star for the New York Giants who now spent off seasons in Muncie, his wife's hometown. Nicknamed the "Hoosier Thunderbolt," Rusie was renowned for his powerful pitching. Imagining the rapturous scene that must have followed in the streets of Rusie's adopted hometown upon reports of a strong performance, the *Journal* cartoon depicted a drunken brawl among hayseeds gathered in front of the local "Harness & Groceries" store. The image, which the *Muncie Daily Herald* reproduced along with indignant editorial comment, clearly stung. The *Herald* angrily suggested that it was a product of the cartoonist's imagination and more likely represented a scene from his youth in New Jersey, or perhaps a scene recalled from the childhood of William Randolph Hearst, the *Journal's* publisher.[34]

No doubt mindful of such views, the city's civic and business leaders emphasized the ways in which Muncie was becoming a more refined community. The same 1890s boosters who extolled the city's economic achievements also trumpeted its cultural attractions. These included "an elegant opera house," "stately school buildings [that] show educational enlightenment among its masses," and "a well filled public library, where all the leading papers and periodicals are kept on file, [which] interests and instructs its inhabitants and gives a pleasant loitering place for the strangers within its gates." While the city's intellectual development put it on par with any metropolis, boosters claimed, its strongly Christian character prevented the moral decay associated with big-city life. Citing "imposing churches [that] raise their spires to heaven, and proclaim the morality and liberality of its citizens," they depicted Muncie as "a Christian cultured community." Yet they were also at pains to note that the city was neither prudish nor intolerant. Residents embraced a "wide range of religious beliefs" and were in "no sense

puritanical," displaying a "broad, liberal, religious sentiment." These representations were clearly exaggerated booster rhetoric, but they nevertheless
articulated the ambitions of those local residents anxious to position themselves as participants in the broader cultural developments of the fin-de-siècle United States.

That provincial sense of connection was evident in the local art scene. It
centered around the work and teaching of J. Otis Adams, an Indiana-born
landscape and portrait painter who secured patronage from a Muncie physician and opened a studio there in 1876, after spending two years studying
in London. Evidently the time in England was insufficient, for Adams soon
solicited donations to fund another two-year European study trip, and he
set off in 1880 for what turned out to be a seven-year excursion across the
continent. Returning to what was now a booming town in the fall of 1887,
he reopened his studio and in 1889 organized the Muncie Art School with
the help of an Indianapolis colleague. The short-lived school staged semian-
nual exhibitions of student work, which became important cultural events in
the city and evidence that, in the words of one local leader, "the culture and
enlightened taste of our people have kept abreast with [Muncie's] material
growth and prosperity."[35]

After the school closed in 1891, aspiring local artists formed the Art
Students' League, which continued to present exhibitions for a time before
gradually becoming more of a "ladies' club" that held public lectures about art
and culture. Even in that form, it represented an effort to foster engagement
with wider cultural trends among its members. Its purchases included a guide
to the correct pronunciation of 7,000 words, to assist the club's would-be critics in the delivery of their lectures, and a copy of the *Encyclopedia of Painters
and Paintings,* which was placed on hold in the Muncie Public Library, where
it could be borrowed only by club members who received special permission
from the group's president. These acquisitions reflected the nature of local
engagement with the visual arts, and cultural production more generally,
which occurred primarily through the emulation and interpretation of ideas
and trends established elsewhere rather than through the creation of noteworthy original work.[36]

Like many smaller cities and towns across the United States, late nineteenth-century Muncie developed a thriving cultural club movement dedicated to the appreciation of art and literature. Evident as early as the mid-
1870s, when local businessmen and professionals anxious to improve the
community's reputation formed a Literary and Scientific Society and middle-class women formed a reading circle that became the Woman's Club of
Muncie, club life expanded as rapidly as the city's economy over the final

years of the nineteenth century. Numerous literary and cultural clubs formed during the 1890s; by the end of the decade the city had at least a dozen such groups. Most were for women, and several of the more prominent groups were linked to statewide and national organizations such as the Indiana Union of Literary Societies and the General Federation of Women's Clubs.

Groups devoted to musical performance and appreciation flourished as well. Even before the gas boom, the city boasted a Musical Society, and by the 1890s choral singing in schools and public concerts was a staple of local cultural life. The city even had a resident composer, the German-born Matthias Kuechmann, who also owned a music store and taught music. His work was performed locally on several occasions during the 1890s. All of these groups—musical, artistic, and literary—formed connecting links through which middle-class residents imbibed and experienced the cultural production of the world beyond the city's boundaries.

The city's principal theatrical stage provided another means of encountering culture. Even before the gas boom Muncie had been a regular stop for touring shows, which played at the Wysor Opera House, opened by the Wysor family in 1872. In 1892 the Wysors decided to open a more impressive venue, the Wysor Grand Opera House, to capitalize on the city's gas-fueled growth. Its first performance featured the "celebrated tragedian" Thomas W. Keene in a production of *Richard III*. The construction of this new, "grand" theater provided another marker of Muncie's refinement. The Grand Opera House, modeled after some of the best in the country, was "complete in every detail, and with every moderness [sic]." Opening night provided all sorts of opportunities for "the elite of the city" to display their sophistication. Local retailers stocked up on "opera glasses" and "opera gloves," while urging theatergoers to pick up some bonbons on the way to the show. The *Morning News* described the audience for Keene's performance as "the most prettily costumed ever assembled in the city," noting as well that it was "cultured and appreciative" of the first-rate performance.[37]

The new theater not only offered tangible evidence of Muncie's growing sophistication, it also served as a venue for the presentation of a variety of literary, dramatic, and educational productions. National stage stars appeared frequently, as when Helen Modjeska and Otis Skinner performed in a staging of *As You Like It* in 1893. The Grand continued to host nationally touring theatrical productions well into the next century, and during the 1890s and the early part of the new century it presented performances of Shakespeare, Goethe's *Faust,* and Thackeray's *Vanity Fair* as well as more popular shows. The mix of highbrow and popular was evident in the productions at the Grand during the first months of 1900, which included dramatic renditions of *Uncle Tom's Cabin*, *Camille* (based on the novel by the younger Dumas), *Sapho* (an opera production of the novel of the same name by the French writer Alphonse Daudet), a stage version of Marie Corelli's best-selling novel *The Sorrows of Satan*, and another of Frances Hodgson Burnett's *Little Lord Fauntleroy*. The Grand provided a venue for public lectures, political speeches, and community meetings as well, making it an important entry point through which Muncie's citizens encountered the era's civic, cultural, and intellectual currents.[38]

Not every show at the Grand was a highbrow event. Perhaps the most exciting moment in the history of the opera house came when John L. Sullivan, the famed boxer and former heavyweight champion, appeared as himself in the autobiographical play *A True American*. The tour took place near the height of Sullivan's fame, in December 1892, just months after his first and only defeat, in a sensational match with "Gentleman Jim" Corbett. The Muncie performance drew a full house, and the boisterous crowd seemed more interested in seeing Sullivan than in following the play, save for the last act when Sullivan donned gloves and battled a fictional opponent. The presence of famous performers and popular stories on a Muncie stage through the 1890s and into the new century underscored the city's integration into national cultural life.[39]

It seems fairly certain that the audience that packed the Grand to see Sullivan differed considerably from the one that had filled the room on opening night. No doubt they eschewed opera gloves and bonbons. That disparity highlights the degree to which an individual's social and economic position influenced how he or she encountered the cultural currents coursing through Muncie. Most of the literary, art, and music clubs active during the 1890s were composed primarily of members of the middle class. Indeed, participation in such organizations was one way members of a developing bourgeoisie sought to distinguish themselves from their proletarian neighbors. Workers, whose jobs required long hours and yielded modest incomes and limited leisure time, tended not to join in these sorts of activities. This is not to say that they were not connected to wider social trends. Rather, Muncie's workers forged links to the world beyond their community that ran along different lines—those that led to the saloon, the baseball park, or a union hall—and gave shape to different identities.

For many workers, the networks that connected them to the wider society ran through unions. Writing during the 1920s, the Lynds quoted a longtime labor leader who described Muncie during the 1890s as "one of the best organized cities in the United States" (surpassed in his estimation only by Rochester, New York). The significance of these institutions extended beyond the workplace, they added, forming "one of the most active coordinating centers in the lives of some thousands of Middletown working class families, touching their getting-a-living, educational, leisure time, and even in a few cases religious activities." Union locals held banquets, concerts, dances, and baseball games. Some organized libraries for their members, an impulse that eventually led to the formation in 1900 of a short-lived Workingmen's Library in the city's downtown district, which supplied an alternative space for leisure and education. No holiday save the Fourth of July surpassed Labor Day in terms of the scale of celebration. The Knights of Labor thrived locally into the early 1890s, even as the organization's fortunes dimmed nationally. Its most prominent national successor, the American Federation of Labor (AFL), also developed a strong presence in the city by the end of the decade. By 1897 there were thirty AFL locals active in Muncie, representing 3,766 members (a very high number in a town with roughly 6,000 wage earners).[40]

A robust workers' movement not only reached down into the lives of its membership, it also reached outward, forging ties to national labor organizations and encouraging identification with other workers. That sense of connection was evident in the local response to the infamous violent clash in Homestead, Pennsylvania, between steel workers and the Carnegie Steel Corporation during the summer of 1892. Muncie's unions, particularly those representing ironworkers, staged mass meetings to express support and raise money to help the strikers. Employees in the local nail mill, professing sympathy for "suffering humanity" and seeking to "assist their brothers in distress," took up a collection for the Homestead workers as well. That sense of connection could only have been deepened when AFL president Samuel Gompers came to Muncie in 1897, dined with the mayor, and spoke to a capacity crowd at the Wysor Grand Opera House, or three years later when another labor organization, the National Building Trades Council, held its annual national meeting in Muncie.[41]

It is worth noting that the workers represented by these groups were skilled craftsmen—printers, ironworkers, glassblowers, and carpenters—rather than simple factory hands. The 3,766 workers represented by AFL-affiliated locals, along with their families, certainly represented a substantial swath of the city's working class. But there were several thousand other residents who worked as unskilled factory hands or day laborers. These men, along with poor women working as domestics or in other low-wage jobs, had few local organizations to connect them to the wider world. Many were transient, coming to Muncie when jobs were plentiful but moving on quickly in pursuit of other opportunities. A good number of them lived in working-class settlements just south of the city line, which for a time made them ineligible for

Muncie Public Library privileges. Most were literate and likely read newspapers, but their low wages and limited leisure time restricted opportunities to engage more deeply and extensively with literature and the arts.

Gradually, as mechanization took hold, the number of skilled workers would diminish and the proportion of those occupying the very lowest rungs of the occupational ladder would increase. The Balls introduced automated glassmaking machines in their plant in 1898, more than doubling the rate of production within a few years while reducing the number of workers needed. Increasingly, wage work in Muncie would require little in the way of skills or education.[42]

While differences in the way the residents of boom-era Muncie lived and worked influenced the way they experienced the world beyond the city limits, none could be said to be isolated. Muncie at the close of the nineteenth century was a community that was well integrated into national transportation and communication networks. The cultural and intellectual trends coursing through the United States were readily apparent in Muncie, in the pages of its newspapers, in clubrooms and union halls, on the local stage, and, not least, on the shelves of the public library. Some forms of cultural engagement were evident among members of the city's small but growing middle class, particularly the consumption of highbrow and middlebrow material, a fact evident in the group's more frequent use of the public library. But blue-collar residents had their own set of institutions and activities that linked them to aspects of popular culture and gave meaning to those engagements.

One of the main integrating forces in local life was the Muncie Public Library. It was an expanding institution that offered access to a growing collection of books, periodicals, and newspapers from around the country. It served as a portal through which at least some of the city's residents connected with a substantial part of the literary and intellectual output of the day. Civic boosters were quick to cite the library as evidence of the city's prosperity and cultural development. It grew substantially during the 1890s, although it struggled to keep pace with the expansion of the community as a whole. Its success received tangible expression early in the twentieth century when, with substantial help from Andrew Carnegie, the city opened a new, architecturally resplendent library building in the downtown district. An exploration of the Muncie Public Library's history, and of the ways citizens used it as the nineteenth century closed, sheds fresh light on the manner in which residents engaged with the wider world, as well as on the ways a particular local institution of reading mediated that engagement.

2

"A Magnificent Array of Books"

The Origins and Development of
the Muncie Public Library

At a special meeting called for Friday, September 26, 1902, the board of the Muncie Public Library reached a unanimous decision to purchase a Smith-Premier typewriter, at a cost of $100. It was to be used for a specific purpose, preparing the manuscript for a printed catalog of the library's books. The catalog was a priority for the board, since its publication was planned to coincide with the inauguration of a new library building that was being underwritten to the tune of $50,000 by no less a figure than Andrew Carnegie, the Pittsburgh industrial magnate and philanthropist. It was to become one of approximately sixteen hundred libraries across the United States that were among Carnegie's many abiding legacies. The board felt that it should not be sparing in its support of this grand endeavor, which would create for the developing city of Muncie a library in keeping with her other institutions. Though expensive, the typewriter was an expression of the board's commitment to the new library.[1]

Ostensibly evidence of a desire for progress, the decision to purchase a typewriter was in fact overdue. The earliest Smith-Premier typewriter had gone on the market in 1889, a good thirteen years before the board deemed it necessary to buy one, and the first commercially successful typewriter had been introduced by Remington in the mid-1870s. According to a Muncie newspaper of 1895, "The typewriter has made great inroads upon the business of inkmakers," to the point that, in order to retain trade, a local ink seller

had begun offering as an incentive "an imposing array of glass inkstands
. . . to those who purchase a quart of ink." The short article ends with the sly
observation that it is far from clear "why one should need inkstands when
they do not need ink."[2] Across America throughout the 1890s and beyond,
people were encouraged to learn and make use of the technology of typewriting. Indeed, the typewriter had become so omnipresent in the business
world by 1900 that a Muncie-based outfit, the Adamson Typewriter Press
Company, was advertising nationally a small press that could produce "a
perfect fac-simile of the work of a typewriter," so that mass mailings would
mimic the look of individually typed letters.[3]

With such a proliferation, it is legitimate to ask why it took so long for
the Muncie Public Library to order its first typewriter. During its twenty-
eight-year history, from its inception in 1874 up until that Friday meeting in
late September 1902, the board never once discussed the practical advantages
of introducing a typewriter into the library rooms. Of course, it could be
argued that, given limitations of space and the need to maintain an appropriate silence in the reading room, the clack of typewriter keys would have been
grossly out of place and highly disturbing. Yet if used out of hours or away
from the main reading room, a typewriting machine would have aided the
work of the librarian immeasurably in terms of the day-to-day enrollment
of new patrons, the keeping of an updated record of borrowing, the preparation of a now-lost 1893 catalog, and the general management of the library.
Correspondence with publishers and booksellers, with bookbinders, stockholders, and donors, as well as the upkeep of financial records, would have
been greatly facilitated. Instead, everything was handwritten. The library
board seems to have been resistant to technological innovation and was perhaps also constrained by limited funds.

The belated purchase of a typewriter reflected the modus operandi of
the library's leadership during the period stretching from its founding to
the beginning of the new century. They were technophobic and resistant to
change, at least as far as the maintenance and development of the library
was concerned. There was not much that was radical or pioneering in their
handling of library matters. The paradox here is that, wearing different hats,
the same members of the board (or in the case of female members, their
husbands) were captains of industry, branches of a business elite that was
intent on advancing Muncie as a spearhead of the manufacturing boom that
shaped middle America at the advent of a new century. If they were willing
to transform the city by encouraging growth through industry, they also
saw it as their duty to preserve and perpetuate traditional values. Outside
the churches and the schools, there was no better site for the realization of

that duty than the library. Yet the decisions that they reached as a board between 1874 and 1902 were more conservative than innovative, a quality common to other similar institutions across the Midwest in the last quarter of the nineteenth century.[4]

What follows is an account of the development of the Muncie Public Library from its founding until the opening of the new Carnegie building in 1904. Although its founders proclaimed lofty cultural ambitions, those remained chiefly aspirational through the end of the century. The collection continued to be a traditional one; it developed haphazardly, with acquisitions constrained by limited funds as well as conservative tastes. Daily operations, overseen by a succession of local women appointed as librarians, tended to be informal and loose. Muncie's rapid growth during the 1890s created new strains as demand increased, the collection grew, and space became scarce.[5] By the advent of the twentieth century, its leaders had begun planning for a new library, one that would modernize its operations and reflect Muncie's emerging status as a significant city.

Origins and Ambitions

Although scattered and piecemeal, several pieces of surviving evidence indicate that, long before the formal inauguration of the Muncie Public Library in January 1875, the circulation of books and printed matter had become integral to the development of emergent midwestern communities. In Indiana, it is possible to trace the advent of newspapers almost to its earliest settlement by people of European origin. The *Indiana Gazette,* the territory's first newspaper, was published in Vincennes in 1804, and by the middle years of the century many recently established towns (including Muncie itself) had their own daily or weekly papers. According to Mary Alden Walker, during those first fifty years of the century "the newspaper satisfied the primary need for reading matter, and took up almost all the time the frontiersman had for such things." Before the Civil War, she notes, "there were few common schools and no educational system in Indiana."[6] After the war, new legislation mandated the creation of schools. The need for books was tied to the educational requirements of schools in communities, while novels and works of belles lettres were the stuff of leisure hours, particularly for the growing number of women readers.

Muncie's citizens met this demand by taking advantage of a number of developments that predated and were eventually channeled into the creation of its public library. In 1865, the same year Muncie incorporated as a city, an Indiana law mandated the establishment of township libraries, and in consequence the county library "went into the custody of the township trustee." The trustee appointed as librarian in Muncie was Wilson J. Smith, who was later elevated to city sheriff, with the result that for a time books were circulated from his residence at the town jail. Not surprisingly, the good citizens of Muncie were uncomfortable with this arrangement, for there seems to have been a drop-off in interest in the county and township libraries.[7]

Perhaps as a consequence, Muncie's postmaster, Henry C. Marsh, a Civil War veteran, took it upon himself to purchase books for a circulating library, obtaining "permission from the proper authorities to incorporate these books [from the county and township libraries] into his own library and circulate them free of charge." Marsh's library was housed in the post office, a far more convivial location than the town jail. One of the earliest surviving documents is a manuscript register of the books from the earlier library that came into Marsh's possession in 1867. They comprise approximately two hundred volumes, mostly canonical works, and include Gibbon's *Decline and Fall of the Roman Empire*, Macaulay's *History of England* as well as that of David Hume, Sir Austen Henry Layard's account of Nineveh, Plutarch's *Lives*, the works of Shakespeare, a large number of travel works, the writings of Washington Irving, and some Ruskin, Dickens, and Samuel Johnson, along with American histories, biographies, and reference works. At the inception of the Muncie Public Library in 1875, the library committee purchased Marsh's stock of books, which by then had risen to over thirteen hundred volumes.[8]

We also have interesting, though so far scanty, evidence of the parallel existence of an early "Workingman's Library" in Muncie. These institutions had distinctly British origins and aimed to provide moral uplift and intellectual stimulation to manual workers. William Maclure (1763–1840), a Scottish geologist, educator, and philanthropist who joined in the short-lived utopian experiment established by Robert Owen in New Harmony, Indiana, played a key role in their development in the state. After Owen returned to his native Scotland in 1827, Maclure opened a successful school for orphans and published under his own imprint his reformist ideas on education. When he died in 1840 he left specific funds in his will for the setting up of libraries for workingmen. According to Dawne Slater-Putt, "From 1855, when the funds became available, to 1859, donations were made from Maclure's estate to 144 Working Men's, Mechanics', and Literary Association Libraries in eighty-nine Indiana counties."[9] One of these libraries was located in Muncie's Workingmen's Institute, and its contents were transferred as a gift to the Muncie Public Library at the time of its opening.

The new public library would also incorporate the books of the Philalethean Society into its collection. It is likely that the Muncie Philalethean Society was a literary and debating club, perhaps having its origin at the high school. Several nineteenth-century midwestern colleges boasted active Philalethean Societies. Muncie's society donated to the new public library "near ninety volumes of bound books and some magazines" following its opening. The collection included a mix of poetry, fiction, and politics, with authors ranging from Homer to Louisa May Alcott.[10]

These and other endeavors formed the backdrop for the organization of the Muncie Public Library. They reflected the growing importance of printed material in nineteenth-century America, as well as the desire of small, seemingly isolated communities to partake in the intellectual developments of the age. The movement to establish publicly funded libraries gained momentum after the Civil War as the volume of printed material grew rapidly. An early historical account of Muncie's initial organizational meeting states that the citizens who attended were inspired by a high-minded understanding of "the benefits and advantages to communities flowing from the general diffusion of knowledge" that might be achieved in Muncie through the creation of a public library. They saw the new library both as "an ornament" to the growing city and as an educational institution. As one contemporary put it, the library would be "a source from which the people may derive such useful information and acquire such practical education as are suited to the wants and needs of those who do the great business of life, and are called upon to become the working bees of the hive—the hewers of wood and drawers of water of our general, social and domestic system."[11]

These ambitions did not readily translate into substantial material support, a problem that would periodically plague the library over the next quarter century. The initial meeting resulted in the formation of a board of trustees, which offered local residents the opportunity to purchase shares in the library, apparently with no limit to the number purchased. The minimum needed to float the stock company was $50, but the initial subscription raised many times that amount. Lewis C. Naylor, in his history of the library, claims that "a considerable amount of stock was later sold to various citizens of Muncie," though he concedes that "the purchase of stock in the amount of $3,600 by the Common Council [the city's legislative body] virtually placed the library under city control."[12]

Reading more carefully, it is pretty evident that the public sale of stock in the library was an unmitigated failure, the citizens recognizing that it would bring no direct financial return. Buying a share was more a gesture of good will, an investment in the cultural life of the small city that was their home. In turn, the much larger sum provided by the Common Council was an acknowledgment that a public library must be funded primarily through

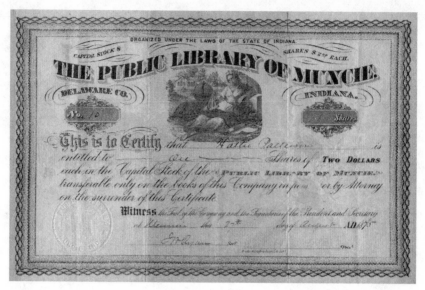

FIGURE 4. Muncie Public Library stock certificate held by Hattie Patterson, the first librarian. Courtesy Muncie Public Library.

local taxation rather than by individual contributions. The terms of the stock merely permitted a holder to receive books equivalent to the value of the share upon its surrender (fig. 4). We know of no stockholder who actually exercised this right.

From the beginning, then, financing the library became the responsibility of the city and ultimately of its taxpayers. Representatives of the newly formed stock company met with the Common Council on July 21, 1874, to argue that the city should buy a majority of the shares. On this occasion, the council agreed to subscribe to 1,500 shares at $2 each, thus ensuring that the proposed new library could go ahead. That was followed in 1876 by a major infusion from the council of $1,500, in 1877 a further $700, and in 1879 the additional purchase of 300 shares, again at $2 apiece. By the end of December 1880, the city held as many as 2,215 shares of stock in the library, compared to just 503 shares held by about two hundred individual stockholders.[13] From then on the library relied in the main on annual funding from the city for the purchase and binding of books, the maintenance of the facility, and the librarian's salary.

The minutes of the library board reveal that the majority of its members, from its inception in 1874 to its dissolution in 1903, were either original stockholders or their spouses or children. The members of the inaugural board, all of whom were male and each of whom had subscribed to five shares apiece, were Hamilton McRae, the superintendent of schools, who was elected board president; two leading local businessmen, William B. Kline, the owner of a flour mill and a city councilman, and Marcus C. Smith, a dealer in grain who was also the city's mayor; a railroad agent, Erville B. Bishop, who had been installed in 1869 as Eminent Commander of the city's Order of Masons; Dr. William Glenn, a Pennsylvania-born dentist with a practice in Muncie; and two lawyers, Massachusetts-born William March and the youngest of the seven, John W. Ryan, who was appointed clerk.

Over the next thirty years, the board would continue to draw from the city's civic and business leaders, or, increasingly, their wives and sisters, for its membership. In 1902, on the eve of the transition to the new Carnegie building and a newly constituted board, the membership included Theodore F. Rose, the president of the board and a respected local lawyer and business-man; Nathaniel F. Ethel, the owner of the *Muncie Daily News;* Nellie Stouder, the wife of another newspaper publisher; Arthur Brady, a lawyer who had served as mayor of Muncie from 1891 to 1895; Mrs. E. B. Claypool, the wife of a prominent horse breeder and local banker; John Rollin Marsh, an engi-neer; and Carrie McCullough, the wife of a well-known businessman. The presence of women on the board was a marked change that reflected a grow-ing perception of the library as a "feminine" enterprise, though no woman ascended to the presidency of the board. Otherwise, in socioeconomic terms, the board's character changed little between 1874 and 1903.

There remained several issues that required urgent resolution prior to the library's opening. A subcommittee of the board produced a set of bylaws governing the library, modeled on those of the Indianapolis Public Library, which had opened in 1873. They included a 3-cent fine for overdue books and a one-book-at-a time borrowing policy.[14] At the final meeting of the board for 1874, with the opening of the library quite imminent, it was agreed that a salary of $250 per annum should be offered for the post of librarian, with the additional privilege of being allowed to sell stationery in the library rooms. At a subsequent meeting on January 5, the board selected Harriet L. Patterson, the thirty-nine-year-old wife of a local telegraph operator, for the position. Like most librarians of this era, particularly those in small cities and towns, Patterson—always known as Hattie—likely had no previous experience or formal training as a librarian, but the fact that she soon bought stock in the library is an indication of her commitment to her new position.[15]

These modest beginnings did not preclude grand ambitions, as the library's inaugural ceremonies made clear. Its reading rooms opened in January 1875, although books would not circulate for several months. Once it was fully operational, the city marked the occasion with a public event that articulated the intellectual and moral aspirations that lay behind the establishment of the library. It took place in the Council Chamber of the City Building, across from the new library's rooms (fig. 5), with a "goodly number of our citizens" in attendance, according to the *Muncie Weekly News.* "The time will come, we hope," the paper declared, "when the size of the library will have grown to such an extent that we will laugh almost incredulously and say, 'why, I remember when that library only had about 3,000 volumes.'" The report also described the decorations for the event, including "a large book covered with evergreens, representing, we suppose, the book of nature," which hung over the library's entrance. Inside, the rooms were "decorated, with the following mottoes fastened to the walls. '*Qui bono?*—Pro urbe' [and] 'Leisure without literature is death.'"[16]

Although a secular institution, the Muncie Public Library operated within the Christian ethos that characterized the entire community. The Reverend Oliphant M. Todd, pastor of the First Presbyterian Church, chaired the opening celebration, and the Reverend Thomas S. Guthrie, minister of the First Universalist Church, offered prayers. Both clerics presided over vibrant and prominent congregations whose members, along with those of the city's Episcopal Church, made up a sizeable portion of the library's initial stockholders. The informally religious character of the library would also become evident in its collection. During its almost thirty-year existence, it acquired a variety of religious texts, including free literature supplied by such denominations as the Christian Scientists and the Swedenborgians.

The ceremonies also made it clear that the library represented concrete evidence of Muncie's intellectual progress. John W. Ryan, the local attorney who also served as the library board's clerk, offered a historical sketch of the library's origins in which he applauded its "magnificent array of books" and characterized it as "the finest public library in Indiana, outside the cities of the first class." Its reading room, he added, was "supplied with the leading current literature from the world whence the comers of both continents [Europe and America] may read in the newspapers and periodicals of their own country the current events of the time." Ryan's plaudits contained a touch of hyperbole—the library at that moment held just over two thousand titles and only a handful of periodicals—but it reflects the prevailing sense that the opening of the public library was an important civic milestone. "The Muncie Public Library Association is now a fixture beyond a doubt," the *Weekly News* pronounced with some pride, "and a success even beyond the expectations of those who conceived the idea, and have brought it to its present state of perfectness."[17]

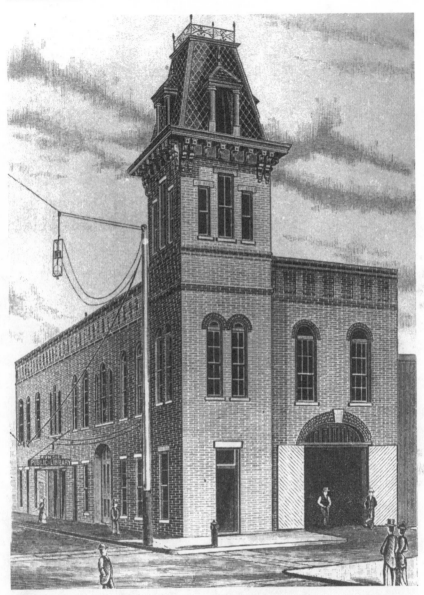

FIGURE 5. The old City Building. The library was housed in two rooms in the left rear of the second floor. Patrons entered beneath the awning on the left side of the building. The wires to the left supplied electricity to the building. Courtesy Ball State University Archives and Special Collections.

Assembling the Collection

The expectation of perfection ultimately ran up against everyday realities. While the library board exhibited a concern for moral uplift, limited funding sometimes left it reliant on donations of all sorts. The materials inherited from Marsh's library and the library at the Workingmen's Institute would soon be supplemented with purchases designed to fill gaps, as well as miscellaneous donations from various sources. Though customarily delegated to the librarian, the selection of new books was formally the responsibility of a three-person Library Committee made up of board members, with the collective board frequently being asked for its opinion on the suitability of a certain volume or to express its gratitude when a particular book was donated. Hattie Patterson and her successors, especially Katherine (Kate) Wilson, who ran the library through the 1890s, seemed more concerned with meeting popular demand than in pursuing any formal strategy for the moral improvement of patrons.

Among the library's initial acquisitions were more than 350 new books purchased from George Andrews, the proprietor of Muncie's Star Drug Store, between May and July 1875. These included many of the novels of R. M. Ballantyne, Charles Dickens, Thomas Hardy, Mark Twain, Jules Verne, and Lew Wallace, poetry by Robert Browning, Henry Wadsworth Longfellow, and Lord Byron, the complete works of Shakespeare and editions of Milton and Dryden, scientific and philosophical works by Charles Darwin, Francis Galton, and Herbert Spencer, moral and religious treatises, histories and biographies, and a number of general reference works. In its opening year, it seems that Hattie Patterson was looking to fill several conspicuous gaps in the library's holdings, while also seeking a mix of popular and highbrow texts that would appeal to a diverse readership.[18]

It appears as well that the board ultimately learned from experience that by buying directly from the different publishers or their wholesalers in Indianapolis, Cincinnati, Chicago, Boston, Philadelphia, and New York, it could take advantage of special terms and save on costs to the library.[19] By the 1890s the library was ordering in bulk almost all of the books it purchased from national distributors.

Simple examples of cost saving by buying directly from the publisher or wholesaler abound. For instance, in 1898 the library paid 79 cents to Houghton Mifflin for a copy of Jeanie Gould Lincoln's historical novel of 1897, *An Unwilling Maid*, a popular book that was to be borrowed 125 times over the next four years. The bookshop list price for the same novel, as printed in the book's preliminaries, was $1.25. Henry Gillman's *Hassan: A Fellah;*

A Romance of Palestine, acquired at the same date from Little, Brown, cost the library $1.34; it was advertised as a newly minted publication for $2. The library purchased the first American edition of Theodore Watts-Dunton's minor classic, *Aylwin: A Poetic Romance,* from Dodd, Mead & Co. of New York for 90 cents; in *Publishers' Weekly,* it was among books promoted in its "Christmas Bookshelf" section for $1.50. Buying books at wholesale or discount prices from the publishers or their regional agents had become the norm for American public libraries by the final decade of the century. According to one widely used contemporary advice book, when buying books, "a library should secure from 25 to 35 per cent discount."[20]

The board's minutes are replete with proposals for the purchase of individual books that may not have been included among those marketed by publishers and wholesalers. Although the librarian usually had the task of proposing what might be bought, it was the members of the board who had the final say. In practice they usually gave the librarian considerable latitude, particularly in the decisions to purchase popular fare, but they nonetheless took it as part of their involvement in library affairs that they would recommend books for purchase. Implicitly, they saw it as their role to act as moral guardians in terms of what might be made available for reading.

The board's involvement in acquisitions ebbed and flowed, often depending on its composition at a particular moment. When it did involve itself in such matters, it most often concerned children's books. At a meeting in 1890, attended by five members of the board including three women, the discussion turned to the acquisition of further books for juvenile readers. Jacob Abbott's Franconia stories (1850–1854), one of the earliest fictional series written specifically for girls, and *The Wide, Wide World* (1850), by Elizabeth Wetherell (Susan Bogert Warner), a best seller promoting Christian values that was often perceived as a kind of behavioral yardstick for young women, were named as desirable purchases. It is an intriguing and perhaps sad reflection of the choice of books here that all three women on the board were in their fifties, several years older than the two men.[21] Their selections appear to reflect the books that were in vogue when they themselves were children, and there seems to have been little or no attempt to delve into more recent juvenile fiction.

After these and several other books were put forward, however, "it was decided that any action be postponed until the next meeting, and that each member of the Board bring a list of Books from which selections shall be made." It took until the following year before the president could report to the board that "the purchase of the Franconia stories had been arranged for, at 57 cts. per volume—nine vols. already received, the tenth to be ordered."

Abbot's Franconia series, which had long been superseded in popularity by other children's series such as the Elsie Dinsmore books, achieved only a moderate circulation among Muncie's readers. A far more popular choice was *The Wide, Wide World,* which was added to the library later in 1891 at a cost of $1, and proved an enduring favorite, being borrowed 123 times within our records. In terms of readership, then, there was often a hit-or-miss quality to the board's selections.[22]

Given the conservatism of the board, it is not surprising to find that its members were far more likely to choose works by established authors. A good example is Louisa May Alcott, whose semiautobiographical novel *Little Women* (1868–69) had cemented her reputation for future generations of readers. At a November 1891 meeting, "the subject of new books was raised." A subcommittee was immediately formed, consisting of "the Ladies of the Board" and the librarian, Kate Wilson, and their task was "to expend the amt. of $50.00 in the purchase of such books as they might see fit to select." The following month, at a meeting that was short of a quorum, they were unofficially able to inform those members present that fifty-six volumes had been ordered and received, "and the Librarian reports the entire number constantly off the shelves in the hands of Readers." The selection included new editions of Harriet Beecher Stowe's *Uncle Tom's Cabin,* Anna Sewell's *Black Beauty,* Frances Hodgson Burnett's *Little Lord Fauntleroy,* and several series books by Harry Castlemon, Horatio Alger, and Edward S. Ellis, all of which achieved a wide and continued readership.

Although pleased with the immediate reception of these books, one prominent member of the board, Mary Goddard, who was present at the meeting in December that lacked a quorum, appears to have been frustrated that the $50 then available for purchases was insufficient to include any of Alcott's works. She pressed for their acquisition as soon as funds would permit, and in March she was finally "authorized to purchase the Books written by Louise M. Alcolt [sic] as far as the Board's Treasury will allow." The library already owned more than thirty copies of books by Alcott, although some appeared to have dropped out of circulation by 1892. During the period for which we have borrowing records, the individual copies of Alcott's works acquired by the library prior to 1889 were, without exception, almost never borrowed. We can assume that, by the 1890s, these earlier volumes were either old and shabby and thus disdained by young readers or, more likely, had been lost or discarded.

The same cannot be said for the volumes bought in 1889. Of that particular purchase, *Little Women* was borrowed 115 times, almost exclusively by female readers; *Little Men* 144 times, with a minority of male readers; and *An Old-Fashioned Girl* 154 times, and among the few men borrowing the book were a couple of Muncie schoolteachers. Only *Aunt Jo's Scrap-Bag: Cupid and Chow-Chow, Etc.*, a collection of humorous tales that had mostly first appeared in periodicals, failed to attract even a single reader. All ten new books acquired at the behest of Mary Goddard in March 1892 were to enjoy significant appeal. Among them was another copy of *Little Women*, which was to attain 111 borrowings, and *An Old-Fashioned Girl* with 128, both having similar proportions of female and male readers to those of the earlier 1889 acquisitions. In this case the board's tastes matched up well with popular demand.

The board's emphasis on Alcott reflected an ongoing concern with providing moral guidance through its collection, particularly for children. The uplift associated with her writing is well captured by an anonymous columnist in the *Muncie Morning Star*, who averred that "it is hard to realize that a girl who has read Louisa M. Alcott's 'Rose in Bloom' or her 'Eight Cousins' can never be other than better for the reading, and how, after she has read these, a normal girl will read obnoxious literature, provided the best is provided for her." Hardly less penetrating is the slightly later evidence of a ninth-grader who signed herself "Cleo," who contributed to *The Munsonian*, the Muncie High School commencement magazine for 1912, commenting on *Jo's Boys* (1886), the sequel to *Little Men*, which imagines the heroine translated into a married woman. Fifteen-year-old Cleo writes: "I consider Jo as my favorite character. Her patience and motherly love are here shown and also her husband's patience. . . . [Their experiences] show the character of these two people who were always planning to give other people pleasure. These are the kind of people that the world needs and it needs a good many of them." Mary Goddard's efforts to buy new copies of Alcott's books for the public library reinforce one's sense that here was a writer who spoke to values that the conservative members of the board wished to promote.[23]

By the same token, there were authors whose works were deemed "obnoxious literature" and therefore unfit for inclusion in the library. Given its notoriety, we should not expect to find the work of, say, Walt Whitman or Oscar Wilde represented, and indeed neither author is present.[24] The minutes of the board offer us few clues as to whether there was ongoing discussion concerning the propriety of including certain controversial authors on the shelves of the library. In practice, board members would have taken to heart the pointed advice proffered by William F. Poole in one of his annual reports on the activities of the Cincinnati Public Library, which he headed. "Novels of an immoral tendency, or even of an equivocal character," Poole wrote, "are excluded from our collection."[25] Older works with a questionable or lubricious reputation, such as *Moll Flanders, Tom Jones, Candide*, and *Frankenstein*, are absent from the Muncie Public Library, but so are controversial contemporary novels such as Stephen Crane's *Maggie: A Girl of the Streets*, Kate Chopin's *The Awakening*, and Theodore Dreiser's *Sister Carrie*. Despite the fact that French was taught at the Muncie High School, works by Zola and Maupassant—perhaps considered too risqué—are also absent. Nor did the library acquire Bram Stoker's *Dracula*, perhaps because of its gory detail.

The single intriguing reference in the board minutes to any overt attempt at policing the content of books in the library occurs in the middle of 1890. As one of her first acts after being appointed as the new librarian (a post that she was to occupy for just over half a year until her resignation in January 1891), Emma Sparr conducted an inspection of the library's holdings and reported to the board that she had detected what she described as "improper books" on the shelves.[26]

Her announcement was treated almost as a health alert. The board hastily set up a task force, consisting of Mary Smith, its secretary, and the indefatigable Mary Goddard, to investigate Sparr's report. Their mission was to search through all holdings and "to lay aside such books as they might consider unsuitable to have a place among the books of the Library." The task was not a small one, and when they reported three months later, the so-called Committee on Improper Books maintained that eight such volumes had been "laid aside." The brief minutes of the meeting do not include the titles of these books nor any rationale that might have guided the two ladies in their moral guardianship of the library's contents. The fate of these eight books is also unknown, though in all likelihood they were discarded rather than being locked away. Consequently, we do not know for certain what kinds of book would have been considered "improper," though the greatest likelihood is that these would have been works of fiction that were reckoned to be too sexually explicit or ones that appeared to compromise the norms of conventional married life.[27]

Arguably, the two major nineteenth-century novels that shocked and undermined conventional moral beliefs more than any other were Gustave Flaubert's *Madame Bovary* and Leo Tolstoy's *Anna Karenina*, which, because of their respective heroines' indulgence in sexual relationships outside marriage, were under frequent attack for their putative moral depravity, even though they also garnered many admirers for their exceptional literary merit. *Madame Bovary* became available in English in 1886 and was issued again in New York in 1902. Constance Garnett's translation of *Anna Karenina*, well regarded at the time, became available in a Philadelphia edition in 1900 and was republished in New York the following year. Significantly, neither book found its way onto the shelves of the old Muncie Public Library, though *Anna Karenina* is included in the 1905 catalog of the new Carnegie Library.

In terms of notoriety, perhaps the nearest equivalent novel written in

English is Thomas Hardy's *Tess of the D'Urbervilles* (1891), which also came under attack by conservative critics for its challenge to the sexual mores of the day. In this case, however, the library acquired a copy of *Tess* in January 1895. As far away from his home as the American Midwest, Hardy was an iconic author, and the library already possessed *Far from the Madding Crowd* and a volume of short stories, *Life's Little Ironies,* both of which were borrowed with some regularity. It therefore comes as something of a surprise to find that *Tess of the D'Urbervilles* was not once taken out from its acquisition through the end of the extant records in 1902.

A first surmise is that Muncie readers spurned the novel because of its notoriety; human experience, however, suggests that notoriety attracts rather than shuns readership. A far more likely explanation is that it was considered by the librarian as yet another "improper book" and not made available for patrons to borrow. The book was not a purchase but a personal gift to the library, along with four other unrelated volumes, from Nathaniel F. Ethell, a member of the library board. One suspects that he and other members privately agreed that *Tess* was too immoral a book to be placed on the open shelves for regular borrowing by all and sundry. We know that it stayed in the possession of the library, for it still remained listed in the new 1905 catalog.[28] As Evelyn Geller has convincingly shown, the open-shelf system adopted by most American public libraries during the 1890s may have been touted as a physical manifestation of passionately held democratic ideals, but freedom of access "literally exposed existing censorship policies, for where all books had once been concealed, closed shelves now remained only for restricted books."[29] In Muncie, where open shelves had been used from its inception, moral oversight of the library's contents was for the most part subtle, but it was ultimately the opinion and moral composition of the board that decided whether what Milton called "that precious life-blood of a master spirit," a good book, might find its way on to the open shelves for the public to read.

As the example of *Tess of the D'Urbervilles* suggests, idiosyncrasies in Muncie's library collection resulted most often from private gifts. From its founding, the library encouraged patrons to donate books of their own to help fill the shelves. Among miscellaneous terms in the "Rules and Regulations" that were drawn up by the board prior to the opening of the library, article 9.2 reads, "Donations of all kinds suitable for the Library Reading Room or Museum are respectfully solicited and will be properly acknowledged."[30] Before she stepped down as the first librarian, Hattie Patterson compiled a detailed list of all subsequent donors between 1875 and 1880, with totals by the year. By the end of 1880, Patterson reckoned the whole number of books in the library to be 3,587, roughly a quarter of which were donated.[31]

In later years, the number of books donated often far exceeded the number purchased. For instance, at the end of 1899, Kate Wilson reported to the board that of the 272 books accessioned during that year, "141 were Government and State documents, 44 were purchased by the directors from the library funds; 87 were gifts from the Authors or publishers and friends of the library." For the following year, 1900, Wilson reported that the library "was very pleasantly and substantially remembered by its many kind friends," counting for the first time among its benefactors the youngest of the Ball brothers, George A. Ball, who selected for donation twenty-five popular works of fiction out of his private library.[32]

As Wilson noted in her 1899 report, authors too were the source of presentation copies given to the library. As well as carrying many responsibilities on the board and donating a variety of other books, Dr. G. W. H. Kemper wrote a fifty-six-page pamphlet titled *The Uses of Suffering*, a copy of which he presented to the library in 1897. An earlier history, *A Portrait and Biographical Record of Delaware County, Indiana*, was donated in 1893 by its publisher, A. W. Bowen of Chicago.[33] It was almost certainly considered a reference volume, for there is no record of its having been borrowed.

A number of other authors donated copies of their own books. Several were travel writers, such as John Wesley Bookwalter, a manufacturer and land owner from Ohio, whose book *Siberia and Central Asia* was published "for private circulation" in Springfield in 1899, and Henry Isaac Sheldon, the author of *Notes on the Nicaragua Canal* (1900), which advocated an alternative to the Panama Canal several years before that structure was begun. Among creative writers, the library received a copy of *In Memoriam*, composed by Charles Dexter (1830–1893) in the same measure as Tennyson's much more famous poem. It had been published in Cincinnati in 1891, and was given in memory of her father by the poet's daughter, Mary, in 1899. In 1900, a local author and schoolteacher, Bessie Lee Blease, who was a patron of the library, presented a copy of her own novel, *Eilene; or, The Invisible Side of a Visible Character*, which had been published in New York earlier that year.

Maintenance of the separation of church and state may have been loosely adhered to during the early years of the library, but in a small city at the heart of the predominantly Christian Midwest, there was pressure from denominational groups for their works to be represented on its shelves. The very first work entered into the accession catalog was a copy of *The Young Converts*, by Julia C. Smalley, recorded as a gift from Miss Lucy Trueworthy. As the work is a Catholic devotional text, the donor's surname may well have been a pseudonymous personification of its contents. The acceptance of the book prefigures the regular donation of a variety of religious texts from different denominations. Particularly during the latter years of the 1890s, donations of books and periodicals from, among others, the Church of Christ Scientist, the Jehovah's Witnesses, and the Swedenborgians became increasingly commonplace.

Two volumes of the *Christian Science Journal* sent by Mr. John D. Wood of Buffalo, New York, "were accepted with thanks" by the board in 1897, followed by another, Mary Baker Eddy's *Science and Health, with Key to the Scriptures,* from the same source in December. In the same year, George W. Maring, a leading glass manufacturer in the city, gave the library three volumes of *The Millennial Dawn,* published by the Jehovah's Witnesses' Watch Tower Bible and Tract Society; a fourth volume followed shortly after. A further concession by the board to the Christian Science Association "granted the privilege of placing periodical literature on the tables of the reading room." Also in 1899, the American Publication Company, publishers of the works of Emanuel Swedenborg, approached the library, offering "if the Board desired" to donate six volumes of *The Apocalypse Explained,* and "the librarian was instructed to order them sent." It has to be said that, of these donated religious texts, only Eddy's *Science and Health* attracted more than a small handful of readers, and even that was borrowed by only twenty-six people between 1898 and 1902. The vast majority of the patrons of the Muncie Public Library did not go there to immerse themselves in theology, despite the ambitions of the donor and, perhaps, at least some members of the board.[34]

One other type of donation received even less interest from borrowers, though it nevertheless helped define and sustain the library. From almost the outset, the library served as a certified repository for official publications issued by the State of Indiana and by the U.S. Department of the Interior. Books and other publications from these sources often arrived in sizeable numbers. Such publications, which were almost never borrowed and likely only rarely consulted in situ, constituted something of a dead weight on the library, but receiving them carried a degree of prestige for the city of Muncie, both as a developing municipality and as the county seat. When the Interior Department proposed to remove the library from the register of official depositories of government papers, the board firmly instructed its secretary "to reply in the Negative, the Board not wishing to have [the] name of [the] Muncie Public Library taken from their list." The receipt of government and state publications was to continue unabated, but with very few exceptions, these were *not* what Middletown read.[35]

Languishing on the shelves was the fate not only of government publications but of many donated books that were read (or at least borrowed) with far less frequency than those that were purchased by the librarian. We can see this by examining a sample of books that were donated in a typical year. Among the books that were received as donations during 1897, Tobias Smollett's classic novel *Humphry Clinker,* given to the library by Frank Everett, a stockholder and the son of the owner of Muncie's main ice-cream saloon, was borrowed but once, confirming the view of the critic Fred W. Boege that by 1890 "Smollett's fortunes . . . were at their nadir."[36]

Other donated volumes that never circulated include *Ab-sa-ra-ka, Land of Massacre,* Margaret Carrington's first-person account of her military husband's battles against Indian tribes as America expanded westward, the gift of G. W. H. Kemper, and *Who Invented the Reaper?,* an undisguised piece of promotional literature from the McCormick Company of Chicago. But when Ernest Davis, the fourteen-year-old schoolboy son of a wholesale grocery salesman, gave the library his own copy of G. A. Henty's *By Pike and Dyke: A Tale of the Rise of the Dutch Republic* in November 1897, he showed himself to be in tune with his generation of readers, for the book was borrowed thirty-three times, primarily by boys of a similar age, between its acquisition and 1902. The previous month, the board had negotiated the purchase of nearly thirty secondhand books at 25 cents per volume from Conway Hemingray, the eighteen-year-old son of Muncie glass manufacturer Ralph Hemingray. Among these was another copy of *By Pike and Dyke,* which was loaned twenty-nine times during the same period. It was not the most borrowed of Henty's enormously popular novels, which for many years were the rage among adolescent males, but it was sufficiently in demand for the library to purchase a third copy in 1900.

The Library as a Contested Space

The same give and take between the Muncie Public Library's official leadership and its users that shaped the collection also defined the library as a space. That process was evident from the moment it welcomed its first patron in 1875. Reporting on the library's opening, the *Muncie Weekly News* emphasized the presence of young boys: "Master George Wilson [was] the first of America's young sons who came to visit and enjoy its privileges. Master Charlie Blackburn came next; then followed one another to the number of about thirty boys and young men, who visited the room during the forenoon, all apparently seeking after knowledge."[37]

Whether that hunger for learning was satiated remains uncertain, but the paper's account made it clear that other, more conventional appetites were satisfied. "There were a few little boys who seemed to think it a nice place to eat apples, nuts, etc.," the paper observed, "which they will please remember will not be allowed hereafter. Boys who visit the room are supposed to go there for the purpose of reading, and such will enter quietly and orderly and remain so as long as they remain in the room. Those who do not observe quiet and order, will not be allowed to remain." The paper also reported that the library welcomed its "first lady visitors," a list that included "Miss Mabel Haines, Miss Lottie Bishop, and Miss Mamie Winans." Presumably these girls maintained a higher standard of decorum than the boys who flocked to the library.[38]

From the first moments of its existence, then, users defined the interior space of the Muncie Public Library as much as the library's leaders did. The board and staff envisioned a quiet and attractive space for reading and learning; the sorts of patrons it attracted defined the library's social character. Like most public libraries of the late nineteenth century, Muncie's was a quasi-domestic space, defined largely by the presence of women and children and the relative absence of men. Its staff was female and its board gradually came to include women. The process of defining it included both the efforts of its leaders to organize the modest, two-room space and to provide the heat and light that made it an appealing setting, as well as the presence (and absence) of particular sets of people.

Hattie Patterson's recollections of these early months give us some sense of the new library's sparse interior and limited resources. Its contents, when she took charge in January 1875, included no more than "one doz[en] chairs, one table, one news board, with six papers." She faced the herculean task, in the months that ensued, of not only entering into the accessions catalog and then labeling and classifying, but also finding shelf space for, the contents of the county and township libraries, the stock of Henry Marsh's books, and the donated volumes from the Workingmen's Institute and the Philalethean Society.[39] An early expense account, presented at the board meeting, includes the sums of $60 for the purchase of five bookcases, a table, and a "Reading stand," $10 for two chandeliers, and $75 for a library desk and the fitting of "twenty five feet [of] counter." To pay for such items, the board had to apply for funds to the Common Council's library committee, which was generally compliant, particularly in the early years.[40]

Over time, the library's interior layout grew more structured. No illustration or photograph of the library rooms has been located, but a detailed description appeared in the *Muncie Daily Times* in 1893, shortly after some improvements had been made. It makes clear the manner in which the staff sought to control access to books. "There are on the shelves of the Muncie library 8,622 volumes on the accessible list," the paper reported, noting that "the books are arranged in a system of cases in such a position that the librarian can tell the exact location of any volume from the title." The article also described a counter that extended along one side of the room and divided the bookcases from the area accessible to patrons. The open area was "provided with tables and chairs and supplied with all the latest magazines, papers and periodicals, to which visitors have access at all times. But within the enclosure, back among the bookcases, there stand rows of books embracing every variety. Beginning at one end of the room th[e]re are four or five cases reaching almost to the ceiling filled with government records and documents. . . . Then there are cases of fiction, history, travel, biography, science and politics." Segregated from the space for patrons were shelves "containing reference books and bound volumes of magazines." The *Times* also pronounced the library "well lighted and ventilated" and "always neat and clean," qualities that made it "a very inviting place for the lover of books."[41]

One of the principal challenges had been illuminating the library rooms. The two large chandeliers that were installed prior to its public opening in 1875 and other oil or gas lighting that was added later provided far more illumination than would have been available in most homes. The decision of the board to keep the reading room unlocked until nine o'clock at night and to constantly renew and expand its annual subscription to a variety of the most popular magazines and periodicals made it an appealing venue for the people of Muncie to visit and browse. To capitalize on this, the Common Council passed a motion at a meeting on March 18, 1887, to put out a "contract for electric light for the Library room and the Council Chamber," the cost being calculated at eight dollars per month.[42] The reading room thus became one of the few indoor spaces in the city that was lighted by electricity, a feature that added greatly to its attraction.

The natural gas boom that prompted homes and businesses to connect to the city's gas system also prompted board members to press for its installation at the library. The minutes record a motion by Mary Goddard asking "that new burners be purchased, that the Rooms may have the benefit of the City's gas, whenever needed." There is no indication in the minutes that the motion was not carried, and during its final twelve years gas probably served as the main fuel source for heating and subsidiary lighting within the library. Just before the same meeting adjourned, the board expressed its gratification for "the well lighted and comfortable, home like appearance of the Rooms." Two years later, a piece in the *Muncie Morning News* takes note that at the center of the library stands "a large, well-lighted reading table [which] contains about twenty-five leading magazines from all parts of the world, together with the best illustrated periodicals."[43]

To some extent, the effort to make the library an orderly and attractive environment succeeded. An 1896 newspaper sketch emphasized the good behavior of its young patrons. "One of the pleasant sights of Muncie," the

Daily Times reported, "is to visit the public library and see the scores of young people, boys and girls, intensely interested in the books and magazines. Seated around the tables or standing up behind the several counters you will observe from thirty to fifty boys and girls either at study or selecting books to take home." The paper stressed the "very excellent order and the fine regard for the proprieties" among the children, noting that "not a word [was] being said above a whisper." It estimated that "up to two or three hundred . . . visit the library during a week," a figure that did not "include the adults who visit the library during the day." Praising the head librarian, Kate Wilson, for "the order and system she has brought about," the report also stressed the need for "more extensive quarters and facilities for doing greater good," an issue that only grew more pressing.[44]

The question of library hours also reflected ongoing friction between the ideal of the library as a conveyor of moral values and the demands of its patrons. The initial rules declared that the library was to be open "on Sundays except for issuing and returning books from 3 p.m. to 6 p.m."[45] In many ways, this represented a bold decision; the matter of Sunday opening later became a perennial hot issue, particularly during the 1890s when a devout minority advocated for the library's closure on the Christian Sabbath. In response, advocates of Sunday hours noted that it was the only day of the week when laborers could visit.

The minutes of a December 1890 meeting record that "the question of closing the library on Sunday was considered, and it was decided that the Rooms be opened during the afternoon as usual." A year and a half later, the same issue prompted a discussion that "occupied some time in regard to closing the Library on Sabbath," the proponents of the retention of Sunday opening for reading heading off a vote by arguing that, with only four members present, the board was only barely quorate. At the following meeting there was further debate and a compromise: during the hot summer months, the library would remain open from 9 a.m. to 9 p.m. during the week but be closed on Sundays. But by the beginning of 1894 the advocates of Sunday closure appear to have extended it beyond the summer, for a notice inserted in one of the city's newspapers announces that "since Jan. 1, the Library is again open from 9 a.m. to 9 p.m., every day except Sundays, not only for readers, but books are issued regularly."[46]

Sunday closure was one of the reasons the city's workers eventually sought their own library, a development that threw into sharp relief the social character of the public library. In 1900, near the end of the period documented by the What Middletown Read database, local unions banded together to open a Workingmen's Library. Launched under the auspices of the Muncie Trades

Council, an umbrella body for the city's trade unions, the new library received the support of prominent local businessmen as well as labor groups and even claimed a donation from Andrew Carnegie as part of his campaign to promote the construction of community libraries. As the name implied, its purpose was to provide a space for leisure and self-culture by workingmen, the group least likely to patronize the public library, although women, children, and even businessmen were ostensibly welcome as well. The Workingmen's Library proved a short-lived experiment. Dogged by political controversies and funding shortfalls, it folded in 1903. But its appearance nevertheless offers the chance for revealing comparisons that can sharpen our portrait of the Muncie Public Library.

The campaign for a new library and reading room dedicated to the needs and interests of laboring men began in late 1899. It grew out of an ethos of working-class autodidacticism that still defined the labor movement in late nineteenth-century Muncie.[47] Initial appeals to local unions garnered seed money, which ranged from substantial donations by the local Typographical Union ($45, one dollar per member) and the Street Railway Employees Union ($50) to a $2.50 contribution by a newly formed box-makers union. The city's business community chipped in as well, with major gifts from two leading manufacturing concerns, the Ball Brothers glass company and the Midland Steel Company ($100 each), along with modest offerings from local druggists, jewelers, and attorneys. The mayor, city attorney, and school superintendent were among the several civic leaders who donated to the fund. Supporters held a series of benefit events, including concerts and entertainments, as well as a ball put on by the local glassworkers' organization. The decisive step in making the library a reality came when Andrew Carnegie agreed to contribute $500, which increased the total funds assembled to more than $2,000. The organizing committee rented five rooms in a downtown office building, hired a local baker, O. S. Tuttle, as librarian at a salary of $600 per year, and opened the library on March 5, 1900.[48]

The promoters of the new institution made it clear that they aimed to serve male workers, a stance that can be interpreted as an implicit critique of the public library. Fundraising appeals to union members promised "a commodious room down town, where you may drop in at any time during the day or evening, to spend your leisure hours in reading or social conversation with your fellow workingmen." It would feature "comfortable chairs," tables for spreading out newspapers and magazines, "official journals of the several trades," and a smoking room. Its collection of books would be "calculated to benefit and entertain" and would include a selection of titles "bearing upon the labor and economic qu[e]stions that are interesting the wage earners of our community." The space would be "YOUR library and reading room," one announcement told workers, "your down town home." It was clear from such suggestions that the new library would be both masculine and working-class in character, in contrast to the more effeminate and middle-class setting provided by the public library, which had few if any trade journals and its collections were notably timid about labor issues. More significant, the public library was not a space conducive to the leisurely smoking and conversation the Trades Council aimed to offer its constituency.[49]

What was implied about the public library in fundraising appeals became explicit in other pronouncements. Speaking at a meeting designed to rally support for the new facility, Professor Franklin Abiah Zeller Kumler, president of Muncie's newly formed college, the Eastern Indiana Normal Institute, noted the public library's shortcomings with regard to working-class patrons. "It has been argued that the city library is ample to accommodate all the citizens of Muncie," Kumler observed, "but it is closed on the only day that the laboring people use it." There was more to a library space than a supply of books, he pointed out. Even if workers could come on other days, "they would not be permitted to smoke and enjoy social conversation." A month later, a supportive local daily put it even more bluntly, declaring it "a matter of congratulation . . . that the library is to be open on Sunday" and adding that it would be useful for the public library to follow suit since Sunday was the only day of the week when "the masses of the people," who supplied "the bulk of the money that supports libraries" were "at leisure."[50]

The masculine and blue-collar character of the Workingmen's Library only grew more emphatic during its short life. When the library first opened, its trustees had to remind the public that it was not solely for union men: "business, professional, and laboring men will at all times be privileged to use the books and papers." The first librarian was male, in contrast with the public library, which had been headed exclusively by women. Indeed, with the exception of a brief interlude, the Workingmen's Library was always managed by a man. The new and relatively large (compared to the public library) space included two "smoking apartments" with $50 worth of oak furniture, an expense that suggests the importance of such accommodations to the overall mission. Within a few days of opening the library added a cigar stand, and discussions soon followed about the prospect of adding a barbershop, both of which were more likely to appeal to men.[51]

The board charged Tuttle, the librarian, with establishing an employment bureau as part of the facility as well, making it clear that the Workingmen's Library was more than just a reading space. Tuttle was to stay abreast of job openings at local factories and refer patrons. Most factory workers were male, but as the *Muncie Star* pointed out, "the bureau would not be confined strictly to securing work for men but would also offer its services to women." The point was perhaps necessary to make because organizers had placed so much emphasis on the new library's role as a refuge for workingmen.[52]

Creating a leisure space for mostly young, mostly single, working-class men was a morally precarious enterprise, so organizers sought to reassure potential supporters from outside organized labor. In a letter soliciting financial support from "prominent citizens," the Trades Council presented the library as a tool of moral uplift that would provide a wholesome alternative to the saloons, dives, and brothels that had proliferated during the city's boom times and would surround workingmen with a "healthy atmosphere" in which to pursue self-culture. The approach to Carnegie strongly emphasized the moral purpose of the library. J. B. Besack, secretary of the Trade Council's library committee, declared in a letter to the philanthropist that "hundreds" of the city's factory workers were "young men, without families, houses, or home influences, taking their meals at restaurants and living in boarding houses." Many spent their evenings "in questionable places, seeking company where their time and money [were] worse than wasted." The library would offer a better place for them to spend their "leisure hours." It is not clear if Besack's appeal influenced Carnegie in any way, but it is evident that when petitioning for support from those who were not members of the working class, the Trades Council put more emphasis on the moral and educational benefits, even as it promoted the library as a space for leisure when addressing the workers themselves.[53]

The Workingmen's Library was everything the Muncie Public Library was not. Despite the protestations, it was clearly a masculine preserve. If not boisterous, it was undeniably a social space, designed more for conversation than for solitary reading. It was also an acknowledgment of class differences, particularly in the way it was used. The new space not only provided workingmen with access to reading material, including labor publications, but also helped define them as a distinctive group. Although the rhetoric surrounding the Muncie Public Library presented it as a unifying institution, its practices, and the users they attracted, gave it a specific social character.

The Carnegie Library

One reason the Muncie Public Library was unable to create the kind of space that served the needs of workingmen was its size. With just two rooms, only one of which was fully open to patrons, it could not accommodate a variety of users. The city's rapidly growing population also strained the library's ability to accommodate demand. The total number of registered borrowers grew from 2,345 at the end of 1885 (the eve of the gas-boom period) to 4,716 a decade later and 6,328 by the end of 1902. The number of books and bound periodicals stored on library shelves increased to more than 11,000 over the same period. By the late 1890s the library was running out of space for both people and books, making the necessity for new accommodations increasingly apparent.

Cramped quarters had in fact long been an issue. An 1880 account of "the Public Library of Muncie" in the *Muncie Daily News* reported that "of late the room has become entirely too small for the purposes for which it was designed, and for two years past the [city] council has had under consideration various plans for more ample accommodations." The article goes on to describe a proposition by James Boyce, a leading Muncie businessman (see chapter 1) who had been involved in the founding of the library, offering "to furnish a suitable room for 99 years" in the new Boyce Block he was building two streets away on the corner on the northeast corner of Main and Jefferson Streets (across the street from the building he would construct so rapidly in 1887). The new library he was proposing would be in a room of "50 by 60 feet" on the third floor of the building, "28 feet high and well lighted from the north and a glass roof. There will be two tiers of windows at the north, the upper of which and the skylight will be stained glass." The result would be "a reading room second to none in the State," without "an equal outside the city of Indianapolis."[54]

In contrast to the cramped condition of the existing library, the proposed new room, because of its size, risked having "comparatively empty" shelves. The article ends by congratulating the Common Council on its "wise act in taking the steps it has toward giving Muncie one of the finest libraries and reading rooms in the northwest," but urging fellow Munsonians, "If we would have the room present that appearance that it should," to contribute liberally by donating their own "books, periodicals, &c. just as soon as the room is fitted to receive them."[55]

The article gives this good news almost as a fait accompli, though that may have been no more than the fervent hope of the newspaper's editor and proprietor, Nathaniel Ethell, a longtime supporter and founding stockholder of the public library. The choice of the Boyce Block as the new location would indeed have placed the institution in the forefront of Indiana's public libraries; according to David Nye, the building was to be the first in the city with lighting powered by electricity.[56] For reasons that remain unclear, this ambitious scheme was scaled down and no third floor was built to accommodate the library. In hindsight, it was probably just as well, since a boiler fire in 1888 resulted in extensive damage to the building. But it seems likely that it was as a consequence of this failed attempt to expand that the case was successfully made for a separate space in the City Building for the perusal of periodicals.

The continued increase in the number books held and patrons served prompted renewed attempts to secure a new location. G. W. H. Kemper, while serving as president of the board in 1893, contacted prominent local developers who were planning a five-story business block to see whether it could include space for the library, but the approach led nowhere. Two years later, a firmer prospect began to take shape when George W. Spilker, a local banker, let it be known that he planned to bequeath his "house on the corner of Jefferson and Adams street as a permanent home for the city library" in the belief that "he should leave some monument, some memorial for the citizens of the city he has loved so long."[57] Spilker died in March 1899 and in his will bequeathed the family's downtown homestead to the city as the dedicated site for a new library building. The structure proved ill suited to house a library, so instead of receiving the property, said to be worth $10,000, the board accepted $6,000 toward a future building.[58]

With Spilker's bequest securely in the bank, the members of the board could engage in speculation, mainly idle and without much sense of direction, about the future of the library. At a typical meeting, held in late 1900, the minutes report that "an informal talk was indulged in, upon the needs and prospects of the Library," but no confirmed resolution or outcome emerged from this convivial discussion. The stasis broke unexpectedly early in the following year when Theodore Rose, the board's president, asked members "to consider the advisability of asking Andrew Carnegie, the Scottish-American Industrialist, for a gift to the City of Muncie, of a sum sufficient to erect a library building commensurate with the needs of the city."[59]

In the same month, Carnegie had sold his Carnegie Steel Company, based in Pittsburgh, to the New York banker John Pierpont Morgan for some $225 million. At the time, it was the biggest deal in U.S. corporate history. Now sixty-six years old and already a generous donor, Carnegie was to devote the remainder of his life to charitable giving. His own rags-to-riches life story, coupled with his passionate belief in the value of education as a primary instrument for cultural and vocational advancement, led Carnegie to channel his benevolence toward the building of public libraries across the English-speaking world. In all, between 1883, when the public library in his native Dunfermline in Scotland was dedicated, and 1919, when funds were given to build a library in the small town of American Fork, Utah, Carnegie donated more than $56 million toward the construction of a total of 2,509 library buildings. Of these, 1,689 were erected in the United States, more than half of them in midwestern communities (768), with the largest number of grants per state going to Indiana (156).[60]

Carnegie himself conceived of his libraries as temples of civic learning. According to Theodore Jones, he "repeatedly claimed that his library donations were not philanthropy" but a dutiful redistribution of wealth so that knowledge could become truly democratic. In a famous speech at the dedication of the Carnegie Library in Washington, D.C., in 1903, he insisted that "free libraries maintained by the people are cradles of democracy, and their spread can never fail to extend and strengthen the democratic idea, the quality of the citizen, [and] the royalty of man. They are emphatically fruits of the true American ideal."[61]

Among working-class Americans there were many who were distrustful of Carnegie's motives. They saw him as sinister figure who was employing a fraction of his wealth in building marmoreal libraries that would serve only to enshrine capitalistic values and beliefs to the detriment of the laboring man. While favoring in principle the creation of libraries, Eugene Debs, the influential leader of the American Railway Union, excoriated "the philanthropic pirates of the Carnegie class," arguing that, once capitalism is abolished, libraries would more naturally spring up as noble temples "dedicated to culture and symbolizing the virtues of the people."[62] Perhaps because the Muncie's library board was so paternalistic in its outlook, there is no hint in the discussions that ensued of any local opposition to the idea of a Carnegie-financed library. On the contrary, as we have seen, the city's labor movement had already received a grant of $500 from Carnegie to support the Workingmen's Library.[63] But discussion took place among local union workers, and, while they did not wish to forestall the construction of a new library that would be financed by Carnegie, they were later unanimous in their adamant opposition to inviting the philanthropist to the dedication in July 1903 of the library that his endowment had financed.[64]

Throughout, at least to the end its tenure in January 1903, the board of the old Muncie Public Library was to remain blithely oblivious to all of this. When Theodore Rose first raised the idea of applying for Carnegie funds, there was nothing of the periodic inaction of earlier meetings when the future of the library had been raised. Members responded enthusiastically, confident in the belief that "Muncie ought to afford to support a $50,000 building." After a full discussion, it was "accordingly . . . decided to ask for that amount," and Rose and Arthur W. Brady, a former mayor of Muncie, were delegated to proceed with the application on the board's behalf. Yet the real impetus to ask for Carnegie funds came not from the board but from the Commercial Club of Muncie, the turn-of-the century equivalent of a Chamber of Commerce.

Rose and Brady found themselves sidelined by the Commercial Club, which had set up its own application committee consisting of hard-nosed Muncie businessmen, including two bankers, John C. Johnson and Hardin Roads, and a real estate developer, James A. Daly.[65]

Johnson, Daly, and Roads wrote to Carnegie in late February 1901 and asked for $50,000. They described Muncie as a city of 29,000 people (including suburbs) and, perhaps anxious to prove their community worthy, emphasized its recent expansion. "It is a manufacturing city, and has grown from a substantial county seat with a population of about 6,000 in 12 years to its present size." They also cited its "public spirit," which they claimed had "developed in a permanent and progressive manner." Noting that they already had a public library, they added that "if we had a building worth $50,000 it could be liberally maintained and would be a perpetual foundation of intelligence and worthy of your noble efforts." Evidently the appeal proved persuasive. His office responded almost immediately and agreed to supply the requested funds, with its standard requirement that the city agree to pay "no less than $5,000 per year" in support of the library.[66]

Anxious to secure such a generous award, the library's supporters arranged for the Common Council to accept these terms. It did so the following week, expressing thanks for the gift. Two weeks later, at its next meeting, the council guaranteed "a perpetual maintenance for a free public library, the annual income to be as required by Mr. Carnegie, i.e. 1/10th of donation." Simultaneously, the council appointed a committee to investigate suitable sites for the new building.[67]

With funding in place, plans took shape quickly. The committee appointed by the Common Council, which included six members of its building committee, three members of the library board, and the city engineer, began to investigate suitable sites. After a summer's investigation, it recommended a downtown location at the corner of Jackson and Jefferson Streets, at a cost of $13,000. The Common Council bought the site, using for part of the payment the $6,000 from the Spilker estate. In September the committee recommended Wing & Mahurin, a prestigious Fort Wayne firm, as the architects.[68]

According to John Rollin Marsh, a board member who also served on the building committee, "The architects made sketches of various plans which were submitted to the Committee and also to a number of citizens of the City, and after careful consideration the Committee voted to adopt for the exterior treatment the plan designed in the Greek Doric order."[69] At the next meeting of the board, Rose, who was also on the Common Council committee charged with overseeing the Carnegie development, reported to the members in slightly more detail that the proposed new building would "be

MUNCIE PUBLIC LIBRARY

FIGURE 6. Muncie's Carnegie Library. The building's classical design, common among Carnegie libraries in the Midwest, was in keeping with architectural styles associated with the City Beautiful movement. From Charles Emerson, *Emerson's Delaware County Rural Route Directory, 1907–1908* (Muncie, Ind.: Central Printing Company, 1907). Courtesy Ball State University Archives and Special Collections.

of stone, one story and high basement, and classical in style." Construction commenced in April 1902, and the building was completed and officially opened on New Year's Day 1904, almost thirty years after the original Muncie Public Library had opened (fig. 6). Like many that were built with the industrialist's funds, it was christened the Carnegie Library.[70]

As we saw earlier, all of this bypassed the library board. When the board met for the first time after the receipt of Carnegie's donation in March 1901, the minutes give no sense that its members might have felt slighted by not having been further consulted at this momentous turn of events. Instead, the conversation turned informally to expressions of "satisfaction, delight, and gratitude . . . over the bright prospects of the City of Muncie soon possessing a library in keeping with her other institutions."[71] The sidelining of the board, however, reflects a familiar pattern among cities that obtained Carnegie libraries. Businessmen and political officials often elbowed aside library boards and educational groups, many of which included substantial numbers of women, in the scramble to attract the industrialist's largesse. For the powerful men who inserted themselves into this process, impressive public libraries represented a form of civic advancement. The common choice of a pillared, classical style of the sort used in Muncie can be interpreted as a glorification of learning, but it was also a form of communal ornamentation in stylistic step with the period's City Beautiful movement. Constructing a monumental library was a way to symbolize the "progressive" spirit that Muncie's businessmen cited in their appeal to Carnegie. It expressed the city's newfound status as a community on the rise.[72]

While the establishment of Muncie's Carnegie Library was in many respects an exercise in civic burnishment, it also entailed the professionalization of its management. As plans took shape in the wake of Carnegie's donation, local leaders invited Mary Eileen Ahern, the influential editor of the journal *Public Libraries,* to address the community. Ahern, who hailed from Marion County, Indiana, was a disciple of Melvil Dewey and a strong advocate of trained professional librarianship. During her visit in April 1901 Ahern met with the library board, and its minutes report "a very interesting and instructive talk . . . abounding in hints and good suggestions for the new library"; that evening Ahern addressed the Commercial Club and library board.[73]

Unfortunately, we have no detailed information regarding her "hints and good suggestions," though she herself wrote about her visit in *Public Libraries,* an article that gives us valuable clues to her thinking. "A Visit to Indiana Libraries" described the public libraries of Anderson, Elwood, Hartford, Muncie, Marion, Wabash, Peru, and Fort Wayne. Ahern was particularly complimentary about the libraries in Marion ("one of the most active and advanced," with a collection of more than fifty thousand books) and Peru ("one of the best libraries visited, considering the small quarters and limited means on which it is administered"). What immediately distinguished the Marion and Peru libraries, and also the one in Fort Wayne, was that they were administered by professional librarians. Leaving aside these "gratifying exceptions," she bemoans the fact that the introduction of new practices in librarianship has been slow in Indiana, and attributes this to the "lack of librarians trained in the latter-day methods, and the fact that the libraries are largely governed by school boards and others too busy with what they consider larger interests to give any considerable amount of attention to the development of library matters."[74]

The summary of her visit to Muncie includes praise for the library board's questions about "up-to-date methods, the best books and modern appliances." (Among the appliances, one assumes, would be a typewriter.) Reporting on her talk to the Commercial Club, Ahern commended "the interest expressed, and the questions and speeches during the meeting," which suggested that "a new day for this library is not far off." Her language is diplomatic, but it is evident that Ahern saw the Muncie Public Library as one that was seriously old fashioned and more than ripe for change. She was quick in praising the generosity of Carnegie "in distributing his gifts for library building over Northern Indiana," above all else as the major factor in stimulating renovation and rethinking across the state and awakening "interest in the mission of the public library."

Overall, she viewed the future of Indiana's libraries as "altogether . . . encouraging, for where matters were not in the best of shape, there was a disposition on the part of those in charge to arise to the occasion." That there was a meeting of minds during her stopover in Muncie boded well, even if she gives the impression of being disenchanted with the present state of affairs. Her visit that early spring day heralded change and was an exhortation to the people of Muncie to take full advantage of the once-in-a-lifetime opportunity that lay before them. For our purposes, it also makes clear the managerial informality, physical limits, and financial weakness of the Muncie Public Library during the first quarter century of its existence.

Muncie's library boosters received much the same message a month later, when a second librarian visited. It may well have been at Mary Eileen Ahern's urging that Merica Hoagland, state organizer for the recently formed Indiana Public Library Commission, came to the city in late May 1901. Another advocate of professionalization, Hoagland also addressed a gathering of library board members and businessmen at the Commercial Club. She, too, "offered valuable suggestions as to what was needed in a building." The board's minutes report that "she was listened to with a great deal of interest" but do not specify her recommendations. Nevertheless, Hoagland was a prominent advocate of professionalization, and she no doubt pushed her listeners to update all aspects of the library's facilities and operations.[75]

In all likelihood responding to this advice, the board of the old Muncie Public Library began preparing for the transition. In the summer of 1902 it sought a professional cataloger familiar with the Dewey classification system and with other modern library innovations that had been so strongly advocated by Ahern and Hoagland. They agreed to employ for the task Artena M. Chapin of Fort Wayne. She was taken on with a salary of $75 per month, considerably more than the $250 per year that Hattie Patterson had enjoyed less than thirty years before and undoubtedly more than Kate Wilson's salary (which in 1893 was less than $40 a month, although the exact figure remains unknown).[76]

The selection of Chapin also represented a new commitment to profession-alism in library matters. She had graduated from the University of Michigan in 1896 and then earned a degree from the Library Science program at the Armour Institute in Chicago. She had worked in libraries in Indianapolis and Fort Wayne. Now in her late twenties, Chapin showed both a maturity of vision and the necessary enthusiasm and drive to transform the Muncie library out of its seemingly antediluvian ways. In her faintly condescend-ing assessment of things as they were at the time of her appointment, she declared that Kate Wilson had fulfilled her role according "to the standard of library work as it was understood when she entered upon it," adding that "the patrons of the library during her regime, will always remember her with kindness" for the faith and conscientiousness with which she worked "long hours, [with] no extra help, and very little pay."[77]

According to Chapin, the Muncie Public Library of 1902 under Wilson was in dire need of a complete makeover. As she recalled a few years later, "The fact that great strides had been made in the technical work of libraries in the past ten years with which one could not keep pace unless she had received special training, led the Board to send for some one [meaning her-self] who might re-organize the library according to modern standards."[78] Chapin made her presence felt at the very first board meeting following her appointment, when she was "empowered to order all necessary equipments" for her cataloging work. Within a few weeks she had ushered the board back for a further meeting at which she asked members to agree to purchase such supplies as "were necessary for the work of cataloguing," the star item being the typewriter described at the beginning of this chapter. If that were not enough, she persuaded them to invest in "a rubber tired book rack or truck . . . , price not to exceed $25." Finally, she succeeded in getting permission at the same meeting to appoint an assistant cataloger to work under her, at a salary of $20 per month, to help with all the work that needed to be under-taken. Chapin's energy and new ideas appear to have expedited Kate Wilson's retirement.[79]

Chapin succeeded Wilson as librarian and quickly tightened the rules governing operations. She proposed a series of changes in late 1902 that elim-inated much of the informality that had characterized the library's manage-ment under the prior regime, and the outgoing board quickly accepted them. The first was to require that patrons present a card when borrowing a book. Seemingly anodyne, this measure in fact represented a complete departure from what had been the customary practice. Wilson had always taken a lais-sez-faire attitude to library cards, allowing visitors or patrons who had for-gotten to bring in their own cards to borrow books under her name. The circulation records show that between November 11, 1891, and November 26, 1902, Wilson used her own card on a total of 464 occasions, the vast majority of them for books that were being borrowed by other people. It is evident that the professional Chapin would never allow such laxity to be introduced into the new Carnegie library. In fact, the "Rules and Regulations" included in the 1905 printed catalog, when Chapin was firmly installed with the title of City Librarian, specify that "Books cannot be transferred from one card to another. A person returning a book cannot take it out on another card." In addition, "any one abusing the privileges of the Library or violating these rules shall be temporarily suspended from the enjoyment of these privileges."[80]

Hardly less casual had been the board's attitude toward patrons who failed to return books by their two-week due date and in enforcing payment for the cost of books that had been damaged or lost while checked out. Already in 1875, even before the library was open to borrowers, the board had endeavored to anticipate future problems by making it "lawful for the librarian to employ a messenger to collect books from delinquent borrowers" and setting the messenger's payment at 15 cents per book The board minutes and the library's fine books indicate some success with this arrangement.[81]

Depending on circumstances, however, it was no less common for the board to waive or reduce a fine. Late charges were normally accrued at 3 cents per day, but when, in early 1895, Rudolph Bloom, a thirteen-year-old schoolboy from a working-class home to the south of the city, borrowed and kept for three weeks beyond its due date a copy of *From Peasant to Prince*, a juvenile fiction based on the life of the Finnish-born nobleman Alexander Menshikov, the board opted to fine him but a nickel. On another occasion, seven "special cases" were discussed by board members. Two fines of $2.66 and $3.20 were excused, but with all the other cases, the notices to the delinquent readers were "repeated" and the expense of sending these out was added to the charge. In its apparent desire to make ad hoc adjustments rather than blanket enforcement of its regulations, the board was more than once willing to accept a donation of books in lieu of imposing a fine. Yet when Nellie Campbell, a young housewife who had joined the library in December 1897, accrued a debt of $2.87, her offer to pay $1.00 was accepted but her card remained "discounted," and no further books were ever issued to her. Sentiment, more than logic or a blind insistence on enforcement, seems to have dictated these decisions.[82]

Correspondingly, it was largely left to the librarian to decide what to do about books that had been damaged while in the care of a patron. An exception to this was in 1894, when two separate canine episodes were brought before the board. On July 5, it was moved that "Mrs. Hemingray pay twenty-five cents for the book destroyed by her dog." Mrs. Hemingray was the wife of a prominent Muncie glass manufacturer, and the fine imposed seems to have been nominal. On October 17, Maggie Smith, a patron of about three months' standing, "was asked to rebind the book injured by her dog." It is reasonable to assume that the intention here was that she should pay for the cost of rebinding rather than attempt the task herself. By showing more of a palate for books than their pooches, each of these ladies was allowed by the board to remain in good standing and continue borrowing from the library.[83]

Under the new regime inaugurated by Chapin, such infractions were to lead automatically to fines. The rules she imposed spelled out without ambiguity that patrons were responsible for paying for any books they damaged or lost. Moreover, she insisted, "All penalties shall be rigidly enforced, and the librarian shall deliver no books to any person who shall be delinquent by non-payment of fines or unsettled claims for damage or loss of books."[84] What is implicit here is that the responsibility for overseeing these actions has been subtly shifted from the board to the librarian.

The new rules instituted in late 1902 also place restrictions on the circulation of fiction. Borrowers were now allowed to take home two books at a time, but only one could be a work of fiction. While the customary loan period remained fourteen days, new fiction could be kept for only seven days and could not be immediately renewed. This policy was in part an attempt to accommodate the demand for new fiction, but it also aimed to curb the reading of best sellers and steer patrons toward material of a higher literary quality. Here Chapin was following the received principle of many professional librarians at the turn of the twentieth century that patrons should be actively encouraged to extend their reading to nonfiction. Several years later, in her *Sketch of the Muncie Public Library*, she makes this clear. Noting that "as [was] the case in every public library," fiction constituted the "largest part of the whole" in Muncie. "Whether this is to be deplored, as some librarians think, or whether it is merely as it should be, as other librarians contend, it is always gratifying to find that through the instrumentality of the library its patrons have been led to more serious reading than is found in the average novel."[85]

The annual report of the library for 1906 shows that Chapin's methods produced at least a small decrease in fiction reading In 1903, 87 percent of loans involved works of fiction. By 1906 that figure had dropped to 84 percent, suggesting that she had achieved at least some degree of success in promoting what she called "more serious reading."[86]

The final part of the transition from the old Muncie Public Library to the new library housed in the Carnegie building resulted from a change in state law. In 1901, the state of Indiana had passed a law designed to ensure that Indiana's cities and towns met Carnegie's financial requirements. The legislation was introduced before the state's General Assembly by Representative Elmer Ellsworth Mummert, a Republican from the small city of Goshen, and it became known as the Mummert Law. At the time, according to a local historian, it was "considered one of the best acts of its kind in any state, and upon the strength of which Andrew Carnegie has given between forty and fifty libraries to Indiana."[87]

One of the provisions of the law, which received full backing from the recently established Public Library Commission, decreed that towns or cities must levy an annual tax "not to exceed one mill [a tenth of a cent] for each dollar of all the taxable property assessed" for library purposes, and that libraries be governed by a board of seven citizens, three appointed by the judge of the circuit court and two each by the Common Council and the trustees of the local schools. It also specified that "not less than three of the members appointed shall be women." The boards were to be entrusted with the control of funds "and the custody of all of the books and other property," and were to "direct all of the affairs of such public library . . . [and] enforce rules for the management . . . as they may deem necessary, and to employ librarians and assistants."[88]

By slow evolution rather than through statutory legislation, the Muncie Public Library of 1902 conformed to almost all of the main provisions of the Mummert Law. Its board was made up of seven members, even though they were selected by the stockholders; three of the members were women; and the city's tax levies sustained most of the library's financial needs. But the incorporation of the library as a stock company was not in conformity with the new law. In December 1902, at the board's final meeting of the year, one member, John Rollin Marsh, proposed a resolution that would transfer the ownership of the library to the City of Muncie on January 1 of the new year. He pointed out that the city was already "practically the owner of the entire stock of the Muncie Public Library, consisting of 13,000 to 14,000 volumes, an amount greatly in excess of three-tenths of a mill on each dollar of valuation of the [city's] taxable property." Under the Mummert Law, he argued, it was therefore necessary for the current board to transfer the library, at no cost, to the city and to cede control to a "legally qualified Board of Directors." A similar motion had already been ratified by the Common Council, and Marsh's resolution passed unanimously. All that was left now was to call a meeting in the new year at which the old board would meet the new "to settle up the unfinished business of the year and hear the treasurer's final report."[89]

That meeting took place on January 6, 1903. The new board, no longer the appointees of a stock company that had now ceased to exist, accorded exactly with the Mummert Law, and it was made up of Theodore Rose and Nellie Stouder, representing the city school board; Lewis W. Cates and Belle Thomas, who were appointed by the city council; and Abbott L. Johnson, Nettie Wood, and Dr. Cassius M. Carter, who had been chosen by the circuit court judge. Rose and Stouder, the president and secretary of the old board, were the only holdovers, and their presence on the new board, in which they were elected to the same offices, must have helped to give continuity to the proceedings.

The membership of the new board included the secretary of the People's Home and Savings Association of Muncie (Cates), a schoolteacher who became secretary of the Art Association of Muncie (Thomas), a capitalist and business leader (Johnson), an 1891 graduate of the Muncie High School (Wood), and the minister of the First Baptist Church (Carter). Cates was to become the treasurer and Carter the vice president of the new board. All five new members had either been patrons of the old Muncie Public Library themselves or had partners or siblings who were. The three new men had each in turn had school-age children who had made good use of the old library.

The proceedings of the new board have not been preserved, so we cannot tell directly what impact the constitutional and personnel changes may have had at that time. Just over twenty years later, however, the Lynds were to criticize the fact that the library board of 1924, still appointed by the same procedure but prey to conflicting political pressures, "contained no college-trained person or outstanding business man in the city."[90]

3

Cosmopolitan Trends

Print Culture and the Public Library
in 1890s Muncie

By choosing the city of Paris of the flapper era as the setting of her adroit short story "Forty-Five" (1922), the Ohio-born author Fannie Hurst creates a deliberate contrast between the brittle sophistication of the French capital and the small midwestern hometown of her protagonists. Escorting her daughter to Paris, Edith Whatley, an 1899 graduate of Muncie Central High School, faces constant reminders of her upbringing, not least through her chance encounter with two of her fellow classmates, who, like her, have reached the age of forty-five.[1]

On her first trip to Paris nineteen years earlier, Edith had sailed across the Atlantic with "a group of time-and-money limited teachers and librarians from Muncie" and had shared a cabin with three of them. While on board she was wooed and compromised into shotgun matrimony by Gordon Whatley, a New Yorker of considerable affluence, and endured "ten years of unmitigated married hell" from which she was liberated only by Gordon's death. Following her marriage Edith had relocated from Muncie to New York City, where she took up the well-heeled and leisurely lifestyle of "the smart tea and shopping districts of the slightly east fifties." Now she was accompanying her nineteen-year-old daughter, May, to what the author paints with mock adulation as not the real Paris but an "*American* Paris" where the daily routine might include "a massage and a look-in at Cartier's in the forenoon. Snails and Amer Picon at Prunier's for luncheon. Longchamps. Wood strawberries at tea-time on the Bois. Dinner at the Ritz. . . . Dancing at Café Madrid and Maxim's."

The "*American*" conception of Paris, May sardonically notes, differs from that of true Frenchmen whose activities are confined to "running the show. They sit behind the scenes, scrape in American dollars and eat tripe." For New York–raised May, a half generation removed from the Midwest, "the Indiana burr" shared by her mother's former classmates and their small-town talk grate on her sensitive ears and cause her embarrassment, whereas for Julie Bell, one of Edith's class of '99 who is still living in Muncie, the vibrancy of Paris is a pleasant release from "intellectual isolation" and an opportunity to harvest some seeds of its cultural glitter to bring home with her. It is through traveling to and experiencing such centers of culture as Paris or New York that a middle-aged woman like Julie can realize the dream of "carrying the first banners of the real intellectual awakening" to inelegant Muncie. At the women's discussion club to which she is proud to belong, "my very first paper next winter," Julie proclaims, "is going to be on Rodin and the pieces on the Rodin Museum here. . . . Our little culture clubs and art circles that afford you sophisticates so much amusement are in a way the Rodins of American culture."

Hurst's fine story risks articulating a definition of the cosmopolitan that promotes Paris and New York as intellectual and cultural hubs while consigning Muncie to the outer reaches of provincialism. Here, the notion of what might be deemed "cosmopolitan" may more exactly find a substitute in the word "metropolitan," with its emphasis on the influence of major capitals as founts of urbane and sophisticated cultural production. Late nineteenth-century Muncie might have been beholden to New York, Chicago, and Cincinnati (or even Paris or London) as metropolises that held a kind of centripetal pull which was hard to see, or even absent, in a provincial midwestern small city. Yet in the midst of the gas boom and after, Muncie did not wish to project itself as anything less than a beacon of progress at the frontier of a great nation that was endeavoring to forge a new and progressive character for itself following a divisive and terrible civil war.

Our working employment of the terms "cosmopolitan" and "cosmopolitanism" in this discussion is more pragmatic than theoretical, though it is indebted to present-day philosophical debate on these concepts and their varied meanings. The editors of a 2011 essay collection on the topic begin by defining *cosmopolitan* as "a term that is often used to describe a citizen of the world: an enlightened individual who believes he or she belongs to a common humanity or world order rather than to a set of particular customs or traditions." As the same editors point out a few pages later, however, the related term *cosmopolitanism* comes across as "inherently complex": "the kind of political and philosophical concept that eludes a single, absolute, and authoritative definition." They conclude that "cosmopolitanism is therefore bound to frustrate any attempt to establish a grand and universal theoretical system." It connotes what the theorist Bruce Robbins has called "habits of thought and feeling" that forge a sense of connection which carried beyond national boundaries. But, as Robbins and others have also noted, the precise character of this mentality is difficult to pin down, particularly because the boundary between national loyalty and cosmopolitanism is blurred. The processes that produce national solidarities can also generate loyalties that extend beyond the nation.[2]

Our articulation of these two closely related terms attempts to mediate between them by stressing "cosmopolitan *trends*." By trends we mean the increasing efforts of local citizens to comprehend and appreciate the world beyond the limits of their community through a perception, albeit imperfect, of its place in the order of things. It manifested itself in Muncie as a communal sense of belonging to a wider civilization. If such thinking did not constitute a full-fledged cosmopolitanism as it has been defined by various theorists, it nevertheless suggests an outlook that we cannot simply dismiss as provincial.

It is almost customary to view Muncie in such condescending terms, the equivalent of the fictitious town of Plattville in the Hoosier writer Booth Tarkington's wildly popular first novel, *The Gentleman from Indiana* (1899). Tarkington created a small town of the 1890s, a county seat like Muncie, seventy miles from the nearest big city, in which "the people lived happily; and, while the world whirled on outside, they were content with their own."[3] The response to the Lynds' Middletown study only reinforced the perception of Muncie as an unsophisticated place, "a city in Moronia," in H. L. Mencken's cutting words.[4] But residents of late nineteenth-century Muncie would not recognize such a portrait. Enthused by their community's remarkable transformation during the gas-boom period, they imagined themselves as participants in a process of national, international, and perhaps even universal cultural development. Muncie during the final decade of the nineteenth century was a rapidly growing city with grand ambitions. Citing its cultural institutions as well as its economic development, Muncie's boosters saw their city as becoming a constituent part of an advancing civilization. Such boasting represented more than an expression of municipal pride; it also reflected an impulse to identify with broader segments of the world, even those that stretched beyond national boundaries.

It is perhaps no less the dilemma today of a small city to find itself torn between a desire to compete with its larger urban rivals, against which it is likely to be (or at least risks being) belittled, and a countertendency to glorify its provincial roots and endangered rural character. Arguably, the crucial invention that sustained Muncie in the years following the gas boom was the motor car. By 1910, the city—previously a mecca for carriage building—not only built automobiles but was also, and remained through the twentieth century, a principal center for the manufacture of automobile parts. Throughout the whole existence of the old Muncie Public Library, when the automobile was still being invented, and into the first decades of the twentieth century, when it became ubiquitous, there remained a nostalgia for small-town values and a simpler lifestyle that was nonmechanized and, to a degree, anti-cosmopolitan. The nostalgia for this far less complicated, almost bucolic existence is captured in a poem titled "The Gay Nineties," published many years later by Dr. Hugh Cowing, one of Muncie's leading physicians and himself a patron of the library:

> Yes, the Nineties were gay;
> Then life was geared to a trot;
> There was time to laugh and play
> When the honk of the Ford was not.
>
> The clatter of horses' feet,
> The rumble of wheels in the street,
> Glad sounds of that other day,
> Back when the Nineties were gay! . . .
>
> You wonder how could they be gay
> When rouge and lip-stick were rare;
> When girls wouldn't dare bob their hair—
> How could the Nineties be gay?
>
> I answer, the Nineties *were* gay;
> There was time to laugh and play;
> A horse to drive, and a hand to hold,
> Helped make the Nineties gay.[5]

Cowing acknowledges the inevitability of progress while ruing the loss of a slower and less developed pace that is denoted audibly by "the clatter of horses' feet" instead of "the honk of the Ford." With poetical hindsight, the 1890s are made to encapsulate the transition from an era that measured itself by the gaiety associated with simple country pleasures to a more complex, and inevitably more cosmopolitan, milieu and lifestyle that lay in store with the advent of the new century. Unlike the nostalgia in Cowing's verses for an older, more leisured way of life, the commoner response is one that hails technological advancement and the growth of cosmopolitan values.

These cosmopolitan aspirations were generally linked with the material and intellectual advancement of Eurocentric ideas of civilization. In his *Twentieth Century History of Delaware County, Indiana* (1908), G. W. H. Kemper, a former president of the library board, employed the word "cosmopolitan" in this fashion. Discussing what might have prompted pioneer families to settle in the county and whether their places of origin would have had an impact on their chosen destination, Kemper obliquely invokes the progress of "this modern age, when men are becoming more cosmopolitan in their conditions, when provincialism and the influence of state and section are less plainly impressed on individuals." Here, what is "cosmopolitan" is seen as a counter to provincialism, even though it still operated within national boundaries. It represented the progress of civilization through the inexorable westward drive of the United States during the nineteenth century. The places where a settler family lived before coming to Delaware County, Kemper notes, "were intermediate points in the westward migration, to which the family made the first stage of its journey, or stopped a few years until civilization caught up with them, and then pushed on deeper into the wilderness."[6]

Some pages later, Kemper again invokes the word "cosmopolitan" in a complementary way:

> The men who developed Delaware county did not own any particular section of their previous home. The settlers were perhaps as cosmopolitan as those of any county in the middle west. Here were united in society and often in family ties those whose lives had been molded by Puritan New England and those who had no influences and customs outside of Cavalier Virginia. Yankee thrift and southern liberality became valuable elements in the new social order growing up in the middle west. So far as the recognized sections of the United States have produced each a somewhat different type of people, Delaware county has received samples of each of those types, and has developed a thoroughly American civilization, equally removed from the dominant characteristics of the north or the south, and from the peculiarities popularly ascribed to the eastern and to the western people.[7]

What emerges here is an understanding of the cosmopolitan that stresses notions of commonality, and sees the inhabitants of Delaware County as representatives of an emergent civilization that is made up of largely diverse elements that were being annealed into unity in the Midwest.

It should be pointed out that Kemper was not talking about what today would be deemed multiculturalism, because the origin of all the people he has in mind is European. In a study published in 2006, Margaret Jacob defines cosmopolitanism in today's world as translating into a "meaning closer to home, a way of living in our own multiethnic towns and cities."[8] If such a postcolonial definition is not germane to the present context, and particularly to a city that received few immigrants, one can nonetheless see a comparable pattern of thought that imagined bonding across then-salient cultural differences. The subtext of Kemper's use of "cosmopolitan" was that the American Midwest was a location in which the warring factions of north and south, which had so nearly riven the United States but forty years or so before, were able to live together and harmonize more easily than in the primary battleground states of the Civil War. In that sense, the Midwest provides for Kemper, himself a Union veteran, a model of the cosmopolitan ideal and a promising blueprint of the notion of America as a country that was strengthened by healing its earlier divisions through fostering a caucus of citizens from divergent backgrounds.

While to some degree residents of a city such as Muncie forged this sensibility through face-to-face interaction or, for a lucky few, through travel, to far greater extent they developed and sustained it through print. Only a small portion of the printed output consumed in Muncie was produced locally; most of it emanated from the metropolitan centers of the anglophone world. One facet of the city's feverish growth through the 1880s and 1890s was the increasing availability of printed materials. The number and size of local newspapers grew, the circulation of magazines increased, and opportunities to acquire books multiplied. Newspapers, magazines, and books conveyed experiences of the world beyond the city's limits that were otherwise only rarely available. The public library, which as we have seen was growing rapidly through these years, provided access to all of these forms of print, and local commentators linked its continued development to the cultural and intellectual character of the city. The access to broad cultural currents that such print production provided allowed people living in boom-era Muncie to conceive of themselves as participants in an expanding civilization, a preference sustained largely through reading.

Printers and Newspapers

Although Muncie never gained traction as a publishing center, it was hardly short of either printers or printing presses. Most of the publications to emerge from these presses catered to local needs. As early as May 1837, David Gharky, a German-born immigrant and perhaps the city's first printer, had initiated

a newspaper, *The Muncietonian,* though he could not attract enough subscribers to keep it going.[9] In the ensuing years other printing firms set up in
Muncie, often engaging in jobbing work and sometimes combining this with
the production of a newspaper. In the 1870s an enterprising local businessman, Charles Emerson, who had previously been the supervising agent in
Muncie for the Singer sewing machine company, began publishing city and
county directories, which usually included brief listings of townspeople and
their occupations. *Emerson's Muncie Directory* for 1876–77 lists at least half a
dozen individuals who were working in the printing trade, two of them, John
C. Clark and William H. Messick, as compositors for the *Muncie News,* and
one, Emma E. Taylor, in a similar position for the rival *Muncie Times.*[10]

As these listings suggest, most printers were engaged in the newspaper
business. Muncie's growth had been accompanied by an expansion of local
newspaper production, to the point where the city had four active dailies by
the end of the 1890s, as well as several weekly sheets. Over the course of the
gas boom, the size of these papers—typically eight pages during the early
1890s—expanded as well; by the end of the decade sixteen-page editions were
not uncommon. Locally written accounts of community life filled some of
these pages, but the larger share was advertisements (for both local and, by
mail order, national products), serialized stories, and national news reports.

One gains a sense of the growth and development of Muncie newspapers
and the confidence instilled by technological innovations in this field from
Thomas Helm's account in his local history. Writing in the early 1880s, Helm
begins by taking a retrospective glance back to Muncie fifty years before,
affirming that one "would scarcely recognize the relationship between the
make-up of a newspaper office then and now." His account predates the gas
boom of the final years of the decade, but already it is driven by the sense of
an inexorable progress from the period of early settlement:

> Journalism then had not acquired the distinction which characterizes the
> profession and practice of it accorded by the world of mind and of letters
> now. Half a century or more ago, it was the exception, rather than the rule,
> to find even in a county seat, in those early days, a printing office and news-
> paper. . . . The retrospect . . . enable[s] the reviewer to trace the upward
> movement of the profession through many stages of development, from a
> condition akin to starvation, when "ink-balls" occupied the place of "com-
> position rollers," and the old "wooden hand-press" foreshadowed the pres-
> ence of the "lightning power-press" propelled by steam, from which the
> printed sheets come forth to-day at the rate of from 3,000 to 20,000 per
> hour, to the high position and mighty enginery co-operating to mold and
> control public opinion, as manifested now in the usages of society at large.[11]

We know of more than thirty different newspapers published in Muncie before 1904, most of them short lived. Precise circulation figures are difficult to gauge, though Helm tells us that the *Muncie Daily News* sold several hundred copies daily around 1880. Its proprietor, Nathaniel F. Ethell, was a staunch advocate of the Republican Party, and rival papers such as the *Courier-Democrat* (later renamed the *Observer*) and the *Democrat-Herald* (later shortened to the *Herald*) were set up with the specific aim of offering a different political perspective. According to Kemper, the newspapers of the mid- to late nineteenth century may have "reflected a more strenuous partisanship and devoted more space to political affairs" than became the norm in the new century, but that zealousness would prompt "an organization to publish a paper during a campaign and then suspend."[12]

By the 1890s the character of the press was changing, both nationally and locally. In the largest cities, entrepreneurial publishers such as Joseph Pulitzer and William Randolph Hearst found profitability in a formula that combined political independence, sensational reporting, and popular fare such as comics, sports, and light fiction. These innovations did not fully penetrate the pages of Muncie's newspapers, but their effects were nonetheless evident. The local dailies—the *Daily* (later *Morning*) *News,* the *Times,* the *Herald,* and, when it launched in 1899, the *Morning Star*—retained their political ties, but increasingly supplied reporting and commentary on national affairs.

While they devoted a substantial portion of their space to local events, ranging from business and civic developments to reports on club meetings, they also increasingly incorporated material produced elsewhere and provided by wire services. An 1898 advertisement for the *Muncie Morning News* captured this shift, as well as the emphasis on timeliness that reduced the sense of distance between Muncie and the rest of the world. Noting that "the *News* has a special telegraph operator receiving associated press telegrams from 7 p.m. until 3 a.m.," it promised to give its readers "the news of the world before breakfast." The paper had "more local news, more home and foreign advertising and also more circulation than any paper in eastern Indiana."[13]

It was not only by printing the latest news that publishers sought to convey a cosmopolitan sense of connection to readers of the local press. The ads for local businesses reflected close attention to commercial trends—notices for the "New York Store" offered the most current clothing and other dry goods for sale—while others, such as a pitch for subscriptions to the *Family Fashion Journal* that promised women guides to "La Mode de Paris" and other examples of the latest French styles, were part of national marketing schemes. Editors filled space with all sorts of wire service articles, often reflecting the national trends of the moment. The 1893 Chicago World's Fair dominated the inside pages of the local press for months, as did the Spanish-American War a few years later.[14]

When attention-grabbing national and international events were not as prominent, newspaper editors reported more often on literary and artistic matters. A turn through the pages of the *Muncie Daily Herald* during the early months of 1898, before the war took center stage, finds profiles of popular writers of the day such as the Polish novelist Henryk Sienkiewicz, reports on the Dreyfus Affair and in particular the libel trial involving the French naturalist writer Émile Zola, gossip about authors (under headings such as "The Writers" or "News of Novelists"), and excerpts from or descriptions of new publications. Advertisements for new books, or luxuriously bound editions of the classics, also appeared routinely.[15]

When Richard Le Gallienne, the English poet and novelist considered the foremost figure of group of writers known as the Decadents, embarked on a series of U.S. lectures, the *Herald* featured a short article profiling him, analyzing his latest novel, and announcing his tour. The headline, "Leader of the Decadents: Le Gallienne, Poet and Esthete, Will Lecture to Us," was telling. The celebrated writer was not scheduled to appear in Muncie but rather in New York and other major cities. The choice of the first-person pronoun was likely a product of editorial haste, as was the text of the article, which gave no indication of where the writer would speak. Yet it also reflected the ways provincial anxieties and cosmopolitan aspirations could mix, and how the fast-paced, networked character of print journalism was shrinking time and space. For residents of Muncie during the 1890s, the pages of the local paper were a place where they could imagine themselves as part of the "us" when it came to cultural matters.[16]

Although we have no direct record of newspaper circulation in 1890s Muncie, local editors routinely proclaimed that their circulation was growing. The *Muncie Daily Times* claimed a circulation of 1,790 per day in late 1892, and the *Morning News* boasted of 2,300 daily readers early the next year. While these exact numbers must be taken with a grain of salt, claims of growth are plausible, given not only the rapid increase in the local population during these years but also the expanding size of the papers themselves. No doubt seeking to boost advertising sales, the editor of the *Muncie Morning News* played up the success of an advertisement for W. A. McNaughton's Big Store in an August 1898 number. In a front-page ad, the store reported that 1,243 people had read their ad in the Sunday edition of the paper and showed up for its hourly sales. Inside the paper, on page 5, a notice for the paper itself appeared, citing the success of the McNaughton's ad and quoting a ringing endorsement from the store's manager. Though clearly a promotional gambit, the sense of an expanding circulation rings true in a period when the newspaper business, like much of the rest of the city, was booming. And there is little doubt that these readers could gain some sense of the world, however slanted or circumscribed, in the pages of the local press.[17]

Books and Bookstores

While it is safe to say that newspapers were the most widely read printed material in 1890s Muncie, books became much easier to obtain as well. The expansion of the national book trade made available cheap, mass-market fiction to a wide array of readers. Before the gas boom Muncie had a handful of drugstores that sold books, primarily textbooks for schoolchildren, and it was possible to obtain books (or subscriptions to a series of books) through mail order or from a door-to-door salesman. By the late 1890s the city had at least two stores that marketed the latest and most popular titles, newspapers were filled with advertisements for books available through the mail, and locals could order titles through outlets such as the Sears catalog. These changes were not simply the outgrowth of changing local conditions; they also reflected developments in the national book trade system.[18]

During the 1880s Muncie had two booksellers.[19] Both were listed in a local directory under the heading "BOOKS AND DRUGGIST," and it is no less true then than now that drugstores sometimes doubled as purveyors of books, particularly in small towns such as Muncie. The first of these, C. M. Kimbrough, was listed in the directory as having his premises at 27 and 29 South Walnut Street. He was described as a "Dealer in School-Books, Bibles, Albums, Miscellaneous Books, Fine Gold Pens and Stationery, Wall Paper, Window Shades, Picture Frames, Curtain Poles, Art Goods, etc." It adds that he "will furnish any book at publisher's price," though he does not appear to have acted as a supplier to the Muncie Public Library.[20]

Charles Maberry Kimbrough, according to Kemper's local history, "came to Muncie in 1876 and opened the first exclusive book and paper store in this city," and in the 1880 U.S. census his occupation is given as "Dealer in Books and Stationery."[21] At that time he was a relatively young man of thirty, married, with three children. The family's home, at 311 East Jackson Street, was on a site that was later occupied by the new Carnegie-funded public library that was opened in 1904. In a transformation that is indicative of the incentives created by the gas boom and which suggests that the book trade was not particularly lucrative in a small city, Kimbrough closed his retail business in 1887 in order to become manager and, shortly afterward, president of the Muncie-based Indiana Bridge Company, which he was to lead successfully until his death more than forty years later. He also became for a period a Republican state senator, and remained throughout an active member of Muncie's Methodist Episcopal Church. Kemper describes him as "distinctively a man of broad human sympathy, clearly defined principles and high intellectuality."[22]

We have far less personal though far more business knowledge about the second bookseller. His name was George H. Andrews, and the local directory listed him as the "Proprietor of [the] Star Drug Store, No. 2 South Walnut Street. Wholesale and Retail Druggist and Newsdealer. Books, Wall paper and Stationery, etc."[23] Both the 1870 and the 1880 U.S. censuses give his occupation as "Druggist." In 1870, he was twenty-three years of age.[24] The minutes of the library board show that for several years he was the supplier of choice to the library for magazines and periodicals. Although it is uncertain precisely why the library turned to Andrews as a supplier of books rather than to Kimbrough, it seems likely that Andrews, who purchased stock in the library when it opened and was among its earliest patrons (he was no. 24), had established a relationship with the board before Kimbrough even arrived in town in 1876.[25]

A surviving inventory of merchandise held by Andrews's Star Drug Store, dated June 9, 1885, affords us a rare and intriguing glimpse of what was being stocked by a midwestern druggist at the time.[26] Beyond toiletries and medicines, regular articles for sale included one dozen combs, an identical quantity of toothbrushes, a duster, three pairs of scissors, five boxes of dominoes, and twenty-two purses. Among everyday stationery items, the store had available a large quantity of blank books, letter books of different sizes, and half a dozen drawing books. Aids to elementary education included pocket slates, a box of spelling blocks, and a box of picture blocks.

The store carried books, including a number that taught reading and grammar. The inventory reported eight copies of *Swinton's Word Primer*, a guide to spelling for youngsters.[27] For slightly older children, Andrews kept multiple copies of McGuffey's popular *Readers* and *Spellers*, a widely used series of graded primers based on the phonics method.[28] To complement these, it also stocked copies of Thomas W. Harvey's *Elementary Grammar and Composition*, a standard work used by American teachers for many decades. Books for more advanced readers included four copies of Webster's *Academic Dictionary*, two "High School Dictionaries," one "School Etymology," and three copies of "Shaws English Lit."[29] There was also a small choice of letter writing manuals, such as *The Universal Letter Writer*.

The assortment of books in other subjects was no less diverse and catered to different levels of ability. Forty-six copies of Emerson Elbridge White's widely used *Primary Arithmetic,* fourteen of his *Intermediate Arithmetic,* and the same number of his *Complete Arithmetic* were inventoried.[30] Andrews also had six copies of Joseph Ray's *New Practical Arithmetic,* a common curricular work that went through many editions. Among books of science, the store stocked six copies of "Browns Physiology," three of "Kiddles Elem. Astronomy," eight of an unidentified work that is transcribed in the ledger as "Electric History," and single copies of "How Plants Grow" and "Cooley Philosophy."[31] Politics is represented by one book on "Civil Government," the classics by "Chase & Stewarts Virgil" and "Ceasars Commentarys."[32] There are also singing books, a "Glee & Chorus Book," and unspecified primary and intermediary works of geography, three copies of a "1st Bk. In German," and two of a geology textbook.[33] History and the fine arts were poorly represented, as were foreign languages.

The stock of books represented only a small part of the Star Drug Store's total inventory. Most were recently published texts, more often than not titles that were likely to be part of, or a supplement to, the school curriculum. Andrews does not appear to have dealt in secondhand books, which, given the uncertainty of their source, might have been considered out of place in a drugstore. His supply of schoolbooks was not comprehensive, nor does he appear to have had so much as a small shelf of new books, including fiction, that would have been of appeal to the general reader.

It is revealing that, if we compare the books for sale at the Star Drug Store in June 1885 to what was available at the Muncie Public Library, we find that only Thomas Shaw's *Outlines of English Literature* and Noah Webster's *American Dictionary of the English Language* are jointly represented. Webster's dictionary was one of more than 350 new books that were purchased for the library through Andrews between May and July 1875. It would appear that Andrews could obtain a wide range of books, including popular titles, through the 1870s and 1880s, but there was not sufficient demand for him to sell them in his store.

The rapid growth of Muncie during the final years of the century appears to have broadened the local market for retail books. Although Kimbrough abandoned bookselling (and the drugstore business) to pursue opportunities in manufacturing, the Star Drug Store continued and even expanded its trade. By the 1890s, it was advertising its "new books this week," including popular titles such as *A Laggard in Love* (1890) by Jeanie Gwvnne Bethany and *The Tale of Chloe* (1879) by the English novelist and poet George Meredith. (The library did not acquire either book.) Clearly something had changed in the operations of the Star between the mid-1880s, when it stocked only schoolbooks, and the following decade, when it advertised popular titles geared toward a general audience.[34]

A similar evolution can be glimpsed in the development of Shick's Bookstore. Its proprietors were two brothers, Charles and Leonard Shick, though every indicator points to Charles as the active partner in the business. His varied career included working in the hardware business and farming before he opened his bookstore. The store opened for business in downtown Muncie during the late 1880s or early 1890s and was well established by 1894, when a published profile of Charles reports that "he now handles all grades of books, stationery and materials, wall papers, etc., and is carrying on a very successful trade."[35]

That list makes clear that Shick's relied on a mix of products even though it billed itself as "the only bookstore in the city." Books were clearly a staple, including inexpensive copies of the latest from popular authors such as E. P. Roe, as well as titles by established authors such as Dickens. But the trade in books alone appears to have been insufficient to sustain the business, even during the early 1890s when the city was growing rapidly. A Christmas ad from 1891 listed books as only one of a number of available items that also included "pictures, games, dolls, baskets, and toilet sets," as well as wallpaper and stationery. If advertisements are any gauge, books became a more central part of the business over the next few years. Pre-Christmas notices nearly a decade later emphasized books (and stationery) but did not include the other items once listed. By that time, the store described itself as Muncie's "Headquarters for the Latest Books" or as "the place to go for the latest books." Its ads also highlighted new and popular titles, such as Lew Wallace's *Ben Hur* (published in 1880 but still popular) or the best seller *Janice Meredith* by Paul Leicester Ford. By this time Muncie was a big enough market, and publishers were able to distribute books cheaply enough, to make selling recently published and enduringly popular books the principal basis of a retail business.[36]

Even though it increasingly emphasized the sale of books, it is difficult to know just what titles Shick's sold and in what quantities, not to mention the significance of its books in the lives of its customers. There is no doubt that the store was a purveyor of cheap, mass-market editions of top-selling titles. As early as 1892 it trumpeted discounted prices for books by Dickens and H. Rider Haggard (19 cents each, marked down from 25 cents). The store also sold family Bibles, as well as morocco-bound Oxford Teacher's Bibles and "fancy bound" juvenile books. These items were as much status-defining consumer products distinguished by their physical character as they were texts conveying particular ideas or stories. The books that Shick's sold to its customers no doubt served a variety of purposes, but the nature and substance of those reading experiences remain elusive.[37]

One can conclude from the evolving marketing strategies of the Star Drug

Store and Shick's that popular books became more widely available for purchase in Muncie. This shift was likely the result of the interplay between the
city's growth, which made it a bigger market for many commodities, and the
increasingly dense and efficient national book trade. These factors combined
to ensure that even residents of a small city in eastern Indiana were, by the
end of the nineteenth century, active participants in a national, and in some
respects international, print marketplace.

The Public Library as a Cosmopolitan Institution

Although we have no business records for Shick's Bookstore, we can be confident that its sales did not match the circulation figures of the Muncie Public
Library, which remained the dominant supplier of books to the city's residents. The 22,000 loans the library made in 1899 easily dwarfed any such
figures for the smaller private libraries and in all likelihood far exceeded the
number of books sold by Shick's, the Star Drug Store, and other outlets in
that year. It provided to its users a broad, though as we have seen selective,
segment of the print output produced in the United States and Great Britain.
These texts represented links to the broader fund of knowledge and cultural
production that reached back in time and across national boundaries and
defined the civilization to which educated Munsonians were increasingly
confident they belonged.

Muncie was never itself a publishing center, and the books held in the
public library were almost all published in distant places. The exceptions
include a city directory and a two-volume local history, as well as the ubiquitous Dr. Kemper's pamphlet *The Uses of Suffering*. Published outside Muncie
but within the state are 257 volumes that display an Indianapolis imprint.
The majority of these are annual reports, documents of the Indiana General
Assembly, legislative manuals, and the like. A sizeable number of Indianapolis-
published books that were not official documents (and a few that were) bore
the imprint of the Bowen-Merrill Company, which became Bobbs-Merrill in
1903. These were all acquired between 1896 and 1902, and included volumes
of verse by the Indiana poet James Whitcomb Riley and, among works of fiction, *The Redemption of David Corson* by Charles Frederic Goss and Maurice
Thompson's *Alice of Vincennes*, both runaway best sellers. Within the same
six years, Bowen-Merrill often acted as an agent for the library in its purchase of books that were published elsewhere. As the American book trade
historian Hellmut Lehmann-Haupt accurately observes, it is because of this
single noteworthy publisher that Indianapolis "furnishes a solitary example
of successfully continued, general publishing outside the great centers."[38]

It was the "great centers" that supplied almost all of the books and periodicals available in the Muncie Public Library. Of the 11,458 books for which we have a record of the place of publication, less than 3 percent were published in Indiana. Of the remainder, we find that, apart from New York, by far the most common imprint, with a total of 3,664 books—nearly 32 per cent of the total—was Washington, D.C. Since the nation's capital never put itself forward as a major center of the commercial book trade, that figure may seem surprisingly swollen, until we remember that the library was a designated government document depository, and the vast majority of Washington imprints contained there were publications of the Government Printing Office, almost none of which were ever borrowed.

Inevitably, it is New York City, the established center of the American book trade, that was the origin of the largest share of the books that found their way into the Muncie Public Library. A total of 4,611 books, more than 40 percent of those for which we have a record of the place of publication, had or included New York in their imprints. Of these, we have circulation records for 3,338, or 72.4 percent of the total number of library holdings published in New York. The number of recorded transactions of New York–published books adds up to 97,863, out of approximately 175,000 surviving borrowing records. Thus approximately 56 percent of books that circulated during the period for which we have records bore the imprint of a New York–based publisher. The hegemony of New York in the American publishing trade of the latter years of the nineteenth century can hardly be more succinctly illustrated. It is more difficult, of course, to gauge the extent to which cosmopolitan trends and values we associate with New York rubbed off on Muncie.

After Washington, D.C., and New York, the next most prolific publishing source of books in the library is Boston, with 1,593, or 13.9 percent, of the books for which we know the place of publication. Of these, we have circulation records for 1,166, which were borrowed a total of 36,256 times by 3,342 discrete patrons. Next is Philadelphia with 707 (6.17%), of which 561 circulated 32,371 times among 3,017 patrons, and by smaller figures for a number of other U.S. and foreign publication centers, including Chicago (434) and London (419). The latter was the only significant source of publications produced outside the United States. The collection also contained a handful of books published in other U.S. locales, including Buffalo, Cleveland, Hartford, Los Angeles, San Francisco, and St. Louis, as well as those bearing European imprints from such places as Paris, Leipzig, and Edinburgh.

Muncie's access to the wider world through print is evident in a remarkable archive of the working correspondence of Hattie Patterson, the first librarian. It provides firsthand evidence of the library's endeavor from its

inception to reach out well beyond its small-town roots and of a tacit understanding of the value to be gained through such contacts. Here are a couple
of fairly typical examples from her correspondence. Still in the early stages of
building up the collection, probably in 1877, Patterson wrote to Little, Brown
& Company in Boston, requesting a copy of their latest catalog. A reply from
one of their employees only three days later, accompanying a now lost copy
of their "holiday catalogue" and offering to supply any of their books "with
a few exceptions" at "a discount of twenty per cent" to the library, shows the
speed with which such requests could be handled. Correspondence of this
sort—and there are many other similar letters to publishers and booksellers
in New York, Philadelphia, and Boston—shrank the geographical distance
between Muncie and the cultural conurbations of the east coast. Through
these specific relationships, the library became at once a place for Muncie's
citizens to capture and feel the pulse of the new and to connect with the
wider world.[39]

Patterson also engaged in correspondence with the famed bibliographer
and library agent Benjamin Franklin Stevens in London, who informed her
that British imprints—London still holding sway as the center of the English-
speaking publishing world—could with ease be ordered for the library. "I
have the pleasure," Stevens writes from his office in Trafalgar Square, "to hand
you a copy of my revised List of English newspapers & magazines in which
largely increased facilities & economics for ordering books[,] apparatus etc.
are indicated." The accompanying printed catalog, a small single-stitched
hand-set pamphlet printed at the Chiswick Press in London, lists the subscription cost, including postage, for a dozen daily papers and over one hundred "Weekly English Newspapers" ranging from *Punch* and the *London
Illustrated News* to the *British Medical Journal* and the *Gardeners' Chronicle.*
It also includes more than two hundred British magazines, and promises pro-
spective buyers that "English and Continental Newspapers and Periodicals
are mailed to Subscribers in the United States on the days of issue." Although
there is only scanty notation in the accessions catalog that Patterson availed
herself of this service, the surviving correspondence and catalog are yet one
more manifestation of the impulse from the library to reach outward and to
procure for its patrons printed works from the English-speaking world at
large.[40]

Loose copyright law made it possible for American publishers to translate and distribute the work of European authors extensively during the late
nineteenth century. Library users in Muncie thus had access to many books
by authors from England, France, and Germany, although the literary output
of the rest of Europe, not to mention the rest of the world, was mostly absent.

The collection included only a tiny number of foreign-language publications, in French and German, but there were numerous translations. The largest portion of this material was popular fiction, although there were also works of western European poetry, history, religion, philosophy, and science.

British books naturally predominated. The common language, as well as economic and cultural ties between the United States and Great Britain, encouraged publishers to make English, Scottish, and Irish books available to the American market. The lax enforcement of international copyright permitted U.S. firms to produce editions of popular English books without permission from the author or original publisher. Not surprisingly, popular British writers such as Charles Dickens, Sir Walter Scott, and Robert Louis Stevenson were in demand among Muncie's library patrons. They borrowed books by Jane Austen, the Brontë sisters, and Shakespeare with some regularity as well, along with a wide range of historical and other nonfiction work.

The necessity of translation ensured that only a fraction of the literary output of France and Germany was available to American public libraries, particularly those such as Muncie's with modest budgets. Nevertheless, popular French writers such as Jules Verne, Alexander Dumas, and Victor Hugo were regularly translated and earned substantial audiences, in Muncie as elsewhere. Hugo's *Les Misérables* gained a particularly strong readership among Muncie's public library patrons, as did Dumas's *Count of Monte Cristo*. On the other hand, more demanding writers such as Honoré de Balzac captured only moderate interest and, as we saw earlier, the library did not even have copies of books by Gustave Flaubert or Émile Zola.

German books were more heavily represented, largely because of the popularity of translations of German romances. The library did have an English version of Goethe's *Faust*, which was loaned twenty-nine times between 1891 and 1902. Just two people borrowed any of the library's three volumes of Friedrich Schiller's *Sämtliche Werke* (Complete Works). This set was among the small number of books in German in the library's collection. Another was Berthold Auerbach's novel *Edelweiss*, which was never borrowed between 1891 and 1902, although a translation of it circulated nineteen times. The library also held nine volumes of the illustrated weekly *Die Gartenlaube*, which gained a small following among the handful of German immigrants residing in the city. What circulated the most were books that were much different from *Faust*: translations of popular German romance novels by writers such as Adolf Streckfuss, Wilhelmine Heimburg (Bertha Behrens), Wilhelmine von Hillern, and especially E. Marlitt (Eugenie John). Marlitt in particular was extremely popular, and the library made a point of acquiring her books to meet this demand.

Muncie's library users did not generate an interest in Marlitt and her fellow German writers out of thin air. Rather, they came to their attention through a specific marketing strategy. Most of them, though not all, were translated by Anna Lee Wister and published by the firm of J. B. Lippincott in Philadelphia. Wister was a member of a prominent Philadelphia family that included several major literary figures. She translated thirty-nine novels by eighteen different authors between 1868 and 1907, all for Lippincott's, and gained a wide following in her own right. Wister was a brand name of sorts: her translations were well known as light, romantic, domestic entertainments geared toward a female readership. The publisher featured her name in advertisements as prominently as it did the actual author, and marketed her books alongside other domestic romances written by Americans. The Muncie Public Library, which was very responsive to the demand for Wister's books from its patrons, acquired twenty-nine volumes of her translations, and they circulated heavily—a total of 2,809 times. If we were to consider her as an author, she would ranks as the eighth-most popular writer in the What Middletown Read database.

Whether we should consider the circulation of Wister's translations or the reading of translations of Hugo or Dumas as evidence of a cosmopolitan outlook is open to debate. In a meditation on this question that weighs evidence from Muncie, Lynne Tatlock concludes that Wister's translations likely did not instill in her readers the embrace of cultural differences that many definitions of cosmopolitanism require. These German romances followed a formula familiar to readers of American domestic fiction, and Wister employed subtle techniques that diminished the distinctively German qualities of the books. But as Tatlock notes, they may well have promoted a sense of common values and experiences that transcended national distinctions, an impulse consistent with the cosmopolitan trends evident elsewhere in Muncie. At the least, the reading of translated German fiction, or French novels, constituted yet another way in which print made traces of the wider world visible in Muncie.[41]

Beyond its stock of books, the Muncie Public Library also provided access to up-to-date issues of contemporary magazines and journals. In most cases, these chiefly monthly publications were collected together and bound sometime after the end of any given year. Unlike newspapers, the bound issues were then added to the accessions catalog and assigned an accession number. Also unlike the Muncie newspapers, none of these were local publications, so that their inclusion in the library should be seen as so many tiny portals on the outside world. A good proportion of the bound periodicals were transferred in 1904 to the new Carnegie Library, and the 1905 catalog lists more than 150 separate serial publications. Popular titles such as *Harper's Magazine,* the *Atlantic Monthly,* or the new series of the *Century Illustrated Monthly Magazine* were retained as complete runs, their binding usually preceding their entry into the accessions catalog. For magazines such as these there was a steady demand, individual volumes of the *Century* (as a good example) being taken out as many as fifty or sixty times.[42]

It became an end-of-year ritual for the library committee to vote on which journals and magazines should be subscribed to and which should be dropped for the ensuing year. In the early years that choice, or at least the execution of subscriptions, was left to the librarian. From Patterson's correspondence with Benjamin Franklin Stevens in London we do know, for instance, that, between 1876 and 1878 he was commissioned by her to obtain for the library two volumes of the *London Graphic* and three bound volumes of J. Erskine Clarke's weekly paper *The Chatterbox,* a once popular British children's magazine.[43] We have no borrowing records for any of these volumes, which likely circulated before 1891, and only the *Graphic* survived the transition to the new Carnegie Library.

More commonly, Patterson was in correspondence with U.S.-based publishers and booksellers. By way of example, in December 1876 Patterson mailed an order and a bank draft made out to the Graphic Company of New York for the renewal of the library's subscription to the New York *Daily Graphic,* a popular illustrated evening newspaper, and several magazines, including the *Atlantic Monthly, Frank Leslie's Illustrated Newspaper, Galaxy: A Magazine of Entertaining Reading,* and *Scientific American;* five days later the company replied, returning the draft "as we have made no arrangements this year to take subscriptions for other periodicals."[44] Patterson was able to secure most of the periodicals that she requested but had to resort to other sources of supply for her purchases. In the early years, getting beyond Muncie was a learning process that became easier with experience.

An 1885 bill for periodical subscriptions that was remitted to the city's Common Council gives some sense of the range of periodicals the library received. It included twenty-five titles at a cost of $74.25. Six were newspapers: the *Toledo Blade, New York Independent, New York Tribune, Chicago Inter Ocean, Cincinnati Commercial Gazette,* and *Indianapolis Sentinel.*[45] Among the magazines, eight—*Little Folks Reader, St. Nicholas, Pansy, Baby Land, Wide Awake, Harper's Young People, Youth's Companion,* and *Golden Days*—were intended for children of different ages, attesting to the high ratio of young people using the library. That left only ten magazines for adult readers, and evidently these were in demand for borrowing almost as soon as they arrived in the reading room, though they also achieved a continuing later circulation in bound volume form. The least requested volumes from this list were the *American Agriculturist, Scientific American,* and *Blackwood's Edinburgh Magazine. American Agriculturist* claimed a national subscription of 85,000 copies per issue in 1877, with an actual readership of well over a million farmers, but these figures did not translate into Muncie library patrons two decades later.[46]

In 1890 the lack of demand led the board to drop *American Agriculturist* in favor of *Art Amateur,* though that too failed to attract a readership and its subscription was allowed to lapse after a trial year.[47] We know that *Scientific American* was prized by the young diarist Tom Ryan (see chapter 7) but not, it seems, by most other Munsonians. It is ironic that, in a city that had its roots in agriculture and its expansion in industry, so few library borrowers turned to these two leading publications in their respective fields. The American edition of *Blackwood's,* published in New York, may have been highly valued for its literary content and its link with Great Britain, but its presence in Muncie probably had to do more with reputation than readership. The other technological magazine, *Popular Science Monthly,* retained a small but steady readership; occasional bound volumes, such as volume 43 for 1893, were borrowed a total of eighty-one times, mainly by schoolchildren, who may have been directed to one of its articles by a teacher. The library continued to renew its subscription to both *Scientific American* and *Popular Science Monthly,* but *Blackwood's* seems to have been dropped after 1886. It followed in the footsteps of *The Gentleman's Magazine,* another iconic British periodical, which was no longer taken after 1882.

Of those that are listed in 1885, the most popular monthlies available were the *Atlantic Monthly,* published by Houghton Mifflin in Boston, the *North American Review,* originally out of Boston and later New York, *Lippincott's Monthly Magazine,* out of Philadelphia, and the *Century* and *Harper's Magazine* out of New York. *Harper's Weekly* in bound form was borrowed only a small fraction of the number of times of its monthly parent magazine. The popularity of the five main monthlies points to a readership that wished to keep up with the latest trends and enjoyed reading serialized fiction by contemporary authors and reviews of recent books.

We do not have primary evidence that the library board consulted magazine reviews prior to ordering new books, but the library did respond to demand, and on occasion, particularly during the 1890s, extended the number of periodicals to which it subscribed. When *Cosmopolitan* began publishing in 1886, it soon became one of the most popular of family magazines, and the library added it to the subscription list in 1891. Other literary magazines, such as *The Forum,* also started in 1886, the *Review of Reviews,* published for

the first time in London in 1891 but only available from New York the following year, and *Current Literature,* begun in 1888, were added in 1892.[48]

At various times, too, but for shorter periods, the library subscribed to
such periodicals as *Frank Leslie's Illustrated Newspaper,* the *Contemporary
Review, The Nineteenth Century,* and the *Fortnightly Review.* With some gaps,
the library took *Scribner's Magazine,* which also had a healthy borrowing
record. To cater to a demand from women readers, the *Ladies' Home Journal,*
which had begun publishing in 1883, was subscribed to from 1892, though its
contents were too ephemeral to attract readers after it was bound into volumes several years after the individual issues first reached the library.[49] It was
followed by the *Woman's Home Companion* as well as *McClure's Magazine*
(which only later became a women's magazine), both first taken in 1899.[50]

Although not recorded in the accessions register, the library also received
a number of newspapers. Copies of most daily and weekly local newspapers
were delivered to the library and immediately made available in the reading
room. A report in the *Muncie Daily Times* from January 1895 notes that at that
time, when Muncie ranked "fifth [of] the cities having public libraries in this
state," as many as eighteen daily and weekly newspapers were being received.[51]
The 1905 printed catalog of the new Carnegie Library includes a shorter list
of a dozen papers. These included three Muncie papers (the *Muncie Herald,
Muncie Star,* and *Muncie Times*), three Indianapolis papers (*Star, News,* and
Sentinel), two from Chicago (the *Record-Herald* and the *Daily Tribune*), the
Commercial Tribune out of Cincinnati, the Louisville *Courier-Journal,* the
Washington Post, and the *New York Weekly Tribune.*[52] Although there is no
way to know how many times individual newspapers were consulted, the
continued subscription over a period of thirty years to several well-respected
titles from major cities east of the Mississippi, along with the Lynds' finding
that "the circulation of out-of-town papers [in Muncie] . . . was negligible in
1890," provides confirmation that the library was Munsonians' window on
the world.[53]

Indeed, what the subscription lists for magazines and newspapers clearly
show is that, whether seeking entertainment or instruction, the Muncie public used these publications to look outward. Periodicals such as *Harper's,
Leslie's,* and the *Century* were the source of news from around the world,
illustrations of national and international events and individuals, commentary, and serial fiction set in both familiar and exotic locales. Even if they
often depicted distant lands and peoples from an imperialistic perspective,
they nonetheless encouraged an awareness that was, if not cosmopolitan, at
least tending toward a fuller sense of connection and involvement with the
wider world. At the very least, it suggests that the library board members

who continually renewed these subscriptions imagined themselves serving a community that wished to learn about the world beyond its city limits and even beyond the boundaries of the nation.

As a principal purveyor of books, magazines, and newspapers in Muncie, the library also operated as a symbol of the city's cosmopolitan aspirations. Boosters regularly tied its development to the general growth and cultural progress of the city. More specifically, the knowledge provided through the printed materials assembled within it constituted a direct link to the larger civilizing project that late nineteenth-century American imagined to be under way at that time.

That a library might serve such a purpose is a point made by James Raven in a study of social libraries and their contents in late eighteenth-century America. Raven argues that such institutions cultivated a sense of belonging to a broad, geographically extensive community, forging a sense of community and identity that "reached back and forth across the English countryside, the Irish Channel, *and* the Atlantic." This collection of books and the institution that housed them allowed members to imagine themselves as part of this broader social unit defined by shared values and a common fund of knowledge. Though operating in a decidedly different historical context, Muncie's public library had a similar effect. Its assemblage of histories, travelogues, scientific treatises, poetry, and fiction represented a significant sample of the cultural inheritance of western Europe and America. Simply by their physical presence in this small midwestern city, these texts offered assurance that Muncie was an up-to-date community that was tied to and even embedded within the broad cultural formation that they described as the civilized world. The *Muncie Daily News* echoed this sentiment in 1897 when it observed that "our public libraries are plainly destined to be a leading feature of the civilization of the future" and that "as a library grows the public grows up to it."[54]

The sense that the progress of the library embodied the larger cultural development of the city was a central theme in local public discourse, evident in the celebratory rhetoric surrounding the founding of the Muncie Public Library in 1875 and again in the inauguration of the new Carnegie Library in 1904.

It was in such terms that Margaret Rose, the wife of the library's president, defended the institution in 1897, in an impassioned address before "four hundred energetic club women of . . . [Delaware] county, who are alive to all the issues that make for intellectual and moral improvement," assembled at a gathering of women's clubs. "The condition of its library," Rose declared, "is the intellectual pulse of a community." Casting her mind back to its foundation in 1874, she recalled that, at that now seemingly distant era, "Muncie was a town of less than five thousand inhabitants with a little brick court house

and a hitching post fence around it." Since then, and particularly following the discovery of natural gas, the city had undergone what Rose called a
"booming evolution," with "the uttermost limits of the town burst[ing] their
bounds." Here she voiced her apprehension that without substantial additional funding, the library risked lagging behind in its mission of promoting "higher, intellectual development," while the city advanced "in material
affairs." Her plea for a new building to house the more than ten thousand volumes contained in the existing rooms was backed by "the earnest solicitation
of the library board," who wholeheartedly shared her belief in the need of the
city to try to achieve a balance of its material and intellectual aspirations.[55]

An article published in the *Muncie Morning News* in 1893 offered a fuller
sense of the way Munsonians connected the public library to a perception of
civilizational belonging. The anonymous author of "A Brief Resume of Our
Public Library" extolled it as "the pride of our city" and the "chief" of "our
educational aids." But the value of an institution such as the Muncie Public
Library extended beyond the support it provided for local schooling: its collections represented the "best index to the intelligence, culture and business
ability of a community." Libraries were "storehouses for the mind when skill
is required beyond that which is possible to be acquired in the narrow gauge
of experience." The books arranged on its shelves provided "an abridgment
of the best practical ideas, tabulated and of easy access, connected by the
life-time toil of some veteran genius or artisan, who [together] mould our
public opinion and leave in history the primary digests upon which each
succeeding generation is based." They "make permanent the reason, law and
philosophies of the ages, giving us historical inferences by which to construct
our sciences, and elevate our nation to a higher and better civilization."[56]

The significance of this knowledge was not simply practical, the author
maintains; "a library is an emporium of arts, the only veritable paradise in
the material construction of man." Those who did not, at least on occasion,
"enjoy a good book" were living "a semi-barbaric life in which reason is
crudely formed." Absent this fund of knowledge and collective experience,
a person lacked "the basis of a philanthropic life of usefulness." In its place
would arise "a mind that becomes a narrow receptacle for the legendary riff-
raffs and hearsays gleaned from the lower currents of the world's ideals."[57]

The highfalutin rhetoric of these paragraphs deserve some unpacking, for
they represent the cosmopolitan ideals that helped to define the very ethos
of the library. Books are seen as the key to self-improvement. The edification
to be gained from reading and study is interpreted as the primary means
by which the people of America at large, and those of Muncie in particular, have overcome their "semi-barbaric" state and elevated themselves "to a

higher and better civilization." Implicit here is the belief that, through the life experiences and the accumulated knowledge and insights recorded in books, Muncie's residents became far better equipped to lead useful and socially meaningful lives. More significantly, they become inheritors of a mature civilization because they have access to its ideas and experiences through the contents of the public library.

Without the knowledge and experience supplied through libraries, the author contends, the pursuit of human happiness would risk becoming a disorderly and potentially retrogressive affair. Along with commending the role played by the public library, the author extends his inquiry to "Notes on Some of Our Leading Private and Professional Libraries of Special Merit." Among these are a number of law, medical, and theological collections that contributed to the bibliothecal ranking of Muncie as "among the best in the State, and [they] speak well for our professional men whose business is to educate, protect, and enlighten the people of our city." The article is upbeat in its emphasis on the role of libraries as a kind of guiding light or leading indicator of the cultural character of a community.

Writing from a metropolitan perspective, the philosopher Kwame Anthony Appiah warns that "celebrations of the 'cosmopolitan' can suggest an unpleasant posture of superiority toward the putative provincial," but, as we have seen, late nineteenth-century Muncie endeavored to project itself as a small city that near-perfectly combined aspects of the rural and the urban. In introducing his theme, Appiah argues well for a twofold definition of cosmopolitanism that encompasses "the idea that we have obligations to others" and that, as citizens of the world, "we take seriously the value not just of human life but of particular human lives," that we reach a recognition that "people are different, . . . and there is much to learn from our differences."[58] In the context of the public library, the board took very seriously its custodial obligations to the citizens of Muncie, both in terms of the choice of books that it deemed appropriate for them to read and in encouraging them to make best use of the institution.

Whether regular use of the library helped to make its patrons into "citizens of the world" as Appiah understands the concept remains moot. But again, it seems likely that many individuals gained through the library a fuller sense of what and who lay beyond their small, bustling city. For the majority of patrons, the Muncie Public Library offered what the British book trade historian Catherine Armstrong has aptly dubbed the positioning of "the town and its readers in a global community of knowledge," and which, no less forcefully, the Lynds described as a "vicarious entry into other, imagined kinds of living."[59]

II
Reading Experiences

4

Borrowing Patterns

The Muncie Public Library
and Its Patrons

An 1895 brochure titled *Muncie of To-day* extolled "the comfort and advantages possessed by the home owners of Muncie over cities outside of the gas belt." In many cities coal remained the main energy source, but in Muncie "the millennium of comfort and cleanliness" had arrived. Once essential items such as a coal bucket or a fire shovel were now merely decorative, while "the ash heap ha[d] disappeared" and "the wood pile no longer adorn[ed] the back yard." One need only "light a match and turn a key to secure heat and light in parlors, dining rooms, kitchens, and bedrooms, which go on and on at pleasure, at a cost of $25 per annum. In such a home the poet could find the ideal of comfort, and Muncie has thousands of such homes in the full enjoyment of nature's greatest blessing."[1]

In the Muncie of the 1890s, where gas was so readily and cheaply available, electricity could not compete except in the powering of the city's newly constructed network of streetcars. Yet, as David E. Nye points out in describing Muncie during that era, even those houses that were lighted by gas lamps were "poorly illuminated": "A gas flame or a kerosene lamp gave off only seven candle power. The Welsbach gas burner, for sale in Muncie in 1890, was considerably better, having 250 candle power. Nevertheless, most gas illumination was inflexibly mounted on the wall or ceiling, burning up the oxygen in a room and heating it uncomfortably in summer." Yet by 1899, according to Nye's reckoning, "only twenty-two Muncie homes had electricity."[2]

As late as 1903, an art nouveau–style invoice billhead for brothers John and Milt Retherford, Muncie-based producers of gas, electric, and combination fixtures, depicts an ornate gas chandelier that was still being manufactured and sold in the city and beyond (fig. 7). If, as seems likely, John Retherford installed similar lighting fixtures at his home on East Jackson Street, they would have served his wife, Cora, a patron of the Muncie Public Library from December 1901, when she borrowed books by Sarah Orne Jewett and Ellen Glasgow. But such deluxe fixtures were the exclusive province of the privileged in turn-of-the-century Muncie homes, beyond the means of the majority. Indeed, the makeshift and often dangerous condition of domestic gas fixtures, widely used for heating and lighting, was the cause of numerous explosions, some of them fatal. The frequency of these was noticeably more common in working-class neighborhoods.[3]

Despite the relatively poor general quality of domestic lighting, the rising number of book borrowings from the Muncie Public Library during the gas-boom era suggests that home reading was a prized activity, enjoyed both as a means of whiling away one's leisure hours and for extending one's knowledge in the pursuit of a hobby or for furthering one's education. It is clear from the diaries explored in chapter 7 that much of this reading was individualized and private. Yet, as we are well reminded by Guglielmo Cavallo and Roger Chartier, "reading is not a solely abstract intellectual operation; it involves the body, is inscribed within a space, and implies a relationship to oneself or to others." Reading aloud, they add, embraces the "dual function of communicating the written word to those who are unable to decipher writing and reinforcing the interlocking forms of sociability—within the family circle, in convivial social intercourse or in literary discussion among like-minded persons—that make up private life."[4] Judging both by the books that were borrowed and by the borrowers themselves, it can be argued that the late nineteenth-century home, with its lighting often limited and unwieldy, was often more conducive to communal reading, most obviously to children gathered together around a light source so that their parents—most commonly their mothers—could read to them aloud.

The What Middletown Read database offers us some evidence of the challenges associated with reading at home. Katie Seldomridge, the wife of Edward Seldomridge, a paperhanger, took out Howard Pyle's *Merry Adventures of Robin Hood* on March 21, 1900, most likely with the intention of reading it aloud at home to her six-year-old daughter, Beatrice. Katie Seldomridge's personal choice of reading was usually more adult and sophisticated, including such works as *The Cloister and the Hearth* by Charles Reade, George du Maurier's *Trilby,* and Honoré de Balzac's *Père Goriot.* On this particular visit to the library, she was accompanied by her mother-in-

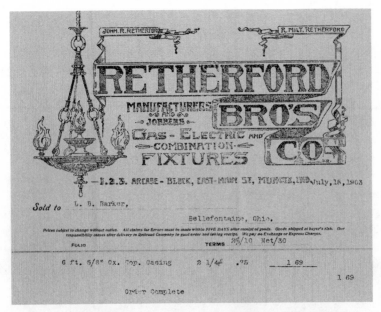

FIGURE 7. Retherford Brothers' Company billhead. The chandelier depicted
was an example of a lavish gas fixture. More modest versions supplied
indoor light that made reading at home easier. Courtesy Ball State University
Archives and Special Collections.

law, Lydia, who took out Helen Hunt Jackson's *Hetty's Strange History,* and by
her unmarried brother-in-law, Delbert, who borrowed Mary Jane Holmes's
novel *Ethelyn's Mistake;* both were popular adult novels. Three generations,
comprising seven family members, lived in the same crowded house on West
Jackson Street, so nighttime reading probably had to be staggered. Young
Beatrice grew up in a household that obviously cherished books—there are
just short of four hundred combined borrowing records for the three listed
library patrons—but may have been in competition for undisturbed and ade-
quately lighted nocturnal reading space at home.

From a more genteel background, with three young children at home,
Susan Ryan Marsh, known as Suzie, the wife of future library board member John Rollin Marsh, borrowed on June 19, 1900, *Cross Patch; and Other
Stories, Adapted from the Myths of Mother Goose* by Susan Coolidge (Sarah
Chauncey Woolsey), a profusely illustrated book for young folks that lent
itself to reading aloud at home. Marsh was only one of 146 borrowers, mainly
women, who were loaned the book between its accession in 1894 and the
end of our records in 1902. In her study of women's book clubs, Elizabeth
Long has helped to show the importance among late nineteenth-century

middle-class American women of reading as a *social* rather than an exclusively *solitary* activity. Her otherwise comprehensive examination of book clubs does not, however, consider that women often began their social reading in the nursery. From reading books to her young children, Marsh went on to become an influential Muncie clubwoman, a member of the Women's Club and president of the Pegasus Poetry Club. She was also the initiator of the Muncie branch of the National League of American Penwomen, and the founder and first president of the Muncie Art Students' League.[5]

Yet another notable example of a patron for whom reading aloud at home was a requisite need, if for a totally different reason, was Elmira Kuechmann, who joined the library as early as 1878 and remained a prolific borrower through most of the 1890s; she also did a stint as a board member. Kuechmann's German-born husband, Matthias, a respected local music teacher and composer, had been blinded by the measles at the age of fourteen and relied on his wife and two daughters, all patrons of the library, to read to him.[6] Borrowing statistics show that many of the books they borrowed were brought in for renewal, sometimes more than once, suggesting that reading aloud can often prove a much slower process than silent reading. It is highly unlikely that a library in the Midwest of the 1890s would have even considered making special provisions for clients with disabilities, though the Muncie library's willingness to renew books more than once (the usual limit) does suggest a sympathetic understanding of a particular need. It is no surprise that we lack statistical evidence to substantiate whether the Kuechmann's situation was unique.

These examples illustrate both the potential and the limitations of the What Middletown Read database as a tool for exploring reading. We can at times infer individual and collective reading behavior from the borrowing patterns it documents. Yet even with such evidence, the reading experiences of ordinary people remain largely elusive. We know a good deal about authors, publishers, and intermediaries such as libraries and booksellers. We know considerably less about the other node in that complex of connections, the readers. They occupied a distinctive, often overlooked place within the labyrinth of formal and informal exchanges that determined the circulation of printed material. But they were not simply autonomous actors. Their choices were also constrained by local mores and influenced by the extensive marketing efforts of publishers that increased so notably during the during the late nineteenth century. The social dimensions of reading also mattered, as our examples suggest. As the borrowing of the Seldomridges, Marshes, and Kuechmanns indicate, choices were made and reading experiences took place within the context of families, as well as among friends and neighbors. Making sense of how readers developed their tastes and how they participated in the exchange and consumption of printed material is a complex but essential task if we are to comprehend the progress of modern print culture.[7]

The information assembled in the What Middletown Read database allows us to make more sense of the role of one set of readers in one time and place. It provides us with evidence of a substantial body of borrowing (and, one presumes, in most instances reading) choices made by individuals and by particular groups of library patrons residing in one community in one historical period. Exploring them gives us a better sense of what readers sought, and how their preferences mattered. It also gives us hints, if not definitive evidence, of why they chose to borrow what they did.

Two broad patterns emerge from an analysis of the Muncie Public Library's circulation data. The first was the massive circulation of children's literature. Although the board expressed an interest in limiting the acquisition of morally questionable children's books, the library nevertheless catered to this demand, at times edging close to the line that divided what some considered moral from immoral fiction. Children from every socioeconomic level raided its shelves for popular juvenile literature throughout the 1890s and the first years of the new century. Horatio Alger's books were easily the favorite; they were borrowed more than nine thousand times during the nine years for which we have circulation records—more than 5 percent of all transactions. Louisa May Alcott's *Under the Lilacs* was the most popular book for girls (and the single most popular volume overall), with L. T. Meade's *A World of Girls* a close second. Women from white-collar households—Suzie Marsh and her peers—borrowing substantial numbers of books of romantic and domestic fiction constituted the second major segment of readers.

The What Middletown Read database also gives us some sense of the ways different sexes and different social groups interacted with an expanding literary marketplace. As we have seen, the late nineteenth century saw an enormous growth in the distribution of printed materials, not only books but magazines and newspapers as well. Muncie's public library served as a conveyor, as well as in some instances a filter, of this material. Though open to all city residents, it primarily served the middle classes, and women more than men. The demographic contours of that connection give us some sense of how both its frequent users and, more obliquely, those who used it rarely or not at all, consumed printed material.

Social class and gender clearly mattered in relation to patterns of library use and borrowing choices, but not in simple ways. Children of all backgrounds frequented the library, though those from blue-collar households exhibited slightly different tastes from their white-collar counterparts. (For an explanation of how occupational status is classified in the database, see the appendix.)

Among adults, the library drew the interest and patronage of women from white-collar homes, but relatively few who might be considered working-class. Men from professional ranks and the business community borrowed occasionally, often, it appears, on behalf of other family members, but as we have observed, the library rarely attracted working-class men. There were subtle but meaningful differences that ran along class lines, with those from more comfortable socioeconomic circumstances more likely to select the latest books. That tendency suggests the role that reading and, more generally, engagement with popular culture played in the process of middle-class formation.

Yet these patterns, along with the ever-elusive character of the experience of reading, resist easy generalization. Borrowing choices were too varied, usage too limited, and the meanings of texts too open and too dependent on what Chartier has called "appropriation" by readers to argue that Muncie's library served as a tool of social control. Nor is there much evidence that users were actively subverting the generally conservative thrust of the library board and the collection it assembled. Rather, the collective character of reading and library use that emerges from the circulation records assembled in the database suggests that borrowers found in the library's material a variety of ways in which to entertain, escape, learn, and engage. Sometimes, though not always, they ventured in directions other than those mapped out by the library's leadership.[8]

As we noted in the introduction to this volume, Wayne Wiegand has argued that we must examine the role of a library in the life of its users rather than the role of users in the life of the library, a strategy that can help us better understand how these institutions function in their communities and in our society. Here too, simple formulas fail. Depicting public libraries as forces for democracy and social mobility (or as agents of social control) cannot encompass the range of interactions between the Muncie Public Library and its patrons. Reintroducing borrowers as active agents whose tastes and demands helped shape a library's catalog and operations, as part of what Wiegand has called "a balancing act," allows us see these institutions in more complex and credible terms, as entities that both shaped and were shaped by the communities they served.[9]

The Library and Its Collection

There was considerable public debate during the later nineteenth century over what sort of reading material public libraries ought to provide for their patrons, but it had little impact in Muncie.[10] As we have seen, the Muncie Public Library assembled its "magnificent array of books" through several processes. Librarians absorbed other local collections, accepted donations, and, especially, responded to public demand for popular fare by ordering books in bulk from publishers. These acquisitions took shape within a traditional and fairly conservative context. A visitor scanning the shelves would find plenty of classic literature but would struggle to find much in the way of recent avant-garde fiction or a wide range of social criticism. Nor would a patron encounter heavy-handed guidance from librarians. While the library board demonstrated some concern for the kinds of books acquired, the women who ran the library on a day-to-day basis, particularly Kate Wilson, were friendly amateurs who apparently did little to direct users toward what the moral pundits of the day deemed proper reading. The library did not supply the cheapest and most scandalous titles of the era, but books with less than sterling literary reputations were readily available and often borrowed.

At the end of 1902, the shelves of the Muncie Public Library held 11,591 books and bound volumes of magazines, only a fraction of which were borrowed regularly. The collection had increased from 5,585 in November 1891, when the circulation records contained in the What Middletown Read database begin. The majority of these circulated only rarely. In fact, only about half—5,972, or 52 percent—of all the books in the collection circulated at all, and many of these were borrowed only a handful of times. More than 20 percent of those (1,301) were borrowed just once, and over half (3,057) circulated fewer than ten times during the nine years covered by the database. A substantial number of these largely unborrowed titles (3,580) were government reports, placed in the library when it became an official repository of federal documents in 1893.

Among the books available to borrowers were an abundance of classics and volumes by well-regarded nineteenth-century writers. A twelve-volume edition of the works of William Shakespeare had been acquired shortly after the library opened in 1875 and remained in circulation well into the twentieth century. It was supplemented by several other collections of his work, including Charles Lamb's adaptation for children. Milton, Austen, Scott, Tennyson, and Dickens were among the other standard British writers available on the library's shelves. Figures from the canon of prominent American writers such as Emerson, Hawthorne, and Thoreau, as well as contemporary figures, such as Mark Twain, Henry James, and William Dean Howells, were well represented.

Less common were books that broke new literary ground. Muncie's librarians apparently saw no need to acquire any Whitman, but collected numerous volumes of more conventional verse by Henry Wadsworth Longfellow, Oliver Wendell Holmes Sr., James Russell Lowell, and the Hoosier poet James Whitcomb Riley. The growth in realist fiction during the latter part of the nineteenth century received at best inconsistent acknowledgment. While

Twain and Howells were well represented, the library did not acquire some of their more sharply critical works. Neither *The Gilded Age*, Twain's jointly authored satire of the U.S. public life during the early 1870s, nor Howells's novel *The Rise of Silas Lapham* had appeared on the shelves by 1902. The collection also held five books by Henry James but included neither *The Portrait of a Lady* nor *The Bostonians*. As we have seen, literary naturalism, a provocative outgrowth of realism that emphasized the impact of social conditions on human experience, received scant attention.[11]

In an era when public discourse was characterized by sharp debates over the impact and consequences of industrialization and the moral character of capitalism, Muncie's library offered only a scattering of material that engaged such issues. It received as a donation in 1891 Edward Bellamy's immensely popular utopian novel *Looking Backward*, which imagined a statist future without class conflict, and bought its sequel, *Equality*, in 1897. It purchased an edition of *How the Other Half Lives* by Jacob Riis in 1898, nine years after the exposé of life in New York's slums first appeared. It circulated twenty-seven times during the period documented by the database. There were also two copies of Henry George's single-tax manifesto, *Progress and Poverty*, which was borrowed nineteen times. These texts engaged the social problems of the day, but they spoke chiefly to a middle-class audience and gained little traction with the library's patrons.

Sharper critiques emanating from working-class perspectives, such as the Populist radical Ignatius Donnelly's *Caesar's Column*, a dystopian counterpart to Bellamy's novels, did not find a home in Muncie's library. Nor did the collection include such left-leaning social critiques as Henry Demarest Lloyd's *Wealth against Commonwealth* or William T. Stead's *If Christ Came to Chicago*. Works by Karl Marx were notably absent as well. More conservative fare was easier to come by. Andrew Carnegie's *Gospel of Wealth* was part of the collection, as was John Hay's anti-labor novel, *The Bread-Winners*. Neither circulated much: the database records just one loan of Carnegie's book and only ten of Hay's. It is not clear whether the acquisition of these books reflected an effort to promote particular social or political views. Public demand, along with donations and other factors, appears to have weighed more heavily. *Caesar's Column* was a popular book but by no means a match for the best-selling *Looking Backward*. Hay's book was a donation (from Muncie industrialist George A. Ball), as was a second copy of George's *Progress and Poverty* (curiously, from Ball's local rival in the glass manufacturing business, Robert Hemingray).

Where the Muncie Public Library did defy convention to some extent was in its willingness to cater to popular tastes. Although most of the cheap, short "dime" novels that flourished in the United States during the later nineteenth century did not find their way to the shelves, Muncie's librarians were not overly discriminating in their selections. There seemed to be little hesitation to acquire books that had earned condemnation elsewhere as inappropriate or overly sensational. They made titles by Horatio Alger, Harry Castlemon (Charles Fosdick), and Oliver Optic (William Taylor Adams) available in abundance. Not quite "dime novels," works by these authors represented a "respectable," Christian alternative to more sensational fare. Their books retained a degree of adventure and suspense, but leavened those qualities with a heavy dose of Christian moralism, Alger and Optic more so than Castlemon. Nevertheless, some critics and librarians elsewhere still expressed disapproval of them as lacking in both literary and moral quality. Castlemon's books featured boys who rejected formal schooling; Alger faced condemnation for promoting excessive materialism and individual autonomy, as well as for poorly contrived plots and unconvincing characters. Alger's biographer concluded that his books, which were dismissed by one contemporary librarian as out-of-date "literary pablum," resided "at the fringe of middle-class respectability."[12]

Such openness to less elevated fiction was at variance with the emerging professional norm for a public library's holdings. A comparison of the Muncie library's accessions with the model collection prepared by the America Library Association (ALA) for the 1893 World's Fair illustrates that Muncie's, like most small-town libraries, diverged substantially from this paradigm. To serve as a source of "expert advice in making the first collection of books" for smaller towns and cities that, like Muncie, lacked professional librarians, the ALA put out a list of about five thousand titles. The distribution across subjects, said to be "the result of careful study," tilted toward nonfiction, with just 15 percent (809 of 5,230 books) devoted to fiction. The remainder included history (756 titles), literature (694), biography (635), sociology (424), travel (414) natural science (355), and a handful of other categories. Only Muncie's collection of 535 history titles and 300 travel books bore any resemblance to the recommended distribution. The library held a limited selection of books under subject headings such as science (37), natural history (47), and sociology (10), a breakdown that reflected its concern for supplying the works its patrons sought rather than the kinds of educational and reference books professionals recommended.[13]

Even within the realm of popular fiction, the Muncie collection diverged from the ALA model. Absent from the national group's recommendations were any children's books by Alger, Optic, Castlemon, Edward Sylvester Ellis, or girls' author Martha Finley (who often wrote under the pen name Martha Farquharson). Muncie's shelves held not only an abundance of titles by each of these enormously popular writers, but in many instances two or more copies of individual titles. The ALA's recommendation for women's fiction also contrasted with the sorts of books to be found in Muncie's library. It held a dozen volumes by Charlotte Brame (some published under her American pen name, Bertha Clay) and another dozen by Mary Jane Holmes, and by authors of romantic fiction who wrote originally for the disreputable story papers that thrived after the Civil War. Other supposedly sensationalistic writers for women, such as E.D.E.N. Southworth and Augusta Evans, were well represented. Books by more respectable writers for women, such as E. Marlitt and E. P. Roe, who received token inclusion in the ALA list, were also extensively available in Muncie.

There is no indication that the Muncie Public Library even took notice of the ALA catalog, much less that it influenced its approach to building a collection. If anything, the library responded to local popular demand by increasing its holdings of fiction of questionable literary and moral merit (at least as the ALA and many outside critics saw them). Between 1900 and 1902, the library obtained sixteen Alger books and eighteen by Castlemon, mostly as replacements for worn-out copies of popular volumes. It also ordered women's fiction by Charlotte Brame, Marie Corelli, Augusta Evans, and others who not only failed to earn a place on the ALA list but generally earned condemnation from literary critics, arbiters of popular morality, and professional librarians. It seems abundantly clear that Muncie's staff worried more about what their patrons wanted to read than about which books they ought to read.[14]

The loose attitude taken by Muncie's librarian was evident in another practice as well. While each patron received a library card and was assigned a patron number, a degree of informality governed their use. Friends and family were able to use each other's numbers to borrow books and, as we saw in chapter 2, librarian Kate Wilson routinely permitted visitors to use her account. Of the 464 times her card was used, only 38 appear to have been choices for her own use. Several dozen others appear to be for family members, including her sister and nephew. But the bulk were for unrelated patrons, and the books in question include numerous Optics, Algers, and Castlemons, along with romances by Brame, Holmes, Evans, and Amelia Barr. So permissive an attitude suggests that Wilson not only tolerated borrowing choices driven by individual taste rather than by literary or moral merit, but that she gave her tacit approval to those selections.[15]

Users and Usage

The What Middletown Read database offers substantial documentation of library use and reading choices. Between its opening in 1875 and its reconstitution at the end of 1902, the Muncie Public Library enrolled 6,347 patrons.

The database includes entries for 6,328 of them (the remaining names were indecipherable in the register of borrowers). Of those, 4,008 patrons borrowed at least one book or magazine during the nine years of extant circulation records. In total, they borrowed 174,641 titles, an average of just under 44 per person, during that period.

Library patrons represented only a fraction of the community. In 1900, when the city's population had reached 20,942, males constituted a slight majority in the city's residents (10,856 to 10,086). About a third of the total population (6,436) were under the age of twenty-one. No precise breakdown of the jobs held by residents is available, but in 1900 the federal census reported 6,294 people (5,703 adult men and 591 women and children) earning wages at manufacturing establishments, making it clear that well over half of the city's families earned a living either as factory workers or through other forms of manual labor. Muncie was also overwhelmingly white and substantially native born. Only 739 African Americans resided in the city in 1900, and the census of that year recorded just 1,235 inhabitants as foreign born (among whom eight were Chinese). Most local residents appeared to be at least minimally literate. Census statistics for Delaware County, of which Muncie was by far the largest city, report that 96 percent of native-born adult white men and 88 percent of foreign-born adult men claimed to be literate. The figure for African American men was 88.4 percent.[16]

The men, women, and children who used the public library were far from a representative sample of the community. Library patrons were a bit more likely to be women and much less likely to be from the city's burgeoning population of factory workers and manual laborers. Of the 4,008 active borrowers, we could determine the sex of 3,574 of them through U.S. census or other records. A clear majority (1,998, or just under 56%) were female. We were able to locate demographic information from the 1900 U.S. census for 2,579 active borrowers, including occupational information for their households.

As table 1 shows, a substantial majority of these borrowers, some 62 percent, came from families whose chief breadwinner worked in a professional, managerial, or other white-collar capacity. Just 17 percent came from families headed by semiskilled and unskilled workers, most likely employed in a factory or as a low-level laborer. The remainder came from families headed by skilled workers, in occupations ranging from blacksmith to baker to carriage maker. Many of these jobs were remnants of a preindustrial period, and those who held them occupied an intermediate, fluid position on the occupational ladder. Some were self-employed; others occupied special niches in the developing industrial economy. Local glass factories, for instance, still employed highly skilled blowers to make glassware. Many of these types of

TABLE 1. Library borrowing by occupational status

	HIGH WHITE-COLLAR	LOW WHITE-COLLAR	SKILLED BLUE-COLLAR	SEMI-SKILLED BLUE-COLLAR	UNSKILLED BLUE-COLLAR
Registered patrons	829	1,177	673	321	239
Borrowers	646 (25%)	955 (37%)	529 (20%)	257 (10%)	192 (7%)
Books borrowed	4,132	4,373	3,715	2,939	2,507
Transactions	34,347	47,586	26,385	13,657	10,434
Transactions per borrower	53.2	49.8	49.9	53.1	54.3

NOTE. Includes only patrons for whom we were able to determine individual or head-of-household occupation. Percentages in the second row indicate the proportion of all such borrowers; they do not total 100 because of rounding.

workers retained a level of status and economic independence that distinguished them from other factory operatives.[17]

Gender intersected with socioeconomic position in relation to library use as well. As noted, females constituted a slight majority of users for whom we collected demographic information.[18] But consideration of occupational rank provides an interesting twist to this pattern. Women and girls from white-collar families were more likely to borrow books from the library than were their husbands, sons, and brothers (58% to 42%). The opposite was the case among patrons from blue-collar families. Males from that group were more likely to check out books than were their female counterparts by a similar ratio (55% to 45%).

Closer examination suggests that children made up a disproportionate share of the patrons coming from wage-earning households. Table 2 breaks down usage by patrons born after 1880, the oldest of whom would have been ten when our records begin in November 1891 and twenty-one at the end of the records in December 1902. The youngest may have been no more than ten in 1902. In comparing these figures within their respective groupings, it is clear that the proportion of working-class children is far higher than for those from a white-collar background. In fact, more than half of the total number of active patrons who came from an unskilled or menial blue-collar household turn out to be children. By comparison, only about 40 percent of the active patrons from skilled or semiskilled families are children. That figure drops to 30 percent among low white-collar patrons, and to about 25 percent among patrons from a high white-collar family. Although the library attracted relatively few readers from an unskilled blue-collar background,

TABLE 2. Library borrowing by occupational status: patrons born after 1880

	HIGH WHITE-COLLAR	LOW WHITE-COLLAR	SKILLED BLUE-COLLAR	SEMI-SKILLED BLUE-COLLAR	UNSKILLED BLUE-COLLAR
Registered patrons	162	299	212	106	113
Borrowers	158	289	209	103	110
Books borrowed	2,375	2,874	2,510	1,907	1,699
Transactions	5,012	15,668	10,898	6,036	6,399
Transactions per borrower	61.3	54.2	52.1	58.6	58.2
Children as percentage of borrowers	24.5	30.3	39.5	40.1	57.3

NOTE. Includes only patrons for whom we were able to determine individual or head-of-household occupation.

within that individual occupational grouping it drew a far higher proportion of children than for any other group. Library borrowing was apparently of minimal importance to many of their parents. On the other hand, for children from white-collar families, there were other ways of gaining access to print, often by purchase rather than through borrowing from the library.[19]

Another surprising statistic to emerge from the data is that many fewer girls than boys patronized the library, particularly in the case of children from unskilled blue-collar backgrounds. Overall, boys outnumbered girls 512 to 408 (56% to 44%) among active borrowers born after 1880. That pattern was particularly pronounced among children from unskilled households: just 29 of the 110 children (26%) in that category were female.

The proportions are more balanced in other occupational groups, ranging from 43 percent female among children from semiskilled and skilled families to 47 percent female among low white-collar children. Only in the high white-collar group did female borrowers constitute a slim majority (52%) among children. This pattern may be explained in part by the fact that by 1900 some of the older boys were working at entry-level, perhaps menial, jobs. It is that occupation, rather than the occupation of the head of their household, that applies in the database, thereby lowering their occupational status in a manner that may belie or conceal their social position. On the other hand, the socioeconomic category of many of the girls, who were less likely to work outside the home, is often based on the occupations of their fathers, who were indeed unskilled or menial blue-collar workers. Nevertheless, the gap in library use between girls and boys is, by any standard, a sizeable one. As a caution, however, it should be remembered that the data do not include demographic entries on every borrower. Nor do the figures given here take account of the fact that library cards, more particularly among borrowers, were often shared by different family members.

Records of borrowing do not capture every aspect of library use. The Muncie Public Library also made reading space available, and its monthly records suggest that a considerable, and steadily increasing, number of people visited without borrowing a book. They likely spent time in the reading room examining recent newspapers and magazines, or even perusing books from the shelves. A few others came to the library for reference queries, which library staff reported were a growing portion of their daily activities during the 1890s and early 1900s. The availability of heat and light in the library's rooms during winter months, when both were in short supply elsewhere in the city, and the corresponding drop in the number of people spending time in the library during the summer, suggest that many users may have found the library an inexpensive and warm place to spend their leisure time. It may also reflect that children often used the library as a space for academic pursuits during the school year.[20]

Borrowing Patterns

If a patron visited the Muncie Public Library and left with a book, it was most likely a work of popular fiction. More specifically, it was probably a children's book or a domestic romance written for women. Titles from those two categories were easily the most often selected by the library's patrons. Adult men were less active as borrowers, and when they did take a book from the library it was quite often one written for women or children, suggesting that they were borrowing on behalf of a family member. Yet the demand for ephemeral fiction does not mean that the library failed to provide its patrons with access to what authorities insisted was more substantial literature, both fiction and nonfiction. There was steady, if comparatively modest, demand for classics, for well-regarded American writers such as Twain and Howells, and to a limited degree for books that addressed the social and political questions of the day.

The popularity of fiction confirms research by other scholars on patterns of library use in this period. As Wayne Wiegand, Christine Pawley, and others have noted, the overwhelming preference among library users, then and now, has been for fiction. Seventy-seven percent of the books borrowed from the Muncie Public Library in the period covered by the records are classified as fiction (according to current Library of Congress subject headings). That preference held across occupational lines almost uniformly. Seventy-seven percent of loans to blue-collar patrons were for fiction, while white-collar borrowers chose fiction 76 percent of the time. High white-collar borrowers borrowed fiction 75 percent of the time, and the proportion for users who fell into the unskilled/menial category was 77 percent. Among younger readers—those born after 1880—81 percent of loans were for fiction titles.[21]

Children's Borrowing

A review of the titles most often issued during the years covered by the What Middletown Read database illustrates the extent to which the library functioned as a supplier of literature for children. The single most popular title was Louisa May Alcott's *Under the Lilacs,* taken out 479 times by 374 people (some of whom borrowed the book more than once). Of the top twenty most frequently loaned titles, sixteen were geared toward children, mostly boys (table 3). Ten were books for boys (five by Alger and five by Castlemon). Finley's Elsie Dinsmore series accounted for another four. Louisa May Alcott and L. T. Meade each had one on the list.

TABLE 3. Most borrowed books

AUTHOR	TITLE	TIMES BORROWED	BORROWERS
Louisa May Alcott	*Under the Lilacs**	479	397
Horatio Alger	*The Young Adventurer*	422	341
Martha Finley	*Elsie Dinsmore**	421	393
L. T. Meade	*A World of Girls*	373	271
Horatio Alger	*The Telegraph Boy*	364	321
Harry Castlemon	*Frank on a Gun-Boat**	363	319
Horatio Alger	*The Young Circus Rider**	359	269
Harry Castlemon	*George at the Fort**	349	305
Martha Finley	*Holidays at Roselands**	342	311
Marie Corelli	*The Sorrows of Satan**	342	280
Martha Finley	*Elsie's Womanhood**	327	292
Augusta Evans	*St. Elmo**	327	291
Harry Castlemon	*Frank on the Lower Mississippi**	325	290
Martha Finley	*Elsie's Girlhood**	315	289
Harry Castlemon	*George in Camp**	310	279
Horatio Alger	*Ragged Dick**	308	283
Harry Castlemon	*Frank in the Woods**	299	261
Horatio Alger	*The Young Miner*	297	263
Amelia Barr	*Bernicia*	291	262
Edward Westcott	*David Harum*	289	267

NOTE. An asterisk indicates that the library held two or more copies of the title.

TABLE 4. Most popular authors

AUTHOR	TIMES BORROWED	PATRONS	AVERAGE LOANS PER PATRON
Horatio Alger	9,230	1,361	6.8
Harry Castlemon	7,399	1,169	6.3
Oliver Optic	5,067	945	5.4
Martha Finley	4,734	718	6.6
Edward S. Ellis	3,039	894	3.4
Edward P. Roe	2,991	1,031	2.9
Louisa May Alcott	2,976	1,022	2.9
F. Marion Crawford	2,120	822	2.6
Rosa N. Carey	1,992	819	2.4
E. Marlitt	1,823	755	2.4
G. A. Henty	1,814	533	3.4
Charles King	1,626	749	2.2
L. T. Meade	1,580	622	2.5
Francis H. Burnett	1,462	849	1.7
Clara Louise Burnham	1.444	618	2.3
Susan Coolidge	1,316	516	2.6
Augusta Evans	1,315	633	2.1
John T. Trowbridge	1,200	509	2.4

Authors of books for boys were easily the most widely borrowed. Horatio Alger led with 57 books loaned a staggering 9,230 times to 1,361 readers (table 4). Harry Castlemon was the second most popular author, and Oliver Optic and Edward Sylvester Ellis remained popular through the end of the century. Only Martha Finley rivaled any of these boys' authors in popularity among Muncie's library users. Her 39 books, all from the Elsie Dinsmore series, circulated 4,609 times among 742 borrowers. The most popular authors also commanded a substantial loyalty among young readers; those who took out Alger, Castlemon, Optic, and Finley books borrowed on average five or more titles from that author.

These data suggest that one reason for the high circulation figures for boys' authors was the brevity and simplicity of their books. An Alger or Castlemon book could be read in a single sitting and was often part of a series, making them prime candidates for binge reading. Alger's books in particular were the shortest and easiest to read among the books that circulated most frequently.[22] Earl Nutting was one boy who read in this way. During a two-week span beginning February 12, 1892, the fourteen-year-old borrowed four books from Castlemon's "Frank Nelson" series—*Frank the Young Naturalist, Frank on a Gun-Boat, Frank before Vicksburg,* and *Frank on the Lower Mississippi.* He switched to an Alger book, *Phil, the Fiddler,* on the first of March, before returning to Castlemon (*Frank in the Mountains*) on March 3. Beginning in late March, he latched on to Alger's stories, borrowing four of them inside three weeks (and two more in May).

Another example par excellence of this mode of reading is Harry Ritter, the son of an upholsterer, who joined the library on Saturday, February 25, 1899. He took home *Cadet Days* by Charles King that day and evidently finished it quickly, returning on Monday to borrow Alger's *Luck and Pluck.* This initial pattern held. During his first two months as a member, Ritter visited the library three or four times per week, carrying out a new title each time. He borrowed, and almost certainly read, twenty-eight books over that span, all of them fiction written for boys. Twelve of them were by Alger and others were by Optic, Castlemon, and Ellis. The database documents the better part of four years of Ritter's borrowing, through early December 1902, and it records 396 loans to him, an average of two per week.

The sometimes insatiable demand for books by Alger, Castlemon, and their peers clearly influenced the library's approach to acquiring new books. The immediate popularity of books by these authors during the first months of 1892, for instance, was likely the result of their recent acquisition. All of them were part of a large shipment of new children's books that arrived in the library on December 30, 1891. It included fifteen by Castlemon, thirteen by Alger, and five new titles by Ellis. None were new releases, and all of them appear to have come from the same publisher or distributor at the modest price of 84 cents per clothbound volume. Kate Wilson had by now assumed her position as librarian, and her acquisition of so many children's titles fore-shadowed the approach she was to follow in the coming years. As the enthusiasm of Nutting, Ritter, and their fellow borrowers demonstrates, there was strong demand for these books that outweighed any criticism they might have received on moral or aesthetic grounds.[23]

The circulation records also suggest that local parents were supportive of this permissive attitude toward popular fiction. Adults regularly borrowed juvenile books; nearly 15 percent of all loans of Alger and Castlemon books were made to patrons born before 1871, and thus at least twenty years old at the beginning of the period documented by extant circulation data. Some were no doubt borrowed by children using the patron number of one of their elders, but it is clear from circulation records that list both the name of the borrower and the account number that the bulk were taken out in person by adults. Even in those instances where a child employed an adult's number, it

seems likely that the adult gave the child free rein in selecting reading material. It was also the case that some adults borrowed these books for themselves, particularly if they possessed only rudimentary reading skills.

One curiosity emerging from the circulation data among males is Alger's
relative lack of popularity among those occupying the lowest rungs of the
occupational ladder. Among the fairly small pool of male borrowers from
families headed by unskilled workers (130, all but 13 of whom were born after
1870), only one Alger title, *The Young Circus Rider*, made the list of the top
ten. Five of the first ten were books by Ellis, and the remaining four were by
Castlemon. Ellis's *Storm Mountain* topped the list. Conversely, among the
248 male users classified as belonging to high white-collar families, the nine
most popular books were all by Alger, and his titles constituted a majority of
the ten most popular choices in every occupational category except unskilled
blue-collar.

It is difficult to draw broad conclusions from this disparity. Since the
sample is small, it may simply be a statistical anomaly. Alger and Castlemon
were hardly unpopular among readers from unskilled households—fifteen of
their books were borrowed at least 29 times (compared to the 42 times that
Ellis's *Storm Mountain* circulated among unskilled male borrowers). But the
prominent popularity of books by Ellis among boys from unskilled laboring
families suggests a different reading dynamic at work at the lower end of
the socioeconomic scale. No doubt less well-to-do homes had fewer books
in the house, and those boys who were inclined to read relied on the public library for a greater array of fiction than did their middle-class counterparts with access to shelves of books at home. Ellis was also a product of the
dime-fiction industry, more so than Alger or Castlemon. Michael Denning
has argued that dime novels circulated more extensively among the working
class in nineteenth-century America, so Ellis may have been more familiar
to the parents of these working-class boys, who in turn steered their sons to
his books.[24] But in the absence of other corroborating evidence, such conclusions are at best speculative.

Girls zeroed in on just a handful of authors as well, although they did
not borrow from the library at quite the same pace. Table 5 ranks borrowing
choices by females born after 1880. Among these patrons Martha Finley's
immensely popular Elsie Dinsmore series ruled; eight of the eleven most
borrowed titles were from the Dinsmore series. Alcott's *Under the Lilacs* and
The Rose in Bloom also circulated heavily among younger female borrowers,
as did L. T. Meade's *A World of Girls*. The latter was in fact the single most
popular title among younger female borrowers.

The popularity of these books cuts across socioeconomic lines. Young

TABLE 5. Most borrowed books, by female patrons born after 1880

AUTHOR	TITLE	TIMES BORROWED
Martha Finley	Elsie Dinsmore*	159
L. T. Meade	A World of Girls	131
Martha Finley	Elsie's Womanhood*	131
Martha Finley	Elsie's Girlhood*	127
Martha Finley	Holidays at Roselands*	125
Martha Finley	Elsie's Motherhood*	124
Louisa May Alcott	Under the Lilacs*	119
Louisa May Alcott	An Old-Fashioned Girl*	112
Martha Finley	Elsie's Widowhood*	110
Martha Finley	Grandmother Elsie*	96
Martha Finley	Elsie's New Relations*	96

NOTE. An asterisk indicates that the library held two or more copies of the title.

women and girls from both blue-collar and white-collar families borrowed *Elsie Dinsmore* and its successors on a regular basis, although the volume of white-collar borrowing was far greater. Nevertheless, Finley's books made up at least half of the top ten most popular titles for every occupational group, from families headed by an unskilled laborer to those whose breadwinner was a high white-collar professional or prominent businessman. Six of the ten most borrowed books among girls and young women from families headed by unskilled workers were from Finley's series and, at the other end of the scale, they made up seven of the ten most borrowed books among those coming from high white-collar families. The popularity of Meade's *A World of Girls* and Alcott's *Under the Lilacs* remained strong at all points on the occupational scale, though on the whole Elsie Dinsmore stories swamped the works of Meade, Alcott, and other authors writing for girls and young women.

Women's Borrowing

Differences in reading choices arose along occupational lines as girls matured into young women. Those from white-collar families shifted from children's literature by Finley and her peers to romances geared toward an adult audience. Romantic and domestic fiction by E. Marlitt (*The Second Wife*, translated from the German by A. L. Wister), E. P. Roe (*Opening a Chestnut Burr*), Augusta Evans (*St. Elmo*) and Marie Corelli (*The Sorrows of Satan*) circulated more than fifty times apiece among white-collar women. Comparatively few women from blue-collar families, and particularly those from families headed by semiskilled and unskilled breadwinners, borrowed these books. As we have noted, it was not the case that they preferred other books, but rather that they used the library far less frequently. Indeed, nearly all of the library use among females from low-skill families took place among school-age children. At the point when these girls stopped going to school, they usually ceased to be active borrowers at the Muncie Public Library.

By contrast, white-collar women continued to borrow as adults. For the most part from comfortable circumstances, these women possessed the leisure time to read, and the records suggest that they consumed in large quantities the romantic, sentimental, and domestic fiction that circulated widely in late Victorian America. Their tastes ran toward the popular fare often dismissed by critics, and their borrowing of this sort of fiction constituted the second largest category of loans by the library (though in numerical terms it was a distant second to children's borrowing). As table 6 shows, the four most popular book titles among white-collar adult women were largely forgotten best sellers by Edward Noyes Westcott (*David Harum: A Story of American Life*), S. Weir Mitchell (*Hugh Wynne, Free Quaker*), Booth Tarkington (*The Gentleman from Indiana*), and Marie Corelli (*Sorrows of Satan*). The popularity of Tarkington's novel must be ascribed at least in part to the Indiana origins of the author and its Hoosier small-town setting, which closely resembled Muncie.

A striking thing about all four of these books is that they circulated almost entirely in the latter half of the period documented in the database. Corelli's novel was acquired earliest, in August 1897, and a second copy arrived in 1900. The library purchased two copies of *Hugh Wynne* simultaneously in December 1897. The first of four copies of *David Harum* arrived in August 1899, just two weeks before *The Gentleman from Indiana* reached the library's shelves. Three more copies of Tarkington's novel followed within two years. Part of the reason that the circulation figures for these books were so high was the availability of multiple copies, a further indication of the library's interest in catering to popular demand rather than attempting to shape it.

That these four relatively recent acquisitions top the list of books borrowed by white-collar adult women suggests these readers were drawn to new titles, and that tendency distinguishes them as a group. None of the books was an especially popular choice among the modest number of women from blue-collar households who patronized the library. Whether through advertising, word of mouth, or both, women from more prosperous households responded swiftly to the release of new fiction.

Not all of the popular selections among Muncie's white-collar adult women were recent best sellers. They also read avidly the works of well estab-

TABLE 6. Books most frequently borrowed by white-collar adult women
(born 1809–1870)

AUTHOR	TITLE	TIMES BORROWED
Edward Westcott	*David Harum**	48
S. Weir Mitchell	*Hugh Wynne**	46
Booth Tarkington	*The Gentleman from Indiana**	40
Marie Corelli	*The Sorrows of Satan**	40
Louisa May Alcott	*Under the Lilacs**	39
Israel Zangwill	*The Master**	38
J. M. Barrie	*The Little Minister**	37
Amelia Barr	*Bernicia*	37
Martha Finley	*Holidays at Roselands**	36
Martha Finley	*Elsie's Motherhood**	34
David Dwight Wells	*Her Ladyship's Elephant*	33
Rosa Nouchette Carey	*The Search for Basil Lyndhurst**	33
E. Marlitt	*The Little Moorland Princess**	32
E. Marlitt	*The Owl's Nest**	32
Martha Finley	*Elsie's Womanhood**	32
Martha Finley	*Elsie Dinsmore**	32
Martha Finley	*Elsie's Girlhood**	32
E. Marlitt	*The Second Wife**	31
Frances Hodgson Burnett	*The Fair Barbarian*	31

NOTE. An asterisk indicates that the library held two or more copies of the title.

lished, if not always critically acclaimed, writers. Amelia Barr, E. Marlitt, Rosa Nouchette Carey, and Clara Burnham were among the popular authors whose books circulated regularly among white-collar women. Three of Marlitt's books appear in the list of the top twenty books most often borrowed by this group. Marlitt, Carey, Burnham, E. P. Roe, and Louisa May Alcott were the most popular authors among Muncie's better-off women. White-collar women borrowed books by each of them at least 250 times, with Alcott topping the list. With the exception of Alcott, whose appeal included younger women and whose books were likely borrowed in some instances for children, all of these writers were dismissed by such arbiters of literary quality as the American Library Association as producers of unworthy fiction, yet they attracted considerable interest and attention among the white-collar women of Muncie.

One of the ways the city's white-collar women may have learned about these books is through popular magazines. The "magazine revolution" of the late nineteenth century, which made weekly and monthly publications accessible to a much wider range of readers, provided consumers of middling means with access to a new range of printed material. It seems likely that some middle-class residents of Muncie subscribed to such publications as *Scribner's, Cosmopolitan,* and *Harper's Magazine.* But women from this group also borrowed them from the library in substantial numbers. If no individual issue necessarily circulated to the extent that best-selling books did, these magazines were nevertheless popular among white-collar women (but not, it should be noted, especially so among their blue-collar counterparts).[25]

The magazines that circulated most among these women were well-established general interest and children's magazines. The top choice was *Harper's New Monthly Magazine;* individual issues were taken out 215 times. Assorted numbers of the *Century Illustrated Monthly Magazine* and the well-known children's serial *St. Nicholas* each circulated 171 times. *Lippincott's* (146 times) and *Harper's Young People* (136 times) were popular as well, while *Scribner's* (86), *Cosmopolitan* (75), and the *Atlantic* (73) were less avidly borrowed but nevertheless in demand. All of these periodicals featured fiction as well as general nonfiction, poetry, and illustrations. Their circulation figures suggest that any account of the demand for fiction among middle-class women must consider magazines as a source as well.

The most popular magazines, including both those geared for adults and those oriented toward children, featured an ample supply of fiction. *Harper's Magazine,* the *Century,* and *Lippincott's,* as well as the less widely circulated (in Muncie) highbrow periodicals such as the *Atlantic,* published works by the most celebrated literary figures of the day. William Dean Howells, Hamlin Garland, Israel Zangwill, Stephen Crane, and the prolific but now seldom read F. Marion Crawford were among the popular and well-regarded writers whose work appeared in their pages. Among the publications that circulated heavily among Muncie patrons, only *Lippincott's* eschewed serial fiction, preferring instead to publish complete stories in a single issue, including novella-length works such as Oscar Wilde's *The Picture of Dorian Gray* or Arthur Conan Doyle's early Sherlock Holmes tale, *The Sign of Four.*

White-collar adult women were also regular borrowers of books geared toward children, and it seems reasonable to assume that they borrowed many of these titles on their behalf. But the frequency with which they took home Louisa May Alcott's *Under the Lilacs,* J. M. Barrie's *The Little Minister,* or Martha Finley's *Elsie Dinsmore* and its sequels suggests that older women were reading some of these books themselves. The circulation ledgers offer little indication that white-collar children were using their mothers' accounts to borrow books. Only 11 of the 104 circulation transactions that involved white-collar women borrowing those titles appear to have entailed one person using another's library account. Women from this cohort borrowed Finley books a robust 704 times during the period covered by the extant circulation records. And on the whole, adult women of all occupational categories borrowed Alcott's *Under the Lilacs* more often than did younger females, despite an episodic narrative oriented toward juveniles. The book was checked out 479 times in all, but only 119 times by females born after 1880.[26]

If women from the upper reaches of Muncie's social and economic order consumed popular, female-oriented fiction at a high rate, their counterparts on the lower end of the occupational scale did not. That distinction was more than a matter of numbers or the rate of borrowing. While women from blue-collar homes, to the degree that they borrowed, consumed fiction geared for feminine readers, they tended not to select newly published popular fiction anywhere near as often as their white-collar counterparts.

The What Middletown Read data offers a limited record of reading choices among adult women from households headed by unskilled and semiskilled workers. It documents the selections of sixty-five such borrowers. Among their leading choices were *St. Elmo, Vashti,* and *Macaria* by Augusta Evans, *Master of Greylands* and *Verner's Pride* by Mrs. Henry Wood (Ellen Price Wood), and *A Penniless Girl* by Wilhelmine Heimberg (Bertha Behrens). These titles were popular among adult women from households of all occupational categories. Largely missing, though, are the best sellers. Corelli's *Sorrows of Satan* circulated nine times, a total that makes it one of the three most popular books among adult women in this group (behind only *St. Elmo* and *Master of Greylands*). They borrowed the homegrown *Gentleman from Indiana* seven times. But the library loaned *David Harum* just five times to women from this demographic category, and *Hugh Wynne* did not circulate among them at all. Together these totals suggest only modest engagement with the mass literary marketplace among working-class women around the turn of the century.

That impression is supported by the lack of interest in periodicals. *Harper's Young People* circulated twenty-two times among adult women from households with semiskilled breadwinners but not at all among those in families headed by unskilled or domestic workers. *St. Nicholas* was also fairly popular. It was borrowed seventeen times by semiskilled women, though never by their unskilled counterparts. A few adult periodicals attracted interest, particularly the *Century* (taken twenty-nine times), *Harper's New Monthly* (nineteen times) and *Lippincott's* (ten times). But of these, only *Harper's* drew the interest of any women from unskilled households: just one of them borrowed three issues of the magazine. Only six issues of *Cosmopolitan* and two of *Scribner's* circulated among low-skill women—no surprise given the middle-class orientation of those magazines. For the small percentage of Muncie's working-class women who patronized the library, its appeal lay less in the availability of the most current fiction, and more in its supply of established, and perhaps familiar, material.

The somewhat larger sample of women from households headed by skilled workers offers an interesting test of this pattern. Eighty adult women from these homes borrowed at least one book from the library. Their families occupied an intermediate, perhaps even indeterminate, position on the occupational ladder in a city making the transition from artisanal to large-scale industrial production. Skilled workers—blacksmiths, glassblowers, and the like—were experiencing a gradual loss of workplace autonomy and status as they were replaced by machines and the unskilled workers who tended them.

The collective reading choices of these women had similarities with the patterns seen among both their fellow blue-collar library patrons and white-collar female borrowers. The relatively small number who borrowed at all—80, compared to 388 women from white-collar families—mirrored the limited library patronage of their counterparts from lower-skill households. They also exhibited a shared taste for déclassé fiction. The most commonly borrowed book (16 times) among this group was *Vashti* by Augusta Evans, a critically panned writer of domestic fiction for women. Many professional librarians discouraged their patrons from borrowing her books, and a few sought to have her titles removed from the shelves.[27] Several other of the top choices of these women were in a similar category, including the two books by Mrs. Alexander (Annie French Hector), *Barbara: Lady's Maid and Peeress* and *By Woman's Wit*, as well as Mrs. Henry Wood's *Verner's Pride*. Four of the ten most borrowed titles were from Finley's Elsie Dinsmore series.

Yet at least a few of these women sought out new fiction in a fashion similar to their white-collar counterparts. They borrowed Corelli's *Sorrows of Satan* ten times, placing it among the twenty most sought after books in the library's collection for that group. Women from skilled families also checked out *The Gentleman from Indiana* nine times. They showed an interest in popular magazines as well; between them these eighty women borrowed *Lippincott's* seventy-six times, while *Scribner's* (twenty-nine) and the *Century* (twenty-five) were reasonably in demand as well. These figures suggest that at least a share of the women from these families gravitated to best sellers, even if many others from their demographic did not. Given the blurred boundaries that divided skilled blue-collar families from white-collar households, such commonality is not unexpected.

Patterns of magazine borrowing suggest another way women from white-collar and skilled blue-collar households interacted with the literary market-place. Many of them, it appears, were frequent readers of serialized fiction in popular magazines. This form of publication originated during the eigh-teenth century and, according to many accounts, peaked in the middle of the nineteenth century in Europe, as masses of readers awaited installments of the latest work by Charles Dickens, the elder Alexander Dumas, and a host of other authors. Both magazines and newspapers delivered serialized stories, helping create a market for popular fiction. While both market pressures and literary trends emphasizing an approach to literature as an aesthetic whole began to undercut installment publishing by the 1890s, the form remained popular in the United States and Europe into the twentieth century. The surge of magazine circulation in the United States during that same decade generated new demand for serial fiction and helped popularize such writ-ers as Rudyard Kipling, William Dean Howells, and Hamlin Garland among American readers.[28]

A closer look at magazine borrowing in the What Middletown Read data-base provides circumstantial evidence of the continued attraction of serial fiction. Without the direct testimony of borrowers, we cannot know with certainty that they selected a series of issues of a particular magazine in order to follow the installments of a specific story. But the data include numer-ous instances of patrons borrowing sequential issues of the same magazine, sometimes just as they became available and sometimes over short periods of time. At least twenty-one patrons borrowed consecutive numbers of *Harper's Magazine,* and forty did the same for the *Century.* In many cases, these pat-terns correspond to the running of a particular serial, with the first and last issue borrowed containing the first and last installments of a novel. Even when the borrowing does not overlap perfectly with a particular serializa-tion, it seems likely that the choices were made because of the serialization. In some cases, gaps in the data (and there were many, since not all magazine transactions could be recovered) may obscure borrowing choices; in others it may be that the borrower had other ways of accessing the magazines or even that he or she waited until the book was published in a single volume.

One such example is Minnie Bell Hoover's sequential borrowing of *Harper's New Monthly Magazine.* Hoover, the fifteen-year-old daughter of a paperhanger, took home the January 1901 issue of the magazine on February 15, 1902, a Saturday. On the following Monday she borrowed the February issue, and she returned for the March issue the next day. Her pace slowed a bit from there. She did not borrow the April issue until the Friday of that week and only on the next Tuesday, the 25th, did she check out the May issue. From there, in short order, she took home the June, July, and August

1901 issues, so that in the course of eighteen days she borrowed eight consecutive issues of *Harper's*. Those eight issues included installments of Gilbert Parker's novel *The Right of Way*. Parker was a popular Canadian writer, and *The Right of Way* was a suspenseful romance that would go on to become one of the top-selling books in the United States during both 1901 and 1902; the Muncie Public Library acquired a copy in October 1901. The book fits Hoover's tastes: her library record shows that she borrowed Booth Tarkington's *The Gentlemen from Indiana* and James Lane Allen's *A Kentucky Cardinal*, books with similar plots and themes.

Similar patterns emerge among other readers. Sara Bradbury, the widow of a doctor, borrowed successive issues of *Harper's* during the fall of 1901 that match perfectly with the serialization of two stories: Elizabeth Stuart Phelps Ward's "His Wife: A Story in Three Parts," and Mary Eleanor Wilkins Freeman's novel *The Portion of Labor*. Ada Gilman, a secretary at the Delaware County Land Improvement Company, borrowed consecutive (and just released) issues of the *Atlantic* during the fall of 1891 that included the two-part serialization of Henry James's story "The Chaperon." The same issues include the final installments of Mary Hartwell Catherwood's *The Lady of Fort St. John*, and since Gilman borrowed the October 1891 issue on November 6, just the second day covered by the extant circulation records, it is entirely possible that she had borrowed in sequence all of the issues of the *Atlantic* containing Catherwood's novel. Ella Jeffers, a stenographer, borrowed three consecutive issues of the 1900 volume of the same magazine, which together contained the full serialization of Mary Johnston's novel *To Have and to Hold*, as well as a series of articles by the Sioux writer Zitkala Za (sometimes spelled Zitkala-Sa) about Native American life. There is no way to be sure that any of these selections were made for the purpose of reading these serials, but the patterns, and the fact that they occurred as often as they did, make it unlikely that all of these sequential borrowings were coincidental.

In a few instances, the database provides evidence that the reading of serial fiction was a family affair. Emma Goodin, a schoolteacher, and her widowed mother, Sarah, jointly borrowed every issue of *Harper's Magazine* for the year 1900. While those twelve issues contained a number of full stories, it seems most likely that they made their selections in order to read the twelve installments of Mrs. Humphry Ward's *Eleanor*. Sarah borrowed the January issue, containing the third installment, on March 8, 1900, and returned for the February issue on March 22 and the March issue on April 13. Thereafter either Emma or Sarah borrowed successive issues of the magazine each month through the December 1900 issue, which Sarah checked out on January 22, 1901. They obtained each issue about midway through the following month, which likely gave the library enough time to catalog them and make them available to borrowers. Emma Goodin was quite familiar with Ward's work, having been a longtime member of the Woman's Club of Muncie, which had discussed Ward's immensely popular novel *Marcella* on several occasions. Ward was president of the club in 1899, when it presented a dramatization of the novel as part of program on "the Evolution of the Civic Woman" (see chapter 5).[29]

The shared borrowing evident in the Goodin household appears to have occurred in other families as well. Dr. Isaac N. Trent and his wife, Cora, were regular borrowers of magazines, including sequential runs of the *Century* and *Harper's*. At times they would go to the library together, typically on a Saturday, and borrow consecutive issues of a publication, as they did when they obtained the March and April 1896 issues of the *Century* on the same day. It is not clear what story they were reading, although another Ward novel, *Sir George Tressady*, had commenced in the November 1895 issue, which was the first of a stretch of loans to the Trents that continued through the May 1896 issue. (Like Emma Goodin, Cora Trent was a member of the Woman's Club of Muncie and likely was quite familiar with Ward.) James Ludlow, along with his adult daughter Ida Ludlow, borrowed consecutive issues of the *Century* spanning December 1894 to August 1895. This series of numbers correspond closely to installments of William M. Sloane's *Life of Napoleon Bonaparte* as well as the serialization of *Casa Braccio* by F. Marion Crawford.

The popularity of magazines, along with circulation patterns that correspond to the serialization of fiction, suggests that Muncie's library users obtained fiction by borrowing periodicals as well as books. Magazine loans most often went to white-collar women, and it seems likely that the marketing methods connected with these serials were aimed at and had the most effect on that audience, a group whose tastes in turn exercised a collective influence on the development of the library's collection.

Men's Borrowing

If adult women of some means used the Muncie Public Library as a source for popular fiction, their husbands and brothers generally did not, at least not for themselves. Among those borrowers for whom we have demographic data, just over 15 percent (392) were adult men (classified as those born before 1871 and thus at least twenty when our records begin). They borrowed books or magazines from the library 18,059 times. Their borrowing patterns suggest that reading was often a family affair. When a man left the library with a book under his arm, it was probably intended for one of his children (most likely a son) or for his wife.

Most of the adult males who took books from the library were married and middle class. Of the 392 men whose borrowing is recorded in the database, we have occupational information for 380. Of those, 256 (65%) held, or came from a family whose head of household held, a white-collar job. Eighty of the remaining 124 blue-collar patrons were skilled workers or their dependents. The vast majority (320, or 82%) of male borrowers were married. Only among the small number of adult men holding unskilled jobs did the likelihood that they were married drop below 80 percent, and this sample of just seventeen men, eleven of whom were married, offers too narrow a base to draw any firm conclusions.

Two sorts of books predominated among the borrowing choices made by men: domestic fiction aimed at women and children's literature, particularly boys' books. The list of the most popular books among men included E. Marlitt's novel *The Second Wife* and the tales of Alger, Ellis, and Castlemon (table 7). Only Tarkington's *Gentleman from Indiana* might be construed to hold any appeal for adult men, though its interest to women was evident from overall circulation figures. Children's reading made up the largest portion of men's borrowing choices. They borrowed Alger books more often than those by any other author, 838 times over the nine years accounted for in the circulation data. They chose Castlemon 647 times and Ellis 299 times. Books for boy eclipsed those for girls, though there were plenty of instances in which a man brought home a girls' book. They borrowed books from the Elsie Dinsmore series 298 times and Louisa May Alcott's books 232 times. Perhaps more tellingly, adult men brought home children's magazines regularly, including copies of *St. Nicholas* (208 times) and *Harper's Young People* (189 times).

The likelihood that books and magazines were often checked out for sons and daughters is reinforced by the fact that nearly all of the men were married, and these men borrowed more frequently than their unmarried counterparts. As table 7 shows, married men account for most of the selections of children's books and women's fiction. Only Ellis's *The Last War Trail*, the third and final entry in his popular Deerfoot series, received much interest from single adult men, perhaps because it told an old and familiar story. It should be noted as well that among the sixty-seven unmarried adult male borrowers there were thirteen widowers, several of whom, it seems, were selecting books for children.

Taking into account occupational distinctions yields two variants of this pattern of borrowing. Among the larger group of white-collar men who borrowed books, titles for women and girls took up a greater share of the top choices. Marlitt's *The Second Wife* (24 times), *The Lady with the Rubies* (also

TABLE 7. Books most frequently borrowed by adult males

AUTHOR	TITLE	TIMES BORROWED	TIMES BORROWED BY MARRIED MALE
Horatio Alger	*The Young Adventurer*	41	36
Edward Sylvester Ellis	*The Last War Trail**	37	24
Horatio Alger	*The Young Circus Rider*	33	28
Booth Tarkington	*The Gentleman from Indiana**	34	28
Horatio Alger	*Ragged Dick**	34	28
Horatio Alger	*The Young Circus Rider*	33	28
Horatio Alger	*Ben's Nugget*	32	25
E. Marlitt	*The Second Wife**	30	29
Martha Finley	*Elsie Dinsmore**	30	27
Edward Payson Roe	*Barriers Burned Away**	30	27
Harry Castlemon	*Frank on the Prairie**	30	23

NOTE. An asterisk indicates that the library held two or more copies of the title.

by Marlitt; borrowed 22 times) and *Elsie Dinsmore* (21 times) were quite popular. The small number of male borrowers from blue-collar homes were most likely to choose books for boys by Alger, Castlemon, or Ellis, whose volumes constituted the top six choices. Whether these men were themselves reading such books remains unclear. Among adult fare of interest to women, only Tarkington's *Gentleman from Indiana* and Augusta Evans's *Vashti* were taken out as many as a dozen times.

Although it appears that most adult men borrowed chiefly on behalf of women and children, there is also some reason to think they read the books intended for these groups. The small sample of single men who used the library yields a list of preferences that includes books by Ellis and Castlemon, alongside the *Encyclopedia Americana* and historical romances by F. Marion Crawford (*Katherine Lauderdale*) and Georg Ebers (*Bride of the Nile*). They may have borrowed those books on behalf of others, but it is also possible that children's fiction, particularly the titles by Ellis and Castlemon known to them from childhood, would appeal to adult men. And the prevalence of romance in English-language fiction during the late Victorian period, even in novels dealing with such male-oriented topics as politics, make conclusions about readership drawn from content, or even intended market, indefinite.

Nearly all of Muncie's active public library patrons were white. Of the nineteen African Americans who held cards, only fifteen (fourteen classified as "black" or "colored" in census records and one listed as "mulatto") borrowed from the library. In contrast to the figures for whites, there were more men than women among black borrowers. Twelve were male and three were female, although one of the men, John L. Morin, a forty-six-year-old barber, let his wife, Nora, employ his number sixteen times during 1894 and 1895. As with all library users, this group's tastes ran largely to fiction. Of the 413 times they borrowed books, they chose fiction 345 times, with their choices scattered more widely. Only three titles drew more than passing interest from the group: L. T. Meade's *A World of Girls* (borrowed five times); *The Works of Daniel Webster* (four), and Tarkington's *Gentleman from Indiana* (four). Their tastes in children's fiction tilted toward Castlemon more than Alger, and toward Alcott and Meade rather than Finley. They did not choose a single book from the Elsie Dinsmore series, hardly surprising given the pervasive racism infusing Finley's portrait of plantation life in the Old South. Likewise, women's fiction popular among whites did not register notably among Muncie's African American library patrons.

Even taken as a whole, Muncie's foreign-born population was small as well. It included 148 registered library patrons, of whom 117 borrowed at least one book. Unlike native-born users, the immigrant population split evenly along lines of sex: of the 117 active borrowers we know were born outside the United States, 59 were female and 58 were male. But in other respects their tastes mirrored those of the rest of the library's users. Alcott's *Under the Lilacs* and Corelli's *Sorrows of Satan* were the top choices (20 times each). Evans's *St. Elmo* (15) and Roe's *Barriers Burned Away* (13) circulated frequently, as did other Alcott books, Meade's *A World of Girls* (13) and Alger's *Young Adventurer* (11). German-born patrons borrowed *Die Gartenlaube,* a traditional German family magazine and one of the few foreign-language items available in the library's collection, quite frequently, but for the most part immigrant borrowers displayed a preference for popular fiction similar to that of their neighbors.

Beyond the Most Borrowed: Reading as Engagement

A survey of the most popular choices among patrons of the Muncie Public Library offers only a partial picture of local reading behavior in these years. Two-thirds of the borrowing done in Muncie during this period did not involve the most popular books; thousands of books and magazines were taken out only once or just a handful of times, suggesting a wide range of motives and interest among library users. In fact, we find almost as many atypical borrowers—meaning those who borrowed none of the most frequently circulating titles—as we do typical readers. In other words, there was more to library borrowing than can be easily summarized in a table showing which books and authors were borrowed most often.[30]

Digging more deeply into the data, we find considerable evidence of borrowing that did not fit the general pattern. Even those enthralled by best-selling fiction at least occasionally dipped into the library's nonfiction collection. Among active borrowers, nine in ten chose a book not classified (by subject heading) as fiction at least once. Some of them were categorized as "literature," which usually meant works of a more elevated reputation. But a substantial part of the remainder was drama, poetry, history, social science, religious commentary, or social criticism. Choices in these areas were restricted, partly because of the conservative outlook that shaped this part of the library's collection, and no doubt partly because the library devoted so large a share of its resources to the purchase of best-selling fiction.

Nevertheless, Muncie's library offered its patrons the opportunity to read both classic literature and well-regarded contemporary fare. And to some extent they did. We noted earlier that borrowers selected works by Shakespeare, Austen, Scott, and Hawthorne, as well as more recent material by Henry James, Mark Twain, and William Dean Howells, on a fairly regular basis. But the circulation numbers for these authors pale in comparison with those of an Alger or a Castlemon. Thirteen books by Twain circulated 877 times. Patrons borrowed Shakespeare texts 268 times (though it should be noted that 85 of these loans were for Charles Lamb's collection for children) and works by Jane Austen 179 times. Sir Walter Scott's adventures drew even more interest, circulating a robust 658 times, with *Ivanhoe* and *Kenilworth* the most popular titles. The library lent books by Henry James 208 times, Dickens titles 672 times, and the thirteen books by William Dean Howells in the collection 538 times.

For the most part, the borrowers of these highly regarded authors were white-collar patrons, though in certain instances the proportion of blue-collar borrowers was larger than expected. On the whole, just under two-thirds (64%) of all circulation transactions recorded in the database involved white-collar patrons. Among loans of Dickens, Howells, Austen, Hawthorne, and James, the rate of white-collar borrowing was roughly the same—within 5 percentage points in each case. But for loans involving books by Twain, Shakespeare, and Scott, there was a somewhat greater likelihood that the library lent them to blue-collar patrons. That was particularly so when Shakespeare texts circulated; just 54 percent of those borrowings were by white-collar patrons, a full ten points less than the overall rate. The reasons for the disparity are not clear, though it is likely that families of means might have owned copies of their works. By contrast, newer works by

James, Howells, or even Twain were perhaps less commonly owned and thus more likely borrowed.[31]

Works of history circulated less often than highbrow fiction or drama. Since a central mission of public libraries was to educate their users in a fashion that prepared them for good citizenship, authorities such as the ALA believed historical works should occupy a prominent place in any collection and, presumably, should make up a substantial proportion of the material lent. (The catalog for the ALA's 1893 model public library included nearly as many history books as it did works of popular fiction.) Muncie's library had a relatively large collection of historical works, but most of them rarely left the shelves. Just 4,290 circulation transactions involved books assigned historical subject headings, making them a tiny part (just over 2%) of the overall borrowing at the library. The most popular history title was *The Boys of '76* by the journalist Charles Carleton Coffin, an account of the American Revolution written for schoolchildren. It circulated 110 times. Oddly, the second most frequently borrowed volume (90 times) was *The War of the Rebellion*, a compilation of reports from the Civil War issued by the War Department. Certainly historical fiction was popular, but no conventional history books ranked near the top of the list of most often loaned books, and only 17 of them circulated as many as 40 times.[32]

Books that addressed the major questions of the day—most of which were tied to industrialization, inequality, and social reform—drew little interest. There was an abundance of such works in circulation by the end of the nineteenth century, yet they constituted only a small portion of the collection, and there is no reason to think the library fostered engagement with these writings in any substantial way. The fact that Muncie was in the midst of a rapid industrial transformation and was beginning to experience attendant difficulties did not spur interest among the library's patrons, or its board, in books exploring these fundamental socioeconomic changes.[33]

Most of the nonfiction books that engaged in social criticism and advocated reform were infrequently borrowed. Henry George's books, including his famed manifesto, *Progress and Poverty*, circulated just forty-eight times in total, and no other title went out more than eighteen times. Only thirty-two patrons borrowed *Prisoners of Poverty*, Helen Campbell's study of women wage workers, and just twenty-five took home Riis's *How the Other Half Lives*, a detailed examination of the plight of the poor in New York City. Users borrowed works by the Social Gospel writer Josiah Strong twenty-one times. Other books offering reform programs barely made a ripple. Lyman Abbot's *Christianity and Social Problems* was borrowed just eight times, while the library logged only seven loans of Richard Ely's *Social Aspects of Christianity*.

The only books to promote social change and achieve even a modest reader-ship through the library were fiction: Edward Bellamy's two utopian novels, both driven by romantic plots, circulated 146 times. Works by Howells and James, which incorporated subtle critiques of American society into their narratives, reached reasonably substantial circulation levels as well.[34]

It is abundantly clear that Muncie's readers were comfortable with fiction in which Christian moralism took center stage. The immensely popular Elsie Dinsmore tales were saturated with religious references, ranging from sus-tained discussions of good and evil to passages from scripture, and explic-itly sought to promote a Christian ideal of woman as submissive wife and pious mother, the so-called angel in the house. Alger's books originated as an evangelical alternative to sensational dime fiction, though in the judgment of some they eventually strayed from those roots. E. P. Roe, a popular novelist whose books were borrowed nearly three thousand times over the course of the extant records, was a Presbyterian minister whose narratives usually featured both a love story and a religious conversion (in which a Christian woman succeeds in winning a man's heart and restoring his faith). The wildly popular, though critically dismissed, *St. Elmo,* by Augusta Evans, followed the same plot line, as did well-circulated domestic fiction by Amelia Barr, Clara Burnham, and Rosa Nouchette Carey.[35]

On matters of race, books chosen often by borrowers reflected prevailing norms as well. Among the most popular books in the library, charged 284 times in total, was *The Planter's Northern Bride,* by Caroline Hentz, published in 1854, a defense of slavery that took the form of a domestic novel. Written in response to Harriet Beecher Stowe's famed antislavery text, *Uncle Tom's Cabin,* Hentz's novel was far more frequently borrowed in 1890s Muncie than Stowe's, which circulated only 115 times. Augusta Evans's books, even more frequently borrowed than Hentz, were proslavery as well. Finley's Elsie Dinsmore books, also set in the pre–Civil War South, exhibited a casual racism, and though racial stereotypes were less pervasive in Alger's work, it was not too difficult to find them in his tales of street urchins and young adventurers. Conversely, Albion Tourgée's *A Fool's Errand,* which included sympathetic treatment of freedmen during Reconstruction, circulated but 68 times.[36]

Despite such fealty to the cultural conventions of the day, it is worth con-sidering the way popular literature chosen by Muncie's library patrons con-tained the rudiments of a more complex and even critical comprehension of industrializing society. Daniel Rodgers offers one such example in his penetrating examination of the interplay between the demands of the liter-ary marketplace and the moral elements evident in books for boys by Alger,

Optic, and their peers. Competition for readers, he notes, forced these writers to avoid heavy-handed moralism and to stress the heroic and even rebellious traits of their heroes rather than their dutiful and industrious qualities. The result, Rodgers argues, was a "divided counsel" that urged discipline and hard work but also prized independence and a willingness to flout authority, an inconsistency that troubled librarians and other critics. Alger never abandoned his emphasis on honesty and initiative, but his stories also painted a picture of a world marked by greed, fraud, and inequality. The goal of *Ragged Dick* was not simply to promote individualism but also to generate sympathy for poor boys in cities. Novels such as *Paul the Peddler* and *Luke Walton* offered critiques of prevailing business practices, including excessive profit-seeking, while *Ben, the Luggage Boy* and *Slow and Sure* endorsed efforts to organize workers.[37]

To classify Alger as an apologist for industrial capitalism is to oversimplify. It was good fortune and the kindness of others, as well as industry, that saw his heroes through. The tension between an emphasis on individual character and effort on the one hand, and the help and good luck that led to success on the other, reflected an unease with industrial life. We cannot say whether Alger's Muncie readers shared this sense of the world, or whether they took anything from such books beyond the thrill of adventure. But it seems clear at least that in reading Alger they encountered a more ambivalent portrait of American society than one might expect from clichés about his books.[38]

Though less tension surrounded the most borrowed books for girls, a few of them encouraged a degree of female independence that challenged prevailing assumptions about gender roles. Despite its ultimate affirmation of domestic propriety as the defining quality of a respectable young woman, L. T. Meade's *A World of Girls* also depicted independence and even rebelliousness with some sympathy. If, in the same fashion, Louisa May Alcott's stories emphasized the qualities of sympathy and kindness that defined the "true womanhood" of the Victorian era, they also featured independent women at their center. Alcott herself was a supporter of women's rights, including suffrage, and her juvenile fiction reflected those commitments.[39]

The mild uncertainties about gender roles evident in juvenile fiction for girls were more pronounced in novels targeting adult women. There were a few popular pieces of women's fiction that argued for more traditional roles. *Marcella*, the popular novel by the English anti-suffragist Mrs. Humphry Ward that circulated regularly (its two volumes were borrowed a total of 222 times), was a case in point. The story of a rebellious young Englishwoman attracted to radical politics who is tamed by her love of a conservative man offered a warning against excessive female ambition and independence. But more often Muncie's library patrons, and particularly its white-collar female borrowers, chose domestic and sentimental fiction that, while celebrating women's piety and virtue in a way that conformed on the surface to conventional gender roles, also conveyed subtle points about the autonomy and moral authority of women.

A novel such as Augusta Evans's *St. Elmo*, the single most borrowed work of women's fiction in the database, offers an example of this sort of writing. In many ways, Evans's stories were conservative. Her novels, including *St. Elmo*, defended Southern life and dismissed women's suffrage. Yet the hero of her most popular story, Edna, is intelligent, well educated, and displays a staunchly Christian moralism. In the book's denouement, she marries and subordinates herself to St. Elmo Murray, but only after establishing herself as an independent figure and persuading him to return to the Christian faith. That narrative formula cannot easily be classified as either feminist or anti-feminist. Its resolution in favor of a conventionally gendered order may not entirely undermine the emphasis on women's moral autonomy.[40]

We do not have direct evidence that the Muncie women who borrowed *St. Elmo* read it in these terms. We know that it was popular. We know that women from white-collar households borrowed it heavily, and that they frequently borrowed books with similar themes by popular writers such as E. Marlitt, E. P. Roe, and Clara Burnham. We know as well that some of these same women engaged in the sort of public reform activism that scholars have linked to the portrayals of women in nineteenth-century domestic fiction. It seems fair to speculate that these parallels represent something more than coincidence, yet even with circulation data we cannot demonstrate precise causal linkages.

What we can conclude with confidence is that the substantial number of Muncie's middle-class women who read these books encountered a more complex cultural calculus than one might think. In much the same way, children reading Alger's fiction were exposed to more intricate renderings of urban-industrial life than is commonly acknowledged. Ultimately, the depth and character of readers' engagement, the impact of their reading on their vision of the world around them, and the collective impact of those experiences are not accessible through library borrowing records. Rather, the richness of the Muncie Public Library archive is in providing us with statistical data of popular borrowing and a unique insight into the vagaries of collective taste.

The circulation patterns evident in the What Muncie Read database make it clear that Muncie's library was not the overtly educational institution that library apologists advocated. Relatively few of its patrons used it as a resource for learning about civics or science, or as a vehicle for self-instruction in a conscious sense. Yet nearly all of the books they did choose to borrow were, if not overtly didactic, at least imbued with values and ideas about how a modern society should function, or even subtle critiques of the prevailing order. The library operated primarily as a supplier of cultural material from which its patrons could absorb the impressions of the world created by popular fiction, not as a conveyor of the knowledge contained in scholarly works and the cultural capital conveyed through highbrow literature.

In its tacit acceptance of this role, Muncie's proved in certain respects more liberal than many other turn-of-the-century public libraries. While some institutions were purging Alger stories and lesser examples of domestic fiction from their shelves, the Muncie library was buying new copies of the same books. Certainly the civic authorities who ran the library sought to supply local residents with respectable reading materials and in doing so limited the kinds of ideas and information one could encounter there. But they were more anxious to meet the demands and desires of local users, even when they flouted the criteria for good reading that prevailed among late-Victorian arbiters of literary taste and morality.

Yet it is important to acknowledge once again that the Muncie Public Library catered to the wishes and tastes of its principal users. Its hours, its atmosphere, and its collections were all geared toward the white-collar portion of the community. The library's responsiveness to user demand created a cycle that reinforced its social character. Since most patrons were from white-collar families, it emphasized the acquisition of books that suited their tastes, such as newly published popular fiction for women. The increasing presence of such works on its shelves in turn made the library even more attractive to middle-class readers. In the case of fiction for women, the library's collection of works that explored domestic experiences likely resonated with the middle-class women who shared those experiences more so than with women from blue-collar families who did not. Ultimately, the very act of reading the latest novels was a form of engagement with the wider culture that helped define the middle class as a separate and distinct group, making the library a tool for group formation rather than a means to level social distinctions.

None of this occurred in isolation. The interactions between local readers and their public library was part of a larger system in which printed materials were conceived, produced, distributed, and consumed. The patterns of borrowing evident in the records make clear that readers gravitated to particular authors and genres. They suggest as well that the marketing efforts of publishers had some effect. The interaction among all of these actors must be taken into consideration as we study the development of print culture, whether in a community such as Muncie or more broadly.

While the precise meaning of individual and collective reading experiences remains hidden, there is little question that reading was central to the lives of a great many of Muncie's late nineteenth-century residents. In a short and evocative memoir of his childhood, Dr. G. W. H. Kemper, who grew up in a rural community about fifty miles south of Muncie, recalled that the rooms in his family's home in the 1840s and 1850s "were lighted by the aid of the open fire, and tallow dips, a rag immersed in melted lard or tallow in a small open dish. Later . . . a new revelation appeared in the neighborhood, a candle mold . . . that would produce six candles, and then twelve, . . . when it seemed that the high tide in lighting had come to our home."[41] In such circumstances, for all but the most affluent families, it would have been challenging at any time of the year to find at home a quiet and lighted space for private reading. By the end of the century, with the advent of gas and the new promise of electric lighting, it was both easier and far more common to read at home, a development that helps explain the phenomenal popularity of the Muncie Public Library. From a twenty-first-century perspective, it is difficult to imagine how dramatic a transformation that was and, consequently, to appreciate the ever-increasing significance of reading in people's lives in this era.

5

"Bread Sweet as Honey"

Reading, Education, and
the Public Library

On March 25, 1896, about five years after Kate Wilson's appointment as city librarian, her work, and the library's success, were recognized in an encomium on the front page of the *Muncie Daily Times:*

> One of the pleasant sights of Muncie is to visit the public library and see the scores of young people, boys and girls, intensely interested in the books and magazines. Seated around the tables or standing up behind the several counters you will observe from thirty to fifty boys and girls either at study or selecting books to take home. The very excellent order and the fine regard for the proprieties of the place are observed by every one present, not a word being said above a whisper. No brighter or more promising body of young people are found anywhere than here. They come and go, night after night, and in numbers must run up to two or three hundred who visit the library during a week. This does not include the adults who visit the library during the day. The good the Muncie Public Library is doing is not fully understood or appreciated. The question as to what to do with the boys and girls is being answered by what the library is doing. The important thing is to have more extensive quarters and facilities for doing greater good. Miss Kate Wilson is giving the library her full time, and the order and system she has brought about deserves the greatest commendation. If parents would drop into the library some evening they would be pleased with the appearance of things and some of them with the brightest boys in the public schools would learn where the boys spend their evenings.

The account made it clear that an essential facet of the library was its employment as an educational conduit. Among its greatest achievements, the *Daily Times* implied, was the inculcation of the habit of reading into the brightest young people of Muncie. The library was the place of choice where boys and girls could go to complete their homework and other studies, while also offering them an extensive array of reading material to fill their leisure hours. A further point of emphasis here is that, without the library as a cultural and social focal point and rendezvous, young boys in particular might be led astray in a city that had comparatively little else to stimulate them.

The shared mission of the library and the city's schools had been made explicit a decade earlier. At that time John M. Bloss, a Civil War veteran, was serving as both superintendent of schools and president of the library board, an indication in itself of the link between the two. He arranged for the board to lay aside fifty-four shares of library stock, one share to be awarded to two pupils in each of the public-school grades 2 to 12, selected for their "good deportment and scholarship." It was also resolved that a share of stock "be awarded to each teacher who shall prove effective and meritorious," further cementing a permanent relationship with the city schools. Bloss and the board were merely upholding the fundamental principle that the twin goals of the Muncie Public Library were to promote readership and augment learning.[1]

In this chapter we examine how the library met those goals. From its inception, supporters cited the library as evidence of the community's commitment to education. It fulfilled that mission by serving as a supplier of morally sound reading material to students, especially to young and impressionable readers. It augmented the more advanced curriculum of the high school, though only in limited ways since, as we have seen, its collection tilted toward popular fare rather than academic treatises. Occasionally the library also provided resources for a patron of an autodidactic bent. For the most part, in keeping with other facets of its operations, the library achieved these ends informally and inconsistently through the 1890s. Only with the appointment of Artena Chapin in 1903 and the opening of the Carnegie Library in 1904 did it begin to approach educational matters in a more structured and aggressive manner.

The Public Library and the Schools

The slow growth of local schooling during the antebellum years is recounted by Thomas Helm in his *History of Delaware County* (1881):

> Education in Indiana, fifty years ago, was in a very backward and unprom-
> ising condition, and the status of Delaware County in that regard was not
> exceptional; yet when education was at low ebb, especially in those dis-
> tricts of [the] country then recently inhabited by the red man, the spirit of
> progress moved even the scattering pioneers in this, as in other localities
> similarly situated, to exert themselves in behalf of their children, toward
> the procurement of the facilities within their reach, for mental training and
> development.[2]

In the early schools, G. W. H. Kemper tells us, "even the first forms of black-
board . . . [and] graphite pencils were . . . unknown," and "paper was coarse
and expensive."[3] The first school in "Muncietown" was set up by Henry
Tomlinson, a native of North Carolina, "in a log cabin that stood at or near the
southwest corner of Main and Walnut streets, during the winter of 1829–30."
It had about twenty pupils, and was paid for by subscription.[4]

Muncie's schools in the years prior to the Civil War were hard pressed
to keep up with the increase in population, and it was only in the late 1860s
that changes of real significance began to take place. In the summer of 1867
Hamilton McRae was appointed superintendent of public schools, and at the
same time Emma Montgomery was named principal of the new high school.
The two were soon man and wife, and Emma McRae played a leading role
in the development of the city's women's clubs before going on to become a
professor at Purdue University (see chapter 6). Hamilton McRae, who by all
accounts was an inspiring administrator, remained superintendent of schools
for sixteen years, until 1883, and during that time he was also instrumental in
the creation of the Muncie Public Library and served an eight-year term as
its first president. He was the first of three presidents elected to that position
while formally employed as superintendent of schools; the others were Bloss
and William R. Snyder. Together, these school superintendents presided over
the board for fifteen of the first twenty-eight years.

The long-term involvement of superintendents in the affairs of the Muncie
Public Library is but one manifestation of the close relationship between the
library and the schools. That such a relationship was considered desirable at
the time can be seen in the writings of Richard Gause Boone, the preemi-
nent late nineteenth-century historian of education in Indiana. Boone held
a professorship of pedagogy at Indiana University and was later appointed
as a college principal in a neighboring state. He devotes a full chapter of his
History of Education in Indiana (1892) to libraries, arguing that they "are
as legitimate a part of a State's equipment of education as are schools and
teachers, universities, and laboratories":

One of the most promising of educational agencies—one dangerously seductive to the unthinking, but that may be made fruitful of good also, though generally poorly understood—is the library. It can easily be made available to the school and the home, to the young and the old, as a supplement to lessons and formal teaching, and as a university in itself. Schools have scarcely begun to use books as their all-sided helpfulness suggests, and the opinion is yet not infrequent that they belong—except texts—to the after-school period.[5]

The children of Muncie knew nothing of Boone, but they used their feet to support his notion that the public library should be seen as a laboratory of learning. Perhaps because their parents were still at work or because of its superior lighting and free heating, the library was the locale of choice for a healthy number of the city's children in their after-school hours. Social or recreational inducements may have played a role as well, but there were also tangible academic reasons for children to make a beeline from school to the library. "The people of Muncie are a reading people," a contemporary columnist claimed in an appeal for more donations of books to the library. "Education in our admirable public schools is rearing a population of readers and thinkers, and these must have books. They cannot have too many of them." A few years later a prominent Muncie clubwoman characterized the library as the "younger sister" of the public schools.[6]

Children's Reading

If an emphasis on reading appears to us today as self-evident, it had a special resonance in the late nineteenth-century Midwest, where literacy rates had once lagged behind those of the more developed states of the Northeast. Earlier in the century it was not uncommon to find pioneer settlers who had never learned to read or write. A Delaware County land deed dated May 7, 1838, shows the signature of John Dinsmore, one of the purchasers of a farm, but only the mark (in the shape of an X) of his wife, Elizabeth, who was illiterate (fig. 8). Writing at the beginning of the twentieth century, G. W. H. Kemper observed that "in 1840 one-seventh of the adult population of Indiana could not read nor write, and . . . in the matter of literacy, Indiana stood sixteenth among twenty-three states in 1840; in 1850 she was twenty-third among twenty-six states, lower than all the slave states but three." Listing the population of Delaware County in 1850 as 10,976, he computes that 1,069, or approximately one in ten, were illiterate.[7]

By the end of the nineteenth century, illiteracy rates were far lower in a

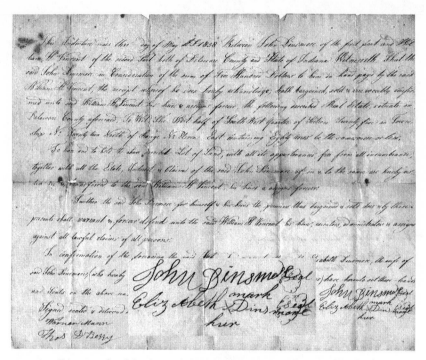

FIGURE 8. Dinsmore land deed. Elizabeth Dinsmore could only mark her name with an X; someone else wrote her name around it. Courtesy Ball State University Archives and Special Collections.

conurbation like Muncie but were marginally greater in more rural parts of the county. Among urban blacks, it should be noted, the illiteracy rate was somewhat higher. Charley Streeter, a white boy who joined the library at age twelve, in March 1894, came from a family that included a widowed father, James, who was a grain dealer, and an older sister, Edna. All three were literate (according to the 1900 census return) but they were joined in the household by Mary Wilson, a twenty-six-year-old Kentucky-born black servant, who could converse in English but was unable to either read or write. For all its pedagogical aims, the Muncie Public Library was not designed to reach out to Mary Wilson's segment of the population. Neither the library board nor the predominantly white citizens of the Muncie of 1900 would even remotely have considered this as a problem that needed to be addressed or fixed. It was a challenge that was to belong to the political and societal agenda of a far later generation.[8]

The ability to read and write was seen by the middle classes in nineteenth-century America as the most basic stepping-stone toward the fulfillment of career aspirations and personal or social advancement. It was a perception that was repeated many times. One of the best known and most emblematic indicators of the importance accorded to literacy appears in Horatio Alger's *Ragged Dick* (1868), which describes the eponymous hero's successful quest to surmount the adversities of street life and (in his own memorable words) "to grow up 'spectable." Escorting his new friend, Frank, a well-to-do boy of thirteen or fourteen who is from out of town, Dick shows off to him some of the sights of New York, including "a very large building of brick, covering about an acre of ground":

> "Is that a hotel?" he [Frank] asked.
> "No," said Dick; "that's the Bible House. It's the place where they make Bibles. I was in there once, —saw a big pile of 'em."
> "Did you ever read the Bible?" asked Frank, who had some idea of the neglected state of Dick's education.
> "No," said Dick; "I've heard it's a good book, but I never read one. I ain't much on readin'. It makes my head ache."
> "I suppose you can't read very fast."
> "I can read the little words pretty well, but the big ones is what stick me."
> "If I lived in the city, you might come every evening to me, and I would teach you."
> "Would you take so much trouble about me?" asked Dick, earnestly.
> "Certainly; I should like to see you getting on. There isn't much chance of that if you don't know how to read and write."[9]

Alger's brand of Christian paternalism, as articulated here through the voice of Frank, paralleled that of the members of Muncie's library board, who saw reading as an essential tool for moral improvement. Many of the children's books acquired for the library were tinged with a flavor of biblical humility that was oxymoronically coupled with recipes for upward mobility. The board no doubt hoped that the rags-to-riches message to be found in Alger's books struck exactly the right chord, appealing equally to middle-class meritorious instincts and to the unrealized aspirations of working-class readers. Whether the children who read them so voraciously drew from them these lessons is a moot point. But these themes, along with the book's popularity, would certainly have encouraged the board to agree to purchase more Alger titles.

The What Middletown Read database provides plenty of representative examples of the most popular reading matter that was chosen by or for the children of late nineteenth-century Muncie. In fact, a good example is *Ragged Dick*. According to Carl Bode, "no later novel [by Alger] aroused the excitement that *Ragged Dick* did," though the evidence from the Muncie library shows that several of his later novels were at least as much in demand and sometimes more so than *Ragged Dick*.[10] The library's accession records for the years

1875–1903 show that it owned sixty-nine separate volumes by Alger, a number of which were duplicate copies. For instance, it had two copies of *Ragged Dick*, the first acquired as part of Marsh's Library in 1875 and the second purchased on December 30, 1891, as one of fourteen books by Alger acquired at a cost of 84 cents per volume. This second copy was checked out on the same day it was registered; between then and February 26, 1900, after which the book vanishes from the circulation records, it was borrowed 285 times.

Omitting the more than two-year gap in our records between March 1892 and November 1894, that copy of *Ragged Dick* was borrowed almost 44 times per year until 1900. It was rarely left on the shelf for more than two or three days and, given its comparative shortness as a novel, was usually returned well within the two-week borrowing period and only very occasionally renewed. Its absence from the circulation records after February 1900 suggests that the volume had become too deteriorated for further borrowing. Although an extra batch of twelve juvenile books by Alger was added in July 1900, a replacement copy of *Ragged Dick* was not among them. Probably because the work had been reissued and was now readily available as a "dime novel" rather than because its popularity in Muncie was already on the wane, no copy of the book is listed in the 1905 printed catalog of the recently opened Carnegie Library.

Of the sixty-nine Alger volumes held by the library from its inception through 1903, we have borrowing records for fifty-seven.[11] As we have noted, they were borrowed heavily, by a total of 1,361 patrons in 9,230 transactions. Thus of the nine-year total of 174,641 recorded transactions, more than one in nineteen was of a book by Alger. That in itself is an extraordinary affirmation of Alger's popularity. Among the fourteen Algers the library purchased in 1891, *Ragged Dick*'s popularity was roughly matched by *The Young Explorer* (borrowed 237 times), *Slow and Sure* (264), *Phil, the Fiddler* (270), *Tattered Tom* (286), and *The Young Miner* (297).

Yet all these titles fell short of *The Young Adventurer,* which was loaned a total of 422 times, as well as *Ben's Nugget,* loaned 324 times. Clearly, then, the popularity of *Ragged Dick* was not an isolated phenomenon, and the detailed records show that many of the same readers worked their way through Alger. The lesson that was taught and retaught by him in novel after novel—that honesty, hard work, and optimism can triumph over adversity—was particularly appealing to young America at the turn of the century. The titles alone of many of Alger's novels—*Strive and Succeed, Shifting for Himself, Bound to Rise, Luck and Pluck, Try and Trust, Brave and Bold,* and *Struggling Upward*—encapsulate the formula.

The borrowing records of the Muncie library corroborate this explanation, and they underscore that Alger's paradigm worked wonderfully well as a powerful reiterative myth that was needed by America in an era of seemingly relentless industrial and commercial expansion. It acted as an excellent counter to the often pitiless reality of the working world, in which prosperity and success were frequently more elusive than actual. Here again, as Daniel Rodgers and others have demonstrated, we must acknowledge that Alger's stories contained a more complex set of ethical precepts than the simple "rags to riches" framework allows, and we cannot pin down precisely what meanings young readers assigned to these texts. But their high demand suggests that their recipe of hard work and upright behavior, leavened by adventure, excited the tastes of both Muncie's young readers and the library's leadership.[12]

The least borrowed of the fourteen Alger volumes acquired at the end of 1891 was *Rufus and Rose; or, The Fortunes of Rough and Ready*, which was taken out but forty times between January 1892 and June 1897, an average of about seven times a year. There is no record of its having been borrowed after that, but it is the single one of the fourteen to have been preserved for transfer to the new Carnegie Library, where it appears, along with eighteen other Alger books in the 1905 catalog. The other thirteen volumes disappeared one by one from the circulation records between December 1897 and September 1901, suggesting that they had fallen into disrepair and were discarded. These books had been purchased at a heavy discount, and the board had by then given up on having inexpensive books repaired or rebound. When there was demand and funds permitted, popular titles could be reordered new.[13]

The database allows us to look more closely at the readership of any particular book that was borrowed, and an examination of the transaction history of the widely circulated second copy of *Ragged Dick* tells us something more about its appeal both to adults and to young readers. Table 8 includes the gender and occupational categories of 261 of these borrowers, and among them the male readers outnumber females by a ratio of more than two to one. In line with this, the occupational classification of these borrowers indicates that *Ragged Dick* attracted approximately one female white-collar borrower for every two male borrowers, but among blue-collar borrowers, males outnumbered females by almost four to one.

A separate search shows us that fifteen of the women borrowers were born in or before 1870. That would have made them adults by 1891, when our circulation records begin, and likely taking out the book for their children. Of the fifteen, ten designated themselves as "Mrs." when they registered for a library card. Ten came from a white-collar and five from a blue-collar back-

TABLE 8. Borrowers of *Ragged Dick* (accession no. 7727)

BORROWERS (LOANS)	MALE	FEMALE	WHITE-COLLAR MALE	WHITE-COLLAR FEMALE	BLUE-COLLAR MALE	BLUE-COLLAR FEMALE
261 (285)	140 (154)	58 (60)	65 (76)	36 (36)	75 (79)	22 (24)

NOTE. Social classification figures include only borrowers for whom gender and occupation data could be found (198 out of a total of 261). Figures in parentheses indicate the total number of transactions in each category.

ground. The remaining forty-eight female borrowers were younger, although some were old enough to have become mothers by 1900, when the book was last loaned. Among male borrowers born in or before 1870, fifteen were of white-collar and twelve of blue-collar origin.

The truly significant factor that emerges from the statistics is that *Ragged Dick* attracted both male and female readers, if not necessarily in equal numbers. Alger may have pitched his juvenile novels to an audience of adolescent boys, but many girls were keen to read him too.[14] This conclusion takes on further significance if we examine similar statistics for four other popular contemporary children's authors.

The next most widely read writer of children's books after Alger is Harry Castlemon, who had served in the Union Navy during the Civil War and drew on that experience in many of his adventure stories for boys. As a writer, he adhered to a simple blueprint. "Boys don't like fine writing," he is quoted as saying; "What they want is adventure, and the more of it you can get into two-hundred-fifty pages of manuscript, the better fellow you are."[15] Avowedly, then, his was an adolescent male readership—he was described by a contemporary as the "boys' own author"—and that is confirmed by the borrowing statistics for two copies of *Frank on a Gun-Boat* (1864), the first tale in his Gun-Boat series, which were constantly being loaned by the library. The first, which may have been a replacement for an earlier copy that came from Marsh's Library, was acquired on December 30, 1891, in the same lot as the second copy of *Ragged Dick*. Our records show that it was borrowed 259 times through July 15, 1899. A year after it was deaccessioned a new copy was bought, and that was borrowed on 104 occasions between June 27, 1900 and the end of the extant records on November 28, 1902.

Table 9 shows the statistics for these two copies of *Frank on a Gun-Boat* among borrowers for whom we have demographic information. Of the thirty-five women borrowers of the first copy, fifteen are identifiable through census records as married by 1900, and of the fourteen who borrowed the second, five were married, widowed, or divorced. The likelihood is that each

TABLE 9. Borrowers of Castlemon, *Frank on a Gun-Boat*

ACCESSION NUMBER	MALE	FEMALE	WHITE-COLLAR MALE	WHITE-COLLAR FEMALE	BLUE-COLLAR MALE	BLUE-COLLAR FEMALE
7704	141 (161)	35 (38)	70 (78)	25 (27)	71 (83)	10 (11)
11848	55 (64)	7 (9)	28 (34)	4 (6)	27 (30)	3 (3)

NOTE. Social classification figures include only borrowers for whom gender and occupation data could be found (176 out of 229 for book 7704 and 62 out of 90 for book 11848). Figures in parentheses indicate the total number of transactions for each group.

of these women borrowed *Frank on a Gun-Boat* not for herself but for a boy in the family to read, so that the number of women as primary readers of the story was probably less than half what the figures indicate. As we have seen, Castlemon aimed at an audience of young males, and his female borrowers were relatively few.[16] Some of these, such as Pearl Snider, the nineteen-year-old daughter of a well-to-do business contractor and a member of the graduating class of Muncie High School in 1896, or eleven-year-old Minnie Gainor, the daughter of a watchman at a mill, might be described as tomboy readers, who immersed themselves in boys' books and largely avoided (or, in Pearl's case, may have outgrown) the kind of "sissy" reading that was associated with girls. Both borrowed boys' adventure books by the score. Anything by Harry Castlemon was a particular favorite, and the disparity in their ages when each took out *Frank on a Gun-Boat* may be an indication of the range of its appeal. Horatio Alger followed closely after; in each case, *Ragged Dick* was one of their selections.[17]

A third hugely popular boys' author was Oliver Optic (William Taylor Adams, a Massachusetts state legislator and prolific writer). The borrowing figures for two of the most frequently loaned of the eighty-eight copies of his books the library owned are summarized in table 10. *The Young Lieutenant; or, The Adventures of an Army Officer* (1874) was a sequel to *The Soldier Boy;* it continued the story of Thomas Somers, a handsome and courageous young soldier in the Union army during the Civil War. *On Time; or, The Young Captain of the Ucayga Steamer* (1870) was the third volume in Optic's Lake Shore series. The Lake Shore stories first made their appearance in *Oliver Optic's Magazine,* which was intended for both boys and girls, and in its early days the Muncie Public Library had subscribed to the magazine, but by the 1890s Optic's stories were available in book form, usually six books to a series. The borrowing records for *The Young Lieutenant* and *On Time* are complete from 1894 through 1902. Despite Adams's apparent hope that his stories would appeal to both sexes, his figures (again for borrowers whose

TABLE 10. Borrowers of Optic, *The Young Lieutenant* and *On Time*

TITLE	MALE	FEMALE	WHITE-COLLAR MALE	WHITE-COLLAR FEMALE	BLUE-COLLAR MALE	BLUE-COLLAR FEMALE
Young Lieutenant	80 (85)	16 (17)	45 (47)	8 (9)	35 (38)	8 (8)
On Time	125 (141)	22 (22)	62 (71)	15 (15)	63 (70)	7 (7)

NOTE. Social classification figures include only borrowers for whom gender and occupation data could be found (96 out of 127 for *The Young Lieutenant* and 147 out of 207 for *On Time*). Figures in parentheses indicate the total number of transactions for each group.

occupation and sex are known) are in many ways comparable to Castlemon's. At least in Muncie, these two authors, unlike Alger, were unable to make significant inroads when it came to female readership.

The paragon among late nineteenth-century American children's books intended for girls was Martha Finley's *Elsie Dinsmore* (1867). Finley was born in Ohio but grew up in South Bend, Indiana. Her pietistic series of twenty-eight Elsie books centers on an angelically beautiful but lonely southern girl, who "in spite of all her trials and vexations, . . . had in her heart that peace which the world can neither give nor take away; that joy which the Saviour gives to His own."[18] Whether despite their cloying religiosity or because of it, the Elsie novels were well represented in the corpus of books read by young girls in the turn-of-the-century Midwest. Table 11 lists the borrowing and demographic statistics for two copies of *Elsie Dinsmore*. As one might expect, they show a reversal of the figures for Castlemon and Optic. More than 40 percent of the male borrowers for whom we have demographic information were adults born before 1870, and in many cases they were the fathers of young girls. For example, on January 26, 1895, Dr. A. J. Phinney, a Muncie physician, let his fourteen-year-old daughter, Louise, use his card to borrow *Elsie Dinsmore*. On the same card, she went on to borrow at least eight other Elsie books over the next six months. She became a library patron in her own name in August 1895; five of the first six books she borrowed were also from the Elsie series, though it was not long before her reading had advanced beyond them. Although she was a regular user of the library, the novels of Alger, Castlemon, and Optic appear nowhere among the books that she borrowed. For Louise Phinney, as for many others, *Elsie Dinsmore* was the bedrock of a young girl's reading.

Finally, Louisa May Alcott is the only one of this group of five nineteenth-century popular children's authors to achieve lasting acclaim. Although widely read, her novels were less in demand than those of her four contemporaries. As is well known, Alcott was highly critical of the unrealistic nature of boys' adventure yarns, taking aim in particular at Oliver Optic, whose stories she

TABLE 11. Borrowers of Finley, *Elsie Dinsmore*

ACCESSION NUMBER	MALE	FEMALE	WHITE-COLLAR MALE	WHITE-COLLAR FEMALE	BLUE-COLLAR MALE	BLUE-COLLAR FEMALE
8365	37 (38)	131 (143)	20 (20)	77 (81)	17 (18)	54 (62)
9196	30 (34)	87 (89)	14 (15)	51 (53)	16 (19)	36 (36)

NOTE. Social classification figures include only borrowers for whom gender and occupation data could be found (168 out of 222 for book 8365 and 117 out of 171 for book 9196). Figures in parentheses indicate the total number of transactions for each group.

punningly delineated in *Eight Cousins* (1875) as "optical delusions": "Now, I put it to you, boys," asks Aunt Jessie in that novel, "is it natural for lads from fifteen to eighteen to command ships, defeat pirates, outwit smugglers, and so cover themselves with glory, that Admiral Farragut invites them to dinner, saying, 'Noble boy, you are an honor to your country!'"[19] Alcott's slap, although it provoked an incensed response from its target, did little to undermine the popularity of Optic's adventure stories for boys.[20] Indeed, the tomboy characteristics of Alcott's heroine, Jo, in *Little Women* may owe something to the influence of boys' adventure stories.

Table 12, which compares the borrowing and demographic statistics for *Little Women* and *Little Men*, helps suggest whether Alcott's appeal, a given for girls, also extended to boys. The library held several copies of *Little Women* over the years, but most were discarded prior to the surviving circulation records. Only two copies, acquired in 1889 and 1900, respectively, were in regular circulation during the period of our records, and their borrowing numbers appear relatively low considering that the book had already achieved iconic status as a novel for girls. But because it was often part of the school curriculum, *Little Women* was one of only a small number of books that would have found its way to readers without the help of the library. Nevertheless, what is striking is that, for the borrowers at the Muncie Public Library, *Little Men* (of which there were three copies in circulation during the same period) was more in demand than *Little Women*.

For each novel, males represented approximately a third of the borrowers, as might be expected a noticeably higher proportion than for *Elsie Dinsmore*. The number of blue-collar borrowers of *Little Men*, both male and female, is relatively high, although of the five authors Alger is not only easily the most popular but also the one who comes closest (though still not very close) to achieving gender balance among borrowers. That finding is confirmed by an early survey of children's reading at the public library in Stockton, California, published in 1899, which observed that Alcott and Alger were "the only ones who enjoy at all anything like equal favor" among boys and girls.[21]

TABLE 12. Borrowers of Alcott, *Little Women* and *Little Men*

TITLE	MALE	FEMALE	WHITE-COLLAR MALE	WHITE-COLLAR FEMALE	BLUE-COLLAR MALE	BLUE-COLLAR FEMALE
Little Women	55 (62)	109 (138)	33 (39)	69 (84)	22 (23)	40 (54)
Little Men	68 (80)	119 (145)	34 (44)	76 (91)	34 (36)	43 (54)

NOTE. Social classification figures include only borrowers for whom gender and occupation data could be found (164 out of 225 for *Little Women* and 187 out of 246 for *Little Men*). Figures in parentheses indicate the total number of transactions for each group.

In assessing the demand for children's literature, we should acknowledge that British and European writers of boys' adventure stories such as Daniel Defoe, G. A. Henty, H. Rider Haggard, Robert Louis Stevenson, R. M. Ballantyne, and Jules Verne were also among those whose books were widely borrowed. Defoe's classic adventure story *Robinson Crusoe* was represented in the library by four copies, but its popularity was eclipsed by such American-based spinoffs as *The Prairie Crusoe* and R. M. Ballantyne's *The Dog Crusoe and His Master: A Story of Adventure in the Western Prairies.* For beginning readers, the library also possessed two copies of Lucy Aikins's adaptation, *Robinson Crusoe in Words of One Syllable.* Among American authors, we can add such figures as John Trowbridge, Edward Eggleston, Jacob Abbott, Edward Sylvester Ellis, Howard Pyle, E. P. Roe, Charles King, and Mark Twain. Among American and European writers who attracted girl readers, Frances Hodgson Burnett, Mary Mapes Dodge, E. Marlitt, A. D. T. Whitney, Isabella Macdonald Alden, Julia Horatia Gatty Ewing, Susan Coolidge, Margaret Sidney, Rosa Nouchette Carey, and Marguerite Bouvet each had a significant following.

Much more to the point, we should recognize as of fundamental importance that the five writers of the second half of the nineteenth century discussed here, and others in the same spirit, were able to create books for children that were distinctly American in tone, setting, and ethos. If a novel like *Ragged Dick* was set on the streets of New York City rather than Muncie, Indiana, that surely did not make it seem anything less than an all-American fable. The reading habits of the children like the ones in Muncie were formative in establishing many of the cultural reference points that were the shared patrimony of a whole generation of Americans entering the new twentieth century.

Profiling those broader reading habits by taking a small selection of the patrons of the Muncie Public Library who borrowed *Ragged Dick* can be revealing. Among the middle-aged white-collar men holding a library card was Taylor V. Moore, a contractor born in 1852. He and his wife, Anna Farrel Moore, married in 1877 and had four children, Charles (born in 1878), Lucy (b. 1879), Harry (b. 1880), and Mary (b. 1886). Taylor Moore had become a patron on March 5, 1881, long before his children would have been old enough to make use of the library. As we have no borrowing records for the 1880s, we cannot identify any of his reading from that time. In the 1900 U.S. census, Charles, by then a twenty-two-year-old, gave his profession as a telegraph operator, and his younger brother, Harry, is described as a clerk.[22] No profession is given for Lucy, and Mary was still at school. Neither Taylor's wife nor his four children appear to have separately become patrons of the library, but they used Taylor's card to borrow books.

The first recorded loan, out of a total of 157, was *A Book for Boys*, on December 5, 1891. This was followed by a series of other boys' books, such as Castlemon's *Frank in the Woods* and Alger's *Slow and Sure* and *Ben, the Luggage Boy*. The titles strongly suggest that most of these books were destined for thirteen-year-old Charles, and it is likely that his mother would have accompanied him to the library and helped him with his book selections.

By 1895, when Lucy was sixteen, a similar process was taking place: books such as Charlotte Brontë's *Jane Eyre* and Elizabeth Wetherell's *The Wide, Wide World* were being taken out, presumably for her to read. The Moore's second son, Harry, was not much younger than Lucy, and perhaps such books as *The Count of Monte Cristo* and *Pudd'nhead Wilson*, both borrowed in 1897, were chosen with him in mind. In 1898, however, although his father's card was still the one used, Charles Moore's name is listed as the borrower of two children's books, *Five Little Peppers and How They Grew*, by Margaret Sidney, and *What Katie Did*, by Susan Coolidge (Sarah Chauncey Woolsey). He could not have taken these books out for himself; most likely he accompanied his twelve-year-old sister, Mary, to the library and helped her pick out books. He later borrowed *Ragged Dick*, perhaps judging from his earlier pleasure in reading Alger that this juvenile classic would go down well with his sister, although of course we have no way of knowing whether that was so.

All of the books that were signed out by the family during the latter part of 1899 and throughout 1900 were in Charles's name, though again still using his father's card. They comprise a gallimaufry of books that suggest that members of the Moore family took it in turns somewhat randomly in selecting what to borrow from the library. In the following two years, however, Charles appears to have returned the library card to his parents, and the final books that were borrowed, which include *Pride and Prejudice* and Richard Harding Davis's *Soldiers of Fortune*, seem to have been their selection. Charles must have left school before the age of eighteen in order to become a telegraph operator, and in 1902 he married Ada Cammack, who graduated from Muncie High School in 1896 and was also a library patron. She was the daughter of Muncie's postmaster and the niece of Emma Cammack, the high school's treasured English and Latin teacher. By 1910, according to the U.S. census, they had moved to Atlanta, Georgia, and Charles was working as a traveling salesman. Both Lucy and Harry Moore graduated from the high school in the class of 1898. In 1910, Harry was an employee at the Delaware County surveyor's office, and Mary had become a teacher.[23]

It may seem surprising that, in a household of six, none of the children took out a separate library card, but the Moores were in no sense atypical of white-collar readers in having only one family member as a registered patron. It certainly made it easier for parents to oversee and perhaps even control what their children were reading. The Moores were also typical of many Muncie families in their choice of reading—primarily fiction—and their borrowing was fairly representative of what was popular in fiction with their different age groups. The dynamics of their reading reinforce our notion of the integrative nature of middle-class family life in late nineteenth-century America and the place of reading within it.

When George N. Peterson, a forty-eight-year-old laborer in a Muncie factory, borrowed *Ragged Dick* on August 29, 1896, he was, as far as we can tell, taking it out for himself. Although a juvenile book, Alger's most famous novel, with its inspirational fable of hard work and honesty leading to the promise of upward mobility, was read by some working-class adults too. Peterson was born in Denmark, immigrating to the United States in 1872 when he was in his early twenties. Before coming to Muncie he had been living in Oregon, where three of his children were born. It is not known what happened to his first wife, but in 1897 he remarried, and he and his new wife became the parents of another boy. In the 1910 census, George is described as a machinist in a glass factory, and in 1920, when he was seventy-two years old, as a mold maker in a factory. He died of acute bronchial pneumonia in 1930 in his eighty-second year, and is buried in Muncie. As a blue-collar worker living in a rented house, George Peterson had not been able to afford to retire and probably worked until shortly before his death.[24]

The records from the Muncie Public Library show that Peterson's leisure pursuit was reading, for between May 12, 1894, when he became a patron, and November 3, 1902, when our records cease, he borrowed a total of 232 books, an average of almost precisely 31 books a year. A review of the subject categories of these books reveals that the vast majority of them were juvenile fiction, and it raises the question why novels aimed at school-age readers, such as Edward Stratemeyer's *A Young Volunteer in Cuba*, R. M. Ballantyne's

The Dog Crusoe and His Master, and J. M. Barrie's *Tommy and Grizel,* would have appealed to him. All of these books and scores of other works of juvenile fiction were borrowed by Peterson long after his two older children had themselves become library patrons, and it is unlikely that he borrowed them simply to supplement their own choice of reading. Rather, it seems that, in common with other blue-collar readers who had not been able to avail themselves of a high school education through graduation, juvenile fiction akin to the works of Horatio Alger and "dime novels" or their equivalent catered to his needs better than sophisticated or complex works of literature.

It might be argued that English was not Peterson's first language and thus that juvenile works were more at his reading level, but he was also borrowing such tomes as Richard Proctor's popular astronomical treatise *Other Worlds Than Ours* and Helen Campbell's *Prisoners of Poverty: Women Wage-Workers, Their Trades and Their Lives,* an important work of social reform and an early call for women's rights. We come to realize that juvenile fiction accommodated the reading needs of a far wider market than just the younger generation at whom it was aimed.

Several books that were withdrawn using George Peterson's card seem to have been taken out by his wife, a few of these having Mrs. Peterson as the designated borrower, and it is also likely that a small number were taken out for his children, but we can say with some confidence that he was the main reader. His eldest son, Newton, joined the library in his own right in December 1896, and his daughter, Anna, followed suit almost two years later. Since Anna was only ten at the time she joined, it is not surprising that the circulation ledgers show that brother and sister would visit the library together.[25] Unlike the middle-class Moores, who shared a single card, in this working-class family and in many others as well, each person seems to have shown a proprietary interest in becoming a card holder in his or her own name. There were fewer books in a working-class home, and the library had the role of making up for that deficiency. Newton's borrowing was also prolific, totaling 162 transactions in just over five years, and Anna, with 89 loans over four years, was not too far behind. Between the three designated library patrons, the blue-collar Petersons made a little short of five hundred transactions, almost triple the number made by the white-collar Moores.

In his seminal study *The Intellectual Life of the British Working Classes,* Jonathan Rose has shown that, in nineteenth-century Britain, "a promiscuous mix of high and low [culture] was a common pattern among working-class readers of all regions, generations, and economic strata. Their approach to literature was a random walk."[26] If the Petersons typify their American equivalent (and of course they may well not), similar claims may be put forward regarding working-class reading in the United States. In the case of the Petersons, however, works of high culture appear merely as seasoning sprinkled on a repast of mostly juvenile fiction.

One final example of a reader of *Ragged Dick* is Gertie Foorman, a nine-year-old twin, who borrowed the book on July 21, 1896, in the midst of her discovery of the seductive pleasures of library membership. Gertie was the daughter of Eli and Flora Foorman; her father was a successful cigar and tobacco dealer and her mother (née Younce) a descendant of one of Muncie's first settlers. They can be classed as white-collar. As well as a twin sister, Edith, Gertie had an older brother, Fred, but neither sibling is recorded as a library patron. She herself had registered for a borrower's card only three weeks before she took out *Ragged Dick,* and by then she had already devoured a dozen other books, turning up at the library counter with a new pick on an almost daily basis.

Those first dozen books, read with breathless speed, began with Martha Finley's *Elsie Dinsmore* and several of its sequels, *Little Lord Fauntleroy* and two other works by Frances Hodgson Burnett, a couple of novels by Louisa May Alcott, Edward Eggleston's *Hoosier Schoolboy,* and a book of children's verse by James Whitcomb Riley. Gertie's binge reading continued unabated for another four weeks and included a plethora of other books in the Elsie Dinsmore series, a generous selection of further works by Alcott, and two short novels by Horatio Alger, *Fame and Fortune* and *Paul the Peddler.* On August 18, she withdrew Marguerite Bouvet's *Sweet William,* her thirty-second book in the space of seven weeks, and then inexplicably stopped borrowing until the following April. After that, she was to become a nonstop patron, borrowing books on almost two hundred and fifty occasions over five years, a figure dwarfed only by her extraordinary first foray into library book reading in 1896.

The phenomenon of what he calls "reading crazes" was explored in the following decade by the pioneering American psychologist G. Stanley Hall (1844–1924), who shows us that Gertie Foorman was far from unique among her age group:

> It usually occurs just before or perhaps in the early teens when it seems that the soul suddenly took flight, awakening with a start to the possibilities of transcending the narrow limitations of individual life and expanding the personality . . . as if trying to become a citizen of all times and a spectator of all events. . . . Those who experience this in full measure are never the same thereafter. It seems to occur somewhat earlier in girls than in boys, and to more often cause a bifurcation of the inner life of idealization and fancy with the outer life of dull and often monotonous daily routine, especially

of a girl's life in school or home. In reverie, she dreams of wealth, splendor, heroic wooers who take her away to a life where all desires are fulfilled, where the possible becomes actual and castles in the air materialize. This also often makes the future seem so rich and full that some disillusion is inevitable later.[27]

Gertie's early teenage reading shows consonance with girls of her age, but extends to a precocious penchant for the novels of Charles Dickens and individual works by Edward Bulwer-Lytton, Charlotte Brontë, and George Eliot. She continued borrowing occasional volumes of poetry, and in one instance took out a work in German, strongly suggesting that she was studying the language at school.[28] Her sentimental attachment to the Elsie books prompted her to reread *Elsie Dinsmore* in 1900. The lion's share of her later reading was of age-appropriate light fare.

The High School and the Public Library

The link between the library and the schools was in some respects most noticeable in terms of the high school. Under the superintendency of Hamilton McRae, a handsome new four-story high school building had been completed in 1880 on a site less than three blocks from the library. It became a prominent feature of the city's landscape and was cited regularly by boosters as evidence of Muncie's cultural development.[29] High school students certainly used the public library, both in connection with their academic work and as a source of leisure reading. But the library had only a modest collection of books that supported the curriculum, which featured mathematics, science, and the liberal arts and offered little in the way of practical preparation for a working life in the industrial economy developing locally.

Not surprisingly, the vast majority of Muncie's children did not pursue schooling beyond elementary grades, and those who did generally dropped out before their senior year. In 1882, when the city's total school enrollment was 868, the high school had 245 pupils, but only 18 graduated that year.[30] In 1890, according to Laurie Moses Hines, "the 170 high school students accounted for only 8 percent of the total school enrollment in the city."[31] There were but 14 students in the graduating class of that year. Clearly, high school and library were not in the vocabulary of the greater part of the young people of Muncie, many of whom put traditional education behind them at a young age in order to enter the workplace directly or to receive vocational training. Until state legislation was passed in 1897, schooling was not compulsory, and even after that, as the Lynds point out, "only twelve consecutive weeks' attendance each year between the ages of eight and fourteen was at first required." Although the school year was extended over the next thirty years, compulsory education still ended at fourteen.[32]

For those seeking further preparation for the world of work, the Muncie Business College, established in 1890, represented an alternative to high school (fig. 9). It provided, in its own words, "a live school for the training of successful business men and women," and offered courses in such areas as bookkeeping, banking, commercial law, commercial arithmetic, shorthand, penmanship, telegraphy, and typewriting. It was open year-round, with no vacations, offering a "Day and Evening class for both Ladies and Gentlemen" and advertising that during enrollment periods "applicants may enter any week day with equal advantages."[33] There was also a rival school, Ball Business College, which opened in February 1893 and offered individual courses in business, shorthand, "pen art," and telegraphy, counter-advertising that its "young men and young women are continually going out into the world far better prepared for the duties of life, for having attended the 'B.B.C.' "[34] These and other vocational establishments, and the opportunities for apprenticeship in Muncie's factories, drew many young students away from the high school long before the end of their senior year.

The curriculum offered in the Muncie school system followed state guidelines and was, in every sense, thoroughly traditional. An 1895 promotional pamphlet describes it in hyperbolic terms:

> No greater triumph has been chronicled in the history of any city, or placed to the credit of any people in school advantages, than are now afforded the citizens of Muncie. There are employed in these schools at this writing seventy-six teachers, giving instruction in all branches of Common School Education, including Algebra, Geometry, Trigonometry, Astronomy, Physics, Chemistry, Latin, Book-keeping, Rhetoric, Literature, Music and History. Students graduating from the High School of the city are admitted to the Freshman class of the State University without further examination, which fact alone establishes beyond question the high standard and excellency of the Muncie schools.[35]

The tenor of this piece leaves it without question that the curriculum was devised with the humanistic intention of preparing students for higher education and for the life of the mind. The Arnoldian thinking that nourished the curriculum is well expressed in another of the city's promotional pamphlets: "The educational facilities of a community mark its advance towards a higher civilization and Christian culture. Gauged by this standard, Muncieites have passed many white stones upon the highway of intellectual progress."[36] Apart

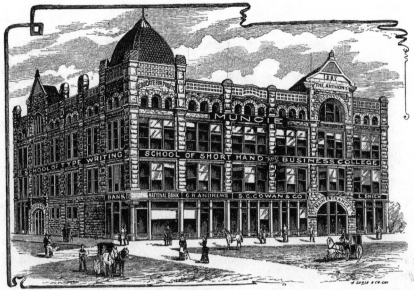

ANTHONY BLOCK.

FIGURE 9. The Anthony Building, 1897. The building was home to the Muncie Business College, as well as the Star Drug Store, owned by G. H. Andrews's drugstore (see chapter 2). From *Muncie Illustrated* (Muncie: Commercial Publishing Co., 1897). Courtesy Ball State University Archives and Special Collections.

from the option of studying bookkeeping, which was offered as an alternative to Latin in the first term of the junior year at the high school, there was little or nothing that was vocational in the curriculum.

The Muncie High School course of study, which is summarized in the 1894 edition of the *Zetetic*, a student-sponsored annual, included four years of Latin, with one-term alternatives such as English grammar or bookkeeping. The pure sciences and different branches of mathematics were covered during the first three years. Despite their enthusiasm for their teachers, however, the scarceness of facilities for science education led the student editors of the *Zetetic* to plead that extra cash "be appropriated for new laboratories" to replace the inadequate resources that were then available: "the remnants of an old electric outfit, and a few worn-out apparatus." It may have come as a relief that the senior year was devoted primarily to the higher study of literature and the humanities.[37] It was here that the curriculum reached its apex. At the end of the twelfth grade, a graduate of the Muncie High School would be lauded in true classical style with the Latin dictum *Palmam qui meruit ferat* (loosely translated, "The reward belongs to him who has earned it"), and acknowledged as having "satisfactorily completed the English [or Latin] course of study . . . [and] sustained a good character and made such attainments in Science and Literature as entitles him [or her] to this Diploma."[38]

Apart from Latin, foreign languages were not taught in the high school until 1899, when German was introduced as an option, one or the other being a requisite for graduation. As many midwesterners could trace their ancestry to Germany, this was to become a popular alternative. The Muncie Public Library, however, made no attempt to stock Latin or German texts. The Latin holdings consisted merely of an edition of Horace and a couple of preparatory readers, all of which were donations. Books in German were also very few in number and again were gifts. None of these donated books had anything beyond a minimal circulation. Some German classics were available in English translations, though only Goethe's *Faust* attracted borrowers.

Far more popular, as we have seen, were translations of German fiction, in particular the romances of E. Marlitt and Ossip Schubin (Aloisia Kirschner), which had a significant readership. Demand for these now almost forgotten women authors vied with that for their better-known American and English contemporaries. Their readers were usually adults rather than children, whose exposure to German authors was limited to English translations of the fairy tales of the Brothers Grimm. In children's fiction, however, the German-speaking world (in its loosest sense) was invoked for Muncie's younger readers in such works as Oliver Optic's *Down the Rhine; or, Young America in Germany* and Johann David Wyss's classic *Swiss Family Robinson*, of which the library possessed several copies.

If the holdings of the Muncie Public Library were intended to complement anything that was being taught in the high school, it would have been in the field of English and American literature. The study of English was seen as central to the high school curriculum. A later annual from 1916, published more than a decade after the opening of the new Carnegie Library, spells out the importance of English as a language in a manner that would have resonated no less for the class of the 1896. "English," it proclaims, "is the most essential course in High School. It is the language of the English speaking race, and the language which every man, woman and child in this country should know." Lest the conservative and ethnocentric implication of this declaration be missed, the account concludes by asserting that "if we wish to have good citizens in this country we must have a good English speaking race."

The English curriculum in 1916, which appears to have been barely modified from that of twenty years earlier, began with spelling and rhetoric in the freshman year, followed the next year by exposition, oratory, and debating. American literature was studied in the first term of the junior year, with the opportunity in the spring to "dwell in Shakespeare's country and breathe

Shakespearean air, and play Shakespeare's plays and dream of Shakespeare at night." Finally, in the senior year, an initial reading of essays and novels was capped by the study of *Paradise Lost,* so "that the students can know and understand so well as never to forget the greatest epic the world has ever produced." A less detailed endorsement of the study of English ("one of the crowning glories of humanity"), which had appeared in a 1902 school publication, concurs with the belief in the value of a humanistic education out of which "it is expected that the student will have an intelligent acquaintance with the best that has been written in the language, and that there will be nourished in him a sympathetic appreciation and sincere love for our English literature."[39]

The masculine pronoun belies an important truth. The lists of alumni of the Muncie High School from 1868 to 1903 show that there was a huge preponderance of graduating girls over boys. In 1896, for example, a typical year chosen because it was the senior year of Norene Hawk, whose diary is discussed in chapter 7, thirty students graduated in the senior class, seven boys and twenty-three girls. The proportion of male and female students reaching graduation is not out of line with other years. For instance, in the class of 1890, from which Tom Ryan, another of our diarists, had dropped out, there were three boys and eleven girls who graduated. Only in three of the years between 1868 and 1903 did boys outnumber girls, and in two early years there were no male graduates at all.[40] We will return shortly to a consideration of possible reasons for this extraordinary gender imbalance.

We were able to identify the social upbringing of most of the thirty pupils who made up the graduating class of 1896. At least thirteen, approximately half of the total, came from families that may be deemed high white-collar, with fathers whose occupations included physician, city postmaster, Methodist minister, grocery merchant, lawyer, architect, and civil engineer. In one instance, a pupil was living with her older sister who was the head of the household and a schoolteacher. Nine students, or approximately a third of the total, were low white-collar; their fathers included a shipping clerk, a livestock trader, a traveling salesman, an insurance agent, and a landlord. Those from a skilled blue-collar background included the children of a streetcar driver, a glass flattener, a carriage maker, a carpenter, and a brick mason. There were no graduating pupils from an unskilled blue-collar background.[41]

A humorous article written by one of the pupils when the class of 1896 was reaching the end of its sophomore year allows us to identify at least by name as many as fourteen further students of the class who dropped out before graduating, six boys and eight girls.[42] They included two gifted male students who (if we may give credence to the literalness of the statement) "were tie[d] for first honors, each having an average of 99 9-10 per cent." One of these, Edward T. Coney, was born out of wedlock; after he left school without graduating, he was apprenticed as a clerk to a druggist in Indianapolis, and by 1920 had become the manager of a wholesale druggists' business. The other, Thomas Hussey, the son of a grocer, is listed in the 1900 U.S. census as a laborer in a creamery. Among the remaining twelve nongraduating students were the daughters of the county's recorder of deeds, a farmer, and a carpenter; and a young man, Ora Miller, whose mother was a milliner. With exceptions, the dropouts tended to be students from families that were less affluent and more often than not blue-collar, and the reason was almost always economic rather than academic. Staying on in high school may not have been excessively expensive in itself, but doing so deprived a family of a potential income earner.[43]

Out of the total of forty-four graduating and nongraduating members of the class of 1896, twenty-six were patrons in their own name of the Muncie Public Library, and an additional three are recorded as having borrowed books using a parent's or sibling's card. Three more had immediate family members who held cards and may well have borrowed books without having their own names entered into the circulation register. Counting those three, then, approximately three-quarters of the class members are likely to have taken out books from the library, twenty-three of the thirty who graduated and nine of the fourteen who dropped out. It is likely too that the dozen students for whom we have no data that connects them to the library had occasion to use the reading room without having borrowed books. Statistics culled from the meetings of the library board show that in 1895 and 1896 the number of users (including repeat users) of the reading room averaged well over a thousand per month, with significantly more than a hundred reference inquiries each month.[44] A large proportion of those users and inquirers were likely Muncie High School students, whether or not they held library cards.

Is it possible to discern any patterns of borrowing by the members of the class of 1896? The simple answer is no; their choice of books was dictated by personal taste and, as far as we can tell, was not directed by what was being taught at school. It would have been impossible to assign library books to a class of forty-four, or even thirty, because students were permitted to borrow only one book at a time, and the library had only a single copy of most of its books. Any multiple copies of books that were to be studied would likely have been kept by individual teachers or in the school library.[45] The surviving 1885 inventory of merchandise from the Star Drug Store (discussed in chapter 3) shows us too that local druggists and bookshops kept multiple copies of schoolbooks in stock. Although well provided with literature, the

Muncie Public Library did not attempt to compete with local shops, or the high school itself, by building up collections of individual schoolbooks.

As we have seen, the vast majority of Muncie's children did not continue their education into high school, and even among those who did there was substantial attrition. The school's *XYZ Annual* for 1903 contains short reports on the junior (1904) and sophomore (1905) classes. The "band of one hundred and twenty-five Freshmen" that had entered the school in the fall of 1900 as the class of 1904 was now reduced "at the end of the third year . . . [to] only fifty-five." That number was augmented, perhaps by the late influx into Muncie of new families, to a graduating class of sixty-one in the following year, still fewer than half the number of those who had enrolled as freshmen. The class of 1905 had commenced in the fall of 1901 with over eighty members, but at the beginning of its sophomore year had been whittled down to fifty, and only forty-four reached graduation.[46] In the 1880s and 1890s the situation had been no different. In his diary, Tom Ryan records his delight in quitting school at the end of his sophomore year in 1888, and when, two years later, he joined the audience to witness the small cadre of his peers who graduated in 1890, he expresses his considered opinion that he had done the right thing in leaving when he did.

Tom Ryan's forte was practical subjects, and here we have an important clue as to why so few of Muncie's children, and in particular so few boys, availed themselves of a complete high school education. The classical curriculum, which placed Latin at its heart and stressed the value of humanistic ideals, may have provided appropriate training for those students who aspired to continue on to university or college, but it completely failed to address the needs of the majority of young people preparing to enter the world of work. The glaring divergence between the humanistic and the vocational was a real drawback in a rapidly growing small city with an economy that was increasingly dependent on its industrial base.

The point was not lost on Muncie's educators, though it was not until the turn of the century that the problem began to be addressed. In 1899, Walter E. Ervin, a twenty-nine-year-old Muncie-born teacher who was a graduate of DePauw University, was appointed principal of the high school. Ervin advocated the introduction of manual training for those high school students of both genders "whose minds have no inclination for the so-called liberal arts, [and who] might find an educational uplift in the mental development obtained through manual work." He recognized that too often "the community's needs are overlooked by the makers of our High School Courses in an effort to make the High School a feeder for the colleges of the State." Since Muncie was a manufacturing town with factories that offered "inducements for Muncie boys," he recommended that the curriculum "be adjusted as soon as possible, so that even better inducements than the factories offer may be given the boys and girls."[47]

Intriguingly, Ervin elided the fact that the city had only developed its manufacturing base over the previous fifteen years and had drawn much of its labor force from rural areas; in fact, he asserted that most of the city's children had "fathers and grandfathers [who had] been factory men." Muncie's "boys and girls have the same blood in their veins, and this environment is a lodestone pulling them away from Grammar, as well as High School, into the factory." While primarily concerned with the need for more science-based and practical classes, Ervin's complaints were also an oblique acknowledgment that a humanities-oriented secondary education had not been a significant part of the experience of most local children.[48]

During the ensuing years, the Muncie High School did move toward a more practical curriculum. It first introduced manual training courses in woodworking, furniture making, and foundry practice, as well as other vocational subjects such as mechanical drawing for the boys and "domestic arts" for the girls. In the spring of 1913 a Commercial Department was established; it included courses in practical electricity and art pottery, subjects intended to attract both boys and girls. The intent was to draw in a wider demographic, and the endeavor appears to have met with some success. It also brought about what Laurie Moses Hines describes as a gradual change in the mission of the school over the next few decades, as "the curriculum shifted from humanistic to practical, and ideas about child study and adolescent development infused discussion of the school's function." Rather than displacing the teaching of the traditional humanities, the new vocational subjects were introduced as complementary to the existing curriculum. Teachers still emphasized the superior value of humanistic study, and students responded by giving them preference. A set of "senior statistics" compiled by the class of 1913 found that the favorite subjects were mathematics, history, and English. At the bottom of the list were domestic science and manual training.[49]

The broadening of the curriculum and the advancement of secondary education in Middletown drew the attention of the Lynds in the 1920s. "While the city's population has increased but three-and-one-half-fold since 1890," they wrote, "enrollment in the four grades of the high school has mounted nearly elevenfold, and the number of those graduating has increased nineteenfold." Their statistics showed that the number of children enrolled in the high school in 1889–90, as a percentage of the total population, was one in sixty-seven, or 8 percent of the total school enrollment, but by the academic year 1923–24 these figures had been increased to one in twenty-one residents, or 25 percent of the total enrollment. They also noted that in 1882, one in every 1,110 residents was among those receiving a high school diploma that year, but by 1924 the equivalent ratio was one in every 161 residents.[50]

The figures found by the Lynds can be valuably juxtaposed with the success of high school graduates in obtaining work, by comparing the class of 1896 with that of 1916. Of the thirty pupils who graduated from Muncie High School in 1896 and whose later occupations are still traceable, only two are known to have gone on to college; one of them, Orville Spurgeon, eventually obtained a medical degree and followed his father as a Muncie physician. Six others, all of them female, became schoolteachers (which at the time did not require a college degree). At least three worked as salespersons. Others had individual occupations as an electrician, a newspaper reporter, a railroad office clerk, and a brick mason. Out of the twenty-three girls in the class, approximately half are listed in census returns as homemakers or equivalent.

Twenty years later, the class of 1916 totaled sixty-eight graduating seniors, twenty boys and forty-eight girls. We do not have long-range statistics of their later working lives, but a high school annual published a year after their graduation reveals their immediate situations. Fifteen (the vast majority of them boys) had found jobs in manufacturing, at the Ball Brothers glass factory, the Warner Gear Company, and the Muncie Foundry Company, among other plants. Twenty were students, several of them out of state, and a further eight held local jobs as teachers. Three worked as telephone operators, and two each in the retail trade and as stenographers. One individual worked in a newspaper office, and three others as a farmer, a chauffeur, and a nurse; another became an assistant librarian at the Muncie Public Library. Only five, all girls, are simply listed as "at home."[51] Similar figures are provided by the Lynds, confirming that high school attendance increasingly came to be seen as a prerequisite for obtaining a good job, and, more broadly, as a means to better oneself. They quote a father's "emphatic assertion" that "a boy without an education today just ain't *anywhere!*"[52] That sentiment was also shared by the girls, for whom a high school education was increasingly perceived as a portal to a middle-class life that had been exceptional only a generation or two earlier.

If the city's high school saw it as desirable to expand its demographic intake and to introduce vocational subjects, the public library developed similar aspirations as it moved into the new century. Given the cramped conditions of the old library, however, these aspirations would come to fruition only after the opening of the new Carnegie building in 1904. The old library was of limited usefulness for those seeking training or occupational manuals. For instance, the single book in the library on the subject of nursing, a calling that attracted many young women, was Florence Nightingale's landmark work, *Notes on Nursing: What It Is, and What It Is Not,* inherited from Marsh's Library. That book was not borrowed during the period covered by the extant records. Equally, a woman trying to find books on, say, stenography or typewriting (both of which promised career opportunities) would come away from the library empty-handed.

Occasionally, though, a patron could discover useful vocational material. When Edward Noland, a thirty-six-year-old Nevada-born laborer, joined the library in March 1900, a primary reason for doing so was to find books that might help him enhance his manual skills. In the 1900 U.S. census Noland is described as a gravel roofer. Among the books that he borrowed in his first month as a patron were Jean Baptiste Baille's *Wonders of Electricity*—a translation of Baille's *Les merveilles de l'électricité,* purchased by the library only a month before—and Philip Atkinson's *Electricity for Everybody: Its Nature and Uses Explained.* He found *Electricity for Everybody* of such value that he renewed it seven more times between April and September 1900. The following year he was the first to take out W. Perren Maycock's *A First Book of Electricity,* another new acquisition, which he later borrowed again, and in 1902, toward the end of our records, he took out T. O'Conor Sloane's *Electricity Simplified: The Practice and Theory of Electricity* and two further books on electricity. Noland was obviously studying hard, and when we find him listed in the 1910 U.S. census, he now describes himself as a roofing and heating contractor.[53] Whether he obtained formal qualifications is unknown, but the library records leave us in no doubt that he was at least partially self-taught in his knowledge of electrical work.

None of the library's stock of books on electricity was widely borrowed, and it is evident that, with the occasional exception, patrons did not think of making their way there to seek out professional training manuals or other vocational guides. In that sense, the function of the library was disconnected from Muncie as a manufacturing city. Thus, though going to the library was always an important leisure and learning activity, it was not a place to seek out books to teach you a trade.

With the appointment of Artena Chapin as librarian in 1903 and the opening of the Carnegie building the following year, the new Muncie Public Library began more strenuously to reach out to working-class children who until then had had little exposure to reading. Chapin was able to appoint a separate children's librarian, Gertrude M. Clark, who had graduated from Muncie High School in 1900.

With her firsthand experience of the local educational system, Clark took it upon herself to visit the schools to explain to both children and their teachers the benefits of library use. In particular, she and Chapin worked hard to establish branch libraries in working-class neighborhoods. The venture began modestly. In one suburb, a local grocer agreed to house a small bookcase from which children could borrow books. In another, an initial supply of fifty books was placed in a school that enrolled five hundred children. "The eager interest which was taken by these little ones in the books we sent," Chapin wrote, "and the disappointed faces when there were not enough for all, told us plainly how great was the thirst of these children for books."[54] As more books were added, they found that mothers and fathers were joining their children in reading all they could lay their hands on. Chapin and Clark may appropriately be described, using Joanne Passet's resonant term, as "cultural crusaders," pioneers in carrying the gospel of books into the Midwest.[55]

Chapin illustrated the deprivation in some of the poorer outer suburbs by recounting an anecdote about a boy who was admonished for defacing a school desk and "asked if he did that to the furniture at home. He looked up surprised and said: 'Furniture! Why Mister, we ain't got no furniture!'" It became the object of the librarian and her staff to provide for such children "stories which will take them out of their home surroundings and will show them a life beyond their narrow horizon."[56]

By providing books for these youngsters, they hoped to instill in them a sense of moral discrimination—"How pliable are the minds of these children," Chapin wrote, "and how easily they are moulded for good and evil"—and create a generation that would carry the library habit into their adult lives. Because Chapin was aware that the content of many books for juveniles did not achieve "a very high standard" and often lacked literary merit, she urged an involved "co-operation between school and library," suggesting that teachers work with librarians to help ensure a good choice of reading matter for the schoolchildren in their charge. She took very seriously the selection of children's books for the new library, and she encouraged Clark in her efforts to set up a "Children's Literary Club," which had the express purpose of bringing the young to the library and making reading a central part of their lives—in Clark's words, "to promote an interest in the good and beautiful things in nature, literature and art, making books a means to that end."[57]

A particular focus of the librarians' attention was the high school. For Chapin, consolidating the link between the school and the library was all-important. She saw the library as the source of "supplementary reading in the High School," recognizing that "teachers depend largely upon the public library to supply the books." The informal understanding that had existed under the regime of Kate Wilson, whereby high school pupils were merely encouraged to patronize the library, became for Chapin an opportunity for much closer cooperation. Teachers were encouraged to learn "what great uses can be made of this library," and Chapin promoted such interdependence by increasing the number of copies of books that high schoolers were being encouraged to read.[58]

With characteristic energy, she also involved herself in the development of a separate library in the high school building. By 1906, the year after the publication of the catalog of the Muncie Public Library and a separate catalog of its children's books, she could report the completion of another catalog, classified according to the Dewey Decimal system, that listed more than two thousand books that were now available in the Muncie High School library.[59] Those books were there exclusively for the school's students and teachers, and they most likely included multiple copies of certain set texts. Gertrude Clark was shortly after appointed as the school's librarian, before moving in 1914 to a position at Chicago University's library.

In no real sense did this new collection at the high school compete with what was available in the public library, which continued to expand. During 1903, the final year of the old library, when we no longer have personal borrowing records, it was calculated that there were 1,777 individual borrowers, and that 1,063 of these were new patrons. If those figures are correct, we can be certain, given previous trends, that a large proportion of the new card holders were schoolchildren. During that year, in preparation for the opening of the Carnegie Library, the book committee purchased approximately two thousand new volumes, all but two hundred of them works of nonfiction. The emphasis on nonfiction was in response to Chapin's extension of the number of books that could be borrowed at any one time to two, of which no more than one could be a work of fiction. In 1903, circulation transactions numbered 35,077, an average of 118 per day. When the new Carnegie Library opened on January 1, 1904, it contained 15,291 volumes.[60] By 1906, the second full year of the new library, circulation had more than doubled from three years before, with 77,765 transactions, an average of 254 per day. In the same year the reading room, containing 114 magazines and 12 newspapers, hosted 15,078 visits. By January 1, 1907, the total number of books in the library had reached 22,750.

The "Brief History of the Muncie Public Library" that prefaces the 1905 printed catalog gives us a glimpse of the enhanced comprehension of the importance of promoting children's reading at the beginning of the new century. It extols the fact that, for the first time, Muncie's Carnegie Library now contained a separate children's room with its own shelf space. An allotted place in the library for children and children's reading may seem a commonplace today, but it was novel then. The city's schoolteachers were being encouraged to send in lists of appropriate books and set texts that they wanted to see on the shelves. Among new rules and regulations is the proviso that teachers in public and private schools could be issued a special privilege card "entitling the holder to draw six books at a time," but only for "subjects immediately related to school work."[61]

Within the year, the success of the new arrangement led to the opening up of the lower floor of the library as an all-inclusive "juvenile department . . . with shelves and delivery desk, at a cost of $700." Chapin noted that the children's room was "the most attractive in the building," adding "Here they are apart from the rest of the library and have a freedom which could not be allowed them while upstairs." The proposed Children's Literary Club was started and "conducted entirely by the children." Emulating the adult board, it had its own elected officers and constitution. Younger children enthusiastically attended the Saturday story hour each week, and the older ones arranged a program of "discussions and papers on literary subjects." Several boys, who took "a greater interest than the girls" in manual tasks, volunteered "to help arrange the books on the shelves" and to lend a hand with other related tasks. Among the girls, one high school senior put her name forward to help on Saturday afternoons, leaving the children's librarian "free to give some of her time to the personal supervision of the reading of the children." "In this way," Chapin concludes, the children "seem to feel that the library belongs to them."[62]

All in all, the opening of the Carnegie Library heralded a golden age for the children of Muncie and for the advancement of reading. The ambiance of that era is captured in a dictum quoted from Ruskin by one of the high school's seniors in 1912: "Bread of flour is good, but there is bread sweet as honey, if we would eat it, in a good book."[63] She could hardly have chosen a more fitting sentiment to delineate the new mood.

6

Reading and Reform

The Role of Fiction in the Civic Imagination
of Muncie's Activist Women

Close to one hundred people gathered to celebrate the nineteenth anniversary of the Woman's Club of Muncie in late January 1895. Filling the main parlor, library, and back parlor in the well-appointed home of Mrs. W. S. Richey, they listened to a musical number, a recitation of poetry, and an opening prayer by a local minister before settling in for the evening's main feature, an address by Emma Montgomery McRae, professor of English literature and the "Lady Principal" (equivalent to the dean of women) at Purdue University (fig. 10). In a talk titled "The New Democracy in Literature," McRae traced a transition from the day "when the poets, even the thousand souled and thousand tongued Shakespeare, wrote only of the purple, of the kings and nobles," to the present time when literature addressed the lives and experiences of "those who need the elevation of the writer." McRae spoke approvingly of "Burns, the simple Scot, who wrote of his life and those with whom he lived," and of Dickens, "the true friend of the poorer English, who saw their wrongs and tried to right them."[1]

That this particular event featured a talk by McRae on such a topic seemed especially appropriate. McRae, perhaps the most prominent female academic in the state at the time, was more than just a visiting dignitary. A one-time Muncie resident and the widow of Hamilton McRae, the former superintendent of Muncie schools, Muncie Public Library board member, and the library's first registered patron, she had been a founding member of the

Emma Montgomery McRae
Our Honorary Member
Prominent personage and noted educator
for whom the McRae Club was named
Born: February 12, 1848 in Loveland, Ohio
Died: September 21, 1919 at Newton Center, MA

The McRae Club
Organized 1894
Federated 1896 I.U.C. 1899
Consolidated I.S.F.C. 1906
Affiliated with General Federation 1922

FIGURE 10. Emma Montgomery McRae, on the cover of a McRae Club history. McCrae was a founder of the Woman's Club of Muncie before leaving the city to take a post at Purdue University. She remained in regular contact with many of the women active in the city's club life. Courtesy Ball State University Archives and Special Collections.

Woman's Club and had served as its president before departing to take up her academic post across the state. The club's first meeting had taken place in her home in early 1876. Beginning as a reading circle for a small group of women, the club evolved over the ensuing two decades into a substantial civic presence in Muncie that devoted much of its energy to improving local educational and social conditions.

By the time McRae came to visit in 1895, the club had begun to take a more prominent role in Muncie's public life. During the years following McRae's talk, members examined race relations, discussed municipal reform, researched school improvement, debated immigration, investigated conditions in sweatshops, and considered the intertwined issues of child labor and compulsory education. In some cases, discussion turned to action. During the late 1890s the club assigned a committee to inspect local schools, promoted sanitary measures as a means of reducing the spread of disease (a matter of some urgency in the wake of the city's smallpox epidemic in 1893), sought reforms to protect "the working girl," and even launched a program of classes open to the public that offered opportunity to study French, German, parliamentary procedure, literature, and current events. By the end of the decade, the club had organized itself into separate Civics, Education, and Literature departments, and had established itself as an influential force in local public life, a role it would sustain well into the twentieth century.

The evolution of the Woman's Club of Muncie is a familiar story. During the years following the Civil War, women's clubs devoted to literary matters formed in cities and towns around the country. Many of them developed gradually into social reform bodies, calling attention to the inequities that arose in urban-industrial settings and demanding public remedies. By the beginning of the twentieth century, activist women with ties to the club movement spearheaded campaigns for sanitary regulation, environmental reform, workplace oversight, child labor restrictions, educational improvement, and a host of other initiatives designed to ameliorate the inequities and difficulties of a rapidly industrializing urban society. Some scholars argue that this work laid the foundations of the modern American welfare state. Activist women were able to do this by insisting that such efforts were a customary part of the feminine domain. Charged with maintaining a healthy and virtuous home, they naturally had a responsibility to ensure that the surrounding social environment did not deteriorate to the point where it threatened the well-being of their families.[2]

Most of these scholars have noted the literary antecedents of women's clubs but have paid relatively little attention to the reading behavior of these groups. They have pointed out that the opportunity to read seriously, to make formal public presentations, and to engage in literary discussions created for women their own public space and allowed them to gain experience as organizers, speakers, and critics. These skills served them well when they ventured forth into the wider civic realm. But beyond that training, the literary life of the era's women's clubs has attracted little analytical attention among those concerned with the social reform activities of these groups.[3]

A few scholars have trained their sights on the role of reading in the development of women's clubs. Anne Ruggles Gere has argued that the literary practices of these groups helped equip them for civic activism and helped them influence public debate on a variety of topics. In her examination of clubs in Houston, Texas, around the turn of the twentieth century, Elizabeth Long has identified shared reading as a means of forging solidarity among members and, through the idealized depictions of human experience found in fiction, an inspiration for reform work. Barbara Sicherman has also emphasized the role of literature as a spur to public engagement and to the literary practices of women's clubs as the platform for civic campaigns.[4]

McRae's anniversary address hints at an even more direct, integrated relationship between clubwomen's reading and their activism than these studies articulate. She suggests that fiction provided a means of understanding the experiences of ordinary people and, she hints, of helping to "uplift" them. Close inspection of the activities of the Woman's Club of Muncie, as well as the record of their members' reading contained in the What Middletown Read database, suggest that club life encouraged women to read novels in part to comprehend the world and attempt to reshape it. To do so, the club's members turned not only to literary realism, with its emphasis on depicting true-to-life social conditions and experiences, but to other genres of literature, which in their hands became records of social experience and the basis for social reform.

Exploring the interplay between reading and reform among Muncie's clubwomen tells us something about both. It highlights a facet of the civic imagination that animated the middle-class women's groups which did so much to reshape American public life around the turn of the twentieth century. Members of clubs like the one in Muncie treated fictional texts as tools for understanding the world rather than simply as diversions from it. Although our concern in this chapter is the reading activity of the club and its members, a review of club records and library circulation data suggests that the club fostered an approach to reading fiction that distinguished club members from other middle-class women. Clubwomen did not necessarily read fiction in this fashion all of the time, but the reading they did in the context of club activities tended in this direction. An examination of this pattern of textual consumption also indicates that the literary pursuits of women's club members were not a separate, preliminary act to the work of reform but an integral part of how they comprehended social problems, both in their own communities and in the wider society.[5]

The Woman's Club Movement in Muncie

Local women's clubs became prominent as Muncie urbanized. They began slowly, starting with the organization of the Woman's Club of Muncie in 1876, but expanded as the century came to a close. Muncie's was among the first groups of its kind in Indiana; one report listed it as the second such organization in the state, following another formed in nearby Cambridge City. The gas boom and subsequent industrialization and population growth, as well as the emergence of a more substantial middle class in the city, produced a spate of new women's literary and culture clubs during the 1890s, a period when similar groups were forming throughout the United States. Six new groups formed in 1894 alone, and by the end of the decade there were more than a dozen active women's organizations in a city of twenty thousand people, with membership rolls ranging from two dozen to over one hundred. The Woman's Club was the oldest, largest, and most prominent, and it took the lead in creating a Federated Club of Clubs in 1896, with Caroline McCulloch, a charter member of the Woman's Club, appointed as the first president of the new umbrella body. McCulloch was wife of a prominent physician and the mother of George McCulloch, one of the city's most successful businessmen. The Federated Club was the first of its kind in Indiana, and it acted as the collective voice of the city's clubwomen. It took a particularly active role in public matters, as did several of its constituent groups, most notably the Woman's Club.[6]

The public prominence of Muncie's clubwomen during the 1890s bears witness to a remarkable change in the organization since its inception. When the Woman's Club formed in 1876, it was a decidedly modest undertaking: a handful of women who met in one another's homes to discuss cultural topics. The model for the new groups was Sorosis, the well-publicized women's literary organization formed in New York City in 1868. Like its metropolitan inspiration, the Muncie club kept to cultural matters during its early years. Discussions focused on literature or history, with U.S. and European history, Shakespeare, and biblical texts among the topics explored. Participants gave formal papers on these subjects and discussion followed before adjournment for refreshments. The purpose of the club was self-improvement: "the promotion of literary and social tastes" and "the general advancement of its members," according to its initial constitution.[7]

Membership in the Woman's Club remained small and mostly middle class. Attendance at regular meetings rarely exceeded twenty through the 1880s and sometimes dropped to as few as ten. When the city began to grow rapidly, participation increased as well, although the club limited membership for a time during the early 1890s, removing restrictions only as the group's agenda shifted to incorporate public activism. Even then, membership was largely self-selected. Most members were married, from white-collar households, middle-aged, and attended a Protestant church. Research into a list of members active in January 1895 found that just two of the thirty-one women for whom such data is available were from blue-collar households. Only six of the forty-five members were single, and women older than forty made up the majority of the club's roster.[8]

One episode outlined in the club's minutes offers a hint of the social boundaries in play. In 1899 an unnamed member proposed Fannie Cohn, the wife of a wine merchant, Henry Cohn, for membership. The Cohns, originally from Michigan, were recent arrivals in Muncie. To this point nominations for membership had been approved routinely, nearly always unanimously. But in this instance, with thirty-eight members in attendance, Cohn received just twenty-eight votes, with five nays and the remainder evidently abstaining; this meant that Cohn was rejected, because club rules denied membership to any applicant receiving five or more votes in opposition. Three other women proposed as members during the same meeting were elected unanimously.[9]

The reasons for this unprecedented rejection—unique in the annals of the club at least through 1902—remain unclear. One possibility is that Cohn was rebuffed because she was Jewish, although there is no definitive evidence that the opposition to her proceeded from that motive. At the very least, she was a newcomer of German descent whose husband sold wine (a point that likely did not sit well with pro-temperance club members). Two months later, at a less well-attended meeting, Cohn was renominated, and this time she received only three nays out of a total of nineteen votes and was accepted as an active member. Whatever the reason for the initial hostility toward Fannie Cohn, the episode suggests that there were distinct boundaries related to social origin or outlook that shaped the club's composition.[10]

Outside of church societies, the club remained the only women's organization in Muncie until the gas boom. A group called the Ladies' Matinee Musicale, devoted to musical performance, formed in 1889, and a Monday Afternoon Club, which, as its name suggested, met weekly to discuss various topics, launched in 1892, as did an Art Students' League, probably named after the more famous New York City institution. Similar groups continued to organize; by the end of the decade there were women's groups dedicated to the reading of Dante and other classics, to Dickens (and, after they had mined his works to exhaustion, to Shakespeare), to the discussion of travel experiences, to municipal affairs literature, to magazine reading, and to learning parliamentary procedure. The Conversation Club, formed in 1894, forbade the customary presentation of formal papers or even the use of notes during discussions. There were also two clubs exclusively for women living outside the city limits, whose members often traveled eight or nine miles, presumably by horse-drawn wagon or buggy, to attend meetings. A chapter of the Daughters of the American Revolution organized in 1897 and began devoting itself to patriotic activities in the city. Eight of these groups, including the Federated Club, belonged to the statewide Indiana Union of Literary Clubs.[11]

This robust activity formed the basis of a substantial public presence for the hundreds of women who belonged to clubs in and around Muncie. Reports of their proceedings appeared in the local dailies, and prominent events such as anniversary dinners or the first convention of the Federated Club in 1897 earned substantial coverage. The clubs also tapped into a regional and national network of such groups, establishing connections that encouraged civic activism. In addition to their participation in the Indiana Union of Literary Clubs, several of the clubs joined the General Federation of Women's Clubs, a national organization that urged women's clubs to pursue public issues. Formed in 1890, it quickly developed into a powerful national voice for social reform. The Woman's Club of Muncie joined the General Federation soon after its founding and sent delegations to its biannual meetings throughout the 1890s (and after); its affiliation with the national group appears to have encouraged it to take on a greater role in local affairs.[12]

The first intimation of this expansion of agenda was the changing list of topics chosen for club discussions. After nearly two decades devoted principally to literature, history, and art, the club's programs shifted noticeably over the course of the 1890s (fig. 11). Cultural discussions did not end, but contemporary political and social issues began to appear with increasing regularity in the group's minutes. Club records for 1896 cite discussions of race, municipal reform, immigration, sweatshops, and child labor. In subsequent years, members deliberated such topics as education, public health and sanitation, settlement work, tenement housing, sewage disposal, public ownership of utilities, workingmen's insurance, and the power of monopolies. Moral issues, such as the growing prevalence of saloons or the rise of prostitution locally, drew the club's attention as well. The title of one member's paper—"What is Muncie Doing to Help the Unfortunate and Punish the Vicious?"—encapsulated the moral attitude that prevailed at club meetings by 1901.[13]

FIGURE 11. A performance of *Macbeth* by the Woman's Club of Muncie, May 16, 1898. The club staged a variety of performances based on literary works throughout its existence, though increasingly it focused on social reform work during the 1890s and early twentieth century. Courtesy Ball State University Archives and Special Collections.

Some of the other women's clubs in and around Muncie made a similar, though less pronounced, shift. Several joined the Federated Club and contributed to reform efforts in that fashion. The McRae Club, begun in 1894, gradually moved from meetings devoted chiefly to literary and historical topics to discussions of Darwinism, women's rights, kindergartens, the protection of children, and settlement house work. By the mid-1890s the religiously oriented Mary-Martha Club began mixing into its biweekly meetings topics such as the growth of great cities, women as wage earners, the problems of capital and labor, and the need for temperance reform. Not all local women's clubs moved in this direction—the Dickens Club stuck with literature, whether by its namesake or by Shakespeare—but there were at least subtle suggestions of growing social interest and engagement in the records of several of these organizations.

What most distinguished the Women's Club of Muncie from other local women's groups was not simply its social and civic concerns, but the extent of its activism. The club took a special interest in local education (several of its members were former teachers), and its members began to visit the city's public schools and report on their condition. One stalwart member, Elmira Kuechmann, whom we met in a chapter 4 as a frequent borrower and who also sat on the library board, argued during a club debate in 1897 that the "education of the masses" was central to "solving the question of Capital and Labor." Another participant in the same conversation, reflecting the growing influence of the idea that social problems arose from circumstances and surroundings rather than individual moral failure, insisted that education was "the greatest lever for the human race," adding that "against heredity . . . may be set environment and education."[14]

Concern for education was also reflected in the interest taken in the condition of the Muncie Public Library. The club lobbied for improvements in both the library's rooms and its collection; the decision by the newly formed Federated Club of Clubs to take up these matters in 1897, almost immediately after its formation, may reflect the club's influence. The presence of both Hattie Patterson and her eventual successor as librarian, Kate Wilson, on the club's membership rolls no doubt heightened the group's interest in library matters and added authority to its public pronouncements on such questions. Patterson presented a paper to the group in 1897 outlining necessary improvements to the library, including an expansion in size and the addition of new books to the collection. The ensuing discussion emphasized the need for more of the standard books, for more space so that the existing books would be accessible, and for more "congenial surroundings."[15]

Increasingly, the aim of the papers presented at club meetings was to advocate for reforms. An 1897 talk by Kate Garst, reviewing "the management of our city corporations" and comparing it with local governance in England, found "weak points in the administration of the city laws and dangers to the public health" and proposed "remedies . . . for the correction of existing evils." The following year, in conjunction with the Delaware County Medical Society, the club hosted a public lecture by the secretary of the state's board of health, who urged regulations promoting pure air and water as a means to prevent disease. (No doubt his hearers found this to be a compelling topic in a city that had experienced a smallpox outbreak just a few years before.) When the General Federation of Women's Clubs asked the Muncie club "to use its influence in the interests of wage-earning women by appointing a committee to study local conditions of labor and work for better conditions where possible," the club created a group for that purpose within its Social Science department. Over the next few years members took up that issue, as well as tenement house reform, sewage system improvements, and

clean alleys, in each case examining local conditions and publicly proposing changes. Though a bit less likely than their counterparts in other cities
to engage in direct lobbying, the club was anxious to draw public attention
to these matters and often worked through the Federated Club of Clubs to
achieve policy changes.[16]

The internal organization of the Woman's Club reflected its shifting priorities. If, as its early constitution declared, the initial idea behind the club
was to promote literary and social taste, it had developed into something
different by the end of the century. In 1899 the club revised its constitution to
signify its commitment to activism. "United effort to further improvement in
the community in which we live" became part of the official agenda. By then
the club had organized into departments that reflected this new balance: the
Literary Committee, which arranged programming devoted to the discussion of books, was supplemented by a Civics and Social Science department
(later split into two) and an Education department, and each took a hand in
arranging topics for consideration at the biweekly meetings. Programs alter-
nated between cultural discussions and presentations on civic matters.

The Woman's Club trod carefully on the most explosive question tied to
women's activism: suffrage. During the 1880s, when it was a small literary
club meeting in private homes, members demonstrated an openness to the
idea of granting voting rights to women. An 1887 meeting was canceled so
that women could attend a state suffrage convention, after which Susan B.
Anthony and other prominent suffragists traveled to Muncie for another
meeting that was no doubt attended by Woman's Club members. Citing prec-
edents in other states, Anthony urged local women to lobby Indiana's legisla-
ture for voting rights, if only in local school-board elections.[17]

The club held a debate on the question of votes for women the following
year, which produced "a very animated discussion from every lady present.
Some were decidedly for suffrage, a few indifferent, others decidedly against,
and one or two on the fence." In 1891 the club invited the prominent Indiana
suffragist Zerelda Wallace to speak to the group (although the talk had to
be canceled when Wallace became ill). Yet as the club's activism intensified,
discussion of suffrage diminished. In 1894 club member Nellie Stouder gave
a talk on women's suffrage in Wyoming, the first state to grant women voting
rights, suggesting that its success there made it feasible elsewhere, and in
1899 the club debated whether women should have "greater political recognition," which evidently produced arguments both pro and con. Otherwise, the
topic does not appear in the minutes through 1902, an absence that suggests
the club had to proceed cautiously as it took on a greater public role, lest it
appear too radical.[18]

Reading and Reform

At first glance it seems easy to conclude that the rise of activism coincided with a decline in literary pursuits. That certainly is the case if we simply use the topics discussed at club meetings as a measuring stick. In its early days, the Woman's Club dedicated nearly every formal meeting to presentations and discussions of literature, art, and music. By the 1890s that balance had shifted to an even split between civic matters and cultural programming. Club members acknowledged the change as well: "Purely literary work no longer satisfies," one member reported in 1896. "To study, merely for one's self, has ceased to be our ideal standard; being practical, we desire to put into action some of the theories which, as a club, we have advocated."[19]

But the division between reading and activism was less pronounced than such statements might suggest. Reading remained a central element in all of the club's endeavors, and discussion of fiction continued to be a principal activity of meetings, even when reform issues were on the agenda. Members regularly turned to novels when investigating the plight of the poor, the challenges of urban life, or even the role of women in society. In connection with the club's activities, at least, it seems clear that they treated fiction as a tool for understanding the world rather than as a diversion from it.

Such an approach to reading is not surprising given the wider social and intellectual trends of the time and their influence on literature. The interplay of fictional writing and reform activism was extensive during this period in American history. The 1890s was a time of change on many fronts, not least in boom-era Muncie. The national economy was shifting toward large-scale manufacturing and corporate capitalism, cities were growing rapidly and in a seemingly uncontrolled manner, inequality was becoming more visible, and immigration increased. These and many other changes became the subject of public discussion. Shifts in social thought accompanied this upheaval, as writers, artists, and thinkers rejected older, more formalistic understandings of how society worked and embraced more pragmatic modes of argument and activism rooted in the investigation of social problems. This new approach to understanding human experience had broad influence, seeping into much of the popular literature of the day and particularly into the move toward more realistic depictions of the contemporary world in fiction.[20]

The roots of literary realism reach back at least to the early Victorian era, when English writers such as Charles Dickens, Elizabeth Gaskell, and Benjamin Disraeli published novels designed to expose and explore social questions connected with the rise of modern industrial society. These "social problem novels" examined in fictional form the lives and struggles of ordinary people, particularly the poor, a focus that the realist writers of the late nineteenth century would emulate. It was this literary tradition that Emma Montgomery McRae embraced in her 1895 address in Muncie. As her talk suggested, by the time the Woman's Club began to appropriate fictional texts as documentary evidence of social problems in need of reform, this mode of reading had become well established.

Within that context, the club's members approached fiction as a means of investigating social problems and, in turn, pursuing reform. As McRae had noted, much of the popular fiction written during the late nineteenth century aimed to portray contemporary life among ordinary people in stark, realistic terms and to provoke a response. Writers such as Mark Twain, William Dean Howells, and Stephen Crane pursued this agenda, and even authors of popular romantic fare wove touches of realism into their narratives. Reformers such as Edward Bellamy or, a few years later, Upton Sinclair also turned to fiction as a means of spurring popular demand for reform, mixing romantic plot lines into their social criticism. But the consumption of this sort of fiction within the context of the club's activities seemed to have a special intensity, as its members read and discussed books by reform-minded writers such as Albion Tourgée, Bertha von Suttner, Leo Tolstoy, and even Charles Dickens in an effort to better comprehend and refashion the society in which they lived.

Woman's Club members did not rely solely on fiction when studying social problems. The growing body of reformist journalism and social criticism that developed around the end of the nineteenth century attracted their attention. Among the writers with whom they engaged was Josiah Strong, an evangelical clergyman and writer who was prominent in the Social Gospel movement, which advocated Christian-inspired social reform. An October 1897 meeting was devoted chiefly to a discussion of *The New Era; or, The Coming Kingdom*. Club members appear to have found compelling Strong's argument for the necessity of realizing heaven on earth through aid to the poor, and much of the conversation turned toward "practical ways to aid in the establishment of the New Era." Two years later the Civics and Social Science department made Strong's newest work, *The Twentieth Century City*, the centerpiece of a well-attended discussion about local social and sanitary reform. The emphatic religious bent and sense of Anglo-Saxon superiority that pervaded Strong's writings no doubt resonated among the white, middle-class, churchgoing women who made up the ranks of the club. But the more important point for our purpose is that these increasingly reform-minded women relied heavily on books when taking up civic matters.[21]

The What Middletown Read database corroborates the degree to which some club members turned to nonfiction texts to investigate social conditions.

Many of these women, after receiving their assignments, used the holdings of the Muncie Public Library to research papers and prepare for discussions. When charged with preparing a presentation for the club on Dr. Charles Parkhurst, the celebrated New York City moral reformer, Florence Kingsbury appears to have relied on the library's periodical collection as a research tool. Shortly before her presentation, she borrowed in quick succession the June 1897 issue of the *Atlantic Monthly*, which featured articles by the well-known reformers Albert Shaw and E. L. Godkin about social conditions in New York City, as well as the May 1898 number of the *Century Illustrated Monthly Magazine*, which included an article by Mrs. Schuyler Van Renssalaer on reform in greater New York. Kate Garst borrowed Jean Baptiste Baille's *Wonders of Electricity* just before a presentation titled "Electricity as It Affects Daily Life." She may well have prepared for a discussion of women and industrial labor by borrowing the 1892 volume of *Forum*, a reform magazine that included numerous articles devoted to labor questions.

Not all members turned to the library's shelves to prepare for a meeting, but for Garst, a typesetter and one of the few members from a blue-collar household, and for Kingsbury, whose husband sold hides and likely provided only a modest living, the public library was a useful resource for obtaining the latest works in reform journalism and other materials necessary to research a presentation to the club.

As important as nonfiction was in their investigative work, the most striking thing about the reading behavior of the club's members was their reliance on fiction as a tool for reform. Not infrequently, they turned to fiction texts to explore contemporary social questions. Most meetings featuring discussion of civic matters did not explicitly cite novels, poems, and short stories, but enough did use these texts to suggest that participation in club life encouraged an approach to reading that blurred the lines between fiction and reality. These invented narratives provided a means of documenting actual conditions and, in most cases, exemplifying an appropriate, satisfying response. Perhaps more significantly, they provided cover for women's activism at a time when it was greeted with suspicion by many, both by framing club activities in literary rather than political terms and, in a few instances, by offering a rationale for women's civic work.

Literature could offer illustrations of real-world questions and perhaps provide examples of desirable behavior. An 1896 session on appropriate dress included a paper on the character of Hamlet, possibly a rumination on his concern for outward appearances or the way his "inky cloak" reflected his disposition, although no record of the talk's content survives. A series of papers on immigration concluded with a presentation about the biblical character

Hagar, the second wife of Abraham, who was Egyptian (and thus foreign), but after being cast out into the desert returned to bear the patriarch a child, Ishmael, and ensure the dynastic line would continue. One discussion of children's education brought up Mother Goose stories and the works of Hans Christian Andersen, while participants in another reviewed the character of King Arthur as an example of admirable conduct for children.[22]

Such passing uses of literary characters to illustrate and instruct appear quite often in club minutes. Less common, but not infrequent, were meetings during which fiction was used as the central element of a discussion of a contemporary political or social issue. Some of these texts were essentially reform tracts, such as Edward Bellamy's *Looking Backward*. Published in 1888 and reissued several times over the next decade, the best-selling utopian novel imagined American society in the year 2000. Essentially a brief for central planning embedded in a science fiction novel and love story, the narrative provided clever and provocative details about the future that helped distract readers from its pedestrian plotting and extended didactic passages. It was one of several texts discussed in an 1897 gathering devoted to utopias, including Thomas More's *Utopia* and Plato's *Republic*, as well as the imagined pastoral utopia Arcadia. It was the element of advocacy in the book that drew the interest of Emma Walling, who in her presentation to the club read passages from "that part of the book which deals with education and which advocates the *higher* education for *all*." The club took up Bellamy's sequel, *Equality*, the following year, as part of a discussion on working conditions, particularly for women, and labor conflict. Although fictional, both books offered arguments about the importance of education and the need for greater opportunities for women, thus implicitly endorsing the club's civic agenda.[23]

The club approached Bertha von Suttner's novel *"Ground Arms!" The Story of a Life* in similar fashion. The Austrian-born von Suttner, a peace activist who would win the Nobel Peace Prize in 1905, wrote *"Ground Arms!"* (its German title, *Die Waffen Nieder!*, is more often translated as *"Lay Down Your Arms!"*) in 1889 at the outset of her lifelong pursuit of peaceful solutions to political conflicts in Europe. The story of four nineteenth-century European wars told from the point of view of a woman, the novel reportedly relied on von Suttner's careful research to present a realistic picture of war. Extraordinarily popular and influential in Europe (the Pope supposedly read it), the book was translated into many languages, including an English version published in the United States in 1892. The club made it the centerpiece of a program on peace movements and the role of women in war. One member, Kate Patterson, whose husband borrowed the book from the library twice in succession just before the meeting, presumably on her behalf, summarized the book and profiled von Suttner. Another, Eve Kessler, provided a closer examination of the book's plot and themes. *"Ground Arms!"* is the only text referred to in the club minutes for that day—an interesting choice considering the abundant array of published material on war and peace movements. A subject search of the What Middletown Read database shows that the public library alone held 274 books that addressed aspects of war, ranging from children's books to histories to government reports.[24]

The use of von Suttner's and Bellamy's novels in this manner made sense since all three were well known and were, in essence, reform tracts. Muncie library users borrowed *"Ground Arms!"* thirty-four times, and at least seven Woman's Club members (or in some instances their husbands) had signed out the book before the 1898 meeting. *Looking Backward* was, as we've noted, among the best-selling American books of the 1890s, and it was an inspiration to thousands of reformers (who launched dozens of "Nationalist Clubs" around the country to push for the realization of Bellamy's social vision). Library users borrowed it eighty-three times during the period covered by our records, including twice in succession by Emma Walling, the stenographer who led the discussion of its implications for education at a July 1897 club meeting. *Equality,* less popular, still captured considerable national attention and circulated sixty-three times. These novels were written to document social conditions and experiences, and club members used them in exactly that fashion. Though fiction, the Woman's Club treated them as credible evidence of real-world phenomena.

The club displayed a particular affinity for similarly reform-minded fiction written by religiously oriented writers. The Woman's Club was a Protestant Christian group in all but name. Members quoted scripture and offered prayers at meetings, sang hymns, and met in one of the rooms of the First Baptist Church beginning in the fall of 1900. Not surprisingly, they read and discussed a fair number of religious texts, including the Bible, and they often turned to fiction influenced by the late nineteenth-century Social Gospel movement, which aimed to make organized Christianity more responsive to social problems spurred by urbanization and industrialization.

The first such text to be examined by the club was Hall Caine's *The Christian.* The novel tells the story of John Storm, an aptly named English parson, who struggles to reconcile his vocation and his attraction to Glory, a music-hall singer who had once been his childhood sweetheart. The book garnered considerable interest in Muncie: after acquiring a first copy in September 1897, the library lent it 137 times to 114 different people. That level of interest prompted the purchase of another edition, which circulated 46 times among 42 borrowers between May 1901 and December 1902.

The Woman's Club turned to this familiar text during a June 1898 discussion of social and moral reform. The meeting began with papers titled "Social Purity" and "Sociological Bearing of Heredity and Environment," both of which appeared to advance the claim that behavior once condemned as evidence of a person's inherent immorality was better understood as the product of social circumstances. Caine's novel provided backing for that argument, particularly through a sequence of letters from Glory contending that her choice of profession resulted from economic forces rather than her own ethical failings. The melodramatic resolution, which unites Storm and Glory shortly before her death, affirmed the ethical claims advanced by social reformers about the power of environment to shape individual behavior, a perspective evidently shared by the members of the club who selected the text for discussion. That choice does not mean that club members unanimously agreed with the novel's arguments about reform, but rather that at least some of them saw it as a useful means of considering such a question (more useful, perhaps, or at least more engaging, than any of the myriad nonfiction texts of the day that explored these matters).[25]

The following year the club placed another Social Gospel–oriented novel at the center of its discussions of social issues. In a program organized by the Sociology and Civics department for an October 1899 meeting, a discussion of Albion Tourgée's *Murvale Eastman: Christian Socialist* dominated proceedings. The sisters Julia and Eve Kessler, unmarried schoolteachers who shared a home in Muncie's West End neighborhood, headed the meeting, the general theme of which was Christian Socialism. It opened with a presentation by Eve that used Tourgée's novel in a paper she called "Ideal Relation of the Church to Social Conditions." Julia followed with a character sketch of Wilton Kishu, the novel's principal villain, a greedy and imperious businessman who is emphatically pious yet contemptuous of the poor. Kessler described Kishu, suggestively, as a "Churchman, Philanthropist, successful, financier—an American Type." The evening continued with papers on American churches, on "the insufficiency of almsgiving" (which argued in favor of the need for justice rather than charity), and on the ideal of cooperation as "applied Christianity." Here again, in an era when real-life discussions of such matters were plentifully available in the press and in books, the members of the Woman's Club turned to a novel for purposes of illustration and instruction.[26]

Muncie's leading clubwomen also turned to Christian fiction (and some poetry) as they addressed another question of social equality. In a 1901 program on the living conditions and social status of domestic servants, the club chose for discussion Charles Sheldon's *Born to Serve*. Sheldon was the enormously popular writer of *In His Steps: What Would Jesus Do?*, the era's best-selling Social Gospel novel. (The library acquired *In His Steps* in June 1898, and patrons borrowed it sixty-one times through the end of 1902.) *Born to Serve* (which the library had not purchased, at least at that time) told the story of a middle-class female college graduate who became a servant out of necessity. After a difficult experience with the indignities of the work, the heroine is rescued by marriage to the local minister and becomes an advocate for the more humane treatment of young women engaged in domestic service.[27]

The club used the novel to dramatize the plight of such women, including those from their own community. The program opened with an initial paper that examined the working and living conditions of servants in Muncie. It included quotations from "No Classes!," a critique of social and economic distinctions in American society by the popular poet Ella Wheeler Wilcox. The club also heard a recitation of the full poem, with its stirring conclusion that "It is the vain but natural way / Of vaunting our weak selves, our pride, our worth! / Not till the long delayed millennial day / Shall we behold 'no classes' on God's earth." Another member then presented a comparison of domestic service and other employment available to women, particularly industrial work. Sheldon's novel was discussed as part of this analysis. With the exception of Wilcox's poem, it was the only text named in the club minutes for that day.[28]

Aside from the explicit religious dimensions of the fiction texts selected by the Woman's Club, two common features stand out. All of them make romance a central element of their plots, and, with the exception of Tourgée, they present women as an active agent, if not as the narrative's sympathetic protagonist. This includes not only the Social Gospel novels but also those by Bellamy and von Suttner. The romantic elements of each story provide the reassurance of happy endings that affirm the possibilities of social reform.

More than that, women drive the reform activities they portray. Barbara Clark, the lead character in Sheldon's *Born to Serve*, uses her experience as a servant as the spur to providing aid to others in the same predicament. In Caine's *The Christian*, Glory is not the main character, but her letters give voice to the argument that women occupying jobs of low repute are victims of circumstance rather than products of their own moral failure, a contention the novel's resolution affirms. Bellamy's pair of stories trace a man's encounter with a new, utopian society, and the narrator's guide in both novels is a woman; both endorse women's full equality. Von Suttner wrote her antiwar narrative from the point of view of a woman. It seems likely that members of the club found in these stories not only dramatic versions of the real-life social issues they sought to explore and redress, but an endorsement of the idea that women could take a leading role in solving their community's problems and perhaps even implicit assurance that such public work would not disrupt conventional gender relations.

It is reasonable as well to conclude that Muncie's clubwomen identified with the female characters in these and other stories. That seems especially evident when one considers the remarkable program the club staged in May 1899. By that time, the Woman's Club had substantially transformed itself from a purely literary society to one committed chiefly to public activism. The May 29 meeting featured a paper by Rose Budd Stewart, a longtime member, titled "The Evolution of the Civic Woman." Although the Sociology and Civics department sponsored the presentation, it was to the world of literature rather than social science that Stewart turned in her defense of women's public work. Arguing that "there had always been a civic woman," she examined female characters in three novels: Henry Fielding's *Tom Jones*, Charles Dickens's *Bleak House*, and Mrs. Humphry Ward's *Marcella*. The program included more than the mere reading of a paper, however. Most of the proceedings were taken up with a dramatization, in full costume, of a scene from each novel that buttressed Stewart's central claim.[29]

Neither club records nor accounts that appeared in the local press indicate which scenes Stewart selected from *Tom Jones* and *Bleak House*, though one can make educated guesses from the evidence available. A cast list included in the club's minutes indicates that the scene from Fielding featured Sophia Western, the virtuous and beautiful daughter of Squire Western and the true love interest of Tom. It seems likely that the dramatization made some reference to Sophia's good works among the poor in London. The scene also featured Sophia's parents and the parson, which suggests that it involved either the efforts of Squire Western to retrieve her from London or the famous reconciliation scene in which Tom credits his love for Sophia as the source of his improved character, which is followed by their marriage. The selection from *Bleak House* included both Mrs. Pardiggle and Mrs. Jellaby, characters noted for their charitable activities as well as for their unpleasant, overbearing qualities and for neglecting their own domestic responsibilities. (Jellaby is more concerned with helping the poor in distant Borio-boola Gha, in Africa, than with assisting her struggling neighbors.) Both scenes feature women who engage in what might broadly be defined as civic work, but they also likely touched on the resistance to women's activism and the challenges of overcoming it.[30]

A front-page article in the *Muncie Daily Times* offers more details about the third part of the dramatization, a scene from Ward's *Marcella*, a highly regarded popular novel published in 1894. The club had spent a full meeting in 1895 discussing the book and reading selections from it, and at least a half dozen club members had read the book by then. (The McRae Club had also discussed the book during an 1898 meeting.) A local newspaper reported that the finale of the Woman's Club's reenactment included a conversation between Marcella, Lady Winterbourne, and Lord Maxwell that "was very exciting[,] being an argument in favor of the civic woman."[31]

The choice of *Marcella* suggests the subtleties of Stewart's argument. Ward herself was hardly a feminist; she is perhaps best remembered as a vocal opponent of women's suffrage in England. *Marcella* tells the story of a headstrong woman who is attracted to socialism and leaves her country estate to work with the London poor. In the course of her reform work her naïveté is exposed, and the romantic narrative culminates with her marriage to Lord Raeburn, a wealthy landowner and Conservative Party politician. The plot's resolution sounds an ambiguous note: Marcella does not renounce her concern for the poor, for she turns her attention to the rural poor around her husband's estate, but she does assume a submissive role in relation to her husband. The selection of Ward's novel, and her title character, as the culmination of "the evolution of the civic woman" hints broadly at the line the Woman's Club of Muncie (and many other women's clubs) sought to tread. Women had always had civic responsibilities and had always met resistance as they tried to fulfill them. Given its long antecedents, such public work could hardly be seen as a violation of traditional norms of womanly behavior or a threat to customary marital arrangements. It was, rather, an extension of established feminine roles that did not challenge accepted gender roles but instead affirmed them.[32]

Employing fiction to make historical and social arguments of this sort helped sustain the club's balancing act. Stewart clearly sought to justify the activism in which she and her fellow club members were now quite heavily engaged. There were certainly true-life historical examples to which she might have turned, ranging from Joan of Arc to Susan B. Anthony. Instead she trod familiar ground, using well-regarded fiction as the evidence for her argument that women had always been active in public life. (Although *Marcella* has not sustained the enduring literary reputation of the other two novels, it earned critical praise at the time, and Ward was considered one the period's important writers.) As with the club's engagement with other contemporary issues, fiction was often a useful tool for dramatizing the issues involved and for expressing a rationale for women's action. It was also more safely feminine to critique, discuss, and reenact works of fiction than it was to conduct empirical social-scientific inquiry. In an age when women's formal scholarly work was rare and limited largely to literary studies and "domestic science," the discussion of books was safe. Engaging in civic matters through fiction was a way to disguise the political dimensions of their enterprise.[33]

Using fiction to disguise public activism makes sense when one takes into account evidence of resistance to such behavior. Hints of domestic discontent appear in accounts of the club's anniversary celebrations. Until their numbers grew too great, it was the custom of members to invite their husbands or another guest to attend the annual celebration of the club's anniversary. During the twentieth anniversary celebration in 1896, male guests offered a series of toasts, most of which praised the club and its members. But a few husbands sounded a less complimentary note, even if their conscious reversal of traditional gender roles was intended to be humorous. In a toast to "The Clubwoman's Husband," Isaac Trent, a local physician, recited an altered version of "Now I Lay Me Down to Sleep" as "he pictured the husband caring for the babies while the wife attended club meetings." Frank Claypool, publisher of the *Morning News* and a prominent local businessman and investor, delivered a toast to the "Woman at Home," declaring, "I will take her in preference to the club woman; the one who shares the joys and sorrows, makes home pleasant and keeps man where he belongs—at home." Another joked of "The New Man" planning church festivals. Even in the jocular tone they were intended, such protestations laid bare the degree to which these activist women had to tread carefully as they ventured into new, unsettling territory.[34]

Muncie's clubwomen were fully aware of the potential unease their public work created and seemed anxious to allay concerns. As late as 1902 the club still debated whether higher education would "unfit girls for wifehood and motherhood," and a paper on women and business presented at the same meeting argued that matrimony was "the natural vocation of women and as a business arrangement very profitable financially."[35]

During the same year's anniversary celebration the club staged a "frivolous" but nevertheless striking pantomime titled "Bachelor's Romance." It centered on the efforts of a bachelor, Mr. Sherritt (evidently a play on "Share It"), to hire a wife. He interviews a series of applicants, each unsuited to the post for a different reason. Mrs. Shillalah Sarosis—the name a play on the well-known pioneering women's club, Sorosis—describes the wonders of club papers but leaves Mr. Sherritt unimpressed. Mademoiselle Squalliana's music proves unattractive. The "comradeship" of Miss. S. Banthony is found to be undesirable as well. Another candidate, Miss Traveliana Bookiana, realizes in the course of her interview that she is too occupied with books and has no time to mend clothes, so she takes herself out of the running. After several more interviews in the same vein, Patience Homespun wins the job by "devot[ing] her attention to the room and not the bachelor." As she arranges the room, Sherritt's face "lights with joy as he realizes that here is what he has been searching for." The self-deprecation of the skit is striking, and while it was obviously presented with tongue in check, it nonetheless made clear these clubwoman were at pains to affirm fealty to traditional expectations for their sex.[36]

Considered in this context, the frequency with which these clubwomen turned to fiction as the basis for their reform work makes even more sense. Reading stories and exploring culture was to a large extent a "feminine" enterprise according to the gender codes prevailing in late Victorian middle America. Discussing a novel, or even reenacting one, was firmer ground than poring over statistical data or venturing into the street to conduct investigations of their own. To be sure, Muncie's clubwomen engaged in both of these undertakings, as did members of similar organizations spread about the United States around the turn of the century. But the threatening aspects of such work were minimized when it took the form of studying fiction, and when the Woman's Club of Muncie ventured into the touchiest area of all, the role of women in public, the use of fiction and dramatization rather than direct advocacy seemed to have been all but essential.

The Woman's Club and Borrowing Choices

One way to investigate whether and how participation in the Woman's Club of Muncie related to reading behavior is to examine the members' individual and collective reading choices. Library circulation provides an imperfect gauge at best; not all members of the club used the library, and even among those who did, the relative wealth of many members likely allowed them to purchase their own books and subscribe to periodicals. The opportunity to borrow a card, or to rely on a family member to procure a book, complicates matters further. The records in the What Middletown Read database can reveal only a portion of their reading activity, and we can only speculate about how large that portion is in relation to the whole. Nevertheless, these records provide us with some suggestive results.

Members of the club who were also active library users appear to have been a little more likely to borrow books with elements of narrative realism than were other library users and even other white-collar women.[37] The tendency to seek out more realistic writing does not mean that clubwomen eschewed other fare. As a review of a selection of individual borrowing records shows, Woman's Club members used the public library for many reasons, often shaped by personal circumstances. Some used it as a resource for conducting their own research. Mothers with children most often borrowed juvenile literature. A few displayed a taste for literary realism even when not investigating a topic in preparation for a club meeting. And, it must be remembered, some club members did not use the library at all. Only 62 of 120 club members included on the membership rolls in either 1895 or 1901 (or both) had an active library account during the period covered by the extant records. A few had registered with the library but did not borrow books during that interval, and others borrowed just once or twice. But most of those who patronized the library during this time used it regularly: the 62 active users averaged 68 loans each.

Individual borrowing among the club's members varied considerably, in terms of both type of material and frequency. Anna Truitt, a founding member of the club who was also a prominent local suffragist and an enthusiastic temperance reformer, borrowed just four items from the library during the covered period: a new issue of the *Century* (in 1891), two recent issues of *Harper's New Monthly Magazine* (in 1892 and 1895), and a copy of William Graham Sumner's *History of American Currency* (in December 1891). Club minutes offer no clues at to why she might have borrowed these texts, but her extensive civic activism (Truitt was perhaps the club's most publicly active member) suggests that she sought them in connection with that work. If she had any interest in fiction, it was not evident from library records.

On the other end of the spectrum was Edna Keller. A young wife and mother, married to a successful dry-goods merchant and with three children under the age of thirteen in 1900, she was the most regular library patron among the club's membership. After joining in 1897, she borrowed 243 titles in just over five years. Her initial borrowings were almost entirely children's fare, in particular Martha Finley's Elsie Dinsmore series. A few years later she was more likely to borrow popular romances, among them *The Search for Basil Lyndhurst,* by Rosa Nouchette Carey, *A Fair Barbarian,* by Frances Hodgson Burnett, and *Carita: A Cuban Romance,* by Louis Pendleton. There was little indication of any interest in serious or socially engaged fiction, which is perhaps not surprising for a young and busy mother from a comfortable home.

Perhaps more typical of Muncie's clubwomen was Carrie (Andrews) Burt. A patron of the library from its opening in 1875, the year she turned nineteen, Andrews joined the Woman's Club in 1887, two years after her husband died. She also used the library heavily, borrowing 220 times during the covered period. Early in the 1890s she frequently took out books by Horatio

Alger and other children's writers, presumably for her young son, Robert, who was born in 1883. Later in the decade her borrowings included a heavy dose of history, including Congressional reports on such subjects as fraud in the 1875 elections in Mississippi, which may have been taken in connection with young Robert's schooling. (According to the U.S. census he remained "at school" at least through the spring of 1900.) Burt also brought home more than a few light romances, including *The Search for Basil Lyndhurst* and *A Fair Barbarian*. Yet other selections were consistent with the Woman's Club's growing social concern. Late in the decade she borrowed Bellamy's second utopian novel, *Equality,* Mrs. Ward's *Sir George Tressady,* and Rebecca Harding Davis's realist novel *Frances Waldeaux*. Each was a serious commentary on contemporary life, suggesting that her reading taste had developed beyond romantic flights of fancy. It is not clear that the club's shifting agenda had any influence on Burt's changing tastes, which can just as easily be attributed to evolving circumstances at home that gave her more time for intensive reading, but they were certainly consistent with the club's use of fiction to explore real-world questions.

The mixed agenda evident in Burt's borrowing records appears in the circulation details of other members of the club who used the library extensively. Fannie Cohn had joined the library in 1897, two years before she earned acceptance into the club's ranks, and she was a frequent borrower, taking out 171 books or magazines through 1902. She obtained a good number of children's books, which was not surprising given that she had four children, the youngest born in 1888. There was notable interest in her ancestral homeland, Germany, including such translated works as *The Villa on the Rhine, Black Forest Village Stories,* and *Edelweiss*. Cohn borrowed plenty of popular romances, such as *Opening a Chestnut Burr* and *Castle Hohenwald*. But she also displayed a taste for sharper-edged realist fiction, including Richard Harding Davis's story collection *The Exiles* and two novels by Mary Wilkins Freeman, *Pembroke* and *Jerome, a Poor Man*. Titles of this sort did not predominate, but they were a noticeable strand within the mix of books she borrowed.

Another club member, Luella Claypool, displayed a comparatively idiosyncratic set of choices. The Claypools moved to Muncie from their nearby farm in 1892; before that Luella had been a founding member of the Mary-Martha Club, a literary society for women residing outside the city. Both Claypools were active civically in Muncie. Frank, who was a real estate investor as well as the publisher of the *Morning News,* served as an officer in a number of booster groups, while Luella joined both the library and the Woman's Club soon after moving to town. She remained an active club member through 1897 and a regular library patron into the twentieth century. Her borrowing choices were distinctive and included an unusual amount of material on books and reading. Along with the customary array of popular fiction, at various times between 1898 and 1902 she borrowed *The Relation of Literature to Life, Books and Culture, Highways of Literature; or, What to Read and How to Read,* and *The English Novel: A Study in the Development of Personality.*[38]

She borrowed other nonfiction as well, such as William James's *Principles of Psychology,* the autobiography *Life of Genl. Garibaldi,* and a variety of periodicals. Her fiction choices included Howells's *A Hazard of New Fortunes* as well as two novels purporting to show the reality of city politics, *The Honorable Peter Stirling,* by Paul Leicester Ford, and *J. Devlin, Boss: A Romance of American Politics,* by Francis Churchill Williams. As the subtitle of Williams's book suggests, these two stories were heavily romanticized, despite their contemporary reputations as realistic portrayals of the underside of urban public life. Claypool seems to have been serious about her reading and engaged with contemporary issues, tendencies likely reinforced by her connections to the Woman's Club.

Mabel Hagadorn was among the most voracious readers in the club, and her borrowing records suggest several impulses behind her choices. A young, single schoolteacher from a well-off family, she borrowed 248 books during the period covered. Hagadorn was born in New York State, but as a child she moved with her parents to Muncie, where her father became an inspector of railroad bridges. She joined the library in 1879 at the tender age of seven and graduated from Muncie High School a decade later. As an adult she worked as a teacher in the local schools and continued to pursue her literary interests. She joined the Dickens Club during the 1890s and became a member of the Woman's Club in 1900. Her library records suggest an avid reader with a taste for popular romance (*Castle Hohenwald; Sweet Clover*) and translations of German novels (*A Penniless Girl; The Little Countess*), but also one with an interest in realism as well. She borrowed *The Red Badge of Courage, Frances Waldeaux* (twice, in 1898 and 1899), and works of social commentary such as *Samantha among the Colored Folks,* a satirical novel about race relations by the popular humorist Marietta Holley.

Hagadorn's record also shows that she regularly used the library to obtain magazines, frequently borrowing *Lippincott's Monthly,* the *Century,* and the *Atlantic Monthly.* These periodicals included a mix of popular fiction, reportage on current affairs, and social commentary. We cannot know which parts Hagadorn read and which she did not, though her penchant for borrowing sequential issues of a magazine suggests she was drawn to the always respectable, and occasionally ambitious, serialized fiction they included.

Kate Garst provides a last, distinctive example of the relationship between club activity and reading. Garst was a typesetter and the daughter of a saloonkeeper, characteristics that distinguished her from the more well-heeled majority of the club's members. She is also unusual because it appears that her interest in reading as a means of investigating social questions drew her to the Woman's Club, rather than the club's being a spur to reading. Her transaction records suggest that she was a particularly avid reader who found in literature a means of engaging the world and defining her place within it. She became a patron as a ten-year-old schoolgirl, on December 30, 1878. Her surviving borrowing record (153 transactions) runs from 1891 to 1898, when she was in her twenties, and it shows a maturing reader who graduated from juvenile fiction to more serious writers, including Shakespeare, Victor Hugo, Charles Kingsley, Henry James, and Charles Dickens. For three months during the late summer of 1898 she immersed herself in the study of phrenology by borrowing in turn all six volumes of Franz Joseph Gall's *On the Functions of the Brain*. She is the only borrower to have worked her way through this extensive and, by the 1890s, decidedly esoteric treatise. But, from our perspective, a far more interesting choice was J. C. Croly's *Thrown on Her Own Resources; or, What Girls Can Do*, of which she was one of only eight borrowers.

Thrown on Her Own Resources, published in 1891, is partly a polemical treatise and partly a career guide for women, and in many perhaps unanticipated ways Croly's book became something of a loose blueprint for Garst's own life. Jane Cunningham Croly, who also wrote under the pen name Jennie June, was a celebrated journalist—according to some, America's first female journalist—and an early advocate of equal rights between the sexes. She was also a founder of Sorosis, the New York women's club that served as a model for the Woman's Club of Muncie, and, in the historian Karen Blair's words, "the single most important figure in the women's club movement."[39] (In 1994, she was posthumously named to the National Women's Hall of Fame.) In *Thrown on Her Own Resources*, she advises young women to take stock and reevaluate where they stand both in socioeconomic terms and with regard to the male sex.

The book is also a vade mecum for women who are seeking ways, "in this age of advancement," to lift themselves "out of dependence into independence." "Active work," Croly argues, "is a necessity of healthful life," and for those wishing to thrive as independent working women, "your present business is to keep out of the poorhouse—to keep yourself from joining the large, miserable army of absolute dependents." "The reason why the inferior man is practically superior to a woman infinitely beyond him in all essential attributes," she contends, is that "he has assumed his right to earn money, while she has not." But women must do more than earn their own keep, she concludes, "if they are to achieve a place in this money-worshipping world." Croly calculates that women have become the majority in such professions as teaching, telegraph operating, secretarial work, and nursing, but have failed to advance beyond these low-paying occupations. "Work, and work for pay," she insists, "is the motto of to-day for girls who wish to prove themselves true daughters of the nineteenth century, and ready for the responsibility which the twentieth century will be sure to bring," and her words must strike us today as prescient.[40]

Croly's words would have hit home for Kate Garst, particularly when she gave as an example of women's willing self-sacrifice in the workplace a profile of a young woman who worked in a type foundry and, stoically and without complaint, supported her ailing parents on wages of $7.50 per week. This amount would not have been out of line with, or may have slightly exceeded, Garst's own earnings as a typesetter.[41] Perhaps seeing herself in this portrait, Garst was soon to develop into an active promoter of labor rights, joining the local chapter of the International Typographical Union in 1896 and serving as one of its officers, while continuing to work as a manual typesetter and later as a linotype operator for the *Muncie Star*. Following her mother's early death in 1904, she continued to live at home, caring for her increasingly senile and alcoholic father, who lived until 1923. Some years later, she had accumulated sufficient funds to be able to retire on a union pension in 1932. When she died in 1956 she was the oldest pensioner to have availed herself of this scheme.

Toward the end of her treatise, Croly remarks that some are surprised to discover that "'working' girls . . . like to discuss thoughtful books, ethical questions, and subjects connected with political and social economy." One of her primary contentions was that women should "engage directly with the world of active life and struggle" rather than learning about it "through novels, through stories in a weekly paper, or the pages of your favorite magazine." Fiction for her was a needless distraction from the real world. "Fiction is on the decline," she maintains; "the *real* is here, and we are not afraid of it as formerly."[42]

It is unclear whether Kate Garst took to heart Croly's strictures, but, inexplicably, we have no record of her borrowing books from the Muncie Public Library after September 1898, when she was loaned the sixth and final volume of *On the Functions of the Brain*. Until then, the library had provided Garst with a channel to commune with a broader cosmopolitan culture that Croly had also advocated as a necessary means to enhance women's lives outside working hours, through ready access to such things as "libraries, galleries, museums, botanical gardens, and halls where good music can be heard." Statistical and demographic evidence suggests that, in general, too few women from Garst's socioeconomic background availed themselves of the library's offerings. In late nineteenth-century Muncie, with some notable exceptions, insularity rather than cosmopolitanism was the norm among blue-collar and lower white-collar women, and most avoided the library. Garst was one of those notable exceptions.[43]

If an examination of the selections made by specific individuals reflects the range of reading interests and agendas among Woman's Club members, a review of their cumulative activity offers at least the hint of a pattern. Table 13 lists the top nineteen book-borrowing choices among the sixty-two club members (taken from membership lists published in 1895 and 1901) who maintained active accounts at the Muncie Public Library.[44] Since the list was derived from two points in time, it includes those who joined after 1900 as well as early members. Overall, the registered borrowers constitute a bare majority of the club membership, and library use among them ranged from extensive (Hagadorn's 248 circulation transactions were the most of any member) to minimal (two members took out just one book each).[45]

The most striking thing about this list is how it differs from the top choices among women from white-collar households reported in table 6 in chapter 4. With only a handful of exceptions, members of the Woman's Club either held a white-collar job (most often as a teacher) or came from a family headed by someone who did. Yet there is little overlap between their top choices and those of women outside the club's circle who came from similar socioeconomic circumstances. Only three titles, S. Weir Mitchell's *Hugh Wynne*, Israel Zangwill's *The Master,* and Rosa Nouchette Carey's *The Search for Basil Lyndhurst* appear on both lists. Marie Corelli is the only other author who turns up on both inventories, but white-collar women as a whole gravitated toward her most popular title, *The Sorrows of Satan,* while Woman's Club members most often selected *The Master Christian* and *Barabbas: A Dream of the World's Tragedy.*

Two categories that predominate in the top choices of white-collar women in general, children's books (particularly Martha Finley titles) and popular romances (by writers such as E. Marlitt and Amelia Barr), are largely missing from the clubwomen's most frequent selections. Since many club members were somewhat older women with grown children, it seems reasonable that juvenile fare would not appear as often in their collective borrowing record. And while it is certainly possible that they did not need to obtain the most celebrated titles from the library because they could afford to buy them, the same could be said of the white-collar women who used the library but did not join the Woman's Club.

Muncie's clubwomen did not eschew the most popular fictional fare out of

TABLE 13. Most frequently borrowed books among Woman's Club of Muncie members

AUTHOR	TITLE	TIMES BORROWED
Marie Corelli	*The Master Christian*	11
James Lane Allen	*A Kentucky Cardinal*	11
S. Weir Mitchell	*Hugh Wynne, Free Quaker*	11
Helen Hunt Jackson	*Ramona*	11
Samuel R. Crockett	*The Lilac Sunbonnet*	11
Marie Corelli	*Barabbas: A Dream of the World's Tragedy*	10
F. Marion Crawford	*Casa Braccio*	10
Rebecca Harding Davis	*Frances Waldeaux*	10
Victor Hugo	*Les Misérables*	10
Ethel Lillian Voynich	*The Gadfly*	10
Henryk Sienkiewicz	*With Fire and Sword: An Historical Novel of Russia and Poland*	10
Israel Zangwill	*The Master*	10
Rosa Nouchette Cary	*The Search for Basil Lyndhurst*	10
S. Weir Mitchell	*Characteristics*	9
Oliver Wendell Holmes	*Elsie Venner: A Romance of Destiny*	9
Mary Eleanor Wilkins Freeman	*Jerome, a Poor Man*	9
F. Marion Crawford	*Saracinesca*	9
J. M. Barrie	*Sentimental Tommy*	9
F. Marion Crawford	*Taquisara*	9

NOTE. Includes only the 62 members with active and identifiable library accounts.

a taste for the classics. The books they borrowed differed from those selected by other women from comfortable households, but their selections did not necessarily carry greater literary reputations. What may distinguish them is a relatively greater degree of narrative realism. A solid share of the titles on the list in table 13 employ at least some of the hallmarks of realistic writing, including a credible depiction of ordinary life and the social environment, the use of vernacular language rather than more stylized speech and narration, and an emphasis on character development. For the most part, club members did not seek out the starker, more critical realism and naturalism evident in works by William Dean Howells and Stephen Crane. (They borrowed *The Red Badge of Courage* just twice among them, for instance. The library did not even own a copy of *The Rise of Silas Lapham*.)

More often these clubwomen sought out books that blended romance and realism, that seemed to convey faithfully the inner life of characters and the social milieu in which they lived but also relied on familiar story-telling formulas, particularly love stories that end happily after a period of trial. Regional and local-color fiction, historical novels, and works set over-seas predominated among their choices. The degree to which these books incorporated realist techniques varied, but with the exception of Carey's *The Search for Basil Lyndhurst*, Corelli's two fanciful stories, and F. Marion Crawford's three books, all of them might be described as influenced to some extent by realism.

The only authors on the list who qualify for full inclusion in the canon of American social realism are Rebecca Harding Davis and Mary Wilkins Freeman, and even they leavened their work with romantic elements. Davis, a fiction writer and journalist as well as the mother of the prominent jour-nalist Richard Harding Davis, was most famously the author of *Life in the Iron Mills*, a novella serialized in the 1861 *Atlantic Monthly* that offered a stark depiction of industrial work. That story and her subsequent work earned her a reputation as a pioneer of realist fiction. *Frances Waldeaux*, published in 1897, explored the relationship between a mother and son, focusing intently on character and dialogue and offering a plausible portrait of middle-class life (one scholar labeled it a "novel of manners"). Freeman's *Jerome, a Poor Man* blended a sharply drawn portrait of a New England town with a charac-ter study of an impoverished yet charitable man. Both stories ended happily; as one critic reviewing Freeman's book wrote, her "photographic realism" was "not so uncompromising as to refuse absolutely the admission of the elements of romance."[46]

Most of the other top choices for club members used some variation of this formula, usually with a bit more emphasis on the romantic elements. Allen's *A Kentucky Cardinal* and Helen Hunt Jackson's *Ramona* were local color, or regionalist, fiction, a genre that borrowed elements of narrative realism, including a reliance on dialects and a depiction of landscape and folkways to convey a sense of place. Yet for all their attention to indigenous detail, these stories offered sentimental plots and other romantic features. The several his-torical novels that drew substantial interest from Muncie's clubwomen were constructed in similar terms. Literary scholars cite the convincing histori-cal detail in S. Weir Mitchell's *Hugh Wynne* even as they dismiss the heavily romanticized plot. Henryk Sienkiewicz's tale of Poland and Russia during the seventeenth century included intensively detailed depictions of histori-cal scenes and events that provided the background for an equally idealized story. *The Gadfly* was "a melodramatic philosophical adventure set during the Italian *Risorgimento*" that also included a sharp critique of social injustice and inequality. Victor Hugo's *Les Misérables,* arguably a genre to itself, provided compelling accounts of life in an urban environment (among other things) as it relayed a highly improbable—if also gripping—narrative of loss and redemption.[47]

Viewed in these terms, the list includes one especially intriguing title. Israel Zangwill's *The Master* tells the story of Matt Strang, an aspiring artist from Nova Scotia who travels to Europe and becomes part of the bohemian world of avant-garde painters and writers. At its core an exploration of the social role of art and the artist, the novel was a departure from Zangwill's now more famous depictions of the Jewish American immigrant experience. After many permutations, the plot concludes with Strang rejecting the more radical and unsettling aesthetic forms, returning to his family, and embracing a more conventional realism in his own painting. Zangwill's affirmation of a restrained, moderate realism and the implication that such an approach to art jibed with a tranquil domestic life seems especially suited to the approach Muncie's clubwomen adopted. *The Master* can be read as endorsing serious investigation of the social world through cultural production and interpretation, work that was seen as a respectable, morally sound means of cultivating oneself while serving both family and community. We lack the firsthand testimony necessary to demonstrate that local clubwomen read the book in these terms, but the attraction of such a tale among women engaged in a blend of culture and civic pursuits is striking.[48]

It would be easy to make too much of this pattern. While there is some evidence that Woman's Club members gravitated toward fiction with at least a dose of realism, they borrowed their share of romantic, even sensationalistic fiction. Arguably, Corelli's stories were about as far from realism as one could get during the 1890s, although to some degrees they raised questions about religion and the relations between the sexes. The presence of three novels by F. Marion Crawford certainly cannot be construed as evidence of a taste for realism. Crawford, the Italian-born son of an American sculptor, wrote melodramatic stories of aristocratic life in Italy, including the three that appear on the list of books most often borrowed by club members. He also published an emphatic defense of romanticism in *The Novel: What It Is,* published in 1893. Writing in response to William Dean Howells's *Criticism and Fiction,* which asserted the superiority of realism, Crawford argued that fiction was, first and foremost, "a marketable commodity," a luxury, not a necessity, which meant that readers were not obliged to read it. Stories with heavy moralizing, excessive detail, or overzealous social instruction would fail to win an audience. The challenge facing authors was to balance "the requirements of art" and the necessity of telling a good "story or romance."

The "perfect novel," he argued, "must chiefly deal with love; for in that passion all men and women are most generally interested."[49]

Yet it is worth noting that Crawford did not reject every element of realism. His novels about Italy and other distant locales earned high marks for their accurate depictions of those settings. And even in *The Novel*, he acknowledged that good stories should include a degree of reality, although not the quotidian detail favored by the more serious literary realists. A novel's "realism must be real, of three dimensions, not flat and photographic," he wrote. "Why should a good novel not combine romance and reality in just proportions?" Art should "represent the real but in such a way as to make it seem more agreeable."[50]

The formula that Crawford proposed would seem to have hit the mark for Muncie's clubwomen. Fiction that aimed to represent social reality, whether in familiar places or exotic locales, but leavened with a dose of romanticism, allowed them to engage with the wider world without appearing overly aggressive. Stories formulated in this way did not disturb or challenge conventional gender assumptions or promote a radical agenda, an important consideration for women carving out new public roles in a fairly conservative community. But the plots of novels as varied as *Ramona*, *Frances Waldeaux*, and *Les Misérables* all encouraged their readers to consider social distinctions as well as the circumstances and environments that shaped ordinary people's lives, a perspective of increasing importance to members of the Woman's Club. It should be noted as well that romances generally end on a positive note, with a resolution affirming the happiness of the main characters. Blending those reassuring sentiments with supposedly more realistic portrayals of society seems to have implied that both individual and social improvement were possible.

When the Lynds surveyed Muncie's civic life during the 1920s, they noted the continuing presence of women's clubs in local public affairs. The Chamber of Commerce, they remarked, was "wont to turn to the Federated Clubs for help in a community program." But the Lynds also argued that "the essential function of these groups is no more to be found in their civic work than in their study programs." Most were fundamentally organizations intended to improve the social standing of their members. The Woman's Club of Muncie, they noted (without naming it specifically), had enlarged its membership to 168, but many of the newcomers saw it as a means of enhancing their reputation rather than as a vehicle for serving the community. As one of their informants put it, "it has brought in many women who want the social prestige of club membership but are not willing to work for culture." For the Lynds, this shift was the product of changes in the intellectual environment of the city: "In the nineties, when books, magazines, and other opportunities for 'self-culture' were relatively less available, and informal contacts with friends more so, the social aspect was apparently less important; today, with this situation reversed, it must be served first."[51]

That the Lynds were told of the coincidental decline in the significance of civic work for women's clubs and the diminished salience of literary activity reinforces the idea that the two had once been intertwined. The collective reading of texts undertaken by the Woman's Club of Muncie throughout the 1890s, which manifested itself in formal recitations, dramatizations, reports, and discussions, was a central element in the way its members took stock of their community and devised means of improving it. While the degree to which these activities reshaped reading experiences on an individual level is unquantifiable, the evidence we can draw from their library choices suggests it had an impact.

The problem of cause and effect remains when considering the relation between reading and reform for Muncie's clubwomen. It may be the case that women drawn to fiction that claimed to represent social experience and social tensions more forcefully and realistically were also more inclined to join a club that engaged with contemporary social issues—that the club merely reinforced interests that formed in other contexts. For others, the transition the club made may well have sharpened their desire for stories that addressed the questions raised in club meetings. Most Woman's Club members probably fell somewhere in between these two poles. But in any case, participation in a group that joined discussions of texts, including a good deal of fiction, with civic work, seems likely to have encouraged a particular approach to reading.

The blend of realism and romance that distinguished the reading choices of Muncie's clubwomen would seem to make sense under the circumstances. Women were still new to the public stage in many respects, and they still had to advance on this front cautiously. Excessive activism would upset still-prevailing assumptions about women's roles and responsibilities. The selection of reading that made a point of exploring real-world social issues but also used the conventions of romance to affirm customary relations between the sexes may have been a means of reassuring a skeptical husband, or even convincing themselves, that they were on safe ground.

To assert that club members were drawn to a blend of romance and realism does not mean that they made a conscious choice to read this way. As Crawford insisted, these books were commodities, carefully crafted to appeal to a readership that approached fiction as a means of grasping reality but was equally attracted by the reassurances of the romance. Club members did not necessarily seek out Mary Wilkins Freeman's *Jerome* as part of a social-scientific investigation of life in New England towns spurred by their participation in club discussions. It seems more likely that they were, like white-collar women who did not join the club, attracted to romances, but were also conditioned, perhaps by club activities, perhaps by personal inclination or domestic circumstances, but more likely by some mix of these, to seek out texts that also offered at least a veneer of social reality.

There is a substantial degree of speculation in these claims. We lack direct evidence of the interpretive strategies these women adopted in private. They did not leave diaries or other commentary that allow us to engage their reading experiences at that level. Nor were the papers they presented and the discussions they held at club meetings preserved. Instead we have to satisfy ourselves with patterns and the possibilities they suggest. The most striking of those patterns is the greater interest these women displayed in fiction that offered readers a distinctive mix of realism and romance. An interest in using fiction to apprehend the world did not preclude reading of romances, but it seemed to alter in subtle fashion the types of romances they chose and, possibly, the meanings they ascribed to the stories they read.

7

Schoolboys and Social Butterflies

Profiling Middletown Readers

The "Registration of Book-Borrowers" ledger is the primary source for the names and addresses of the patrons of the Muncie Public Library from its inception, when Hamilton S. McRae, superintendent of schools for the city, became patron number 1 on May 25, 1875, to June 13, 1904, when the ledger ends. The What Middletown Read database includes patrons who registered up until December 31, 1902, when patron number 6347, Willard A. Bartlett, a twenty-four-year-old farmer's son from Green Township, a few miles to the southeast of Muncie in neighboring Randolph County, joined the library. Bartlett, who was living with his parents at the time, is described in the 1900 U.S. census as a schoolteacher; he was later to become the proprietor of a mortgage company in Muncie that specialized in aiding small farmers. We have no borrowing records for either of them—McRae died before the surviving circulation records begin, and Bartlett joined a few weeks after they end—and, apart from some biographical details in county histories, no firsthand accounts of their lives.[1]

In common with many families who settled in Muncie, Bartlett became part of what Robert and Helen Lynd were to describe as "the constant process whereby Middletown tend[ed] to recruit its population from the outlying smaller communities about it and . . . to lose certain of its young potential leaders to larger cities."[2] Turn-of-the-century Muncie was a mobile community; although clearly growing in size, it also lost many inhabitants who, for a variety

of reasons, decided to live elsewhere. The city also hosted a transient population of individuals, and sometimes whole families, who were drawn there with
the prospect of work but then moved on. Several of these enrolled as library
patrons. As an example, more than twenty patrons, for most of whom we have
no borrowing records, gave their address as the Kirby House, Muncie's leading
hotel, which also took in boarders and which was across from the library. We
can only assume that most of these were very temporary library patrons.

Turning briefly back to Willard Bartlett, the final patron in our database,
we noted that in 1900 the U.S. census recorded his occupation as "school
teaching," but we also know that, probably with a view to advancing his
career, he was serving under the preceptorship of a local judge. Whether that
qualified him to call himself a lawyer is unknown. But if we follow his occupations as recorded by census takers, we find that in 1910 he is listed as "Agent
Magazines," in 1920 as "President Bond Co.," and in 1930 as an "Independent
Broker."[3] We also know that he was drafted, though did not necessarily serve,
toward the end of the Great War, and so might also have been able to refer to
himself as a soldier. The point is that over the course of a working life, individuals often worked in a variety of different occupations, but the database
records only a single one, most often the one listed in the 1900 census return.
Just as we have seen that the population of Muncie had a mobile element, so
in a different sense we should recognize the mobility of occupations.

That is most obviously true for younger library patrons (none of whom
remained permanent schoolchildren or students), and it is more prevalent
among males, who in many cases moved from job to job. For patrons whose
occupation could be determined from the 1900 U.S. census or the Muncie
city directories of the 1890s, we have a passing snapshot of what an individual
may have been doing with his or her life at the time. Whether an individual
hailed from a blue-collar or a white-collar background, the notion of a single
job for life, which may have become more common later in the twentieth
century, was not the norm in the era of massive industrialization that marked
the Midwest in the final years of the nineteenth century.

Among a plethora of occupations held by only a single patron are a bootblack and a ballplayer. Profiling these and several others will help to demonstrate some of the inherent strengths and also the shortcomings of using borrowing records in conjunction with census and other available information.
Sometimes imperfectly, at other times precisely, it will allow us to come away
with a sense of the role of the library and reading in the life of a representative
sample of its users. That will become even more the case in the second part of
this chapter, when we examine passages having to do with books and reading
in the surviving diaries of four young Muncie residents.

The bootblack was Ohio-born Grant Frazier, who joined the library on February 15, 1894, at the age of fourteen. His guarantor was David Shewmaker, a highly regarded Muncie schoolteacher, who had fought on the Union side during the Civil War. No doubt Shewmaker encouraged his protégé to become a library patron, and that in itself would not be remarkable except for the fact that Frazier was an African American. In the 1900 U.S. census his father, Moses, is listed as a "Day laborer" and his mother, Lydia, as a "Laundress." Although his father was literate, his mother was not.[4]

Grant Frazier is one of only nineteen African Americans who have been identified as patrons of the old Muncie Public Library, and he is one of only two to have a significant borrowing record. Between November 1894 and November 1902 he borrowed books a total of 106 times. These included novels by Horatio Alger, such as *Doing for Himself* and *Mark, the Match Boy* (though not, significantly, *Tom, the Bootblack*, or *Ragged Dick*, in which the eponymous hero fell into the same profession), several of the Frank series by Harry Castlemon, tales of adventure by G. A. Henty, James Fenimore Cooper's *The Last of the Mohicans*, a collection of short stories by Charles Dickens, and a number of works by Louisa May Alcott. Some of the juvenile fiction he borrowed may have been intended for a female readership—examples would be L. T. Meade's *A World of Girls* and *The Palace Beautiful*—and it is possible that he obtained them in order to read them aloud to his mother. Other works show a precocity beyond his age. They include Herbert Spencer's *Recent Discussions in Science, Philosophy, and Morals*, biographies of Edward Preble, William Penn, and Richard Cobden, a volume of Rollins's *Ancient History*, and separate histories of Greece and Rome. There are also several works of a religious nature, suggesting that Christian faith was a powerful motivating force in his life. Sadly, 1890s Muncie was not a place that encouraged the advancement of people of color, and he may have had little chance of obtaining anything better than menial work.

Jasper Poor, a white man who became a patron in February 1892 and borrowed a total of eight books between then and May of the same year, after which he may have left Muncie, exemplifies the type of transient library user we mentioned earlier. Jasper Ethan Poor (to give him his full name) was born in Eaton, on the outskirts of Muncie, on January 27, 1875; his mother was the daughter of a local farmer. Jasper was to become a professional baseball player. By 1899, following several successful seasons, he had risen to manage the Wabash, Indiana, minor-league team, part of the Indiana-Illinois League, and in 1900 he was recruited as player-manager of the Terre Haute Hottentots, another minor-league team in the Central League. He also played for three Illinois teams, though there is little record of his later career as an athlete apart from the 1910 census, where he is still listed as a baseball player, living at that time in New Castle, Indiana.[5] The books he borrowed from the Muncie Public Library are too few to deserve particular commentary and throw no light on his subsequent career. Thus, although they do help to reveal a heterogeneous community of readers, the circulation records are sometimes of fairly limited use in enhancing our knowledge of a particular patron.

If Poor is more interesting as a sports figure than as a library user, the same may be said several times over of Zora (usually known as Z. G.) Clevenger, arguably Muncie's greatest all-around athlete. He came from a working-class family in the city; his father, Frank, was a day laborer and his older brother a cutter in a glass factory. Zora was the only one in his immediate family—he was second of three brothers—to become a library patron, joining as a fourteen-year-old schoolboy on January 6, 1896. During the following year and a half, he borrowed books on an almost weekly basis, though with a significant gap between June 1 and October 3, 1896, when he was probably engaged in summer sports. His library borrowing was arrested once again in 1897, suggesting a second summer on the baseball field, and after that he does not seem to have resumed visiting the library.

During his eighteen months of active library use, Zora's reading was primarily boys' juvenile fiction, including the usual fare of Horatio Alger, Edward S. Ellis, Oliver Optic, and Harry Castlemon. Only very few books that he borrowed—for example, a volume of the *Congressional Globe* and an edition of *The Poetical Works of William Cowper*—give any sense of a reader prepared to explore beyond what was conventional among his peers. Yet Clevenger stayed the course at school and was one of forty students in the high school's graduating class of 1900. From there he went to Indiana University in Bloomington, where his sports prowess really came to the fore. By the following season he was a halfback on the football team, and he also played both baseball and basketball, serving as captain in all three of these sports. After graduating he began a storied career as a baseball coach at various colleges before returning to Bloomington, where he was the university's director of athletics from 1923 to 1946. In 1968 he was inducted into the College Football Hall of Fame, and today the university's top athletic award is named after him. He is buried in Muncie.[6]

Among Clevenger's classmates in the Muncie High School class of 1900 was Rudolph Bloom, who, along with his brothers, offer exceptional examples of avid readers from a socioeconomic background that hovers somewhere between skilled blue-collar and low white-collar. Rudolph was the second son of Jennie Bloom, a widow, who eked out a living by taking in boarders. She had four children: three boys, Louis, born in February 1879, Rudolph, born two years later in November 1881, and Landess, born in April 1884, and finally a girl, Ella May, born in May 1887. The time and circumstance of their father's early death are unknown, but Jennie was already widowed by 1893. All three boys became active library patrons, and each of them in turn was to graduate from the high school.

Louis, who joined the library in 1892, is listed as a member of the Muncie High School class of 1894, though the date here is suspicious as he would have been only fifteen at that time. Between February 1892 and September 1901 he borrowed books continuously from the library, except for a significant gap between the end of November 1894 and the start of January 1896, when his borrowing privileges may have been suspended because of unpaid fines. (That his name is crossed out in the register of borrowers supports this hypothesis.) In the 1900 U.S. census he is still listed as living at home, now working as a laborer in a glass factory, which would place him among unskilled blue-collar workers. There is uncertainty about his later career, though he appears to be the same Louis Ellsworth Bloom who is registered in the 1920 census as an engineer (distinctly white-collar?) in Hot Springs, Arkansas, and who later succumbed to cancer when in San Francisco in 1936, with his body brought back to Muncie for burial.[7]

The frequency of Louis's library borrowing—a total of 291 transactions—shows that reading was a central activity in his life. Even as a twelve-year-old, his choice of books quite often went beyond juvenile fiction; the very first book he borrowed, on the day he joined the library, February 3, 1892, was Jean Baptiste Baille's *Wonders of Electricity*. Within the next two days he had also taken out and returned Harry Castlemon's *Frank before Vicksburg* and Horatio Alger's *Ragged Dick*. Between his enrollment as a patron and April 15, a period of less than two and a half months, he had borrowed twenty-eight books, exemplifying the kind of binge reading by a library neophyte that we described in chapter 4. Most of this borrowing was of boys' adventure fiction, but it also included James Fenimore Cooper's *The Deerslayer*, Harriet Beecher Stowe's *Uncle Tom's Cabin*, and William Goodell's *The American Slave Code*, the similarity in the topics of these last two books probably being more than coincidental.

Louis's later loans include the Reverend H. Moseley's *Illustrations of Mechanics* and Robert Ball's *Wonders of Acoustics,* for each of which he is the only recorded borrower. When the library acquired Charles Cochrane's *The Wonders of Modern Mechanism* and James Lukin's *The Young Mechanic* in 1896, Louis was the first patron to snap up each of these. He was one of only four borrowers of Sir Charles Bell's *The Hand, Its Mechanism and Vital Endowments, as Evincing Design.* He was also one of only four readers (and the single one who took it out twice) who availed themselves in 1900, shortly after its publication, of James M. King's *Facing the Twentieth Century: Our Country; Its Power and Peril*, a fierce attack on the encroachment on "Anglo-Christian civilization and . . . American institutions" by "Politico-Ecclesiastical Romanism" (i.e., the Roman Catholic Church).[8] Louis's religious affiliation remains unknown but is likely to have been Protestant. Among the works of literature he borrowed were novels by Charles Dickens, Henryk Sienkiewicz (*Quo Vadis* and *With Fire and Sword* were particularly popular in late nineteenth-century Muncie), Victor Hugo, Eugene Sue, and Elizabeth Inchbald. He occasionally took out volumes of poetry, including Tennyson and Longfellow. When he borrowed *Elsie Dinsmore* and a number of other books for girls in 1900, it was probably for his twelve-year-old sister, Ella, who was the only one of the siblings not to become a library patron, perhaps because she could piggyback on her three older brothers.[9]

Louis's youngest brother, Landess Aaron Bloom, probably the least nerdish of the three, joined the Muncie Public Library when he was ten years old, on October 23, 1894. From early on he showed a penchant for history and travel works. As well as the usual juvenile fiction, his choice of reading included histories of the United States, Virginia, and Indiana, and volumes on such subjects as glassmaking and the history of great inventions. Among marine-based novels that he borrowed during his first years as a library patron were William H. G. Kingston's *True Blue: or, The Life and Adventures of a British Seaman of the Old School* and Harry Castlemon's *George at the Wheel; or, Life in the Pilot-House*, part of the author's "Roughing It" series.

His reading made him dream of far-off places through, among other works, the evocations of R. M. Ballantyne in *Gascoyne, the Sandal-Wood Trader: A Tale of the Pacific* and *The World of Ice; or, The Whaling Cruise of "The Dolphin," and the Adventures of Her Crew in the Polar Regions*. Further adventure stories with exotic settings that he absorbed included Edward Stratemeyer's *Under Dewey at Manila; or, The War Fortunes of a Castaway*, Claude H. Wetmore's *Sweepers of the Sea: The Story of a Strange Navy*, described by its author as the product of "many a wakeful night while I traveled the seas south of the Equator," and James Otis's *The Treasure-Finders: A Boy's Adventures in Nicaragua*. But the novelist who conveyed his imagination most often to worlds far beyond the humdrum normality of Muncie was G. A. Henty, the prolific British author of boys' adventure stories with a strong imperialist bias. Landess took out at least eight of Henty's historical tales of military service, including *Under Drake's Flag: A Story of the Spanish Main*, *With Buller in Natal; or, A Born Leader*, and *At Aboukir and Acre: A Story of Napoleon's Invasion of Egypt*.[10]

Landess graduated from Muncie High School in 1902. By December of that year he had borrowed books a total of 159 times. His reading gives us strong and convincing clues as to the direction of his life. Sometime after graduating, Landess enlisted in the navy, serving in 1910 on the U.S.S. *Wilmington*, a gunboat that patrolled the Yangtze River and Chinese coastal waters, and was stationed in Hong Kong as part of the U.S. Far Eastern Squadron. As a serviceman, he registered for the draft during both world wars. Returning home after the Great War, he settled first in Muncie with his sister, now married to a railroad engineer, and found employment as a molder in an iron foundry.[11] By 1930 he had followed his oldest brother, Louis, to Hot Springs, Arkansas, where he married and was taken on by the U.S. government as an electrician. The peripatetic lifestyle now behind him, he remained in Hot Springs until he died in November 1967.

Finally, Rudolph himself, the middle brother, was the only one to spend all his life in Muncie. In February 1893, at the age of eleven, he became a library patron, asking George Cummings, a local carpenter who had earlier sponsored Louis, to act as his guarantor. We do not have borrowing records for 1893 and most of 1894, but between November 1894 and December 1902 he borrowed books a total of 340 times. He and his brothers were evidently close enough to share their library cards; almost thirty times during 1895 Rudolph let Louis use his card to borrow books when his own card may have been suspended, and when Landess appears to have had a homework project on Longfellow and had already reached the one-renewal limit for the library's copy of the *Poetical Works*, Rudolph stepped in to renew it again in his own name.

Like his brothers, Rudolph also took out books in the Elsie Dinsmore series around 1900, likely for their sister, who was then in her early teens. As with Landess, to whom he probably passed on the word that these were exciting adventure yarns, he too enjoyed the novels of G. A. Henty, sprinkling his other reading with as many as fourteen of them, borrowed in spurts between 1889 and 1902. Rudolph's surviving borrowing records begin when he was already thirteen, and, in a family of precocious readers, it is likely that he would have matured beyond such writers as Alger and Castlemon by that time. Out of the 340 transactions in his name, only four were of works by Alger, and five (two of them, surprisingly, in his older brother Louis's name) were by Castlemon. But a further twenty-three, with seven of these taken out by Louis, were of works by Oliver Optic, whose tales of derring-do perhaps appealed to a slightly older age group of boys than those of his authorial rivals.

As a schoolboy, Rudolph worked part-time as a carrier for the *Muncie Herald*, a daily newspaper that was owned by Frank D. Haimbaugh, a leading

light in Indiana journalism and an active Democrat. Some of Rudolph's reading, including such works as Edward Bellamy's *Looking Backward* and James
Bryce's *The American Commonwealth,* point to a nascent interest in political
thought, even though, as with his brothers, works of history and historical
fiction were his preferred choices. He also showed a literary bent, borrowing
an edition of Shakespeare (possibly to supplement reading at school) and
works by Washington Irving, Mark Twain, and Herman Melville. He was one
of only three readers who borrowed *White-Jacket,* and one of only two who
took out more than one work by Melville, the other book in his case being
Omoo. His delinquency in failing to return M. A. Pietzker's *From Peasant to
Prince* by its due date was mentioned in chapter 2.

Shortly after graduating from high school in 1900, Rudolph, now eighteen,
found work as a salesman in a feed store.[12] By 1910 he had become a "moulder"
in a foundry, an occupation Landess later took up as well. Although lacking the unique all-around athletic prowess of his classmate Zora Clevenger,
Rudolph was a talented football player, joining and later managing the Magic
City Athletic Association team, a semiprofessional club in Muncie. He was
also an active trade unionist. He died in Muncie in March 1965 at the age of
eighty-three.

This sketch of these three gifted young brothers helps to show how
the library could support the autodidactic bent of many blue-collar and
low white-collar readers. Together the three siblings tallied a total of 790
recorded circulation transactions. That places them among the most prolific
of the library's users; only a few other families exceeded them in number of
transactions. Between them, Isaac B. Saxon, a railroad switchman, and his
school-age son, Loys (possibly a misspelling of Louis), were responsible for a
staggering 1,116 recorded transactions.[13] Close behind them, accounting for a
joint 1,084 recorded transactions, were Addie Knowlton and her far younger
brother, Bobbie, whose late father had made a living as a dealer in lightning
rods. A mother and her son, Dora (born in 1855 or 1856) and Omer Mitchell
(born in 1874), a glassblower at Ball Brothers, recorded a total of 902 transactions. What is distinctive about all these library patrons is not just that their
borrowing was prolific but that they all belonged to a lower middle-class or
working-class (blue-collar) background.

It could be argued that as patrons they gave the Muncie Public Library
its true raison d'être, although, taking readership as a whole, their patronage
and extensive borrowing records were far more the exception than the rule
for the city's manual workforce. The library may have trumpeted the fact that
membership was an amenity freely available to all the citizens of Muncie,
but (as we have seen) the number of working-class patrons in relation to

the size of the population remained disappointingly small. In their idealism, the founders of the library saw it as an institution that would bring untold benefits and advantages to the community through the general diffusion of knowledge, yet it would be difficult to argue that becoming a patron was at any time an automatic pathway to socioeconomic advancement. Rather, the main benefits should be seen as cultural, educational, and pleasurable. For all their use of the Muncie Public Library, the Bloom brothers benefited most from what (in the grandiose words of three trustees who penned a brief history) the library aspired to achieve by "supplying and creating those forces which make for better living, a higher civilization, and the development of the whole man."[14]

In our own day, Ann C. Sparanese has argued that in the United States, such seemingly beneficent motives for attracting blue-collar and labor readers to public libraries during the second half of the nineteenth century can be seen as a covert form of social control. "The intellectual founders of the public library," she writes, saw it as a civic institution that "would provide an antidote to the revolutionary fervor present among the working classes in Europe. The library would not only have a democratizing effect, but . . . would combat the political extremes that they believed were the result of illiteracy and ignorance." If such motives were present in the thinking of Muncie's movers and shakers in the late nineteenth century, they certainly did not express them openly, but rather exercised what Dee Garrison has described as "the elitist nature of public library leadership," and what we would gloss as a form of benevolent paternalism in endeavoring to attract a broader readership that would ideally embrace the whole social spectrum.[15] That they failed to attract a higher proportion of blue-collar readers belies the notion of social control, unless one is prepared to argue that there was a conscious targeting of the intellectual leaders of the labor movement. In conservative Muncie, we have discovered no direct evidence for that. More compellingly, it was through individual choice that blue-collar or low white-collar readers like the Bloom brothers were drawn to the library. If its shelves were largely devoid of radical writings, that did not stop these "bright spark" readers from patronizing the library.

Rosa Burmaster, a close contemporary of the Bloom brothers from the high school graduating class of 1899, provides another valuable example of a gifted individual, one who devoted her life to the city of Muncie. Rosa was the elder child of German-born immigrant parents who had settled some years earlier in Owen County, Indiana, about fifty-five miles southwest of Indianapolis. Her father, Frederick, originally a native of Hamburg, listed his line of work as a "tinner," which seems to mean a tinsmith, a skilled blue-collar occupation. Her mother, Augusta, who hailed from West Prussia, is listed in the 1880 U.S. census as "Keeping House." They may have relocated when Rosa was still a small child, since her younger brother, Huston, was born in Illinois in 1889.[16] In 1895, when Rosa was about fourteen, the family moved back to Indiana, settling in Muncie, and shortly after their arrival she enrolled as a patron of the Muncie Public Library, calling on a German-born local baker to stand as her guarantor.[17] During the next seven years, Rosa's circulation records show well over two hundred transactions, averaging more than thirty books borrowed each year. Huston also became a patron when he reached the age of ten in July 1899, but neither of their parents registered for cards. A lack of fluency in English may have been the reason they never joined the library, although Frederick acted as guarantor for his son, as well as later for at least two other unrelated young people who signed up as library members in 1902.

Rosa Burmaster's borrowing records reveal a number of illuminating particulars about her reading habits. As might be anticipated from a first-generation child of Teutonic immigrants, she showed a fondness in her mid-teenage years for German authors in translation, borrowing in quick succession during the late summer and fall of 1896 such popular romances as Moritz von Reichenbach's *The Eichhofs*, Adolph Streckfuss's *Castle Hohenwald*, E. Werner's *The Alpine Fay*, Ossip Schubin's *Erlach Court* and *O Thou, My Austria*, E. Marlitt's *The Old Mam'selles Secret, Gold Elsie*, and *The Lady with the Rubies*, and W. Heimburg's *My Heart's Darling*. These were all popular works, each borrowed well over one hundred times by library patrons.[18]

Over the spring and summer of the same year, Rosa's choice of books had been Martha Finley's Elsie Dinsmore series, which she devoured religiously, even on occasion returning, perhaps nostalgically, to the works of the same author at a later date. As a more mature choice, she never tired of Louisa May Alcott, whose *An Old-Fashioned Girl* she picked up shortly after joining the library, and to whom she returned by borrowing *Little Women, Little Men*, and *Jo's Boys* in 1901, when she was in her early twenties. It deserves mention that she shunned those beacons of boys' reading, Horatio Alger, Oliver Optic, and Harry Castlemon, not one of their books ever attracting her patronage.[19] Susan Coolidge, the author of the What Katie Did series, and Jacob Abbott, who authored the Franconia stories, briefly gained her attention, though she does not appear to have become a devotee of either. More so too than many other children of her age, Rosa regularly borrowed bound periodicals such as *St. Nicholas, Wide Awake,* and *Harper's Young People*.

In high school, as a fifteen-year-old, she became enamored of Charles Dickens, taking out *David Copperfield, Dombey and Son,* and *Oliver Twist* in successive visits over just a few weeks in 1896. Her love of Dickens manifested itself again more than two years later, when she borrowed in succession *Bleak House* and *A Tale of Two Cities,* and shortly thereafter *Dombey and Son* for a second time, as well as other novels later on. In the interim, her fairly precocious reading included works by Nathaniel Hawthorne, George Eliot, Oliver Goldsmith, Walter Scott, James Fenimore Cooper, and Edward Bulwer-Lytton. But the writer who appears to have intrigued her more than any other was Thomas Carlyle. Beginning with the first of a seven-volume edition of his *Critical and Miscellaneous Essays,* a book that had been in the library almost from its inception and attracted only three other readers in the period covered by the extant records, Rosa took out shortly after the three solid tomes of Carlyle's *History of the French Revolution,* followed by a multi-volume edition of his *History of Friedrich II of Prussia,* which she consumed over two months in early 1898. She rounded off her reading of Carlyle with *Sartor Resartus,* whose mock-German ambience may have amused her, and dipping back occasionally to *Critical and Miscellaneous Essays.*

Among Muncie readers, her preoccupation with Carlyle, whose reputation had been undergoing an inexorable decline by the late nineteenth century, remains unprecedented and unrepeated. All the holdings of Carlyle's works in the library had been given by one donor, T. J. Guthrie, in 1875, and no further acquisitions had been made. That Rosa Burmaster read a good part of Carlyle's oeuvre while still in high school should be reason enough to describe her as exceptional in more than one sense.

Rosa was one of thirty students who graduated from Muncie High School in 1899. Eleven were boys and nineteen were girls, a larger proportion of males than in adjacent years. The book borrowing of many school-age library patrons lessened or even stopped after they graduated, but that is far from the case with Rosa. She continued to use the library regularly until October 1900, and then again from April 1901 to June 1902, with no further transactions until our records end in early December of that year. It is likely that during these gaps she was attending college. An obituary published after her death in 1954 notes that "she was a graduate of Ball State College [at that time the Eastern Indiana Normal Institute] and studied for two years at Columbia University."[20] It is evident that when she returned several years later to Muncie she was qualified as an educator, and her career took her from a position in the city's Washington Elementary School to Spanish teacher at Central High School and finally to the post of principal of the Washington School, which she held until her retirement some twenty-five years later. The obituary adds that "she was active from the start of her teaching career in the National Educational Association" and was prominent in establishing a much admired pension program for Indiana teachers that provided a model for many other states.

Shortly after her high school graduation, Rosa Burmaster joined several of her classmates, including Maude Smith (see the introduction), as founding members of the Tourist Club of Muncie. The club was inaugurated in November 1899; weekly meetings featured presentations on different parts of the world in the form of fictitious letters penned by individual members, as well as occasional visits from "real world travelers, who talked informally of foreign scenes."[21] Apparently diverging from its original objective, when Rosa Burmaster became its president in 1906–7 the club turned its attention to the study of Shakespeare. None of the 425 fictitious letters created by club members between 1899 and 1907 is known to survive, so their exact contents are unknown, but an examination of Rosa's library borrowing between late 1899 and the summer of 1902 reveals an extraordinary preponderance of works of travel, a subject area that was virtually absent from her earlier reading.

The initial meeting of the Tourist Club took place in the home of Rose Budd Stewart, the wife of the Delaware County assessor, on November 23, 1899, and the following day found Rosa Burmaster poring over the shelves of the Muncie Public Library to track down a fitting book for her first presentation to the club. The choice she made, aptly enough for a future teacher of Spanish, was Washington Irving's *The Alhambra,* the classic account of a rambling expedition from Seville to Grenada. Among her later travel-related borrowings were James Dabney McCabe's *Our Young Folks Abroad: The Adventures of Four American Boys and Girls in a Journey through Europe to Constantinople,* Robert Mintum's *From New York to Delhi: By Way of Rio de Janeiro, Australia and China,* and Bayard Taylor's *Views A-foot; or, Europe Seen with Knapsack and Staff.* There is little doubt that these and other books were borrowed and read with club presentations in mind. Those presentations almost certainly would have included oral readings from her chosen texts.

Another feature of the Tourist Club that deserves brief comment is that eight of the nine founding members (Rose Budd Stewart was the exception) graduated with the Muncie High School class of 1899. As well as creating a rendezvous for cultural discussion, it seems that this club (and perhaps others as well) provided an opportunity for old school friends to bond when they were no longer together in the classroom. Most of these first members were also patrons of the Muncie Public Library, and we can see from their borrowing records that they too used the library to research their presentations. For example, Ethel Brady, the daughter of a superintendent at the Muncie Bridge Works, took out George Raum's *A Tour around the World* on four different occasions and was the single borrower of *Seal and Salmon Fisheries of Alaska,* an official government publication that would have been an unusual but instructive source for discussion. Ola Courtney, who, like Rosa, later became a teacher in the Muncie school system, borrowed Lafayette Loomis's *Index Guide to Travel and Art-Study in Europe* just weeks after it had been taken out by Brady, and it is likely that several of the club's presentations turned out as shared readings.

"Our letters describing the various scenes and incidents of travel in almost every country on the globe have been very helpful and delightful," one member reported. "Each week we met to hear, read and approve the letters written—very few letters were sent home behind time."[22] There is more than enough evidence to show how deeply the meetings of the club were indebted to the library. In their endeavors to become citizens of the world, the young women may not have achieved more than a kind of armchair cosmopolitanism, but even that would not have been possible without the browsing potential that the library offered them.

Although our borrowing records end before the opening of the Carnegie library in 1904, there is every reason to believe that Rosa Burmaster and her fellow Tourist Club members made good use of the new facility. With the trajectory of her career assured, there would be little else to comment on about her, except that in the 1920s a couple of budding social scientists found their way to Muncie and began the project that was to make them and their subject quite famous. As they began collecting the data that would result in the first *Middletown* book, they turned to the working people of the city, and many of those workers, now in middle-aged, were of the same cadre of young boys and girls who, a quarter of a century before, had first cut their teeth as library patrons.

Among those the Lynds consulted was Rosa Burmaster. As a more recent scholar notes, she was asked by the Lynds to "comment directly on the manuscript-in-progress," and she also "actively collaborated with the surveyors, reviewing the questionnaires that they distributed in Muncie's classrooms and correcting wordings she thought the locals might not understand." Her terse comments on the unpublished manuscript of *Middletown* seem to have concentrated in particular on the Lynds' discussion of the city's school system, which she confessed "were better than I [thought] they would be" but tended to obscure under a welter of statistics the human aspects of "actual teaching."[23] It is not known whether she also commented on the Lynds' account of the city's reading habits, but Burmaster's involvement with the Lynds provides one particular link between the world of the 1890s and that of the 1920s, a bridge that was often crossed in the published study. If asked her opinion, one suspects that she would have agreed with the sound belief of her intellectual hero, Thomas Carlyle, that "the true university of these days is a collection of books."[24]

The profiles of the Muncie Public Library patrons we have met so far in this book have for the most part been fleshed out with information from census records and city directories. Details about certain high white-collar individuals such as Hamilton McRae and Willard Bartlett can sometimes be gained from the potted biographies (often in the nature of "vanity" entries intended to promote sales) in contemporary county histories, but in what was largely a male-dominated society, these only rarely extend to individual descriptions of their womenfolk. Consequently, working from their borrowing records, it is often more difficult to contextualize the lives of female readers than those of their male counterparts. Yet, particularly among late nineteenth-century middle-class women readers, it was fashionable to preserve the thoughts and ideas that derived from their reading in personal journals and diaries. In *The Importance of Being Earnest*, Oscar Wilde's Cecily Cardew, ensconced in the garden of her family's English manor house, expresses well the notion of a diary as "simply a very young girl's record of her own thoughts and impressions." She keeps one, she earlier confides to her governess, "in order to enter the wonderful secrets of my life" (a declaration she undercuts by adding, "If I didn't write them down I should probably forget all about them").[25]

Wilde was too outré a writer to be represented in the Muncie Public Library, but the fashion of diary keeping, a common practice on both sides of the Atlantic, was shared by several of its young patrons, and we are fortunate to have substantial parts of four diaries. Through them, we are able to comprehend at a far more intimate level the place of books and reading in the lives of Muncie's young people. Two of the four readers were young women and two were young men. The first young man was Thomas Ryan (1872–1956); his diary fits well here since he was the elder son of John W. Ryan, a highly respected local attorney who was also the first clerk of the Muncie Public Library. When John resigned from the position in January 1881, Tom's mother, Lida, took on the role for the next two years, eventually leaving it because of ill health. Thus we can already see that at a personal level Tom's family was deeply invested in Muncie's library, but it was to become apparent—and is reflected in his diary—that his own gifts in the mechanical arts were not particularly well supported by the library's holdings. Nevertheless, we should recognize that Tom grew up in a family where books and reading had a place of primary importance.

A second, and rather shorter, diary was kept by Sarah Heinsohn (1868–

1946), four years older than Tom and from the same upper-middle-class social milieu; indeed, among her girlfriends were his older sisters, Suzie and Mildred. Sarah was the daughter of the owner of Muncie's leading hotel and a granddaughter of pioneer settlers of the city. Despite spending much of her early life in private schools outside Muncie, when she was in the city the library loomed large in her everyday life, both because she made quite frequent use of it and because it was literally across the road from the hotel, where she and her family lived. Her diary and Tom's slightly precede the surviving borrowing records.

The third diary is arguably the most unusual of the four since it was written by a young woman from a blue-collar family. Norene Hawk (1878–1966) was the daughter of a local carriage maker, and a member of the same Muncie High School class of 1896 that is discussed in chapter 5. She is the only one of the four diarists to have graduated from the high school, Tom Ryan choosing not to stay on until graduation and Sarah Heinsohn enjoying a privileged private education in Cincinnati and elsewhere. Norene Hawk's diary survives in two parts, the first of which coincides with the extant borrowing records.

The slim fourth diary, covering parts of 1901 and 1902, was kept by Robert Maggs (1887–1967), whose family, like Norene Hawk's, was skilled blue-collar or lower middle-class. In many respects, Maggs is far more typical of his social class in that the world of books appears less essential to his everyday life. His diary is the record of the happy experience of a child for whom reading has at best only a secondary significance. Unlike Hawk, he shows little intellectual curiosity, although that is perhaps not surprising given that his diary was written when he was only thirteen. In that sense, the diary bears comparison with the first section of Tom Ryan's, which was compiled when he was the same age. None of these diaries was written with the specific intention of recording reading habits, but that fact in itself can be considered valuable for the simple reason that it helps in each case to contextualize library usage and the act of reading as part of the daily experience of living in a small midwestern city at the end of the nineteenth century.

Tom Ryan

Thirteen-year-old Tom Ryan began keeping a diary on New Year's Day in 1886.[26] In all probability it was the encouragement of his parents that led him to this first step, since the earliest volume contains several homiletic entries that appear to be in a different hand than his own. For instance, in the entry for Sunday, April 4, the bottom half of the page begins: "Do at least one good thing each day, that you may look back over the past and feel that you have not lived in vain! God gives us each a certain labor to perform." Normally, Tom would attend church on a Sunday, though on this particular day he records that he did not go because he was still in pain after an accident three days before, when he had badly gashed his head while splitting some wood. The second part of the entry seems to have been written by one of his parents, perhaps his mother, Lida, who we know kept "a diary with more or less regularity during her girlhood."[27] The Excelsior Diary for 1886, which contains these first entries and others for the whole year, was probably given to him as a Christmas gift the previous December, and it is likely that his parents, who believed that schooling should take place as much at home, oversaw its development.

This first volume of Ryan's diary has already provided much of the substance for the opening chapter of Ned H. Griner's *Gas Boom Society,* which affectionately examines life in the emergent city of Muncie during the boom year of 1886.[28] Late in 2009, an anonymous donor deposited at the Muncie Public Library three more volumes of the diary, covering the period from January 1, 1888, through December 31, 1890, so that it is now possible to trace Ryan's life and activities through most of his teenage years. For the first three of those years, until he was sixteen, he was at Muncie High School, and the last two cover the beginning of his working career, as a trainee civil engineer at the recently founded Indiana Bridge Works. The years covered by the diaries all precede the borrowing records for the Muncie Public Library, so we cannot collate the two directly. Nevertheless, the diaries do supply us with a credible picture of an upper-middle-class young man growing up in a typical midwestern small city in the penultimate decade of the nineteenth century and, more to our purpose, of the place of reading and print culture in his life.

Thomas L. Ryan (fig. 12) was born in Muncie on May 4, 1872, the first son of John Wellar Ryan and Eliza (Lida) Jenkins Ryan. He had two older sisters, Suzie and Mildred, and a younger brother, Walter. His father was among the few paid subscribers to the new Muncie Public Library, joining on May 31, 1875, as patron no. 20. According to G. W. H. Kemper, he was one of sixteen original stockholders who each took out shares in the library.[29] He was also appointed to the three-man committee that persuaded Muncie councilmen to pass an ordinance making the city responsible for picking up the vast majority of unsold shares, thus ensuring the future existence of the institution as a free library. During the first six years of the stock company, from 1874 to 1880, John served on the board as clerk, yielding his position in 1881 to his wife. She was to hold the same position for the following two years. Both John and Lida Ryan were active participants in the Literary Fireside Club, which met weekly or biweekly in members' homes to discuss books.[30]

FIGURE 12. Tom Ryan, 1889. Courtesy Ball State University Archives and Special Collections.

During the whole time of Tom's surviving diary, Lida was sickly, often confined to a wheelchair and sometimes not even strong enough to leave her bedroom. On one such occasion, a Sunday, when he was still only fourteen, Tom writes, "Mama wasn't well enough to come down stairs today—and I read some very nice Bible stories to her" (August 22, 1886). His relationship with his mother remained a close one, and even after he had left school but was continuing his studies at home, he would sometimes practice his algebra lessons with her. Though the nature of her malady remains unknown, Muncie burial records show that Lida Ryan finally succumbed in August 1893. Although there is no indication from the circulation records that John Ryan continued to make regular use of the library during the 1890s, we do know that when he remarried, his second wife, Emma, became a patron and irregular borrower, choosing her new stepson, Tom Ryan, to act as her guarantor.

Tom Ryan himself emerges from his 1886 diary as a somewhat indifferent schoolboy, still much more a child than a young man and showing a marked impassiveness to academic learning. As the whim took him, on some days he would shun school altogether. Far more fun was playing tricks on neighbors, as when he and Walter "made a cloth rat and fixed a string to it and put it across the side walk and when the girls & women came past we jerked it alternatively and scare[d] them" (May 3, 1886). He was particularly exasperated when he was made to stay at school one midwinter Monday in order to "write 4 big long paragraphs in U.S. History just because I was incorrect" (January 4, 1886). Rather than showing any real desire to extend his bookish knowledge, Tom soon began to determine that his forte was both in draftsmanship, using his pen and pencil to learn, for instance, how to "draw a cone figure . . . in my Mechanical Drawing Book" (January 23, 1886), and in practical work such as finishing "Mama's spool holder" (February 2, 1886) or deliberately absenting himself from school on a Friday in order to fix up an "old clock so it would run" (January 8, 1886).

In the spring of 1886 his father determined that Tom was old enough to handle the family's horse and buggy, and grooming the horse and tending to the buggy proved further distractions from school. On one pleasant afternoon toward the end of March, he tells us, "Papa let me drive the horse to the Livery Stable—and when I came back I stopped on my way at the Herald printing office—and it is a scene of business to see the immense printing press" (March 25, 1886). Tom was smitten by what he saw. If reading simply for pleasure was not high on his list of priorities, the idea of employing ink and hot type to make text was immensely appealing, as is evident from an entry in his diary about six months later: "As today is Sunday I did not do much but in the afternoon I endeavored to make some printing ink . . . and

I went to boil some linseed oil and it got to smelling bad and they would not let me boil it any more but when they went buggy riding I built a little furnace and boiled it any how" (October 3, 1886). There is no record of this experiment being taken any further.

Physically, Tom was far shorter than most of his peers, which made him self-conscious. In one of the later diaries, when he was well into his eighteenth year, he mentions an overdue growth spurt that pushed him to a full adult height of "a little over 5′ 5″ tall" (December 16, 1889). Early on, he expresses his humiliation when he joined his sisters and brother at an open-air game of "Living Chess": "I was," he says, w[h]at is called a castle and they laughted [sic] at me because I was so little" (January 29, 1886). He describes several times visiting the roller rink to support his classmates in the polo team, but his physical puniness prevented him from being selected to play. For all that, he appears to have had a strong physique, noting rather proudly in an entry on Saturday, March 20, 1886, "I had a fight today with Rob Williams and I whipped him." Coincidentally, the fight took place just after he had gone "down to the Library and looked at some books."

During Tom's schooldays the Muncie Public Library was a regular place of rendezvous with his school friends. In the first three months of 1886, he records visiting it (or sometimes sending his brother, Walter, to pick up a book for him) at least a dozen times. In a typical entry he casually mentions, "I got my Library book renewed today and helped Will Tomlinson water, and feed his horses" (January 18, 1886); in another he records, "I went up to the Library after school—and the duck laid her first egg today and Papa went to the Literary Fireside tonight" (March 12, 1866).

Unusually, most of the books he mentions borrowing were works of nonfiction. They included "a book called Geology" (February 13, 1886), which appears to have been the well-known science primer of that name by Archibald Geikie, J. Hamilton Fyfee's *The Triumph of Invention and Discovery*, and Dio Lewis's *New Gymnastics for Men, Women, and Children*. All of these are books that had been in the library stock almost from its inception, and, during the whole period for which we have borrowing records, none of them was loaned out more than three times. From this point of view Tom was an atypical young reader, though his choice of these books points to an individual with a lively mind and a passion to develop his mechanical skills. The library was able to support his particular interests but patchily. Indeed, if an inducement to visit the library was needed, it may have been the welcome presence in the same building of the fire-engine house, which quickly drew him away from books (March 3, 1886).

For leisure during 1886, Tom also read at least one issue of Oliver Optic's popular periodical *Our Little Ones: Illustrated Stories and Poems for Little People,* as well as J. T. Trowbridge's stirring adventure story for children, *Jack Hazard and His Fortunes,* which he briefly denotes "a good book" (August 11, 1886). Both of these volumes may be categorized as juvenile reading and, in the following decade, were frequently in demand by the young boys and girls who patronized the library. It is not certain, however, that the particular copies Tom read came from the library. His choice of fiction at the ages of thirteen and fourteen does not suggest the sophistication of a reader who is willing to begin coping with more adult literature, and he was obviously not somebody who believed in or understood the value of imaginative reading as a means of extending oneself. On the contrary, it appears that on more than one occasion he resolved to stop taking books out from the library (February 1 and April 19, 1886). What may have drawn him back were books on technical subjects, which, when they became available to him, he absorbed with alacrity. His enthusiasm is indicated in an entry describing an evening when his father came home from Indianapolis with the gift of "a book, which tells all about a Locomotive, and I liked it very much" (January 5, 1886).

Through the Muncie Public Library, Tom was first introduced to *Scientific American,* founded in 1845 and today the oldest continuously published magazine in the United States. Three days after Walter had borrowed on his behalf an unnamed book from the library, Tom very soon returned it and took out instead an issue of *Scientific American* (March 13 and 16, 1886). Within two weeks he had begun purchasing his own copy of the magazine (March 27, 1886), a practice that he continued for a considerable time. An entry in his diary, dated September 29, 1886, reads: "I took 25c. out of my money and paid 15c. for a Scientific American and 5c. for candy." If not on sale at Charles Kimbrough's bookstore on South Walnut Street, this and other magazines could be found on the racks and even offered for subscription at local drugstores. One Saturday in early 1889, shortly after gaining his first full-time employment at the Indiana Bridge Works, he took a significant step: "I went to the Star Drug Store and subscribed for the Scientific American Supplement for three months" (January 12, 1889; on the Star Drug Store, see chapter 3). Even from as far away as Muncie, communication with New York City in the era of the railroad was rapid, for just over two weeks later he records, "I received my first Scientific American Supplement this afternoon" (January 28, 1889).

The following month he was in receipt of "a Scientific American, Architects and Buildings Edition" (February 16), and in March he was able to show his future brother-in-law, John Rollin Marsh (known in the family as "Rol"), who was engaged to his sister, Suzie, "my new book of Scientific American Drawing Lessons." To Tom's delight, Rol "was much pleased with it and thought it was very nice" (March 24, 1889). The following year, he was no less delighted when his brother, Walter, was able to purchase eight years of back numbers of *Scientific American* from Ambrose C. Stouder, the long-time printer and proprietor of the *Muncie Weekly Advertiser.* "They are very interesting," Tom noted, "and I think it was a pretty good bargain" (February 5, 1890). Although the Muncie Public Library received *Scientific American* along with more than twenty other magazines and journals, the circulation records show that it was only sparsely borrowed.

Given that his skills were more practical than academic, it is not surprising that Tom Ryan did not stay on to graduate at eighteen in 1890 but quit school two years before. To leave school early was a common practice among his peers; as we saw in chapter 5, Indiana had no compulsory education law until 1897, and even then it required attendance only until the age of fourteen. The Muncie High School class of 1890 consisted of a mere fourteen graduates, of whom only three were boys.[31] Of these fourteen, at least ten had joined the library before 1885. Tom himself became a patron at the age of eleven, on November 17, 1883. One must assume that other nongraduating members of the class also availed themselves of the library and may even have received encouragement to join from their elementary school teachers. Although no longer a pupil, Tom took some pleasure in attending the commencement exercises on Friday, June 6, 1890:

> This eve is the 22nd annual commencement of the Muncie High School[;] it is my old class that graduates. After thinking the matter over I have come to the conclusion that I have done better in every way than if I had contin-ued. . . . Albert Richey was awarded the scholarship of the class, by a very small fraction of a per cent over Frank Gass. After it had been awarded to Frank, Richey by his mother's help and a good deal of whining around got it changed over to him. After it was over we went around to Hummels and had a dish of ice cream to celebrate the occasion.

Several years before, Albert Richey had been a cherished playmate of Tom's (February 6, 1886), but here, as a newly minted objective observer, Tom expresses his disdain at what appeared as unfair parental lobbying that denied Frank Gass from being declared class valedictorian. After graduating, both Richey and Gass remained active readers, though they did not necessar-ily take their reading to a higher level or endeavor to tackle more challenging literature. During the same period, there is no record of their former class-mate Tom Ryan borrowing any books at all from the Muncie Public Library.

That of course does not mean that Tom stopped being a reader; rather, it suggests that he channeled his reading to reflect his work and his hobbies.

Much earlier on, he had become aware that he could supplement his library loans by ordering books directly through magazine and newspaper advertisements. That option would not have been open to readers without some significant financial wherewithal, but for Tom, coming from a background of relative privilege, it opened up prospects that took him beyond what was available within the confines of Muncie.

A brief entry in his diary for 1886 illustrates the multilayered process by which, already at age thirteen, he was endeavoring to exercise control of his reading: "I sent to Connecticut today for a book and read Burdock's Goat in school and took my library book to the library and stopped taking" (April 19, 1886). Although he does not mention what book he ordered, the likelihood is that it would have been a technical instruction manual of some kind and almost certainly not a work of fiction.[32] "Burdock's Goat," the short narrative he was studying in class, was a frequently anthologized piece, written in a humorous vein, about "an enormous, shaggy, strong-smelling goat of the masculine gender" that ran amok.[33] It was likely employed by his English teacher to test reading and comprehension skills, though, given his own comparatively advanced level of literacy, it would have appealed more as an amusing tale, a distraction in an otherwise tedious class. Proceeding to the library after school to return a borrowed volume and gesturing at terminating his membership was perhaps his way of rebelling against the curriculum. That he resumed membership in the library later in the year, perhaps at his parents' behest, is indicated in his "Expense Account," where he records on October 9 an outlay of ten cents for a new library card.

Despite Tom's indifference to schooling and erratic attendance, his diary provides some insight into the Muncie educational curriculum. In 1886, when still an eighth-grader, he records being "examined in spelling" (January 19); that this was one of his stronger subjects is attested by his diary and by his willingness to participate in an out-of-school spelling contest (April 16). His absences from school may have affected his performance in a grammar examination, where he excoriated his "pretty bad" 51 percent (October 27), and he was still not happy with his achievement when, later in the year, he writes, "I was examined in Grammar today and only got 75%" (December 3). Among his other subjects were history and Latin.

In the spring of 1888, during the final term of tenth grade, his classes also included philosophy and algebra. He found philosophy (or what might also have been known as natural sciences, akin to present-day general physics) particularly immersive because it appears to have had a strong practical element, including experiments with "china paper, pith balls etc." (January 9,

1888), "studying about magnetism" (January 26), constructing "a little Leyden Jar" (January 28), and making "a Gravity Cell" (January 31). After the first test, he could report, "I got a percent of 98 in Philosophy at school which was the highest in the room" (January 26). Here at last was one school course in which Tom was totally in his element. Among books he read, which may have been for his English class, was *Dr. Jekyll and Mr. Hyde* (February 17), though he seems to have derived more pleasure from building a bookcase at home (March 6–9) than giving consideration to what might best be shelved there. In his final weeks at school, with his departure increasingly imminent, he appears to have been counting the days, and his entry for Friday, June 8, contains a broad hurrah: "This is the Last Day of the Term of School and 'Young America' is happy."

As his schooldays drew to a close, the question of Tom's future career continued to come to the fore. His first work experience had been at the age of fourteen, when he took on a part-time Saturday position clerking at the Sun Drug Store at 114 East Main Street, run by Will and Marion Stewart (December 11, 1886). On the strength of that experience, he was offered the opportunity "to learn the druggist's trade" at a drugstore belonging to a Mr. Allen, but decided it was really not for him (January 12–13, 1888).

In the meantime his father had hopes that Tom would choose his own profession and become an attorney. With that in mind, even before the end of the school year Tom had begun his apprenticeship in John Ryan's law office (March 26, 1888), conveniently located in the basement of the Muncie courthouse. When Tom revealed to a close family friend, Ed Coy, the assistant manager at the Western Union telegraph office, "I was going to be a lawyer[,] . . . he didn't like it very well" (March 24, 1888), Coy perhaps recognized that his young friend's aptitude lay elsewhere. Nevertheless, it was to the law that Tom initially turned, and his diary records some of the books his father gave him to absorb. The first was Timothy Walker's *Introduction to American Law, Designed as a First Book for Students,* a hefty tome that went through many editions (March 26). That was followed by, among others, the first volume of Blackstone's famous *Commentaries on the Laws of England* (October 17) and Kent's *Commentaries on American Law,* which Tom claimed he liked very much (October 20). Of these, only Blackstone was available at the Muncie Public Library, though legal works—including constitutional texts and compendiums of Indiana law—were otherwise quite well represented on its shelves. The diary records several evenings when he went to the library to read. He also used the nine months at his father's law office to improve his typewriting skills and to begin to learn shorthand.

Ed Coy was right, however. At the age of sixteen, Tom's heart was not in the law. Through Suzie's soon-to-be fiancé, Rol Marsh, he was "offered a position in the Indiana Bridge Works," which he called "a fine opportunity to be what I have wanted to be a Civil Engineer" (November 10, 1888). He began working there on the final day of 1888, with a starting salary of three dollars per week. Eighteen months later, with his vocational ability as a draftsman well proven, it had risen to forty dollars a month, and, as he notes happily in his diary when talking about his work, "I am getting along very fine" (April 26, 1890). At Muncie High School, the Lynds tell us, drawing had been taught every other day, alternating with penmanship "as an aid to muscular coordination," but here at the Bridge Works, Tom's skills developed exponentially.[34] The diary is full of such comments as "Today I finished my vellum drawing for Logansport and in the afternoon took blue prints of the same" (May 20, 1889), and "I finished up No. 321, (the 100' span for Fayette Co.) this eve. and it is about the best working drawing made in the office yet. I did my very best on it so am receiving a good deal of credit" (May 24, 1890). They are a measure of his involvement with and aptitude for his work.

Tom's reading during 1889 and 1890, the final two years covered by the diary volumes we have, is distinctly secondary, except when he needed books to hone his design and engineering skills at work. For those he no longer turned to the Muncie Public Library but continued his practice of ordering books through the mail. Among others, he ordered a "Mechanical Drawing Book" from New York (March 11, 1889), pored through the latest "Engineering Catalogues" with Rol, now his brother-in-law (November 1, 1889), and received and was "very much pleased" with a new book "on the Locomotive," which he assiduously studied and read (December 9, 1889, and January 20, 1890).[35] Perhaps peripheral though still related to his work was *Through the Shenandoah Valley* (October 20, 1889), an illustrated volume issued by the Passenger Department of the Shenandoah Valley Railroad Company in 1889, which he considered to be "very pretty" (April 3, 1890).

That he kept himself current with the very latest developments in bridge engineering is evident from the fact that, within days of its much-heralded opening, he ordered a "book devoted to a treatise on the wonderful Forth Bridge [which] arrived today and it's a 'daisy.' A great deal finer than I expected" (April 25, 1890).[36] The cantilevered rail bridge over the Firth of Forth in Scotland, deemed one of the true marvels of Victorian engineering, had been officially opened by the Prince of Wales just over a month before, on March 4, 1890.

During these two years, Tom's weekend reading included H. Rider Haggard's *Dawn*, which he found "pretty good, and I hope one that I can profit by" (September 29, 1889), Richard Burleigh Kimball's *Undercurrents of*

Wall Street: A Romance of Business (October 20, 1889), and *The Bosom Friend*, a novel by Mrs. Grey (Elizabeth Caroline Grey), which he pronounced "very good" (April 5, 1890). The likelihood is that these were books that were lying around the house or lent to him by friends rather than ordered from New York or even borrowed from the public library. In the summer of 1890, however, he was persuaded to join a commercial book club, the Chicago-based National Library Association, and on July 16 he records that a certain "Mr. Edwards came around with my new book and certificate of membership in the National Library Assn. The book is 'Stanley's Adventures' and is a daisy." Henry Morton Stanley's *Wonderful Adventures . . . in Africa* was particularly popular in the United States in 1889 and 1890, when it was reprinted in Chicago, Philadelphia, and Milwaukee, and it seems most likely that it was one of these editions he received.

Among Tom Ryan's fellow workers at the Indiana Bridge Works, two in particular deserve further mention. In all respects, he looked up with a blend of awe and passing envy at his brother-in-law, John Rollin Marsh, whom he viewed as a mentor, eagerly showing Rol many of his bridge designs. Marsh's father, John, had been a prominent banker in Muncie, where he had settled as early as 1854. Until his death in 1887 he was the head cashier at the Citizens National Bank, and he was also a leading lay member of Muncie's Methodist Episcopal Church.[37] Rol himself had recently been a student in the School of Mines at Columbia University in New York City, which qualified him to assume at once a senior position at the Bridge Works. Beyond the workplace, Tom chronicles the almost daily visits by Rol to his sister, Suzie, during their courtship, and gives particular attention to their wedding on August 5, 1889, and news of their honeymoon in Europe.

Rol was a talented amateur photographer, and the surviving images that we have of Tom as a young man were all taken by him. Not surprisingly, Tom too soon became an enthusiast of the camera, ordering for himself from Chicago Thomas H. Blair's frequently reprinted *The Amateur Guide to Photography* (November 12, 1890), described by its author as a "pioneer effort," written with the intention of acting as a "guide to the beginner, and one which will teach in the simplest manner how to produce photographs of the highest excellence."[38] During the 1890s Rol and Suzie became the parents of three young children, and we find Suzie's name in the library records as a habitual borrower of such indispensable early juvenile works as Andrew Lang's *The Red Fairy Book* and *Grimm's German Fairy Tales*. Rol himself joined the library's board in 1901, and played an important role in aiding the transition to the new Carnegie building.

The other figure who is frequently mentioned in Ryan's diary is Hal

Kimbrough, one of the sons of Charles Kimbrough, erstwhile bookseller and co-owner of the Indiana Bridge Works. Hal was the same age as Tom and, as is apparent from the 1886 diary, they were already friends at the age of fourteen. Tom and he must have begun their apprenticeship at the Bridge Works at approximately the same time, and they were sometimes made to share basic tasks such as sorting the mail and responding to everyday trade inquiries (March 15, 1889). In the late spring of 1890, to everybody's shock, Hal nearly succumbed to blood poisoning; Tom feared that he "has been so sick . . . [that he] is not expected to live." "If he does die," Tom added ruefully, "it will be an awful blow to his mother and father" (May 19, 1890). Fortunately, Hal made a gradual recovery, with Tom stopping by several times at the Kimbrough household to deliver "some more horse hairs . . . for Hal's arm" (June 21, 1890) and expressing relief to find that "he is at last getting well" (June 26, 1890).

Hal appears to have been a more reflective and intellectual young man than his friend and, Tom notes, became "greatly interested" in a novel that he had spent some time writing (August 2, 1889), although we do not know if he ever completed it. A few years later, in December 1896, he married Lottie E. Wiles of Indianapolis, and the first child of that happy union developed into the popular novelist Emily Kimbrough (1899–1989), whose personal memoir, *How Dear to My Heart* (1944), is a charming account of growing up in Muncie, where she spent the first nine years of her life. For Emily as a precocious young girl, to immerse herself in the books in her parents' sitting room was a near-magical experience:

> How I loved some of these—not for what was in them, I never even asked about that; just the books. The set of Stoddard's *History of the World,* rich red with gold letters, and slippery smooth paper inside. Ruskin's *Principles of Art Criticism,* two volumes to that set. I loved to say the name over, not apropos of anything. Just talking to myself, or to anyone, I liked to say, "Ruskin's Principles of Art Criticism." But the best of all were on the bottom shelf. Three books in that set—*Abbeys, Castles and Ancient Halls of England, Scotland, and Wales.* The times I had put myself to sleep, pretending I was visiting Abbey in one after another of her Ancient Castles and Halls in England, Scotland, and Wales!
>
> There were lots of other books on the shelves, of course, but those were the special ones for me. There were books on the reading table, too, in the bay window. . . . [T]he table was easy to reach, and had the *Muncie Morning Star* and the *Muncie Evening Press* on it every day—and books that Mother was reading.[39]

Among the well-to-do citizens of late nineteenth-century Muncie, finely bound books were treated as evidence of their social status, though it is apparent from Kimbrough's memoir that hers was a highly literate family who put books at the center of their lives. As we have seen, more by design than default, that was not the case with Tom Ryan.

Although he was a minor and unable to vote throughout the whole period of the surviving diary, Tom showed from an early age an enthusiasm for politics. Both his family and their immediate circle of friends and business acquaintances were staunch Republicans, his father seeking but failing to obtain the nomination for a judgeship at the local Republican convention (October 23, 1886). At the time of the National Republican Convention in Chicago in June 1888, the people of Muncie flocked to the bulletin board outside the telegraph office, where they learned within minutes of the announcement that Benjamin Harrison and Levi P. Morton were declared the party's presidential and vice-presidential candidates. "The Republicans [in Muncie]," Ryan notes, writing on the final day of the convention, "are very enthusiastic about it. Tonight the Drum Corps were out and the Delegation train stopped and Bruce made a speech" (June 25, 1888). Blanche Kelso Bruce, a former slave who became a successful plantation owner in Mississippi, was only the second African American to be elected to the U.S. Senate, where he served from 1875 through 1881. At the 1888 Republican convention in Chicago, he was an unsuccessful contender for the vice-presidential nomination, and his short stop and impromptu speech at the railroad station in Muncie were on his return home.

As a supporter of the party of Abraham Lincoln, Tom shows in his diary a tolerant, if inevitably slightly superior, attitude to African Americans, remarking on the "very nice corps of colored waiters" at the marriage reception of Rol and Suzie Marsh (August 5, 1888) and patronizing an African American barber, John Morin ("got a hair cut at Morin's place"; March 18, 1890). Unfortunately, that tolerance does not appear to have been extended to another minority, the Jews. At the age of sixteen, shortly after he had left school, he reports that "Walter bought a shirt of a jew and I got hot at him and gave him a little of my lip" (July 7, 1888). The ambivalences of prejudice are often difficult to fathom, and it would be a mistake to read too much into Tom's reaction to the Jewish street peddler, except to state that minor incidents of anti-Semitism were far from uncommon in the turn-of-the-century Midwest.[40] Earlier in his life, Tom seems to have been unaware that his history teacher, Miss Silverburg, was Jewish (May 5, 1886).[41]

The final year of the diary contains a significant interruption when Tom contracted a dangerous case of what the era's doctors called typho-malarial fever (also known as camp fever because of its prevalence during the Civil War) and remained bedridden or in recuperation for the best part of three months. Perhaps he was too weak to turn to reading during his illness, for the only reference to a work of fiction is to Jerome K. Jerome's good-humored *Three Men in a Boat,* newly published in New York, which he found "very funny and amusing" (October 4, 1890). Not just at this time but throughout the four surviving years of the diary, there is little to suggest that Tom Ryan felt any inducement to whet his intellectual appetite through his leisure reading or to keep abreast of the latest literary publications. Judging only from the extant borrowing records, which cover the decade after the diary ends, Tolstoy, Hardy, Twain, and Stephen Crane were all popular authors, but neither they nor any other "serious" new writing was for him.

We know enough about Tom Ryan's later life to be able to fill in the barest details. An early marriage appears to have led to divorce, though a daughter, Marion, born in 1896, is shown living with him in the 1910 U.S. census.[42] By then he was married to Lenora (née Heighlands, of Clinton, Iowa), and they had four-year-old twins. By the mid-1890s he had left the Indiana Bridge Works, and (after gaining the necessary qualifications) entered into partnership with his father as a lawyer. In 1907 he was advertising himself as an attorney specializing in "Patents, Trade-marks, Copies, [and] Caveats," with an office at 253 Johnson Building in Muncie.[43] He died at the age of ninety in December 1962; Lenora had died in 1956.

Profiling Tom Ryan's reading through his diary enhances our understanding of the place of books in the life of a young man growing up in a small midwestern city during the final years of the nineteenth century. It also exposes a weak point or shortcoming of both of the Muncie Public Library and the system of public education that prevailed in Indiana during his school days. Quite evidently, Tom's skills were far more applied and technical than intellectual or abstract. Neither his school nor the library was set up to cater to his particular abilities, and it is perhaps understandable that he soon tired of both. In this he was not alone. As we saw in chapter 5, the broader question was to be recognized and acted upon by Walter E. Ervin, principal of Muncie High School during the following decade, who promoted the importance of manual training as an integral part of the education of young boys in a manufacturing city like Muncie. The nonappearance of Tom Ryan and a large swathe of his male peers in the graduating roster of the high school class of 1890, and the marked prevalence of girls over boys, enunciates a need that at that time had yet to be addressed. "Strange to say," Ervin wrote in 1902, "practical tests of Manual Training work show that the children of professional men are even more anxious for the manual training than their factory friends."[44] Although speaking a dozen years too late, he could have been talking about Tom Ryan.

Sarah Heinsohn

A fragmentary diary kept by Sarah Heinsohn overlaps the period covered by the first portion of Tom Ryan's, with the happy consequence that it provides complementary descriptions of public events in Muncie that occurred in the same year. She commenced her diary on her eighteenth birthday, May 30, 1886, when she was about to complete three years of education at Mme. Blanche Fredin's Eden Park School for Girls in Cincinnati, Ohio, and move back to rejoin her family in Muncie. For ten and a half months she kept up the diary, often falling behind and having to catch up on a missing week, but on April 12, 1887, it inexplicably and permanently terminates.[45] Keeping a daily journal or diary does not appear to have come as naturally to her as it did to Tom Ryan. Toward the end of her life, however, she penned a thirteen-page personal memoir that helps us reconstruct the outlines of her life.[46]

Among noteworthy parallels with Ryan's diary are their separate descriptions of a great fire that burned down a whole division of Muncie on the evening of Wednesday, July 7, 1886. Tom dramatically describes how his mother was sitting in the buggy about to drive to attend a lecture when "the fire bell rang out its tones of terror" and "Thomas's Livery Stables was seen to be on fire." Within five minutes, he writes, "3 houses perished in the billowing flame. . . . It then spread rapidly and burnt or damaged about 10 of Muncie's Buildings." The following day his mother invited as guests two Muncie women whose home had been lost in the fire, and Tom himself helped by stabling a rescued horse in the family barn.

Sarah Heinsohn's account is far more dispassionate. She was eating supper at a friend's house when "the alarm of fire was heard. After supper we went to the fire; it was a grand sight. A half a square on each side of Walnut street was burned, commencing with Milt Thomas livery stable on one side, and the National Hotel on the other. Fifty thousand dollars is the loss of property. It was the biggest fire ever in Muncie. . . . We went back . . . and danced awhile, then we went home at eleven o'clock." Fires were a common enough occurrence in turn-of-the-century Muncie, and the volunteer fire department with its horse-drawn trucks was as integral to the life of the city as the library, both (as we have mentioned) quartered in the same city hall building.

The element of fire may also be seen as emblematic of the age. Another and far more momentous event shared by the two diarists is the discovery of gas outside Muncie on November 11, 1886. Tom capitalizes the moment in his diary by appending to the day's entry that "THE MUNCIE GAS Well was lighted . . . Ten Min. before 12 [noon]." His description of what he saw is more detailed: "I rode the horse this A.M. and rode to the Gas Well and found that the drillers had struck gas so that there is a good many people going out there. I saddled the horse and went nearly out but the flame wasn't very big so I came back but steadily the flame is getting greater and more forcible." Sarah, four years older than Tom, shows perhaps more comprehension in her diary of the significance of the strike: "A great day. Great excitement prevails. They struck gas this morning at five o'clock at a depth of 888 feet. . . . They lit the gas well at noon. Papa came up in the buggy and took me to see it" (November 11, 1886).

In these two brief accounts of the lighting of the flambeau at the head of the derrick where the first successful strike occurred, we are witness to the inception of the gas-boom years that saw the transformation of Muncie from a quiet backwater into the hectic center of industry that it was to become during the 1890s. Unquestionably, that breathtaking moment was etched into the consciousness of the people of Muncie at large and became a foundation for the optimism and sense of upward mobility that accompanied the ensuing years of growth and rapid change. The flaming derricks provided a lighted backdrop to the thriving city of the late 1880s, where, even in the depth of winter, total darkness could no longer hold sway. In fact, it would require state legislation in 1891 to prohibit the uninterrupted burning of flambeaux. As we noted earlier, the ready availability of gas was to extend and facilitate nighttime reading in the homes of the citizens of Muncie and in its public library.

Sarah Heinsohn and Tom Ryan shared something else. They both came from the same upper-middle-class echelon of Muncie society. Their families were members of the same Episcopal church and, in politics, they were steadfast Republicans. Although she does not mention Tom in her diary, there are at least half a dozen direct references to his sisters, Suzie and Mildred, both closer to her in age and among her friends. Tom several times mentions Sarah, with whom he would sometimes engage in animated conversation (e.g., November 11, 1889), though he considered her to belong more to his sisters' immediate social circle than to his own.

Sarah's diary commences when she was at almost the same age as Tom was when his own surviving daily entries cease. It gives us the perspective of a young woman from a comfortable background who, while not sharing the same career aspirations as her male counterparts, is implicitly conscious that her education should not be allowed to go to waste. In her diary she describes a social milieu in which the notion of having fun is paramount. Sarah was by nature no social butterfly, but the environment in which she found herself during the year following her graduation risked making her just that. The pressure on an eligible young lady of respectable means in a small city of the

Midwest was to find a husband and settle down, and to do so while enjoying a social life that was filled with parties and dancing, dressing up in the latest fashion, theater going, a cookery club, and playing card games. In such a world there was less and less time for reading, and during her year of fun the number of books that she absorbed (or at least recorded in her diary) diminished exponentially. Eventually too, and probably for the same reason, the diary ceased. With the hindsight that we gain through her memoir and through hints in the diary, it is possible to reconstruct how she was able to reclaim certain important life aspirations that her education had instilled in her. The role of reading here is not insignificant as a supporting factor.

Sarah Anna Heinsohn was born in Muncie in 1868, the oldest child of Julius A. and Elizabeth Heinsohn. She had a younger brother, Thomas, born in 1871; two other siblings died in early infancy. Her father was the proprietor of the Kirby House, considered Muncie's finest hotel. An 1882 advertisement describes it as "the only first-class hotel in all its appointments in the city"[47] Julius himself was born in Germany in 1837, growing up and receiving his schooling in the Hanoverian town of Neuhaus before emigrating to the United States at the age of nineteen in October 1856. He went first to Louisville, Kentucky, where he was engaged as a bookkeeper. In 1859 he came to Muncie, where he worked in the manufacturing business for three years, and it may have been during this period that he met his future wife, whom he was to marry in November 1866. He returned to Louisville in 1861 and remained there, working as an accountant in a wholesale dry-goods firm, for over a decade.

Particularly after his marriage, Julius found multiple occasions to pay visits to his wife's hometown of Muncie, and it was there that Sarah was born. Her mother, Elizabeth, was the second daughter of Thomas and Sarah H. Kirby, who resided in a large house on East Jackson Street, about three-quarters of a mile east of downtown Muncie. Elizabeth's father, Thomas, is deemed one of the founding fathers of Muncie, having settled there from Stockbridge, Massachusetts, at the age of twenty-three around 1828. He began his working life as a trader in furs and ginseng, but within years he had opened a general store and then built the Kirby House, which he turned into a city hotel and business center. When he became dissatisfied with the management of the hotel, he offered to give the property to his daughter and son-in-law, on condition that they agree to return to Muncie, and Julius became the proprietor. He very soon garnered a reputation as a genial and hospitable host, and under his ownership the hotel flourished.

Julius also held directorships in a number of small businesses, which helped to make him independently wealthy. He frequently used the rooms of his hotel to sponsor local enterprise. For instance, his response to the discovery of gas was to join with other entrepreneurs in the city to found the Muncie Natural Gas Company. On the words of an admiring contemporary account, "In business circles his presence is always felt, and socially his integrity of character has made him exceedingly popular with all classes of his fellow citizens of Muncie."[48]

During all this time, Julius Heinsohn remained a German citizen and seems to have considered it important that his children be made fully cognizant of their European heritage. Paradoxically, it was for this reason that in April 1883 he applied for and was granted American citizenship. The impetus for his naturalization was that he wished to accompany his daughter, Sarah, then fifteen, on a trip to Germany, where he had arranged for her to stay with relatives for fifteen months in order to learn the language and immerse herself in German culture. "I had German six days in the week," she recounts in her later memoir, "made rapid progress and soon was not only speaking German, but thinking in German also."[49] She does not seem to have felt homesick during her sojourn abroad, likely because of the closeness she established with her German cousins and the parcels and letters she received from her mother in America. She had already spent three years at a boarding school, St. Anne's Episcopal School in Indianapolis, just before leaving for Germany, and on her return to the United States she was immediately enrolled at Mme. Fredin's private school in Cincinnati. This was a school with instruction in French, and soon, she says, "I was speaking French as well as I did German."[50] It had been Sarah's long-held ambition to go to Vassar College, but by then it was considered to be the turn of her brother, Thomas, who was three years her junior, to go away. Instead, she reluctantly returned to Muncie.

"I grew tired of being a social butterfly," Sarah recalled of her time at home, "and wanted to do something, so if ever necessary I could make my own living." But there was no obvious career in the Muncie of the late 1880s for a highly educated young woman with complete fluency in two foreign languages. "[I] conceived the idea," she writes, "of getting a position as foreign correspondent in some business firm, but there was no one in Muncie who required such a person, and mother wouldn't hear of my going away from home, so I was a society girl."[51] Sarah's diary chronicles her first ten months following her return to Muncie and, if her recording of the books she read during that time is complete, shows a marked diminution in her reading.

There is no extant record of Sarah's reading in English, German, or French prior to the beginning of her diary. Presumably she was encouraged by Mme. Fredin to read works by such authors as Victor Hugo, Alexandre Dumas, and Jules Verne, all of whom were very popular in English translation, judging by how frequently such novels as *Les Misérables, The Count of Monte Cristo,* and *Underground City* were borrowed from the Muncie Public Library in the following decade.[52] She had likely read at least some works of French and German literature in the original language. In her final days at Mme. Fredin's academy, she passed exams in German, general history, physics, and French. To mark her graduation, she tells us, she "received two beautiful books from Madame, as a reward of diligence . . . [and] received congratulations from all." Later the same day, as she packed her trunks and fixed her parasol, she was full of reflection: "This is my last day in Cincinnati for some time. I am truly sorry to leave here, and have had many pleasant times here" (June 4, 1886). If she was troubled by the notion of returning from a large city to a small town, that is not evident from any other entry in her diary. The train journey from Cincinnati to Muncie took all of six hours, and in no time at all Sarah appears to have readjusted to home life in the town of her birth.

What she did bring with her from Cincinnati is the evident love of reading that her education had instilled in her. At the end of the very first day back, she records in her diary that she scoured the shelves at the Kirby House and "read and looked at books in the evening" (June 5, 1886). The first book she chose, on the weekend following her return, was George Eliot's *Romola.* She began reading it on Sunday and, between sewing and other activities, had completed it by the following Wednesday evening. It was also available in the collection of the Muncie Public Library, which eventually had five copies of the work, borrowed a total of seventy-four times in the period covered by the circulation records. One of the patrons who borrowed and read *Romola* was Norene Hawk; another was the Reverend William H. Oxtoby, pastor of the First Presbyterian Church in Muncie, who appears to have been so taken by the novel that he borrowed copies of the book on four separate occasions between June 1897 and February 1902.

During the summer of 1886 Sarah's reading was quite prolific. After *Romola,* in quick succession, she turned to Shakespeare's *Richard II* (June 20), Thomas Moore's oriental tale in poetical form, *Lalla Rookh,* which she "got . . . out of the Library" (June 21), Oliver Goldsmith's *The Deserted Village* and *The Vicar of Wakefield* (July 7–11), Elizabeth Barrett Browning's long poem *Aurora Leigh* (July 11), American author Blanche Willis Howard's latest novel, *Aulnay Tower* (August 7), and a trio of recent three-decker novels, Jessie Fothergill's *Healey: A Tale* (August 8), Mary Linskill's *Between the Heather and the Northern Sea* (August 30), and William Black's *Yolande: The Story of a Daughter* (September 24). There were also afternoons devoted to reading in French, though she does not name any titles. Along with *Lalla Rookh,* several of the books on this list may have come from the Muncie

Public Library, but the lack of borrowing records for 1886 makes it impossible to say more than that there were copies of Goldsmith, Browning, and the complete works of Shakespeare there. The majority of books she read at this time were purchased, though unlike Tom Ryan she does not list her acquisitions. The likelihood that she was adding to her own personal library at home is apparent from a diary entry for July 9, 1886: "Fixed my books on my new shelves, and hung up my pictures." The same day she records receiving a catalog from a girlfriend, though she does not specify whether this was a catalog of books.

During the early part of September she engaged in a three-week excursion by train and carriage to visit Kirby cousins in the village of Curtisville, Massachusetts (part of Stockbridge), returning via Niagara Falls and Detroit. Her literary interests were pricked by outings to see "the house where Jonathan Edwards used to live" (September 2, 1886) in Stockbridge, and to Lenox, "where we saw the house where Hawthorne used to live. He wrote the story of 'The House with the Seven Gables,' in this house. It is a small red frame house. One large pine tree furnished all the boarding for it" (September 4).[53] But Sarah was most moved when she visited the cemetery in Curtisville and saw the graves of her great-grandparents (September 2). A week later she traveled by carriage to Niagara Falls, which she "drove all around" in order to see its "interesting sights" (September 9). A highlight of her stay in Detroit was a visit to the Detroit Opera House, where, she informs us, "[I] went to see Edwin Booth in Macbeth; he was grand. I enjoyed it very much" (September 17). Leaving Detroit on September 22, she reached home the same evening.

Life back in Muncie soon took on for her a familiar, if also slightly tedious, routine. A typical diary entry reads: "Got up rather late. Went down town with Gertrude, then came home and wrote letters. Took my bath after dinner, and read all afternoon" (January 8, 1887). Perhaps inevitably, in no time eighteen-year-old Sarah found that the whirl of her social life took priority over any intellectual aspirations that she may have had. Although she never gave up on books, her reading increasingly took second place to parties and dancing. Less than a week after her return from Cincinnati, she records having "an elegant time" at one such party, where she "danced nearly every dance" and "came home a little before two o'clock." When she got up the following morning, she tells us, she felt "nearly dead, I am so sleepy" (June 10–11, 1886).

Soon this had become a pattern. "In the winter," she recalls in her memoir, "we had bob sled parties, and in the summer tally-ho parties and picnics. Then in the winter we had dances which were most enjoyable." In the first four months of the diary she lists each and every book she perused, but during its final six and a half months she mentions only a single book,

Helen Hunt Jackson's recently published runaway best seller, *Ramona: A Story*, about which she comments cryptically, "Think it was lovely" (January 18, 1887). Of course, it is certainly possible that she had given up on recording her reading in the diary, but more likely the absence of such mentions reflects Sarah's swift transformation from diligent student to party girl.

Coming from a family with a strong work ethic and Protestant belief, it does not seem to have taken too long for her to realize that, for all the fun that she was having, she was unlikely to remain altogether happy with her existing situation. She understood that it could only be temporary; indeed, even during the short period of her diary, she felt it incumbent on her to pick up on her studies. In October 1886, perhaps with her father's early career in mind, she received permission to enroll in a bookkeeping class at Muncie High School, where several young women in their senior year (including Mildred Ryan) were among her friends. The books that she needed for this class could be purchased in Muncie (October 7, 1886), and she was to remain a part-time student during the proceeding year. She also took music lessons, though she later recognized that she was "not musically inclined" and would never succeed in making a living as a musician or an artist.[54] The termination of her diary at the beginning of April 1887 means that we have to rely on her much later memoir, her library borrowing records, and other external sources to trace her subsequent life and career.

Sarah stayed in Muncie for the next year, but in 1888 she joined a group that traveled to Ireland, Scotland, France, Germany, and England. Rather than returning with the others, she "decided to stay in Paris in a Pension, studying French and music," residing there for some ten months. What she did with herself immediately following her return to Muncie is unknown, though she may have employed her training in bookkeeping either to help her father at the Kirby House or in another situation. Eventually she came realize that what she wanted was a real career, and that it should be in nursing. In the late nineteenth century it was highly unusual, and in many respects radical, for a young lady from a good middle-class family to choose to go into nursing, let alone any other full-time paid occupation. It took two years of coaxing before she was finally able to persuade her parents to send her to the New York Hospital's training school, from which she graduated in March 1897 with two diplomas and a gold medal. After completing her training, she tells us in her memoir, she truly wanted to stay on in New York City, where she was offered a position in the same hospital and where she was much in demand with foreign patients because of her fluency in French and German.

By then she was approaching the age of thirty, and parental pressure obliged her to return to Muncie, where she soon became engaged to John J.

Hartley, a widower who was eleven years her senior and a successful business-man and real estate agent in the city. John was a first-generation American, both of his parents having immigrated from Germany. His first wife, Anna, to whom he had been wedded for nineteen years, had died in 1896, and two years later, on June 22, 1898, he married Sarah Heinsohn; the couple had four children, three boys and a girl, born between 1899 and 1907.[55]

Unfortunately, much of Sarah's subsequent life was spent as a single mother bringing up her children. As she recounts in her memoir, in August 1910, when her youngest child was barely three years old, she was struck by "a terrible tragedy" when her husband "lost his life in a terrible storm on Carp Lake [in Michigan] where he had gone to fish."[56] Unable to cope with taking care of her children and running her late husband's business interests, she was obliged to sell the latter at a fraction of their value. Although it was now a long while since she had last practiced her profession and "there had been many technical advances in the intervening years," she requalified by passing the state nurses' examination in Indiana, taking charge of the American Red Cross chapter in Muncie and, when the time came, involving herself in the war effort. After the Great War, she was approached to start a school nurses' program for the Muncie City Schools. According to some handwritten notes accompanying her memoir,

> [She] became the only nurse for all the elementary schools and the high school in Muncie. She set up and equipped a nurse's office in each school, made and kept a schedule for visiting each school regularly, gave talks to the children, examined them when necessary, obtained the services of Muncie's physicians and dentists for the free yearly examination of all children, made arrangements and took many children to the Riley Children's Hospital in Indianapolis. She was the only nurse for some time, but gradually added other nurses, but continued to supervise the whole program visiting the schools by street car or bus until 1939 when she was 71 years old—one year past the retirement age. She had stayed on by special request, and didn't want to stop even then.

She died on November 3, 1946, and is buried alongside her husband in the Beech Grove Cemetery in Muncie.

Sarah's library borrowing records allow us a further perspective. She joined the Muncie Public Library on May 16, 1877, when she was not yet eleven and the library itself was barely two years old. Her mother, Elizabeth Heinsohn, was her guarantor. Elizabeth herself was one of the first patrons of the new library, joining as a stockholder on February 12, 1876.[57] She was following in the footsteps of her father, Thomas H. Kirby, who had purchased stock in the library six weeks earlier, on December 29, 1875, and her mother, Anna, who purchased her share on January 15, 1876. During the four years before his death in 1879, Thomas contributed at least ten books to the growing library. His daughter kept up the practice, donating further books in 1891 (a copy of Bellamy's *Looking Backward*) and 1896. For the Kirby family, buying stock in the new library was one significant way of investing in the development of the city of Muncie as a whole. As a minor, Sarah was not eligible to hold library stock at the time, but her regular membership was no less valid. It continued after she reached adulthood and following her marriage.

Interestingly, neither Julius Heinsohn nor his son-in-law, John J. Hartley, became patrons of the library, and it might be argued that this is one more piece of evidence that library-going was seen as a more markedly female pursuit. In Julius's case, given that English was his second language, it is perhaps feasible that he preferred to read German; as we have seen, the library had very little to offer in that line. Both men, however, were aware of the benefits of library membership and may have used this knowledge to further their business interests. John Hartley was the guarantor for Roy Tyler, listed in the 1900 U.S. census as an unmarried man of forty-eight and a manufacturer of wooden novelties, who may have been a business acquaintance.[58] He joined the library on November 8, 1901, and was a prolific reader, borrowing eighty-one books in the ensuing year.

Likewise, as joint owners of the Kirby House, Julius or Elizabeth Heinsohn acted as guarantors for at least half a dozen mainly short-term residents of Muncie who put up at their hotel between 1880 and 1898, when they sold the lease within months of their daughter's marriage. The last of the new library patrons for whom Julius Heinsohn provided his own personal guarantee was Lena G. Dow, the wife of John J. Dow, who came from Ohio and was the lessee and new proprietor of the Kirby House. In the following year Lena was to make almost weekly use of the library. Although perhaps little more than a no-cost gesture of good will that coincided with the sale of the lease, Julius's willingness to act as guarantor was also a neat way of welcoming her into the heart of the Muncie community.

As we noted earlier, until 1902 library patrons could borrow only one book at a time, and it was not unusual for families to share borrowing privileges. Apart from references in her 1886 diary, we do not know which books Sarah Heinsohn borrowed and read before November 1891, when the surviving circulation records begin. But it is clear that she and her mother were familiar with the practice of sharing books, since they each borrowed almost simultaneously a separate volume of Frank W. Gunsaulus's two-volume romance, *Monk and Knight: An Historical Study in Fiction*, in November 1894.

Gunsaulus was a popular preacher and writer, and the library had purchased his novel the previous July. That the first volume was borrowed by the mother four days before her daughter took out the second suggests that Elizabeth was the reader, though it is just as likely that they both read the novel. Indeed, shared borrowing rights must have encouraged shared reading, and in turn-of-the-century Muncie the shared reading of books led to the proliferation of literary clubs in which chosen or favorite authors could be discussed among a coterie of friends.

The circulation records show that between 1894 and 1902 Sarah made twenty-eight transactions and her mother almost the same number, twenty-nine. These are far from prolific numbers, and one must assume that the library supplemented rather than provided their main source of reading, as was often the case for people of means. Given the evidence of Sarah's diary for 1886, it is inconceivable that her reading during the decade for which we have transaction records was limited to her fairly skimpy library borrowing. Those records that we do have show that, in common with most other readers, Sarah favored novels and romances. Prior to her marriage, these included novels by Edward Bulwer-Lytton, who was still quite popular during the 1890s, and Harriet Beecher Stowe. After her marriage and the birth of her oldest child, one might have expected that her borrowing would include nursery books for reading out aloud, but that is not the case. Instead, we find that her choice of books included biographies of Dolly Madison and Confucius, Alice Lounsberry's *Guide to the Wild Flowers,* issues of the *Century Illustrated Monthly Magazine,* and a small selection of popular novels.

For Sarah Heinsohn Hartley, the library had become less of a necessity than an occasional amenity which, as a lifelong citizen of Muncie, she would have considered as a birthright. In a diary entry dated July 31, 1897, she records a busy Monday that included making arrangements for music lessons, attending a public lecture, an unspecified meeting of "the club . . . at our house," conversations with friends, and two separate visits to the library. If sometimes no more than a meeting place close to the center of town and at other times a cultural focal point of study and recreation, for Sarah and her social circle of friends and family, the Muncie Public Library loomed large as an important, though often unsung, feature of their everyday lives.

Norene Hawk

"Am pretty lonesome and have nothing to read," a young Muncie woman complained to her diary on July 8, 1899.[59] This cri de coeur was penned by Norene Hawk, the twenty-one-year-old daughter of George Hawk and Mary

Jennie Walburn Hawk. According to the 1900 U.S. census, George Hawk was a carriage maker, a skilled blue-collar occupation that was, until the advent of the motor car in the decade that followed, a stable profession with a dependable income.[60] Norene and her brother, Winton, attended Muncie High School and, although Winton was a year older, both graduated in 1896. Three years before graduating, on March 3, 1893, Norene joined the Muncie Public Library, where she registered as Nora Hawk. Four years earlier, on April 2, 1889, Winton, then twelve or thirteen, had applied for a card, and about seven years later his name is also inscribed in the minutes of the library board, where he is thanked for the donation of a book.[61] Among Norene's own borrowings as a schoolgirl were Oliver Optic's *Up and Down the Nile* and issues of *St. Nicholas* and the *Atlantic Monthly*. That she was a precocious reader is suggested by her borrowing of Tennyson's long narrative poem *Enoch Arden*, quite a mature choice for a seventeen-year-old. We know that as many as three-quarters of the class of 1896 were patrons of the Muncie Public Library either directly themselves or through their immediate family, arguably a higher figure than at an equivalent high school today.

The Hawk family home overlooked the railroad tracks at 503 South Hackley Street, a row of modest working-class houses that stood at the edge of downtown Muncie. Norene's paternal grandmother grew up in Indiana; her paternal grandfather was born in Virginia. It is not known when grandpa Hawk first came to Muncie, though the family was settled in Delaware County for all of Norene's life. After she left school, Norene secured office work in the real estate business and as a stenographer. The 1890s were boom years for Muncie, and the influx of new residents meant that there was plenty of paperwork to process the buying and selling of properties. Norene was successful at her job, and by 1906 she had been appointed a notary public.[62] Her career reflects her transition from working to middle class.

The Hawks were congregants of the First Baptist Church in Muncie, which had Dr. Cassius M. Carter as its pastor for more than twelve years beginning in 1898. Carter was "three times president of the Indiana Baptist Convention, [and] . . . was asked to preach, lecture, and conduct revivals across [the United States] . . . and Europe. His prominence brought to the Muncie church a recognition not enjoyed previously." He also served as chaplain to the Second Regiment Infantry of the Indiana National Guard. By way of fostering attendance at his downtown church, Carter encouraged the construction in 1900 of an institutional annex to his church that included "a gymnasium, reading room, study, social room, club room for young men, and club room for young women" and was "kept open for long hours during the day."[63]

Even before 1900, it is apparent that the church sponsored several social clubs, and that it included a library, although we have no record of its catalog. It also enjoyed a thriving Sunday school, which, judging from the frequent references to it in Norene's diary, was patronized not just by children but by young adults as well. As Christine Pawley observes in her study of the culture of print in late nineteenth-century Osage, Iowa, the Sunday school had become by that time "an 'American' institution" that "inducted children into a culture of literacy and prepared them to participate in a world centered on print."[64] Even with all that was available to them through their own church, the Reverend Carter and his wife, Martha, both joined the Muncie Public Library in the middle of 1900, between them borrowing nearly eighty books—not quite a book a week—over the next two years. As we saw in chapter 2, several years later Carter himself was elected vice president of the board of the newly built Carnegie Library.[65] Suffice it to say that his and other Muncie churches, most of which also had flourishing Sunday schools, openly encouraged their congregants to extend their reading.

It is not known when Norene Hawk commenced keeping a diary or journal, since only three notebooks survive, covering the periods from November 24, 1898, to August 17, 1899, and January 1 to September 26, 1905.[66] Of course, Norene did not keep her private daily journal with the foreknowledge that more than a century later it would become publicly available for sly eavesdroppers like us, nor did she deliberately give prominence to her reading experience simply for its own sake. Rather, as we will see, the diary provides us with primary evidence of the centrality of reading in the everyday life of a young woman living in an emergent small city of the Midwest at the turn of the twentieth century.

It is fortuitous that the two periods covered by the surviving parts of the diary—1898–99 and 1905—allow us insight into the place in Norene's life of the original Muncie Public Library that was replaced by the new Carnegie Library, which opened its doors in January 1904, shortly before the second period of the diary begins. When she wrote the first part of the diary, Norene was just twenty, turning twenty-one on February 16, 1899; in the second part, she reached the age of twenty-seven and, significantly for a young woman in a small city at that period, still remained single. Here we come to the nub of the two parts of the diary: each chronicles her fraught relationship with an individual suitor. In 1898–99 she was involved with a certain "Mr. W. C. Emerson," who, even though he attended to almost her every whim on a daily basis, is curiously never once referred to in the diary by his first name. Mr. Emerson, it transpires, was Warren C. Emerson, an employee at the Muncie office of the Western Telegraph Company, which Norene visited on several occasions. By the time of the 1910 U.S. census he was forty years old, a hus-band to another woman and the father of two children.[67]

Seven years after her affair with Emerson sputtered to an end, she chroni-cles in her 1905 diary her relationship with another young man, though here she reveals only his first name, Adam. She describes him as "certainly a peach as well as an enigma" (January 11, 1905), and one who "would certainly try the patience of Job" (January 14), and it seems unlikely that he would have been her choice as a boyfriend in our own age of social networking. Yet for a young woman looking for a husband in 1905, he must have seemed a reason-able prospect. The diary reveals that by choice he was an artist or an amateur architect, but by trade a construction worker or house carpenter. He encour-aged her to believe he was serious about settling down by asking to have a portrait of her made especially for him at the Neiswanger Photographic Studio in Muncie (April 1), and by turning up on two separate occasions with "a book of house plans" (August 7 and July 1) to work through with her.

More often than not, though, Norene found herself made "mad" (in both senses of that word) by Adam's erratic behavior, and twice she reluctantly broke off with him. A typical entry reads: "Expected all day and evening for Adam to ring up but he failed to do so and it made me pretty mad, as he had said he would. In fact, I thought he would come up but he seems to have different plans. Why on earth he wanted to ask me for my company again and then not come and see me, is more than I can understand" (March 9). Whether another woman stole his affections or simply because the relationship was going from bad to worse, it seems he may have jilted her, for the diary suddenly breaks off with a date and without an entry on Tuesday, September 26, 1905. If our melo-dramatic theory is right, the shock to Norene caused her to terminate the diary.

As well as recording her twice-broken heart in her dealings with these recal-citrant young men, Norene Hawk's diary provides a picture of life in downtown Muncie in the gas-boom era. Though the 1890s preceded the advent of the automobile as the primary American mode of transportation, there is much in Norene's diaries to suggest that the people of Muncie sensed that major changes were in the offing. And, rather than being resistant to these, they (or at least those of her generation) seem to have greeted with alacrity the technolog-ical innovations, which they perceived correctly as heralds of greater change. In her 1898–99 diary, she mentions the acquisition at the office of "a new Rem-Sho typewriter" (November 28, 1898)—the Remington-Sholes machine, intro-duced in 1896, was among the first to employ a QWERTY keyboard—and six weeks later she writes of putting "in an hour or so on a Caligraph Typewriter, trying to get used to it" (January 11, 1899).

She also records her enthusiastic employment of a Kodak camera (still something of a novelty since its first introduction during the late 1880s), noting, for instance, "[I] had eleven new plates put in my camera today" (January 2, 1899). Although it would be a few years—and a new century— before motion pictures would be more than a novelty, she records that she and Mr. Emerson "went out . . . to see the Cinematographic Exhibition" that was visiting Muncie in June 1899 (June 3). On another occasion she describes being able to look at the bones of her hand on an X-ray plate (March 31, 1899), a process that had been invented only three years earlier, and (paralleling Freud) was popularly seen as revealing our hitherto hidden inner selves.

At home and in the office, the telephone had become an essential accompaniment, and, even in 1898, almost all her friends seem to have had access to one.[68] Telegraphy, however, still remained the primary means by which Muncie communicated with the wider world, and (as we have seen) her 1898 diary includes visits to the telegraph office. On July 26, 1905, she notes that "Papa and Adam . . . got the Graphophon[e] playing"; this was a type of phonograph that had only become popular a few years earlier. Within town, when she didn't catch the "car" (the local electric streetcar service), she whizzed around on her "wheel," bicycling being particularly popular among young people. The impression that we get from the diary is of a young woman who is no less plugged-in for her age than her equivalents are today. The young people of Muncie, it seems, were au courant with trends that, in thinking back to that era, we might more readily associate with life in such cities as New York and Chicago.

Yet there was still much that was comfortably traditional about their small city. Traveling circuses visited Muncie (May 1, 1899), including "Barnum & Bailey's" (June 9, 1905), as well as Buffalo Bill's Wild West show, with excursions into Muncie by big crowds from all around (August 4, 1905). In early June the annual "great street carnival" brought all and sundry to the city (June 5, 1905). Throughout the diary, there are frequent references to stopping by at the candy shop to buy taffy and other confectionery treats. At the opera house, there were new performances of plays and musical events through most of the year. Among Norene's favorites were "The Sewanee River," which she called "a very interesting play," though it drew only a "light crowd" (April 17, 1899), and a dramatization of "Dr. Jekyll and Mr. Hyde", which she "enjoyed very much" (September 4, 1905).[69] (From her borrowing data, we do know that she had already read Robert Louis Stevenson's novella, which she took out in November 1900).

At home, Norene and her family often spent the evening or weekends playing such popular Victorian card games as euchre and progressive pedro, a variant of pitch (January 17, 1905), or a form of dominoes called muggins (February 5, 1905).[70] Sometimes too she would occupy herself with crocheting a doily (December 9, 1898) or with sewing; like many other families, the Hawks owned a sewing machine (April 14, 1905).

But there is little question that Norene's altogether favorite pastime—the one that preoccupied this intelligent and articulate young woman more than any other—was reading. The diary is a record of her avid love of books. To begin with, she was an active member of the "American Literature Coterie" (e.g., February 6, 1899), a reading and discussion group that was centered on her church. In February 1899 it fell to her to lead the discussion, and for that she "spent part of the day writing an essay on Longfellow" (February 20). In her later diary, she reveals that she also wrote poetry (July 15, 1905), though neither that nor her piece on Longfellow has come down to us. It turns out that almost all her reading choices—or at least those she recorded in her diary—were works of fiction, and her pick was often dictated more by what was available than by a desire to read the very latest book.

As we noted earlier, the first part of Norene's diary, covering the period from November 1898 to August 1899, is the only one that coincides with the surviving borrowing data for the Muncie Public Library. On several occasions during this period, she refers specifically to borrowing books from the library. For instance, on Sunday, January 15, she records that she "got a book from the Library, [J. M. Barrie's] 'The Little Minister,' " a popular fiction that tells of the love of a young Scottish pastor for a wild gypsy girl, who (predictably, perhaps) turns out to be of noble birth. The following month, also on a Sunday, she reports that she "got 'Elsie Dinsmore' out of the Library" and read it the next day, "having nothing else to do". By the day after, she had finished it (February 26 and 27).

But although the Muncie Public Library had *The Little Minister* and *Elsie Dinsmore* on its shelves (and both proved immensely popular with patrons), it seems that Norene borrowed them from another library, because there are no transaction records for her on the dates she mentions in her diary, and in fact in each case the library's copy was already checked out on those dates. Given that both books are faith-based and both were borrowed on a Sunday, it seems likely that she borrowed them from the library of the Baptist Church, of which she was an active member. This underscores the fact that the public library was not the only communal repository of popular books in late nineteenth-century Muncie.

Borrowing books from friends, or buying them, was also common. A friend of Norene's lent her a copy of Marie Corelli's *Wormwood: A Drama of Paris*, a book that was not available in the Muncie Public Library. *Wormwood* is a

polemical novel that preaches against the evils of absinthe drinking and its cor-
rupting effect on French society. She describes it as "a wild strange book and
not one adapted to a person subject to the blues [meaning herself]" (March 29
and April 5, 1899). Most of her comments on the books she read, if she made
comments at all, are terse. Thackeray's *Vanity Fair*, which she read in 1905,
strikes her as "anything but a cheerful book" (January 31); she found Booth
Tarkington's *Cherry* "very amusing"; and after finishing reading Kendrick
Bangs's *House-Boat on the Styx* (another book not available at the public
library), she confesses to feeling "very lonesome and blue" (May 2, 1899). None
of her comments on individual books can be deemed profound, and they are
more often indicative of the variety of moods created by her reading.

Although the diaries include many references to books she read, only
a single one coincides precisely with the extant borrowing records. On
Tuesday, August 8, 1899, she writes, "Went to the Library this morning and
got 'The Fair Maid of Perth.'" The circulation records show that Sir Walter
Scott's novel was borrowed on that day, but that it was lent not to Norene but
to her brother, Winton. From the diary, we know that at this time Winton
was quite seriously ill in bed at home. Whether Winton was in a fit state to
read, or whether Norene simply borrowed his card or number, is unclear, but
we strongly suspect that she was the reader. Looking at the records of her
borrowing in the database and in the later 1905 diary, there is no question
that she was an avid and serious reader, one who could count Shakespeare,
George Eliot (*Romola*), George Sand (*Consuelo*), Edward Bellamy (*Looking
Backward*), and Victor Hugo (*Les Misérables*) among the authors that she
borrowed, and not do more than mention Marie Corelli, H. Rider Haggard,
and E. P. Roe among the creators of Victorian potboilers.

After her two failed love affairs, some will no doubt ask what happened
to Miss Hawk. She did eventually marry, becoming Mrs. Peter Quirk. Sadly,
her marriage was not a particularly long one; her husband died in December
1925. She herself lived a long widowhood, finally passing away in March 1966.

Robert Maggs

The recently discovered diary of Robert Maggs, slender as it is, provides us
with a different picture of the life of reading for a young boy just entering
his teenage years. Robert, who was born in Canandaigua, New York, moved
with his family to Muncie in 1891, when he was only four years old, and he
spent most of the rest of his life there. His father, William F. Maggs, was
a tailor, and his mother, Harriett, who had received her schooling at the
Canandaigua Academy, has no occupation listed in either the 1900 or 1910

U.S. censuses and was undoubtedly a housewife. That the family was far from poor is apparent from the fact that, though resident in Muncie, they retained ownership of their family home in Canandaigua, choosing to list themselves through that city in both censuses. The ongoing success of William's business led him to describe himself in the 1910 census as a "Master Tailor."[71] His son's diary makes reference to a bath (which he often used) and a telephone at home, so it would be a mistake to consider the household as in any real sense financially disadvantaged, in the way that many blue-collar families in Muncie were during this period.

Robert himself was the youngest of three siblings. At the time of the diary his sisters were in high school; the older, Harriett, graduated in the same class as Landess Bloom in 1902, and the younger, Emily, in 1904. Robert appears to have been the least intellectual of the three, choosing to leave school before graduation in order to join his father in the tailoring business.

The fragmentary diary, partially written in pen with the latter sections in pencil, is contained in a slim memorandum booklet, and contains daily entries from Monday, February 11, to Wednesday, April 24, 1901. It then has a brief entry stating, "I quit writing for 7 mo[nths]," before picking up on December 6, 1901, and continuing until February 6, 1902. The final entry is on the booklet's end page. It is unclear whether parental encouragement, or possibly the receipt of the memorandum book as a gift from a friend, prompted him to keep a diary in the first place. On the inside front cover he wrote his name and address, as well as his age: "Robert Maggs,/107 Sutton St./Riverside/Muncie Ind/Age 13."[72] The address is of some importance since it shows that the family was living in Riverside, a newly constructed residential suburb that had sprung up as a consequence of the gas boom. Across the White River and more than a mile from the city center, Riverside was away from both from the bustle of the commercial district and the industrial development on the south side. Until 1903, when it became linked to the city by streetcar, access to Muncie was by foot or horse and buggy.

The Maggs family had previously lived closer in to the city center, at 708 East Adams Street, and it was when they were at this address that Robert's mother and elder sister, confusingly both named Harriett, became patrons of the Muncie Public Library. Perhaps because of the move to Riverside, neither Robert nor his younger sister, Emily, registered as library members.

The borrowing record of Mrs. Harriett Maggs, who first joined the library on November 17, 1894, but has no transactions recorded before August 10, 1895, and her daughter Harriett, who was just short of thirteen when she enrolled a few weeks later, on September 14, show that mother and daughter often took out books together, sometimes to the confusion of the librarian.

For example, on Saturday, November 2, 1895, Mrs. Maggs borrowed Martha Finley's *The Two Elsies*, while her daughter took out a volume of *The Forum*, a magazine that was almost certainly intended for her mother. They were next at the library together on Saturday, November 30, when Mrs. Maggs renewed a copy of another volume in Finley's series, *Elsie's Kith and Kin*, which she had taken out on her own two weeks before, and young Harriett borrowed still another, *Elsie's Friends at Woodburn*. It seems obvious that thirteen-year-old Harriett was going through an Elsie Dinsmore phase, for between mother and daughter at least fifteen of the popular series were borrowed within about six months. It is likely too that Harriett would have shared her choice of books with her ten-year-old sister, Emily, perhaps even reading them to her aloud. As we will see, reading books aloud, whether by a parent to the children or by the children to their younger siblings, was a habit encouraged in the Maggs household.

After Martha Finley, to whom she never returned, young Harriett soon graduated to Louisa May Alcott, Frances Hodgson Burnett, Susan Coolidge, and L. T. Meade. She even ventured into boys' fiction, checking out books by Horatio Alger and Thomas Bailey Aldrich. Her reading through July 1902, when she was nineteen and now a high school graduate, was age-appropriate. Her mother's borrowings within the same period show a continuation of her support of her daughters' reading and a fairly widespread choice of books for her own consumption.

Where does that leave young Robert, the third and last of the Maggs children? Because he never enrolled as a library patron, we have no direct access to his reading choices. Sifting through his mother's later borrowings from 1901 and 1902, which include such books as Macaulay's *History of England* and a variety of works of fiction set in colonial times, it seems unlikely that she was supporting her son's reading through the Muncie Public Library. The distance from Riverside made the library that much less accessible, though both of her daughters were traveling in to central Muncie to attend the high school. The library board had taken steps during the 1890s for readers living outside the city limits to obtain full borrowing privileges, but the distance may have deterred many of the residents of Riverside and other new suburbs from making the journey on a regular basis.[73]

Reading his diary leaves one with the immediate impression that traveling into Muncie to visit the library would not have been one of the priorities of thirteen-year-old Robert. Because of the gap in the diary, we have no record of how he entertained himself during the summer months. A characteristic winter entry, which also imparts a sense of the juvenile aspect of the diary as a whole, reads: "Wednesday Feb. 27 [1901] Fed my rabbits and went to school.

After school came home and got my skates and went skating. I skated until 5 oclock. And then came home. Dan Wilsey and Victor Martin came over we plaid crokinole [a board game] until 10 oclock and then they went home. I went to bed."

Typically, his afternoon activities would include playing ball games and marbles and socializing with his friends, but he would also help around the house, and sometimes at his father's shop. On one occasion, he describes how he and his friend Clarence Baldwin, the son of another local tradesman, put on their boots and went down to the White River, where they "broke off a large cake of ice and floated down the river" (February 1, 1902). The life of this young boy growing up in Muncie was jam-packed and fun-filled in a way that left little time for leisure reading or for intellectual pursuits outside school.

In fact, we have found only two mentions in his diary of private reading time, the first on a rainy day, when he sat down and "read until dinner was ready" (December 8, 1901), and the second that he "laid around home and read" while his parents were taking a ride in their buggy (January 5, 1902). On neither occasion does he divulge what he was reading. Far more significant, since it represents almost the only firsthand evidence of reading aloud at home that we have found, are a number of references to members of his family who read to him. We can take it as a given that parents, particularly mothers, read stories to their young children, but it is revealing to learn that, at least in this family, the habit continued into a child's teenage years. On March 10, 1901, also a rainy day, he writes: "After [afternoon] Sunday School Mamma read to me. Then I fed the cow and went to bed." All three of these events took place on a Sunday, when traditional Sabbath observance, without the playing of games or similar entertainments, remained de rigueur for most God-fearing Muncie families.[74]

Later in the same year, however, he records that on a Wednesday evening, "Mamma read—to me out of the book—Dri and I. I then went to bed" (December 18, 1901). The book in question, *D'ri and I,* was the latest best seller by the once well-known writer Irving Bacheller, a novel in the form of the fictional memoirs of an American colonel who fought against the British in the War of 1812. So popular was the book that in September 1901, shortly after it was published, the library acquired two copies. Between them, they were borrowed 111 times in the space of fourteen months, the volumes barely pausing on the shelf before being withdrawn by the next patron. Mrs. Maggs apparently read from her own copy. A passing mention in the diary of "go[ing] out to Shicks," Muncie's leading bookseller (see chapter 3), suggests that the Maggs family could afford to buy their own books and magazines (February 14, 1901).

In another entry Robert writes that his sister Emily "read me two stories out of the Youth's Companion" (March 4, 1901). *The Youth's Companion* was among the periodicals available at the library, but although Mrs. Maggs borrowed magazines not infrequently, this was not one of them as far as our records show. Whether the family subscribed to *The Youth's Companion* is unknown, but having it at home had a positive impact on at least two of the children. Writing about the 1920s, Robert and Helen Lynd were to observe that "there appears to be considerably less reading aloud by the entire family."[75] But to judge from this diary of 1901, it seems more than likely that the custom of oral reading still remained widespread among midwestern families at that time.[76]

From our point of view, the most enigmatic entry in Robert Maggs's diary is his short account of the single visit to the Muncie Public Library he described. After school one freezing Tuesday afternoon, Robert briefly notes, "[I] came home and got my overcoat and . . . then went up to the library for Lister Baldwin[;] he gave me a nickel" (March 12, 1901). He gives no more details than that. Lister Baldwin (born 1885) was the elder brother of Robert's close friend and playmate, Clarence (born 1888). Their father, Oliver Baldwin, was a successful Muncie grocer. Their mother, Sadie (née Lister), was a library patron, though we have no record of her borrowings. Lister himself did borrow books in the latter part of 1899 and early 1900, but not between then and when the extant records end. Neither the borrowing register nor the cash receipt books recording fines for overdue books help to enlighten us as to why Lister paid Robert Maggs to go to the library on his behalf. Since the library served as a reference center, a shrewd guess would be that Robert was sent there to look something up, perhaps having to do with a homework assignment. Statistics culled from the minutes of the library board show that in the first three months of 1901 the librarian fielded as many as 2,012 inquiries.[77]

The glimpse that we have from the diary he kept as a thirteen-year-old gives us no clues as to Roberts Maggs's progress later in life. Leaving school before graduation, initially to go to work for his father exactly as Tom Ryan had done, Robert went on to a varied career that included working for five years as a traveling reporter for the Bradstreet Commercial Agency. Toward the end of the Great War he took up real estate and made his mark in the development and construction of residential housing in Muncie's suburbs. When he died in 1967, a seventy-nine-year-old widower, he was again living in Riverside. His obituary states that "until his retirement, he was a realtor, and for the past several years had served on the Delaware County Tax Review Board."[78] Without his early diary, he would almost certainly have remained unsung. We may feel, however, that the life of Robert Maggs exemplifies the opportunities that lay ahead for a young man of no particular distinction growing up in a close and happy family environment in turn-of-the-century suburban Muncie. If in comparison with his siblings he was the least book-ish, that seems to have made little difference in terms of his later success.

Christine Pawley devotes a section of *Reading on the Middle Border* to the use of diaries as a key to individual reading.[79] The single diary that she was able to locate for her study of reading habits in Osage, Iowa, was kept by a local farmer's son, Charles Miller, and she describes it as both "laconically expressed" and "erratic." But since "any purchase warranted special mention" in the diary, it is valuable as a record of the stationery and newspapers he bought. Without undue modesty, we can say that the four Muncie diaries, examined in conjunction with the What Middletown Read database, provide us with more rewarding material. All four are written by young people, and thus if they lack an important perspective it is that of the older reader. Two other surviving diaries from the same period were copiously maintained by longtime Muncie residents of an older generation.

The first is the diary of Thomas Neely, who was born in Adams County, Pennsylvania, in 1811 and moved to Muncie in 1839, where he opened a black-smith's shop. The father of four children, he was a strong advocate of public education. When he retired from his work as a farrier, he opened a photog-raphy gallery that specialized in daguerreotypes. He started keeping a daily diary in 1860, but only the volumes from 1867 to his death in 1901 survive. Although he himself does not seem to have been a patron of the Muncie Public Library, at least three of his children were. The second diary was kept by Frederick Putnam, born in Charleston, New Hampshire, in 1818, who came to Muncie at about the same time as Neely, where he married and was also the father of four children. Putnam made his living in the hardware trade and took an active part in civic affairs, serving on the Common Council and as a school trustee. Unlike Neely, he did join the library; he is recorded as a stockholding patron from 1886. That he did not become a patron when the library opened in 1875 is perhaps an indicator that his main focus was else-where. He was a consistent though not prolific borrower between 1895 and 1899. The thirteen volumes of his diary date from 1846 to 1900, just a year before he died.[80]

Both the Neely and Putnam diaries are meticulous in recording the daily weather, the state of business, church issues, and local events, including mar-riages and deaths; neither makes mention of books. The circulation records for Putnam never correspond with entries in his diary that might mention visits to the library or his reaction to his reading. This is perhaps a generational thing; though each meticulous in the upkeep of his diary, neither Neely nor Putnam grew up in an era when books could commonly be borrowed from a library, and it is evident that the place of books in their respective lives was distinctly secondary. On the other hand, at least the first three young diarists whom we have profiled took library usage as a given, and their diaries are sprinkled with references and allusions to their reading. The impact of the library on their lives was profound, whereas it was far less central or consequential to the generation that preceded them.

Epilogue

Looking Backward,
Looking Forward

The home page of the Views of Readers, Readership, and Reading History website, part of the Harvard University Library Open Collections Program, is headlined with an observation by Robert Darnton: "Reading has become one of the hottest subjects in the humanities, perhaps because it seems especially intriguing now that so much of it has shifted from the printed page to the computer screen." A quarter of a century earlier, and well before the arrival of the Internet, Darnton had already claimed a shared patrimony between ourselves and our ancestors in the "activity" of reading, while also acknowledging that our own experience "can never be the same as what they experienced" and that our relation to the texts they read "cannot be the same as that of readers in the past." In trying to put ourselves into the same physical, cultural, and mental world of readers in times past, the best that we can hope for, he argues, is to "enjoy the illusion of stepping outside of time in order to make contact with authors who lived centuries ago."[1]

Reading, Darnton writes, "has a history," but the central question that he poses is "How can we recover it?" Unlike, say publishing, for which we have printed works as primary evidence, or the life of an author that might lend itself to biographical study, there is a transient aspect to solitary or even communal reading that makes it an experience less than easy to recover. Strategies that might be employed "to learn more about the ideals and assumptions underlying reading in the past," Darnton suggests, might include the study of "contemporary depictions of reading in fiction, autobiographies, polemical writings, letters, paintings, and prints in order to uncover some basic notions of what people thought took place when they read." However we approach the problem, it is evident from Darnton's discussion that the sources for the study of the historical experience of reading are piecemeal and, for the most part, hard to assemble into a coherent framework or meaningful argument.[2]

In the same essay, Darnton advances what has since become something of a commonplace or truism, that "studies of who read what at different times fall into two main types, the macro- and the microanalytical." The first of these— what he calls "macroanalysis"—finds focus in the mainly Franco-German tradition of analyzing reading tendencies through the broad sweep of "quantitative social history," whereas the primarily Anglo-American approach to figuring out who read what (and, where possible, personal responses to their reading), has relied far more on the "excessive detail" that emerges from the microanalytical study of such things as subscription lists, auction catalogs, and library registers.[3]

The challenge that emerges from each of these disparate approaches to the history of reading, as Darnton acknowledges, is that "the microanalysts have come up with [so] many . . . discoveries, . . . that they face the same problem as the macroquantifiers: how to put it all together?" While ruing the fact that much of the historical experience of reading is unrecoverable, Darnton offers a number of promising routes to learning "more about the ideals and assumptions underlying reading in the past." In addition to making use of portrayals of historical reading in works of fiction, autobiography, letters, works of art, and so forth, his suggestions include, among others, studying literacy levels in particular periods and social milieus, deciphering the marginalia inscribed in books by earlier readers, and conjoining aspects of literary theory (and particularly reader response theories) with the findings of historians of the book. As he concludes, "every narrative presupposes a reader, and every reading begins from a protocol inscribed within the text."[4]

While Darnton's call for a more broadly germinated and multifaceted approach to the study of the history of reading did not go unheeded when it was first made, it has required the advent of the new discipline of digital humanities to begin to realize the full import of his farsightedness.[5] This book arises from the convergence of recent scholarship on print culture history and the availability of technical tools that allow us to discern patterns within a mass of data. Part of our purpose in writing it is to demonstrate the value of the What Middletown Read database, and of similar digital tools, for exploring the history of print culture.

As of 2015, a number of separate projects that have been in various phases of development since around 2000 are beginning to yield their first fruits. One of these, which now can claim more than thirty thousand individual records, is the British-based Reading Experience Database 1450–1945 (RED), which collects and makes available, via an open-access database that welcomes public contributions, the responses of readers "derived from published and manuscript diaries, letters, journals, autobiographies and marginalia." The extensive and ambitious scope of the project inevitably means that there is a piecemeal quality to it, and its creators admit that its true value would remain incremental until the number of entries hit a "critical mass in terms of data necessary for RED to be of use to researchers and to have a lasting impact on the field."[6] Given the broad chronological parameters of the project and the relative haphazardness of its entries, it is perhaps disputable whether that "critical mass" has yet been reached. Arguably, a less open-ended and more focused project would sooner achieve impactful results.

In a 2011 essay, strategically placed as the final selection in a collection devoted to present-day interpretations of the history of reading, one of RED's managers lists eight things or elements that "we need to know" in order to make meaningful claims about the habits of reading of British readers "between 1450 and 1945[,] . . . who for the most part are no longer around to speak for themselves":

1. Who the readers were—their age, sex, class, nationality, region—and anything else we can find out about them
2. What they read
3. Where they read it
4. When they read
5. Whether they read silently or aloud to themselves or to others
6. What they thought of what they read or had read to them
7. How often they read
8. Whether the reading matter was bought, borrowed, or stolen, and from where.[7]

RED endeavors to record as many of these elements as are recoverable. Inevitably, the records of early reading tend to be sparse, and it is rare that all eight sought-after facets can be salvaged for any given entry. Nevertheless, the list provides a valuable template for those engaged in projects aimed at recovering the historical experience of reading.

Employing the same listed criteria throws beneficial light on the strengths and limitations of the What Middletown Read database and its associated material. The What Middletown Read project is at its weakest in being unable, except in the rare instances where we have diary entries, to record what readers "thought of what they read or had read to them," since almost none of the individual copies of books that belonged to the old Muncie Public Library have been traced, and of those that have been located, none contain significant annotations by readers. The closest that we can come to gauging the popularity of a particular work is by the crude measure of the frequency with which it was borrowed and the number of copies that were acquired by the library. Here, RED is potentially far more rewarding, since its primary purpose is to provide a record of readers' responses, whether in diaries, marginalia, or other sources, to the books they read. But the random or fragmented quality of its records at the present time often leaves much to be desired.[8]

Where the What Middletown Read project scores heavily is in providing instruments to establish those sought-after details of a reader's age, sex, social class, and nationality. In addition, through census records and other historical sources, we have been able to list the occupation, parentage, marital status, race, and a host of other details for individual patrons. Admittedly, we were unable to do this for a large number of readers whose names could not be found in surviving census records, city directories, or other sources. The loss by fire of the 1890 U.S. census deprived us of much potential information that would have helped extend the profiles of readers. Nevertheless, of the 6,328 patrons who joined the library between 1876 and 1902, we have gleaned additional demographic information on more than 3,000, and for many of them we are able to record such details as their place of birth, appearance in city directories, and even, in the case of foreign-born patrons, their naturalization status and the year of immigration.[9] The latter details can be useful for tracing patterns of acculturation.

For each individual reader, the evidence of "what they read" is copious, since the database allows a searcher to discover with ease what books were borrowed by any individual patron. In some cases a reader borrowed only a single book in the time covered by the surviving records. At the opposite end, more than thirty individual readers each accounted for over three hundred books borrowed, and two of them for over six hundred; well over one hundred patrons borrowed over two hundred books each.[10]

Experimental research using the What Middletown Read database being conducted by Stephen Pentecost at Washington University in St. Louis, in close cooperation with Ball State's Center for Middletown Studies, presents in a series of online graphic visualizations, a "Market Basket Analysis" of which authors or titles tend to occur together in borrowers' histories. His extraordinary graphics allow us to go beyond reading by individuals and distinguish broader patterns of borrowing by different groups. Pentecost breaks down his analysis by authors and titles, and in doing so lets us visualize important differences "between male, female and age-group reading, and especially between young male and female readers."[11] It is an early example of some of the more sophisticated findings that can be derived from the What Middletown Read database. As should be evident from the present study, selective research into the reading patterns of individuals and groups helps give us a better sense of the role of the library in the life of the user, an approach to public library historiography that, as we noted earlier, has been strongly advocated by Wayne A. Wiegand. The What Middletown Read database privileges the user, while also acknowledging that it is indebted only to a single source (the public library in Muncie) for all the borrowing that it records.

As for other elements put forward by the RED team insofar as they may be applied to the What Middletown Read project, the addresses of patrons recorded in the library's "Registration of Book Borrowers" ledger at the time of joining allow us to ascertain with some accuracy *where* individual books were read, though, unless a new address was entered later, it does not take into account individuals who moved or the possibility that books were read elsewhere.

The recorded location of readers has a more crucial part to play for RED, which has much broader geographical parameters, whereas books borrowed from the Muncie Public Library were self-evidently most often taken out to be read in the immediate locality. We have taken preliminary steps toward employing GIS (Geographic Information Systems) to map the spatial distribution of the residences of the library's patrons. From this, we believe it will be possible to create sociocultural visualizations of the city's demographic divisions. A pilot foray utilizing GIS conducted by one of our team exemplified that the popular expression "from the wrong side of the tracks" holds true for Muncie: the city's old railroad tracks formed a distinct physical barrier between wealthier and more economically privileged patrons, who tended to have homes north of the tracks and south of the White River, and a much sparser population of readers from blue-collar neighborhoods to the south of the tracks. As the Lynds recognized in the 1920s, "the mere fact of being born upon one or other side of the watershed roughly formed by these two groups is the most significant single cultural factor tending to influence what one does all day long throughout one's life."[12] It is surely not without significance that such divisions are already mirrored in the cultural life of the city's readers of the 1890s.

The question of "When they read" again takes on a different dimension in the context of our project. For a database that purports to cover an approx-

imately six-hundred-year period, the chronological dating of entries is crucial, and RED's compilers are quite scrupulous in including this important
detail whenever possible. The What Middletown Read database, although
it contains approximately 175,000 transactions, all dated, covers borrowing
activities for a far shorter period of less than a dozen years, with the consequence that the date of any particular transaction is, in most cases, of far less
consequence to the overall scheme. But "*When* they read" takes on a second
meaning for us, since one of the primary elements of the our database is
its capacity to search for readers of any given age. It has thus allowed us to
explore with some precision what children and older people were reading.
It also gives us almost unprecedented insight into "How often they read,"
through the chronological tabulation of books borrowed by any given reader,
and the answer to "Whether the reading matter was bought, borrowed or stolen" is, in our case unproblematic, since all the borrowing was from a single
institution. Finally, the question of "whether they read silently or aloud to
themselves or to others" remains speculative, although we have endeavored
to address this issue in our discussion of book clubs, in the opening section of
chapter 4, which deals with lighting, and in our accounts of reading activity
derived from diaries.

This discussion may give the misleading impression that the What
Middletown Read project is in some ways in competition with RED. Nothing
could be further from the truth, since the two have different objectives, the
one significant overlapping factor being the desire to retrieve evidence of
historical reading. From that factor alone it should be obvious that there is
much to learn from comparison of the two projects.

Using Darnton's distinction between the macroanalytical and microanalytical, it can be argued that the scope of RED, with its bold aim of revealing "the reading practices of our ancestors," places it in the macro category,
whereas the study of reading habits in late nineteenth-century Muncie,
Indiana, belongs with the microanalytical. Yet, at least implicitly, Darnton's
simultaneous recognition that both types of research share the problem of
"how to put it all together" presupposes that even a study with the kind of
particularity of the What Middletown Read project may contain within it the
seeds or essence of the macroanalytical, insofar as our discrete findings may
typify a far broader picture. At the most rudimentary level, the database and
our monograph can be viewed as no more than a portrayal of fin-de-siècle
reading habits in one small town in the American Midwest. As with debates
about Middletown, it can be argued and remains a moot point whether our
findings can be considered representative of broader reading habits in late
nineteenth-century America. If, in common with other such field work, we

are unable to recover the actual reading experience as it happened, we believe that our database provides a decipherable palimpsest of what people read at a critical moment in the history of the United States and in the development of its public libraries.

It is our deepest hope that the attention the What Middletown Read database has so far gained will prompt parallel research that will go a long way toward refining our understanding of how typical or otherwise are the results from Muncie. The work of such scholars as Dee Garrison, Joanne Passet, Elizabeth Long, Wayne Wiegand, Christine Pawley, Evelyn Geller, Carl Kaestle, and a host of others who have labored in the trenches of turn-of-the-century American library and reading history leads us to believe that there is much that is typical about the old Muncie Public Library as a pre-Carnegie library. No less, the transition to the new Carnegie Library tells what should by now be considered a familiar story. It bears repeating that Andrew Carnegie's prodigious endeavor to implement a democratization of knowledge through the building of public libraries was replicated in more than sixteen hundred communities across the United States and Canada.

The progress of the Muncie Public Library beyond the opening years of the twentieth century remains outside the scope of the present study. The absence of preserved day-to-day borrowing records of the kind that were religiously kept in the era of Kate Wilson leaves a void that effectively relegates the interest of the new Carnegie library to a level no greater than many others of its ilk. In the years following the opening of the new library, there was an exponential increase in the number of its books and patrons. A letter from the library board to Andrew Carnegie dated February 14, 1907, notes that in 1903 "there were 15,291 books in the library; 35,077 books were circulated; 9618 readers used the reading room; and 1777 new borrowers were enrolled. In 1906 there were 22,750 books in the library; 77,765 books were circulated; 23,019 readers used the Reading room; and 1,934 new borrowers were enrolled." The letter goes on to interpret these figures statistically by noting that "the increase in circulation from 1903, the last year in the old quarters, to 1907, is over 42,000, or 120%; and that the increase is more than the entire circulation of 1903. The number of readers in 1906 is almost 2½ times the number in 1903."[13]

The purpose of the letter to Carnegie was secondarily to show to its main benefactor "that the library is highly appreciated by the citizens" of Muncie, but primarily to ask for more money. In making its case, the board averred that when the new library was built, "the needs of the community were underestimated." With a calculated increase of the city's population from just under 21,000 in 1900 to some 35,000 in 1907, the board now wished to build an extension to the library in order to open up more space and also to house a collection of "valuable medical and historical books" that were piled up without ready access in its basement. The letter, which also included details of the city's income from local taxation, ended with a deferential plea of hope that their proposal "will be in keeping with your splendid scheme of public benefaction." Accompanying it was a now-lost architectural sketch of the "proposed extension to our present building, which would cost about $25,000."

The reply from Carnegie's office, dated February 25, is short and begins peremptorily: "Yours of 14th received. Mr. Carnegie cannot consider adding to the amount already provided for a Library Building for Muncie." It also suggests that rather than building an extension, the board should consider as "a wise form of expansion" the opening of a branch library "at some distance from the existing building." As a slap in the face for the proposal to build on to the existing edifice, it added that "a very slight examination shows that what was sought in erecting it was an architectural feature and not the most accommodation that could be had for the money consistent with good taste."[14] The reply, which is both pragmatic and sensible as well as consistent with Carnegie's general policy, reminds us of the competing civic and educational objectives that informed Muncie's pursuit of his support. For the Muncie Public Library, the goose that laid the golden egg had been called upon once too often.

It was essentially the same library that drew the attention of the Lynds in the 1920s, and they tabulated the increase in its use by subject categories in the twenty years since its opening:

> During the twenty years between 1903, the first year for which library circulation figures are available, and 1923, while the population less than doubled and the reading of library books in the adult department of the library increased more than fourfold, reading of library books on useful arts increased sixty-two-fold; on the fine arts twenty-eight-fold; on philosophy, psychology, etc., twenty-six-fold; on religion . . . elevenfold; on the institutional devices involved in group life, sociology, economics, etc., ninefold; on history eightfold; on science sixfold; of fiction less than fourfold. . . . [I]n 1903, 92 per cent. of all the library books read by adults were fiction, as against 83 per cent. in 1923. Under a trained children's librarian the reading of fiction by children has decreased from 90 per cent. of the total of books read in 1903 to 67 per cent. in 1923.[15]

The Muncie of the 1920s described in their book was even more divided than in the 1890s. "The poorer working man," they wrote, entered his "bare one-story oblong wooden box" of a home through the living room, from which "the whole house is visible . . . swarming with flies and . . . musty with stale odors of food, clothing, and tobacco," whereas the typical wealthy owner resided in a home with "large parlors and library . . . an atmosphere of quiet and space . . . [and] open book-shelves with sets of Mark Twain and Eugene Field and standard modern novels."[16] Willy-nilly, industrial Muncie during the early twentieth century did much to perpetuate these distinctions, reserving a culture of highbrow reading, at least for the most part, to those who could afford it.

In broad strokes, these patterns continued through much of the twentieth century, although the role of the library changed to some extent. In their second book, *Middletown in Transition*, the Lynds reported a circulation increase of 145% between 1929 and 1933, a jump no doubt spurred in part by the need to forgo the purchase of books during the Great Depression, as well as a desire for escape. ("Middletown reads more books in bad times and fewer in good times," they noted.) The circulation of fiction nearly doubled during that time.

But the post–World War II period saw a reversion to the trend the Lynds had identified during the 1920s, in which fiction made up a lesser portion of overall circulation. By 1967, it accounted for just over half—55 percent—of books borrowed by adults. More generally, only one in three local residents held a library card by that time, down from six in ten in 1935. The city librarian saw the "present role" of the main (Carnegie) Library as "a sort of central depository for reference, technical, historical, and other informational matter," rather than as a supplier of entertaining fiction. In a pattern that would be familiar to the Lynds, or to observers of library use during the 1890s, borrowing rates were noticeably higher at the branch in the middle-class section of town than they were at the branch located in the city's blue-collar district. Today, the Carnegie Library houses local history and genealogical resources, while its two branch libraries maintain circulation collections, and fiction constitutes a substantial portion of their loans.[17]

In his foreword to the original edition of the Lynds' iconic study, the anthropologist Clark Wissler praised the authors "for their foresight in revealing the Middletown of 1890 as a genesis of the Middletown of today, not as a contrast." Yet the Lynds also gave prominence to the technological divide between 1890 and their own era, speculating in particular on the changes brought about by the advent of the automobile and motion pictures. If they found continuity in their understanding of the cultural life of the city, it was in their investigation of the place of reading, which they interpreted, with the limited exception of a minority of the business class, as "overwhelmingly . . . the reading of public library books." In 1924, they calculated, about 6,500 public library books were borrowed for each 1,000 citizens, compared to 850 per thousand in 1890.[18]

The 1890s were truly an era of genesis. Indeed, as we look back at Muncie's culture of print during the late nineteenth century, it more closely resembles what the Lynds found thirty years later than what had existed thirty years before. The expansion of the book trade during the 1880s and 1890s ensured that people living in a city such as Muncie had access to an extensive array of printed material, something their predecessors at the time of the Civil War could not claim. During the gas-boom era a resident of Muncie could obtain books on loan from the library, purchase them from a local shop, or order them directly from publishers and wholesalers. Magazine circulation grew dramatically, and newspapers increased in both number and size. If residing in a household of at least modest means, one could read at home by gaslight instead of a flickering flame during the 1890s, and within a few years would be able to rely on electricity. By the 1890s, Munsonians were awash in print, and would remain so.

The ubiquity of print allowed Muncie's readers to engage with the world more extensively and, for those who wished to, more intensely than we might imagine. From the perspective of the globalizing twenty-first century, it is tempting to imagine the Muncie of the late nineteenth century as isolated and provincial. But our investigation reveals that the intensification of print circulation made much of the world accessible through reading, including both fiction and nonfiction. The representations of life beyond the city limits found in novels, travel literature, magazine illustrations, and newspaper reports may have presented a picture of the world shaped by the prevailing prejudices of the day, but even so, those depictions cultivated an awareness of distant places and a sense of connection to a broad, ascendant civilization.

Engagement with the world through print was entangled with class formation. Muncie's social order was in the process of being sorted throughout the 1890s and the first years of the twentieth century. As the ranks of the laboring classes swelled, the city's middle-class minority felt more urgently the need to distinguish themselves from the masses. Reading was one way in which they did this. As the circulation data of the Muncie Public Library attests, most of those who borrowed books—particularly recently published books—and magazines came from white-collar households. Reading the latest novel or the most popular magazines was middle-class behavior, or more precisely, middle-class female behavior. It offered women from white-collar circumstances a shared experience and a common fund of cultural knowledge that identified them as a group. The relative absence of blue-collar adult borrowers in our data is not an indication that reading ended when industrial labor began. Rather, they turned to newspapers and other kinds of reading and, if the library records are any indication, were less concerned about reading the newest and most current material.

These patterns shaped the library, both as a social space and as an institution. From the moment it opened its doors, it was a site defined by the presence of children and women. Their presence, and the rules of decorum the library enforced, made it a less attractive setting for adult men, particularly those of a blue-collar background. The borrowers the library did attract created demand for certain kinds of titles, a demand that for the most part the library's leadership strived to meet. Although the library's board members and its most ardent advocates sought books they thought would mold borrowers into morally upright citizens, the informal character of day-to-day operations ensured that in practice the library sought to accommodate its users more than it did to discipline them. To a considerable degree, this indulgent quality diminished under Artena Chapin's professional management and the transition to the Carnegie Library, and, as the Lynds reported, a shift in library borrowing patterns followed.

The experience of reading that unfolded after a book had been borrowed remains largely elusive. Nonetheless, by examining both individual and collective borrowing choices in the context of community life, including schools, clubs, families, and the library itself, we gain some sense of the role of reading and of the public library in the life of Middletown's residents. If in later years reading lost ground to radio, television, and eventually the Internet, it was, during the years spanned by the What Middletown Read database, a central element in their lives, one that helped them define their community and make sense of its place in the wider world.

It took until 2003, when the Carnegie Library was undergoing major renovation in anticipation of its centenary, for the nineteenth-century library records on which the What Middletown Read project is based to be rediscovered. Their survival in the attics was remarkable in itself, given a leaky roof, nesting pigeons, and the presence of vermin. Their fragile condition, let alone their intrinsic documentary value, was reason enough to conserve the originals and to preserve them for later generations in digital form. But the most serendipitous aspect of the trove lies in the fact that, of all places, it was discovered in Muncie, Indiana, the now post-industrial small city that since the 1920s has borne the parallel name "Middletown." The bird's-eye view of the "activity" of reading within that era granted to us by the tools of present-day technology is uniquely complemented by a welter of accrued historical scholarship and knowledge deriving from almost a century of Middletown studies. In its latest manifestation, what is arguably the most widely researched small city in America has revealed itself as a new focal point for the emergent study of reading. As a handy vehicle for deciphering what people read, the "Magic City" of the 1890s still casts a somewhat potent spell.

Appendix

The What Middletown Read Database

The What Middletown Read database arose from the chance discovery during the 2003 renovations of the Muncie Public Library of a set of dusty ledgers. They included a register of the names and addresses of every patron who had joined the library between its opening in 1875 and June 1904, and two volumes of the accession catalog, listing each book acquired by the library for roughly the same interval (1875 to March 1903). Most important, the cache contained twenty-five slim, decaying notebooks with penciled listings recording each circulation transaction for most of the period between November 6, 1891, and December 3, 1902. (Ledgers covering May 28, 1892, to November 5, 1894 were missing, probably because library staff destroyed them as a precaution after an 1893 smallpox epidemic.) Soon after their discovery, Frank Felsenstein visited the library in search of materials for a book history class he was teaching at Ball State University. He found the collection of ledgers in a handful of unlabeled boxes on a shelf. Recognizing their value for understanding reading behavior, he enlisted the cooperation of the university's Center for Middletown Studies, along with Ball State University Libraries, and set in motion a six-year effort to convert the ledgers into a searchable online database. That resource, the What Middletown Read database, is available online at www.bsu.edu/libraries/wmr.

The three interrelated sets of handwritten ledgers form the bedrock of the database. The circulation ledgers (fig. 13) record each loan in a simple man-

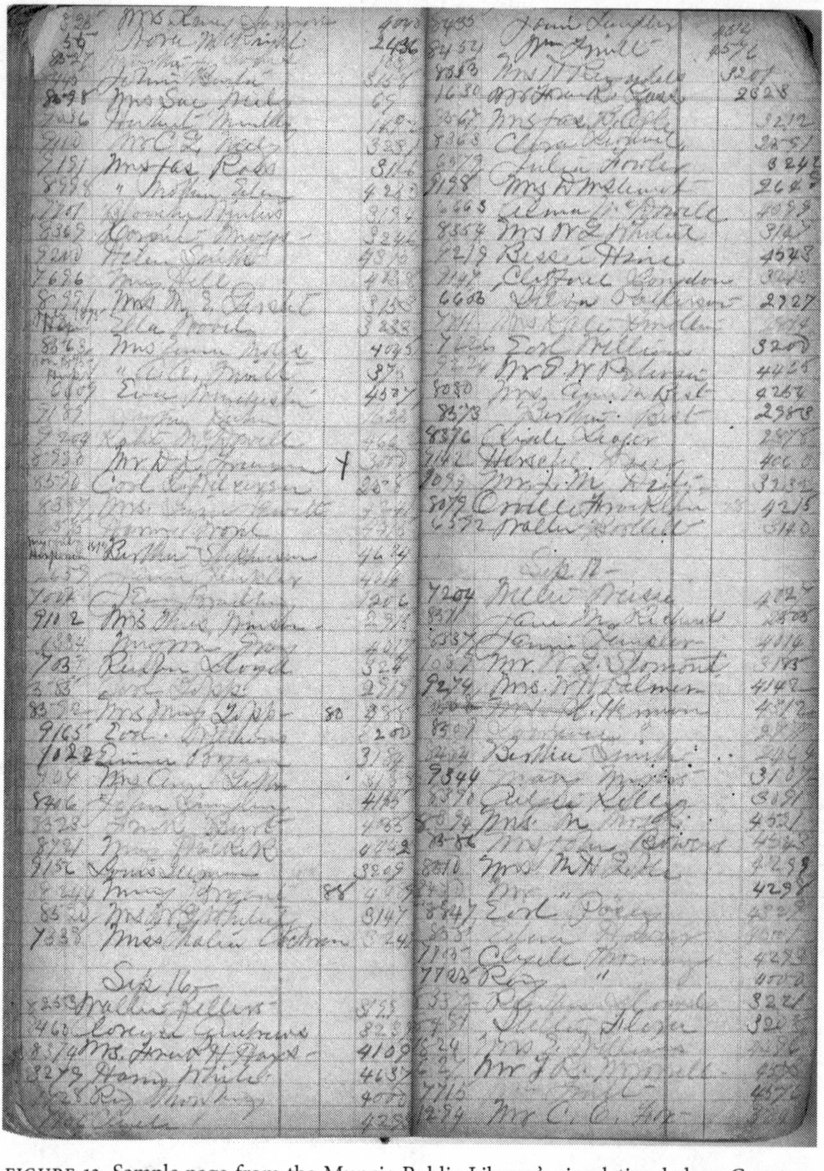

FIGURE 13. Sample page from the Muncie Public Library's circulation ledger. Courtesy Muncie Public Library.

ner. Along the left side of the page the staff ordinarily recorded the number of the book loaned, which corresponded to the number listed in the accession catalog. Along the right they listed the number of the patron borrowing the book, which was the number assigned in the register of borrowers. In

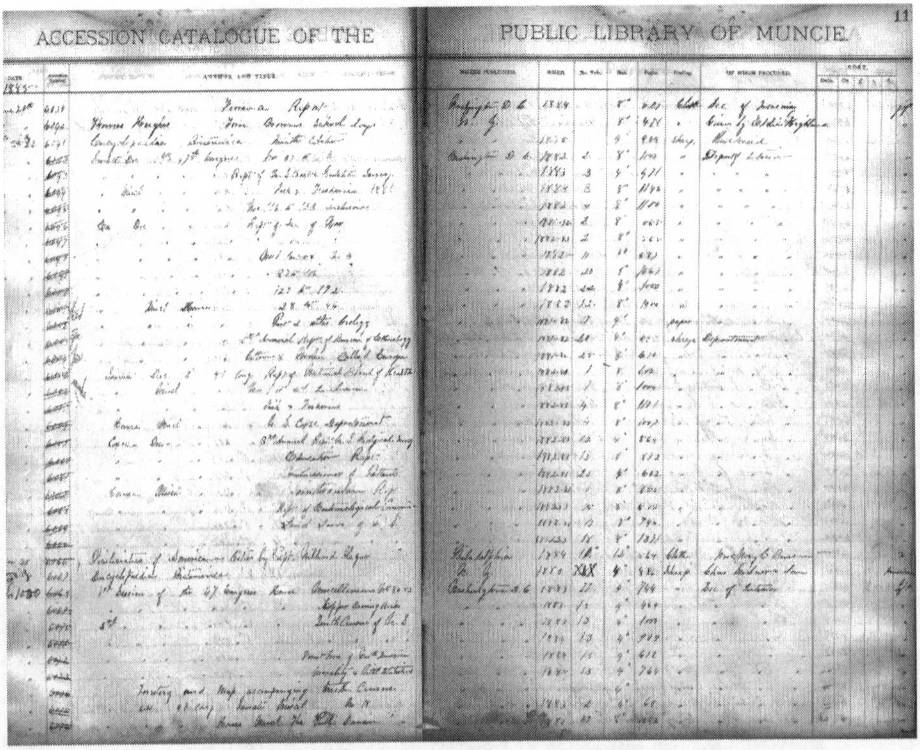

FIGURE 14. Sample page from the Muncie Public Library's accession catalog. Courtesy Muncie Public Library.

a wider central column they wrote the name of the borrower, which, as we will see, did not always correspond to the patron number listed. Surprisingly, no space was left in these ledgers to record the return of a book, though surviving fine books do make it evident that a late return incurred a penalty charge. The borrowers' register assigned numbers consecutively, in the order in which patrons joined the library; the accession catalog employed the same method for the books as they were acquired. The database simply reproduces this system in digital, searchable form.

Each ledger contained space for particular pieces of information. In the case of the two-volume accession catalog (fig. 14), the information recorded changed slightly when the library made the transition from one ledger book to the next. The first volume included listings for the date acquired, number assigned, author, title, location of publication, date (year) of publication, number of volumes, size, number of pages, binding type, the provenance ("Of Whom Procured"), and cost (including columns for dollars and cents as well as for pounds, shillings, and pence). The second volume, which the library began using on March 23, 1900 (beginning with book number 11,672), added a column for the name of the publisher and dropped the columns for British currency. The "Registration of Book-Borrowers" ledger (fig. 15) listed the date a patron joined the library, his or her number, name and address, and the name and address of a guarantor (who vouched for the applicant). (The 364 people who purchased stock in the library, most of whom also joined as borrowers during the 1870s, did not need to supply a guarantor, and word "stock" was listed in that spot.)

Information recorded in the borrowers' register and the accession catalog allowed our researchers to provide additional information about some of the patrons and almost all of the books. Using the addresses listed in the borrowers' register, we located patrons in a city directory for the year in which they joined the library, or, when necessary, the directory with the closest possible year of publication. Using both the information from the original record and from the city directory, we searched for each patron in the 1900 U.S. census and recorded demographic details for each one we located.[1] In total, we provided at least some information on 3,295 patrons, although not all of them were active borrowers during the period documented by the surviving circulation ledgers. Information derived from the census included the name (as recorded in the census data), race, sex, marital status, year of birth, place of birth, year immigrated (if applicable), naturalization status (if applicable), mother's place of birth, father's place of birth, whether owning or renting home, number of servants in household, number of boarders in household, and occupation. Obviously, not every category listed here applied to every patron for whom we found a listing in the census.[2]

The staff involved in the creation of the What Middletown Read database added three additional pieces of information to patron profiles. Two of these derived from occupation listed in the census, either for the patron himself or herself or, in the case of many children and some women for whom such information was not recorded, for the head of the household. We classified those occupations using the scale first developed by Alba Edwards.[3] An attraction of Edwards's twelve-category system is its flexibility; it allows other scholars to reconfigure the data into different groupings as they see fit. The database includes two categorizations: Occupational Group (either white-collar or blue-collar) and Occupational Rank (with a more graduated scale that splits occupations into high white-collar, low white-collar, skilled, semiskilled, and unskilled). These somewhat crude classifications have been used by many past statistical analyses, making the What Middletown Read data more easily comparable to other scholarship.

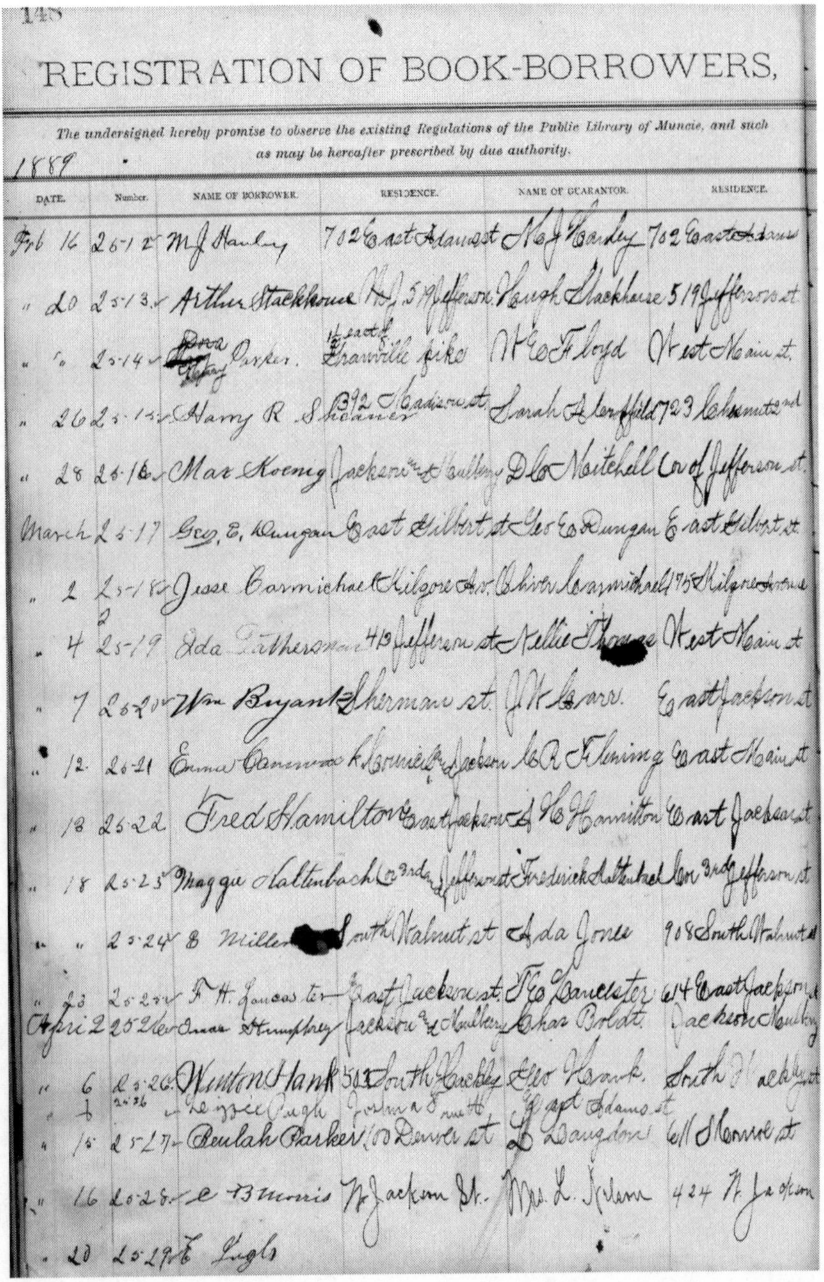

148

REGISTRATION OF BOOK-BORROWERS,

The undersigned hereby promise to observe the existing Regulations of the Public Library of Muncie, and such as may be hereafter prescribed by due authority.

1889

DATE.	Number.	NAME OF BORROWER.	RESIDENCE.	NAME OF GUARANTOR.	RESIDENCE.
Feb 16	2512	M J Hanley	702 East Adams st	M J Hanley	702 East Adams
" 20	2513	Arthur Stackhouse	519 Jefferson	Hugh Stackhouse	519 Jefferson st
" "	2514	[illegible] Parker	east of Granville pike	W E Floyd	West Main st.
" 26	2515	Harry R Skinner	812 Madison st	Sarah Stanffild	723 Chestnut st
" 28	2516	Max Koenig	Jackson & Mulberry	D C Mitchell	Cor of Jefferson st.
March 2	2517	Geo. E. Dungan	East Gilbert st	Geo E Dungan	East Gilbert st
" 2	2518	Jesse Carmichael	Kilgore Av.	Oliver Carmichael	175 Kilgore Avenue
" 4	2519	Ida Patterson	413 Jefferson st	Nellie Thomas	West Main st
" 7	2520	Wm Bryant	Sherman st.	J W Carr	East Jackson st
" 12	2521	Emma Cammack	Cor Mulberry & Jackson	C R Fleming	East Main st
" 13	2522	Fred Hamilton	East Jackson	J H Hamilton	East Jackson st
" 18	2523	Maggie Kaltenbach	Cor 3rd & Jefferson st	Frederick Kaltenbach	Cor 3rd & Jefferson st
" "	2524	B Miller	[illegible] South Walnut st	Ada Jones	908 South Walnut st
" 23	2525	F. H. Lancaster	East Jackson st	F C Lancaster	614 East Jackson
April 2	2526	Emma Humphrey	Jackson & Mulberry	Chas Boldt	Jackson & Mulberry
" 6	2526	Winton Hank	503 South Hackley	Geo Hank	South Hackley st
" 8	2526	Lizzie Pugh	Jackson & Walnut	[illegible]	East Adams st
" 15	2527	Beulah Parker	10 Denver st	L Langdon	611 Monroe st
" 16	2528	C B Morris	N Jackson St.	Mrs. L. [illegible]	424 N Jackson
" 20	2529	E Pugh			

FIGURE 15. Sample page from the Muncie Public Library's register of borrowers. Courtesy Muncie Public Library.

The database also includes one further demographic detail for many of the patrons whose listing we could not locate in the census records. Whenever the matter was clear-cut, we assigned a gender category for patrons based on their names. This step, which allowed us to classify 5,708 patrons according to sex even though we only have census data for 3,295, permits a more robust exploration of male and female reading choices. While it runs the risk that a name will mislead us about the person's sex, such errors are likely to be exceedingly rare.

Working from the author, title, and other information recorded in the accession catalog, staff from Ball State University Libraries searched other resources, including the Library of Congress catalog, the WorldCat database, and the 1905 printed catalog of the Muncie Public Library, to locate additional bibliographic information about each of the 11,591 titles listed in the database, including standardized name and title, standardized publisher listing, and Library of Congress subject headings. Whenever possible, they provided this additional information from records of the exact edition of the book in question. Inaccuracies and incomplete entries in the accession catalog made it impossible to locate every book with precision, however. In other cases, current cataloging sources did not provide information about the specific edition described in the library's records, and in such cases the database includes information about the most comparable version of the book.

It is possible for database users to conduct searches using demographic variables such as sex, race, and occupation, or to formulate queries around bibliographic categories such as author, publisher, or subject. Searches that combine these and other variables are also possible, so that, for instance, a search for married women who borrowed books written by Louisa May Alcott would yield a list of all such women, all of the books they borrowed, and a list of the individual loans that fit these parameters. All of the categories derived from original library records, as well as the information gleaned from supplemental sources such as the U.S. census, are searchable, singly or in combination. Search results can be downloaded as a comma-delimited file, which permits further and more complex statistical analysis. (For further details on search methods, consult the User's Guide on the What Middletown Read website.)

In total, the database records 176,912 circulation transactions, 1,694 of which are incomplete. The 175,218 complete transaction records involved 4,008 patrons and 5,972 books or magazines. As these figures make clear, not every one of the 6,328 patrons listed in the database borrowed from the library during the period covered. Likewise, nearly half of the 11,591 titles listed did not circulate at all (many of them were government reports sent to the library in its role as a federal depository). Among the patrons who did not borrow are many who joined the library in its early days and either died or moved away before the extant circulation records began in November 1891.

Search results derived from the database must be employed with care. While every effort has been made to enter accurate and complete information, errors are inevitable, particularly in a project based on deteriorated paper records. Apart from simple transcription errors, unclear handwriting often required researchers to enter their best approximation of what appears on the page, and this was especially a problem in the circulation ledgers, where names were frequently written with evident haste. Some information was lost because fragments of pages are missing. There were errors in the original sources as well; library workers were not always consistent or accurate in their own record keeping, assigning duplicate numbers to multiple books or patrons, incorrectly recording patron or book numbers in the circulation record, or simply entering erroneous information. When sufficiently clear, we have corrected such mistakes, but in many cases we could not correct with confidence and so have left the information as we found it. In the case of duplicate accession numbers we have eliminated both entries from the database to avoid confusion and misleading search results. With these cautions in mind, we again advise careful scrutiny of results derived from the database. It is also worth noting that we will make corrections as new information becomes available. For that reason the data may change slightly over time. The statistics and other information drawn from the database that we present in this book are up to date as of January 2015.

Two other practices of the Muncie Public Library staff bear mention. As we have noted several times in the preceding chapters, when materials were checked out staff recorded the name of the borrower and a patron number, and in some instances the borrower used a patron number that belonged to another person. To address this "borrowed card" issue, transactions listed in search results include both the name of the borrower and the name associated with the patron number. Comparing the two fields allows users to verify instances of actual borrowed cards as well as cases involving variations of the same name, either in the original record or because of transcription errors.

Another practice of library staff members involved loans of individual issues of magazines. The library subscribed to a number of popular magazines during the period covered by the What Middletown Read database, and patrons were permitted to borrow both individual issues and bound volumes. Individual issues of magazines did not have accession numbers, which were assigned only after a yearly volume was bound at a later date. To record transactions involving unbound magazines, staff simply wrote an abbreviated title and issue date in the circulation ledgers (e.g., "Scrib., Oct. 95" for the October 1895 issue of *Scribner's Monthly*) in the field for the book number. Thus a search for a magazine title in the transaction comments field using the Advanced Search tool may produce additional circulation transactions involving that periodical.

To make transactions involving periodicals more searchable, we have assigned the accession number of the bound volume that includes the relevant issue whenever possible, but this could not be done for every circulation transaction involving a magazine. The titles listed in some transaction records were illegible; others listed issues or titles that were not bound during the period covered by the extant transaction records and thus have no accession number available. Whenever a patron borrowed a single, unbound issue of a magazine, the issue date listed in the circulation ledger is recorded in the comments section included in the transaction search results.

One way to confirm the results of particular searches is to explore digitized versions of the original sources. All search results returned by the database include links to scans of original records stored in Ball State University's Digital Media Repository, http://libx.bsu.edu. Listed under the "Original Documents" heading in the search results table, the "View Page" link for each record opens a new browser window or tab that displays a scan of the original ledger page from which that record was entered. These scans, as well as scans of Muncie Public Library board minutes, circulation statistics, a "check book" recording the library's periodical subscriptions, and mailers from various publishers, are gathered in the "Muncie Public Library Historic Documents" section of the Digital Media Repository. If users discover any errors in the database through their consultation of these sources, they may submit corrections through the "Feedback" link at the bottom of What Middletown Read website pages. We welcome questions and comments about the database through that avenue as well.

Notes

Abbreviations

BSU-DMR
Ball State University Digital Media Repository, http://libx.bsu.edu. Unless otherwise noted, the collection is Muncie Public Library Historic Documents.

BSUL
Archives and Special Collections, Ball State University Libraries, Muncie, Ind.

Carnegie Records
Carnegie Corporation of New York Records, 1872–2000, Rare Book and Manuscript Library, Columbia University Libraries, New York

MDC-DRL
Muncie / Delaware County Digital Resource Library, www.munciepubliclibrary.org

MPL
Muncie Public Library, Muncie, Ind.

MPL minutes
"Muncie Public Library Board Minutes and Reports, 1874–1902," handwritten account book, MPL; scans available at BSU-DMR.

Introduction

1. 1900 U.S. census, s.v. "Maude Smith," Muncie, Delaware County, Ind.; 1930 U.S. census, s.v. "Maude Allison," Toledo City, Lucas County, Ohio; and 1962 U.S. Social Security Death Index, "Maude Allison," all accessed via Ancestry.com. Muncie Central High School class list, Indiana County History, www.countyhistory.com.

2. G. W. H. Kemper, ed., *A Twentieth Century History of Delaware County, Indiana*, 2 vols. (Chicago: Lewis Publishing Company, 1908), 1:485.

3. The What Middletown Read database is roughly ten times larger than the similar body of data compiled by Christine Pawley in her pioneering work, *Reading on the Middle Border: The Culture of Print in Late-Nineteenth-Century Osage, Iowa* (Amherst: University of Massachusetts Press, 2001). That material is not available online.

4. Ibid., 114. Pawley notes that Emily Todd made a similar argument in her analysis of circulation records from the Richmond [Virginia] Library Company in " 'Binge Reading' and Historical Fiction: A Study of the Richmond Library Company's Borrowing Records (1839–1860)," paper presented at the annual meeting of the Society for Authorship, Reading, and Publishing, Madison, Wisc., July 1999, note 97.

5. Robert S. Lynd and Helen Merrell Lynd, *Middletown: A Study in Modern American Culture* (1929; repr., New York: Harcourt, Brace, 1957); Robert S. Lynd and Helen Merrell Lynd, *Middletown in Transition: A Study in Cultural Conflicts* (1937; repr., New York: Harcourt, Brace, 1965). On the issue of *Middletown* and Muncie's typicality, see Sarah E. Igo, *The Averaged American: Surveys, Citizens, and the Making of a Mass Public* (Cambridge: Harvard University Press, 2007), 20–102; and James J. Connolly, "The Legacies of *Middletown*," *Indiana Magazine of History* 101.3 (September 2005): 211–25.

6. Lynd and Lynd, *Middletown*, 229–39.

7. Wayne A. Wiegand makes this point in "To Reposition a Research Agenda: What American Studies Can Teach the LIS Community about the Library in the Life of the User," *Library Quarterly* 73.4 (October 2003): 369–82. See also his essay "The American Public Library: Construction of a Community Reading Institution," in *A History of the Book in America*, vol. 4: *Print in Motion: The Expansion of Publishing and Reading in the United States, 1880–1940*, ed. Carl F. Kaestle and Janice A. Radway (Chapel Hill: University of North Carolina Press, 2009), 431–51. The important example of reader-centered library history is Pawley, *Reading on the Middle Border*, particularly chap. 3. Key works on the movement to create public libraries in the United States that describe it as a democratic impulse include Robert Ellis Lee, *Continuing Education for Adults through the American Public Library, 1833–1964* (Chicago: American Public Library Association, 1966); Sidney Ditzion, *Arsenals of a Democratic Culture: A Social History of the American Public Library Movement in New England and the Middle States from 1850–1900* (Chicago: American Public Library Association, 1947); and Jesse Shera, *Foundations of the Public Library* (Chicago: University of Chicago Press, 1949). Scholars viewing libraries as tools of social control include Michael Denning, *Mechanic Accents: Dime Novels and Working-Class Culture in America* (London: Verso, 1987), 48; Dee Garrison, *Apostles of Culture: The Public Librarian and American Society, 1876–1920* (1979; repr., Madison: University of Wisconsin Press, 2003); and Francis Couvares, *The Remaking of Pittsburgh: Class and Culture in an Industrializing City, 1877–1919* (Albany: State University of New York Press, 1984), 112. For a similar perspective on English libraries during the late nineteenth century, see Martin Hewitt, "Confronting the Modern City: The Manchester Free Library, 1850–1880," *Urban History* 27.1 (2000): 62–88.

8. Michel de Certeau, *The Practice of Everyday Life*, trans. Steven Rendall (1984; repr., Berkeley: University of California Press, 2011). See also Roger Chartier, "Culture as Appropriation: Popular Cultural Uses in Early Modern France," in *Understanding Popular Culture: Europe from the Middle Ages to the Nineteenth Century*, ed. Steven L. Kaplan (Berlin: Mouton, 1984), 229–53.

9. Stanley Fish, "Interpreting the Variorum," *Critical Inquiry* 3.1 (Autumn 1976): 191–96; Roger Chartier, *Forms and Meanings: Texts, Performances, and Audiences from Codex to Computer* (Philadelphia: University of Pennsylvania Press, 1995).

10. A valuable summary of these approaches is Janice Radway, "Beyond Mary Bailey and Old Maid Librarians: Reimagining Readers and Rethinking Reading," *Journal of Education in Library and Information Science* 35.4 (Fall 1994): 275–96.

11. See, for example, Jonathan Boyarin, ed., *The Ethnography of Reading* (Berkeley: University of California Press, 1993).

12. Robert Darnton, *The Forbidden Best Sellers of Pre-Revolutionary France* (New York: Norton, 1996), 181–97; on representations of readers, see Kate Flint, *The Woman Reader, 1837–1914* (Oxford: Clarendon Press, 1993).

13. Jonathan Rose, *The Intellectual Life of the British Working Classes* (New Haven: Yale University Press, 2003); H. J. Jackson, *Marginalia: Readers Writing in Books* (New Haven: Yale University Press, 2001); H. J. Jackson, *Romantic Readers: Evidence from Marginalia* (New Haven: Yale University Press, 2005).

14. David D. Hall, *Worlds of Wonder, Days of Judgment: Popular Religious Belief in Early New England* (Cambridge: Harvard University Press, 1989); Emily B. Todd, "Antebellum Libraries in Richmond and New Orleans and the Search for the Practices and Preferences of 'Real' Readers," in *Libraries as Agencies of Culture: Print Culture History in Modern America*, ed. Thomas Augst and Wayne A. Wiegand (Madison: University of Wisconsin Press, 2001), 195–209; Ronald Zboray, *A Fictive People: Antebellum Economic Development and the American Reading Public* (New York: Oxford University Press, 1993).

15. Radway, "Beyond Mary Bailey and Old Maid Librarians," 276.

16. For more on these developments, see Janice Radway and Carl F. Kaestle, "A Framework for the History of Publishing and Reading in the United States, 1880–1940," in Radway and Kaestle, *Print in Motion*, 7–21.

17. Todd, "Antebellum Libraries in Richmond and New Orleans," 204–6.

1. "Now We Are a City"

1. Robert S. Lynd and Helen Merrell Lynd, *Middletown: A Study in Modern American Culture* (1929; repr., New York: Harcourt, Brace, 1957), 12–14, 16–17.

2. "Muncie's Prosperity," *Muncie Daily News*, January 5, 1888.

3. Lynd and Lynd, *Middletown*, 14; *Muncie: Past, Present, Future, 1892* (Muncie: Muncie Land Co., 1892), 6.

4. *Muncie: Past, Present, Future*, n.p.; *Muncie, Indiana: The Natural Gas City of the West* (Muncie: Muncie Natural Gas Land Improvement Company, ca. 1889), 9; "That's Right, Brother Call," *Muncie Daily News*, December 18, 1891.

5. A thorough history of the city's early development (and that of the surrounding county) can be found in G. W. H Kemper, ed., *A Twentieth Century History of Delaware County, Indiana*, 2 vols. (Chicago: Lewis Publishing Company, 1908).

6. Quoted ibid., 1:86.

7. Ibid., 1:77–94, 277–87; Robert MacDougall, *The People's Telephone: The Political Economy of the Telephone in the Gilded Age* (Philadelphia: University of Pennsylvania Press, 2013), 26–56.

8. Kemper, *Twentieth Century History*, 1:108–9, 278–85; Robert MacDougall, "The Telephone on Main Street: Utility Regulation in the United States and Canada before

1900," *Business and Economic History Online* 4 (2006): 9–10, www.thebhc.org. A fourth daily, the *Muncie Morning Star,* would join the other three in 1899.

9. Dwight W. Hoover, "Roller-Skating toward Industrialism," in *Hard at Play: Leisure in America, 1840–1940,* ed. Kathryn Grover (Amherst: University of Massachusetts Press, 1992), 61–76; Kemper, *Twentieth Century History,* 1:148; see also *Report on the Manufactures of the United States at the Tenth Census* (Washington, D.C.: Government Printing Office, 1880), 225, for a breakdown of manufacturing in Delaware County in 1880, which documents the modest range of industry in and around Muncie at that time.

10. The physical description of Muncie was derived from *Muncie, Indiana, 1884,* bird's-eye map, BSUL; Hoover, "Roller-Skating toward Industrialism," 63; David E. Nye, *Electrifying America: Social Meanings of a New Technology, 1880–1940* (Cambridge: MIT Press, 1992), 4–5.

11. Andrew Yox, "Art and the American Community: Middletown, 1875–1950," unpublished manuscript, February 1988; Kemper, *Twentieth Century History,* 1:126.

12. Kemper, *Twentieth Century History,* 1:140–41; Ned S. Griner, *Gas Boom Society* (Muncie: Minnetrista Cultural Center, 1991), 11–12.

13. Thomas L. Ryan, diary entry, November 11, 1886, in Thomas L. Ryan diary, 1886 (MSS.087), BSUL, scans available at BSU-DMR; Griner, *Gas Boom Society* 13–14.

14. *Muncie, Indiana: The Natural Gas City of the West,* 18; Lynd and Lynd, *Middletown,* 14; "Natural Gas the Attraction," *New York Times,* February 12, 1889; *Muncie: Past, Present, Future,* n.p.

15. Frank C. Ball, *Memoirs of Frank C. Ball* (Muncie: Privately printed, 1937), 67–68, 76–78.

16. *Muncie, Indiana: The Natural Gas City of the West,* 21.

17. Quoted in John H. Mills, *Heat: Science and Philosophy of Its Production and Application,* 2 vols. (Boston: Press of American Printing and Engraving Co., 1890), 1:175.

18. *Muncie, Indiana: The Natural Gas City of the West,* 3.

19. Ibid., 6, 8, 10, 16, 5.

20. *Muncie of To-day: Its Commerce, Trade and Industries* (Muncie: Muncie Times, 1895), 5.

21. *The Story of the Magic City: A Souvenir of Muncie, Indiana* (Muncie: Central Indiana Gas Company, 1912), 34, 10–14, 24. On their choice of Muncie as the subject of their book the Lynds wrote, "In a difficult study of this sort it seemed a distinct advantage to deal with a homogeneous native-born population, even though such a population is unusual in an American industrial city." Lynd and Lynd, *Middletown,* 8.

22. *Census Reports, Volume VIII: Twelfth Census of the United States, Taken in the Year 1900. Manufactures, Part II: States and Territories* (Washington, D.C.: United States Census Office, 1902), 220–22.

23. *Muncie of To-day,* 6.

24. *Census Reports, Volume I: Twelfth Census of the United States, Taken in the Year 1900. Population, Part I* (Washington, D.C.: United States Census Office, 1901), 218, 616, 747–48.

25. Griner, *Gas Boom Society,* 16–17; he cites the diary of Thomas L. Ryan, April 21, 1887.

26. Griner, *Gas Boom Society,* 49; Nye, *Electrifying America,* 11; see also *Muncie of To-day* for a full portrait of the city at the height of the gas-boom era.

27. Griner, *Gas Boom Society,* 41–43, 45: Anthony O. Edmonds and E. Bruce Geelhoed, *Ball State University: An Interpretive History* (Bloomington: Indiana University Press, 2001), 50.

28. Griner, *Gas Boom Society,* 43–44. On the importance accorded churches, see, for example, *Muncie, Indiana: The Natural Gas City of the West,* 10.

29. Lynd and Lynd, *Middletown,* 340–41.

30. Griner, *Gas Boom Society,* 49, 52–66.

31. William G. Eidson, "Confusion, Controversy, and Quarantine: The Muncie Smallpox Epidemic of 1893," *Indiana Magazine of History* 86.4 (December 1990): 374–98. See also Kelly H. Jones, "Vaccination: Who Should Decide When Doctors Disagree? The Muncie Smallpox Epidemic of 1893" (master's thesis, Ball State University, 2008); Kemper, *Twentieth Century History,* 1:178.

32. Jones, "Vaccination," 35, 41–42, 60. On the vaccination issue, see Robert Johnston, *The Radical Middle Class: Populist Democracy and the Question of Capitalism in Progressive-Era Portland, Oregon* (Princeton: Princeton University Press, 2003), 179–90.

33. Untitled article, *Muncie Daily News,* February 10, 1892.

34. "A Street Scene in Muncie, Indiana," *Muncie Daily Herald,* July 30, 1898.

35. Yox, "Art and the American Community," 21; Ned H. Griner, *Side by Side with Coarser Plants: The Muncie Arts Movement, 1885–1985* (Muncie: Minnetrista Cultural Foundation, 1994), 13.

36. Griner, *Side by Side,* 7–26.

37. Advertisement, *Muncie Morning News,* September 11, 1892; "Wysor's Grand," *Muncie Morning News,* September 15, 1892.

38. Kemper, *Twentieth Century History,* 1:175–76; advertisements, *Muncie Star,* February 7, 1900, March 13, 1900, and April 18, 1900. We know from the records of the Muncie Public Library that both *The Sorrows of Satan* and *Little Lord Fauntleroy* were frequently borrowed books. Corelli's novel was taken out 342 times by 280 borrowers, making it the tenth most widely circulated title during the years covered by the extant records.

39. Griner, *Gas Boom Society,* 61.

40. Lynd and Lynd, *Middletown,* 76–78.

41. "Money for Homestead," *Muncie Morning News,* July 26, 1892; "The Homestead Strikers," *Muncie Morning News,* July 28, 1892; Lynd and Lynd, *Middletown,* 78–79; "The Homestead Strikers," *Muncie Star,* January 13, 1900.

42. Frederic Alexander Birmingham, *The Ball Corporation: The First Century* (Indianapolis: Curtis Publishing Company, 1980), 80.

2. "A Magnificent Array of Books"

1. The library's petty cash ledger records the expenditure of 25 cents on December 29, 1902, for "Expressage on Typewriter," suggesting a delay between ordering the typewriter and its arrival.

2. "Sales of Ink Are Decreasing," *Muncie Morning News,* September 8, 1895.

3. *American Printer and Lithographer* 31 (September 1900): 373.

4. Christine Pawley, in *Reading on the Middle Border: The Culture of Print in Late-Nineteenth-Century Osage, Iowa* (Amherst: University of Massachusetts Press, 2001), offers a similar perception of the Sage Library in Osage, where the town's elite "controlled the library's administration" (69).

5. The board originally conceived of the library as also housing a museum, and in the early days several cabinets were reserved for the display of geological specimens and Native American artifacts. These were gradually removed to make space for books.

6. Mary Alden Walker, *The Beginnings of Printing in Indiana* (Crawfordsville, Ind.: R. E. Banta, 1934), 19, 24.

7. Lewis C. Naylor, "A History of the Muncie Public Library," typescript, 1955, MPL.

8. Ibid., 1, 3.

9. Dawne Slater-Putt, *Beyond Books: Allen County's Public Library History, 1895–1995* (Fort Wayne, Ind.: Allen County Public Library, 1995), 2.

10. MPL minutes, April 6, 1875, 22.

11. Thomas B. Helm, *History of Delaware County, Indiana, with Illustrations and Biographical Sketches of Some of Its Prominent Men and Pioneers* (Chicago: Kingman Bros., 1881), 169–70.

12. Naylor, "History of the Muncie Public Library," 2.

13. Helm, *History of Delaware County,* 170.

14. A prohibition on chewing tobacco in the Indianapolis Public Library was omitted in Muncie, perhaps a tacit recognition that it would drive away adult men. That this was to become an issue is evident from a later resolution of the board, giving the librarian "authority to procure six cards prohibiting spitting upon the floor." MPL minutes, January 8, 1895, 192.

15. The earliest American library school was established by Melvil Dewey at Columbia University in 1886–87, several years after Patterson's appointment.

16. "Public Library Opening," *Muncie Weekly News,* June 3, 1875.

17. Helm, *History of Delaware County,* 170; "Public Library Opening."

18. MPL minutes, June 5, 1875, December 14, 1883, and January 5, 1885.

19. Michael Winship, "The Rise of a National Book Trade System in the United States," in *A History of the Book in America,* vol. 4: *Print in Motion: The Expansion of Publishing and Reading in the United States, 1880–1940,* ed. Carl F. Kaestle and Janice A. Radway (Chapel Hill: University of North Carolina Press, 2009), 62–64.

20. Advertisement, *Public Opinion* 24.19 (May 12, 1898): 605; advertisement, *Publishers' Weekly* 54.22 (November 26, 1898): 15; John Cotton Dana, *A Library Primer* (Chicago: Library Bureau, 1899), 65.

21. Present were the board's president, William Snyder (b. 1850), the secretary, Mary B. Smith (b. 1834), and members Mary Goddard (b. 1838), Elmira Kuechmann (b. 1839), and Charles F. W. Neely (b. 1859).

22. MPL minutes, September 2, 1890, 134; and March 31, 1891, 144.

23. "What a Child Should Read," *Muncie Morning Star,* July 1, 1901; "Pages from 9-A English Note Books," *The Munsonian,* Commencement Number, 1912, n.p., MPL.

24. Both Whitman and Wilde were known to the citizens of Muncie. The *Muncie Daily News* reported in 1891 that Whitman was so enfeebled by old age that he was unable to send a few lines of verse to John Greenleaf Whittier on the occasion of his eighty-fourth birthday ("Walt Whitman Growing Weaker," December 18, 1891) and, a few days later, that his death was imminent ("Walt Whitman Dying," December 22, 1891). An article in the same newspaper, "Writers and Writings" (January 13, 1892), makes reference to Oscar Wilde. On Wilde's year-long tour of America in 1882 and his notoriety, see Roy Morris Jr., *Declaring His Genius: Oscar Wilde in North America* (Cambridge: Belknap Press of Harvard University Press, 2012).

25. William F. Poole, "Novel Reading," *New York Times,* July 4, 1873.

26. MPL minutes, July 1, 1890, 130.

27. MPL minutes, October 14, 1890, 135. Dee Garrison cites a list of "sixteen questionable authors" whose fiction for adults was deemed "sensational or immoral" by a panel set

up by the American Library Association in 1882. Garrison, *Apostles of Culture: The Public Librarian and American Society, 1876–1920* (1979; repr., Madison: University of Wisconsin Press, 2003), 74–75. Except for William Harrison Ainsworth and G. W. M. Reynolds, all were present in the Muncie Public Library: Ann Sophia Stevens (13 books), Mrs. E.D.E.N. Southworth (28), Mary Jane Homes (19), Caroline Lee Hentz (14), Augusta Jane Evans Wilson (20), Jessie Fothergill (2), Rhoda Broughton (3), Florence Marryat (3), Helen Mathers (2), Mrs. Forrester (1), Mary Elizabeth Braddon (6), Mrs. Henry Wood (7), George Alfred Lawrence (3), Ouida (9). Some novels by these authors circulated extensively, but others remained unborrowed. There is no indication that any of their books were removed from circulation. As Garrison observes, "The effort to enforce conservative literary standards in the public library . . . was clearly symbolic and ritualistic in nature, rather than instrumentally coercive" (61). See also Frederick J. Stielow, "Censorship in the Early Professionalization of American Libraries, 1876–1929," *Journal of Library History* 18.1 (Winter 1983): 37–54.

28. Evelyn Geller remarks that the ALA removed *Tess of the D'Urbervilles* from its 1904 catalog of 5,000 recommended books for small popular libraries "after a trustee spoke against it in 1896." Geller, *Forbidden Books in American Public Libraries, 1876–1939: A Study in Cultural Change* (Westport, Conn.: Greenwood Press, 1984), 54–55.

29. Ibid., 51.

30. MPL minutes, November 6, 1874, 9.

31. Harriet Patterson, "To the President and Directors of the Muncie Public Library," bound in at the beginning of the MPL minutes.

32. MPL minutes, December 4, 1900, 253.

33. MPL minutes, August 23, 1894, 187.

34. MPL minutes, June 8, 1897, 211; December 1, 1897, 219; June 30, 1899, 234; and October 3, 1899, 238.

35. MPL minutes, October 27, 1891, 148–49.

36. Fred W. Boege, *Smollett's Reputation as a Novelist* (Princeton: Princeton University Press, 1947), 132.

37. "First Day of Reading Room," *Muncie Weekly News*, January 14, 1875.

38. Ibid.

39. Patterson, "To the President and Directors of the Muncie Public Library."

40. MPL minutes, March 5, 1875, 19.

41. "Muncie's Library," *Muncie Daily Times*, January 9, 1893.

42. City of Muncie, Council Records, March 18 and April 1, 1887, 79, 87, BSUL.

43. MPL minutes, October 27, 1891, 148; "Libraries: Brief Resume of Our Public Library," *Muncie Morning News*, May 12, 1893.

44. "Muncie's Public Library," *Muncie Daily Times*, March 25, 1896.

45. MPL minutes, November 6, 1874, 9.

46. MPL minutes, December 2, 1890, 138; June 28, 1892, 157; and July 5, 1892, 158; "Our Public Library," *Muncie Daily Times*, January 17, 1894.

47. The Lynds noted that, among other things, union locals provided libraries for their members. Robert Lynd and Helen Merrell Lynd, *Middletown: A Study in Modern American Culture* (1929; repr., New York: Harcourt, Brace, 1957), 76, 232.

48. J. B. Besack to Andrew Carnegie, January 22, 1900, and February 6, 1900, series II.A.1.a, reel 21, Carnegie Records; "Money for the Library Fund," *Muncie Star*, January 15, 1900; "Donations for Library," *Muncie Star*, February 4, 1900; "Tuttle Named Librarian," *Muncie Star*, February 24, 1900; "Open Today," *Muncie Star*, March 5, 1900; Lynd and

Lynd, *Middletown*, 232n15. Carnegie's donation was contingent on the organizers' first obtaining a sufficient level of support from the local community.

49. "To the Officers and Members of Organized Labor," undated flyer appended to Besack to Carnegie, December 25, 1899, series II.A.1.a, reel 21, Carnegie Records.

50. "Money for the Library Fund," *Muncie Star*, January 15, 1900; "Libraries," *Muncie Star*, February 20, 1900. On working-class sociability see Roy Rosenzweig, *Eight Hours for What We Will: Workers and Leisure in an Industrial City, 1870–1920* (New York: Cambridge University Press, 1983).

51. "Open Today," *Muncie Star*, March 5, 1900; "Reading Rooms Open to Public," *Muncie Star*, March 6, 1900; "A Day in Muncie," March 7, 1900; "Smoking Rooms Opened," *Muncie Star*, March 13, 1900.

52. "A Day in Muncie," *Muncie Star*, March 13, 1900.

53. Untitled flyer signed by the Muncie Trades Council Library Committee, December 1899, appended to Besack to Carnegie, December 25, 1899, series II.A.1.a, reel 21, Carnegie Records.

54. "The Public Library of Muncie," *Muncie Daily News*, April 5, 1880.

55. Ibid.

56. David Nye, *Electrifying America: Social Meanings of a New Technology, 1880–1940* (Cambridge: MIT Press, 1992), 4.

57. "A Liberal Bequest," *Muncie Daily Times*, June 4, 1895.

58. Kemper, *Twentieth Century History*, 1:183; *Public Libraries* 6.1 (January 1901): 12–13.

59. MPL minutes, December 4, 1900, 252; and February 21, 1901, 257.

60. See Theodore Jones, *Carnegie Libraries across America: A Public Legacy* (New York: Wiley, 1997); see also George S. Bobinski, *Carnegie Libraries: Their History and Impact on American Public Library Development* (Chicago: American Library Association, 1969); and Abigail A. Van Slyck, *Free to All: Carnegie Libraries and American Culture, 1890–1920* (Chicago: University of Chicago Press, 1996).

61. Quoted in Jones, *Carnegie Libraries across America*, 6, 4.

62. Quoted in Ann C. Sparanese, "Service to the Labor Community: A Public Library Perspective," *Library Trends* 51.1 (Summer 2002): 24.

63. Kemper, *Twentieth Century History*, 1:192.

64. "Labor Opposes Carnegie," *New York Times*, May 18, 1903.

65. MPL minutes, February 21, 1901, 257.

66. J. C. Johnson, James A. Daly, and Hardin Roads to Andrew Carnegie, February 27, 1901, and James Bertram to Hardin Roads, March 8, 1901, both in series II.A.1.a, reel 21, Carnegie Records.

67. Kemper, *Twentieth Century History*, 1:272–73.

68. John Rollin Marsh, "Record of the Proceedings of the General Committee having in charge the construction of the Free Public Library, known as the 'Carnegie Library,' in the City of Muncie, Indiana," 5–6, manuscript book, MPL.

69. Ibid., 6.

70. MPL minutes, October 1, 1901, 262.

71. MPL minutes, April 2, 1901, 258–59.

72. Van Slyck, *Free to All*, 150.

73. MPL minutes, April 9, 1901, 259.

74. All quotations in this and the following two paragraphs are from Mary Eileen Ahern, "A Visit to Indiana Libraries," *Public Libraries* 6 (1901): 297–99.

75. MPL minutes, May 28, 1901, 260.

76. Caroline Fleming, who succeeded Hattie Patterson, had a salary of $20 per month, paid quarterly, though in 1884 that was raised to $25, paid monthly. "The Library Board," *Muncie Daily News,* January 10, 1884. The board sought a salary of $40 per month for Wilson in 1893, but the Council refused. MPL minutes, August 8, 1893, 174. For some comparable figures of librarians' salaries, see Garrison, *Apostles of Culture,* 182, 226, 228.

77. Artena Chapin, *A Sketch of the Muncie Public Library* (Muncie: Privately printed, 1907), 21–22.

78. Ibid.

79. MPL minutes, September 2, 1902, 274; and September 26, 1902, 275.

80. MPL minutes, November 4, 1892, 277–78; *Catalogue of Books in the Muncie Public Library* (Muncie: Muncie Public Library, 1905), xxii.

81. MPL minutes, January 5, 1875, 18.

82. MPL minutes, January 8, 1895, 192; September 2, 1890, 133; February 13, 1895, 180; December 5, 1899, 241; and March 7, 1899, 230.

83. MPL minutes, July 5, 1894, 185; and October 17, 1894, 189.

84. MPL minutes, November 4, 1902, 277.

85. Chapin, *Sketch of the Muncie Public Library,* 33.

86. Ibid. The Lynds give a higher figure for fiction borrowing in 1903: 92 percent for adults and 90 percent for children. Lynd and Lynd, *Middletown,* 237.

87. Anthony Deahl, *A Twentieth Century History and Biographical Record of Elkhart County, Indiana* (Chicago: Lewis Publishing Company, 1905), 513.

88. *Important Laws of Indiana Relating to Public Libraries and the Public Library Commission,* rev. ed. (Indianapolis: The Public Library Commission of Indiana, 1913), 5–7. Dee Garrison, writing in 1979, noted that "the evidence is overwhelming that public library trustees have been almost exclusively male" (*Apostles of Culture,* 50). If that is the case, Indiana was bucking the trend.

89. MPL minutes, December 2, 1902, 280.

90. Lynd and Lynd, *Middletown,* 425n11.

3. Cosmopolitan Trends

1. Quotations and descriptions in this and the following two paragraphs are from "Forty-Five," in *The Stories of Fannie Hurst,* ed. Susan Koppelman (New York: The Feminist Press at CUNY, 2004), 200–227. The story was originally published in *Cosmopolitan,* December 1922. In Koppelman's edition Muncie is spelled "Munsie," though *Cosmopolitan* has "Muncie."

2. Lee Trepanier and Khalil M. Habib, introduction to *Cosmopolitanism in the Age of Globalization: Citizens without States,* ed. Trepanier and Habib (Lexington: University of Kentucky Press, 2011), 1, 5; Bruce Robbins, "Actually Existing Cosmopolitanism," in *Cosmopolitics: Thinking and Feeling beyond the Nation,* ed. Pheng Cheah and Bruce Robbins (Minneapolis: University of Minnesota Press, 1998), 2, 7. See also Tom F. Wright, introduction to *The Cosmopolitan Lyceum,* ed. Wright (Amherst: University of Massachusetts Press, 2013), 1–19.

3. Booth Tarkington, *The Gentleman from Indiana* (New York: Doubleday & McClure, 1900), 3.

4. H. L. Mencken, "A City in Moronia" (review of *Middletown: A Study in Modern American Culture*), *American Mercury,* March 1929, 379–80.

5. Hugh A. Cowing, *A Meandering Hoosier* (Muncie: Scott Printing Company, 1937), 22–24. The extracts given here represent but half of the poem.

6. G. W. H. Kemper, ed., *A Twentieth Century History of Delaware County, Indiana*, 2 vols. (Chicago: Lewis Publishing Company, 1908), 1:44–45.

7. Ibid., 1:50.

8. Margaret Jacob, *Strangers Nowhere in the World: The Rise of Cosmopolitanism in Early Modern Europe* (Philadelphia: University of Pennsylvania Press, 2006), 5.

9. John W. Miller, *Indiana Newspaper Bibliography* (Indianapolis: Indiana Historical Society, 1982), 88.

10. *Charles Emerson's Muncie Directory for 1886–7* (Muncie: The Muncie Weekly Times Steam Print, 1876), 32, 56, 71. Even books written by locals for local audiences were often printed elsewhere. Thomas Helm's *History of Delaware County* (1881) was published in Chicago. More than two decades later, well after the expansion of the gas-boom era, G. W. H. Kemper arranged with a Chicago firm, Lewis Publishing, to print and distribute his two-volume account of the county's history. Thomas B. Helm, *History of Delaware County, Indiana, with Illustrations and Biographical Sketches of Some of Its Prominent Men and Pioneers* (Chicago: Kingman Bros., 1881); Kemper, *Twentieth Century History of Delaware County*.

11. Helm, *History of Delaware County*, 189.

12. Kemper, *Twentieth Century History*, 1:280.

13. Michael Schudson, *Discovering the News: A Social History of American Newspapers* (New York: Basic Books, 1981); "A Pointer," *Muncie Morning News*, October 19, 1898.

14. Advertisements, *Muncie Daily News*, January 3, 1890, and November 21, 1891.

15. "A Polish Novelist," *Muncie Daily Herald*, January 7, 1898; "No Mercy for Zola," *Muncie Daily Herald*, February 24, 1898.

16. "Leader of the Decadents: Le Gallienne, Poet and Esthete, Will Lecture to Us," *Muncie Daily Herald*, February 15, 1898.

17. "Circulation Report," *Muncie Daily Times*, October 10, 1892; untitled article, *Muncie Morning News*, February 1, 1893; advertisement, *Muncie Morning News*, August 16, 1898; "Hands Up," *Muncie Morning News*, August 16, 1898.

18. See Michael Winship, "The Rise of a National Book Trade System," in *A History of the Book in America*, vol. 4: *Print in Motion: The Expansion of Publishing and Reading in the United States, 1880–1940*, ed. Carl F. Kaestle and Janice A. Radway (Chapel Hill: University of North Carolina Press, 2009), 56–77.

19. Another Muncie business that dealt in at least a limited way with printed materials was the Sun Drug Store, which was owned and run by the brothers Will S. and Marion Stewart. An 1885 billhead describes Stewart & Stewart at the Sun Drug Store as "Dealers in Drugs, Paints, Oil, Varnishes & General School Supplies." Marion Stewart, Plaintiff, Delaware County Court Records, Non-Payment of Debt 1886, Delaware County, Indiana Civil and Criminal Court Records, 1827–1959, MDC-DRL. It is not clear what printed materials the Sun Drug Store sold, although the library's records indicate small payments made to the store, possibly for magazines or newspapers. MPL minutes, November 7, 1899, 22.

20. B. N. Griffing, *An Atlas of Delaware County, Indiana* (Philadelphia: Griffing, Gordon, and Company, 1887), 31.

21. Kemper, *Twentieth Century History*, 2:710; 1880 U.S. census, s.v. "Charles M. Kimbrough," Muncie. All U.S. census records cited in this chapter were accessed through Ancestry.com; unless otherwise noted, the city or township location is Delaware County, Ind.

22. Kemper, *Twentieth Century History,* 2:711.

23. Griffing, *An Atlas of Delaware County,* 31.

24. 1870 and 1880 U.S. censuses, s.v. "George H. Andrews," Muncie.

25. MPL minutes, January 5 and December 14, 1883, 53 and 56. Kimbrough did not become a library patron until 1889, two years after he closed his shop and joined the Indiana Bridge Company.

26. Star Drug Store Inventory of Merchandise, vol. 1 (SC 143), BSUL, scans available at BSU-DMR.

27. The full title of this work, which went through many editions beginning in 1873, was *Word-Primer: A Beginner's Book in Oral and Written Spelling.*

28. The Reverend William Holmes McGuffey's *Readers* were highly moralistic in tone. It has been estimated that more than a hundred million copies were sold across America between 1830 and 1920.

29. "Shaws English Lit." was Thomas B. Shaw's recently published *New History of English Literature: With a History of English Literature in America* (1884).

30. Emerson Elbridge White became president of Purdue University in West Lafayette, Indiana, in 1876. His pedagogical manual *The Art of Teaching* was published in 1901.

31. The first of these was *Elements of Physiology and Hygiene* (1872) by Ryland Thomas Brown. His book was widely used in midwestern schools. The British-born Henry Kiddle was the author of *New Elementary Astronomy* (1868). The third book may have been J. J. Fahie's recently published *History of Electric Telegraphy* (1884). Asa Gray's *How Plants Grow* (1876) was a frequently reprinted botanical primer, and Le Roy C. Cooley's *Natural Philosophy for Common and High Schools* (1871) was a first book of physics.

32. The first of these may have been *A Textbook on Civil Government in the United States* (1875) by George H. Martin. The Chase & Stuart Classical Series included *Six Books of the Aeneid of Virgil,* edited with explanatory notes and a vocabulary by Thomas Chase (rev. ed., 1883). The edition of Caesar was probably *Caesar's Commentaries; with an Analytical and Linear Translation of the First Five Books, for the Use of Schools and Private Learners,* edited by James Hamilton, translation by Thomas Clark (1884).

33. The geology textbook's title is difficult to decipher. It may have been W. M. Linney's recently published *Report on the Geology of Clark and Montgomery Counties* (1884). The price of the book makes it unlikely that it was intended for use in schools.

34. Robert S. Lynd and Helen Merrell Lynd, *Middletown: A Study in Modern American Culture* (1929; repr., New York: Harcourt, Brace, 1957), 234. The Lynds do not specify a date, only that the ad was from the 1890s.

35. *A Portrait and Biographical Record of Delaware County, Indiana* (Chicago: A. W. Bowen, 1894), 438.

36. Advertisements, *Muncie Morning News,* December 13, 1893, *Muncie Daily News,* December 11, 1891, *Muncie Star,* December 8, 1901, and *Muncie Daily Herald,* December 12, 1902.

37. Advertisements, *Muncie Morning News,* December 11, 1892, and *Muncie Daily News,* December 15, 1895.

38. Hellmut Lehmann-Haupt, *The Book in America: A History of the Making and Selling of Books in the United States,* 2nd ed. (New York: R. R. Bowker, 1951), 215.

39. J. W. McIntyre to Mrs. H. L. Patterson, January 21, 187[7?], Hattie Patterson Correspondence, MPL, scans available at BSU-DMR.

40. Benjamin Franklin Stevens to Hattie Patterson, October 21, 1875, Hattie Patterson Correspondence.

41. Lynne Tatlock, *German Writing, American Reading: Women and the Import of Fiction, 1866–1917* (Columbus: Ohio State University Press, 2012); Lynne Tatlock, "Romance in the Province: Reading German Novels in Middletown, USA," in *Print Culture Histories beyond the Metropolis,* ed. James J. Connolly et al. (Toronto: University of Toronto Press, forthcoming).

42. The library's 1905 catalog places an asterisk alongside the *Century,* denoting that, under revised regulations, "the magazine cannot be taken from the library." *Catalogue of Books in the Muncie Public Library* (Muncie: Muncie Public Library, 1905), 175.

43. Benjamin Franklin Stevens to Hattie Patterson, May 8, 1875, and January 10, 1877, Hattie Patterson Correspondence.

44. The reply is addressed to "H. L. Patterson Librarian" and begins "Dear Sir." Letter, bill, and flyers from The Graphic Co. to Mrs. H. L. Patterson, December, 12, 1876, Hattie Patterson Correspondence.

45. By 1894, a year's home subscription to the daily edition of the *Indianapolis Sentinel* was being offered to Muncie readers at $6, half what it had cost the library in 1885. A twelve-page weekly edition of the same newspaper was available for home delivery for $1 a year. The *Sentinel* claimed to have "the largest circulation of any newspaper in the state." See advertisement, *Muncie Daily News,* April 19, 1894.

46. See Adam Ward Rome, "American Farmers as Entrepreneurs, 1870–1900," *Agricultural History* 56.1 (January 1982): 37n1.

47. MPL minutes, December 2, 1890.

48. MPL minutes, November 24, 1891.

49. Helen Damon-Moore and Carl F. Kaestle, in "Gender, Advertising, and Mass-Circulation Magazines," in Kaestle et al., *Literacy in the United States: Readers and Reading since 1880* (New Haven: Yale University Press, 1993), 263, give paid circulation records in 1900 of 846,000 for the *Ladies' Home Journal,* making it the American magazine most in demand at that time. Next in popularity was *Munsey's Magazine* (also subscribed to by the Muncie library), which had a paid circulation of 650,000. Of the top ten magazines listed by Kaestle for 1900, the only other one the library subscribed to was *McClure's Magazine,* which—in tenth place—achieved a paid circulation of 369,000.

50. Richard Ohmann observes that magazines "provided mass urban readership for Robert Louis Stevenson, Rudyard Kipling, Thomas Hardy, Mark Twain, William Dean Howells, Hamlin Garland, and others. . . . [The publisher] Henry Holt worried that monthly magazines would 'kill off' books, and indeed, growth in magazine readership in the 1890s far outpaced that of books, especially among the new monthlies." Ohmann, "Diverging Paths: Books and Magazines in the Transition to Corporate Capitalism," in *A History of the Book in America,* vol. 4: *Print in Motion: The Expansion of Publishing and Reading in the United States, 1880–1940,* ed. Carl F. Kaestle and Janice A. Radway (Chapel Hill: University of North Carolina Press, 2009), 108–9.

51. "Shortest of the Year," *Muncie Daily Times,* January 22, 1895.

52. *Catalogue of Books in the Muncie Public Library,* 192.

53. Lynd and Lynd, *Middletown,* 471.

54. James Raven, "Social Libraries and Library Societies in Eighteenth-Century North America," in *Institutions of Reading: The Social Life of Libraries in the United States,* ed. Thomas Augst and Kenneth Carpenter (Amherst: University of Massachusetts Press, 2007), 49; untitled editorial, *Muncie Daily News,* July 6, 1897.

55. "Muncie Public Library," *Muncie Daily Herald,* June 23, 1897.
56. "Libraries: Brief Resume of Our Public Library," *Muncie Morning News,* May 12, 1893. The author of the piece is almost certainly Nathaniel F. Ethell, the longtime editor and owner of the *Morning News.* As we've seen, Ethell was among the Muncie Public Library's early stockholders and, perhaps as a result of his spirited editorial defense of the library, was elected to its board on July 10, 1894, and later served as treasurer. MPL minutes, March 1, 1899.
57. "Libraries: Brief Resume of Our Public Library."
58. Kwame Anthony Appiah, *Cosmopolitanism: Ethics in a World of Strangers* (New York: Norton, 2006), xiii, xv.
59. John Hinks and Catherine Armstrong, eds., *Book Trade Connections from the Seventeenth to the Twentieth Centuries,* vii; Lynd and Lynd, *Middletown,* 237.

4. Borrowing Patterns

1. *Muncie of To-day: Its Commerce, Trade and Industries* (Muncie: The Muncie Times, 1895), 57, 37.
2. David E. Nye, *Electrifying America: Social Meanings of a New Technology, 1880–1940* (Cambridge: MIT Press, 1992), 16–17.
3. Fatalities of this sort in Muncie are recorded in the diary of Norene Hawk: on January 9, 1905, she wrote, "Last night about 10:45 Frank Parsons home blew up," and on February 7, 1899, she had registered another death in a similar gas explosion. Norene Hawk Diaries, MPL, scans available at BSU-DMR. The inherent danger is humorously captured by Mark Twain in an 1891 letter to the Hartford Gas Company, in which he complains of being moved "almost to the verge of irritation by your chuckle-headed Goddamned fashion of shutting your Goddamned gas off without giving any notice to your Goddamned parishioners. Several times you have come within an ace of smothering half of this household in their beds and blowing up the other half by this idiotic, not to say criminal, custom of yours." *The Portable Mark Twain,* ed. Bernard DeVoto (New York: Viking, 1946), 776.
4. Guglielmo Cavallo and Roger Chartier, eds., *A History of Reading in the West,* trans. Lydia G. Cochrane (Amherst: University of Massachusetts Press, 1999), 4.
5. Elizabeth Long, *Book Clubs: Women and the Uses of Reading in Everyday Life* (Chicago: University of Chicago Press, 2003). On Marsh, see the obituary transcribed on the page "Susan Ryan Marsh" on the Find a Grave website, www.findagrave.com. In our database her borrowing records are listed under Suzie Ryan, patron number 5463.
6. Joann Jameson, "Kuechmann, Kuchmann, Schroeder, Lock, Freudenstein, Martin," May 1, 2000, German-American-L Archives, http://archiver.rootsweb.ancestry.com.
7. Carl F. Kaestle and Janice Radway, "A Framework for the History of Publishing and Reading in the United States, 1880–1940," in *A History of the Book in America,* vol. 4: *Print in Motion: The Expansion of Publishing and Reading in the United States, 1880–1940,* ed. Kaestle and Radway (Chapel Hill: University of North Carolina Press, 2009), 7–21; Robert Darnton, *The Forbidden Best-Sellers of Pre-Revolutionary France* (New York: Norton, 1996), 183.
8. One of the key divides in the study of reading experiences arises between those who link texts to social groups and those who reject such an approach. Prominent among the former is Michael Denning, who ties dime novels to the American working class. The latter include, most notably, Roger Chartier, who insists that we cannot simply

label texts and other cultural artifacts as either elite or popular, since the patterns of their usage are complex. As noted, the borrowing patterns evident in the What Middletown Read database clearly have class dimensions, but as this and subsequent chapters show, there is also enough variety in patron choices to make it difficult to find any exclusive association between particular social groups and particular texts, authors, or genres. The city's middle class, and especially women from white-collar homes, read books that were not seen as having literary merit and were not classified as elite reading, a behavior that distinguished them from their blue-collar counterparts. Michael Denning, *Mechanic Accents: Dime Novels and Working-Class Culture in America* (London: Verso, 1987); Roger Chartier, "Culture as Appropriation: Popular Cultural Uses in Early Modern France," in *Understanding Popular Culture: Europe from the Middle Ages to the Nineteenth Century,* ed. Steven L. Kaplan (Berlin: Mouton, 1984), 229–54.

9. Wayne A. Wiegand, "To Reposition a Research Agenda: What American Studies Can Teach the LIS Community about the Library in the Life of the User," *Library Quarterly* 73.4 (October 2003): 369–82; and Wiegand, *Main Street Public Library: Community Places and Reading Spaces in the Rural Heartland, 1876–1956* (Iowa City: University of Iowa Press, 2011), 134. See also note 7 in the introduction to this book.

10. On the degree to which public libraries limited rather than facilitated access to printed material and the disputes among library professionals on that question, see Dee Garrison, *Apostles of Culture: The Public Librarian and American Society, 1876–1920* (1979; repr., Madison: University of Wisconsin Press, 2003), 67–87; and Evelyn Geller, *Forbidden Books in American Public Libraries, 1876–1939: A Study in Cultural Change* (Westport, Conn.: Greenwood Press, 1984), 17–51.

11. Malcolm B. Jones, "Translations of Zola in the United States prior to 1900," *Modern Language Notes* 55.7 (November 1940): 520–24.

12. Gary Scharnhorst with Jack Bales, *The Lost Life of Horatio Alger, Jr.* (Bloomington: Indiana University Press, 1985), 118. See also Dee Garrison, "Cultural Custodians of the Gilded Age: The Public Librarian and Horatio Alger," *Journal of Library History* 6.4 (October 1971): 327–36.

13. *Catalog of "A.L.A." Library: 5000 Volumes for a Popular Library* (Washington, D.C.: Government Printing Office, 1893), v, vii. For comparable libraries see Wiegand, *Main Street Public Library,* 133–72.

14. On efforts to discourage the reading of books by these authors, see Denning, *Mechanic Accents;* Geller, *Forbidden Books,* 29–40; Garrison, *Apostles of Culture,* 67–87; and Garrison, "Cultural Custodians of the Gilded Age."

15. The Muncie library conforms to the looser approach of libraries in the West and Midwest noted by Garrison, *Apostles of Culture,* 93.

16. *Census Reports, Volume VIII: Twelfth Census of the United States, Taken in the Year 1900. Manufactures, Part II: States and Territories* (Washington, D.C.: United States Census Office, 1902): 205, 220–21; *Census Reports, Volume I: Twelfth Census of the United States, Taken in the Year 1900. Population, Part I* (Washington, D.C.: United States Census Office, 1901), 616, 977. On the reliability of federal census data for claims of literacy, see Carl F. Kaestle, "Studying the History of Literacy," in Kaestle et al., *Literacy in the United States: Readers and Reading since 1880* (New Haven: Yale University Press, 1993), 23–24.

17. Given their limits and uncertainties, such classifications can serve only as a loose proxy for the more complex phenomenon of socioeconomic class. See the appendix

to this volume for further discussion of occupational categories. For comparable results, see Christine Pawley, *Reading on the Middle Border: The Culture of Print in Late-Nineteenth-Century Osage, Iowa* (Amherst: University of Massachusetts Press, 2001), 69–77. On the difficulty of distinguishing skilled workers from clerical workers and the petite bourgeoisie in this era, see Robert D. Johnston, *The Radical Middle Class: Populist Democracy and the Question of Capitalism in Progressive Era Portland, Oregon* (Princeton: Princeton University Press, 2003), 3–17.

18. Christine Pawley found that two-thirds of library users in Osage, Iowa, during the years 1890–1895 were female. Pawley, *Reading on the Middle Border,* 69.

19. These findings match the conclusions drawn in David Paul Nord, "Working-Class Readers: Family, Community, and Reading in Nineteenth Century America," *Communications Research* 18.2 (April 1986): 156–81. See also Herbert Putnam's report of similar patterns of library use among the working class in Geller, *Forbidden Books,* 49.

20. Counts of reference queries were compiled by library staff in "Books Issued Each Month with Table of Classes" (1875–1903), MPL, scans available at BSU-DMR.

21. Pawley, *Reading on the Middle Border,* 91–105; Wayne A. Wiegand, "The American Public Library: Construction of a Community Reading Institution," in Kaestle and Radway, *Print in Motion,* 431–51.

22. Data on reading levels were compiled by Stephen Pentecost as part of his Reading What Middletown Read project. See "Reading Levels," in "Presentation at Ball State," http://talus.artsci.wustl.edu. For a description of Pentecost's project, see the epilogue to this book.

23. The same shipment included a new copy of Augusta Evans's *St. Elmo* (discussed later in this chapter), a romance that rarely passed muster with those setting reading standards but consistently met with popular enthusiasm, along with a number of similarly themed books. Kate Wilson was clearly attuned to the desires of her library patrons.

24. Denning, *Mechanic Accents,* 27–46.

25. On the changing character of magazines see Frank Luther Mott, *A History of American Magazines,* vol. 4. (Cambridge: Harvard University Press, 1957). Magazine circulation numbers are likely undercounted because it was not possible for us to assign an accession number to every single-issue loan of a magazine; for an explanation see the appendix.

26. Ruth K. MacDonald, "Louisa May Alcott," in *American Writers for Children before 1900,* ed. Glenn E. Estes, vol. 42 of *Dictionary of Literary Biography* (Detroit: Gale Research, 1985).

27. Bradley A. Johnson, "Augusta Jane Evans Wilson," in *American Women Prose Writers, 1820–1870,* ed. Amy E. Hudock and Katharine Rodier, vol. 239 of *Dictionary of Literary Biography* (Detroit: Gale Group, 2001). See also Bradley Johnson, "Dueling Sentiments: Responses to Patriarchal Violence in Augusta Jane Evans' *St. Elmo,*" *Southern Literary Journal* 33.2 (2001): 14.

28. On the trends working against serialization during the late nineteenth century, see Lindsy Lawrence, "Seriality and Domesticity: The Victorian Serial and Domestic Ideology in the Family Literary Magazine" (PhD diss., Texas Christian University, 2008), 246–89. See Richard Ohmann, "Diverging Paths: Books and Magazines in the Transition to Corporate Capitalism," in Kaestle and Radway, *Print in Motion,* esp. 108–9, for the claim that serial fiction fueled the popularity of these and other writers.

29. Minutes, May 29, 1899, box 2, folder 4, Woman's Club of Muncie records and photographs (MSS 008), BSUL.

30. For more on typical and atypical readers, see Stephen Pentecost, "(A)typical Readers," in "Ball State Presentation," http://talus.artsci.wustl.edu, part of the Reading What Middletown Read project.

31. See Lawrence Levine, *Highbrow/Lowbrow: The Emergence of Cultural Hierarchy in America* (Cambridge: Harvard University Press, 1990), 11–82. On the reading of Shakespeare in Muncie during the 1890s, see Tara Olivero, "Shakespeare in Middletown, 1890–1899" (honors thesis, Ball State University, 2014).

32. For circulation details, see "Books Issued Each Month with Table of Classes."

33. A desire for these books was evident in the formation of the Workingmen's Library discussed in chapter 2. Its collection included a variety of titles devoted to labor, economics, and social reform that were not held by the Muncie Public Library. The Workingmen's Library also subscribed to several trade journals and union papers. "New Books for Workingmen's Library," *Muncie Star*, March 24, 1900.

34. Books by the social Darwinist Herbert Spencer, which offered a more conservative take on contemporary social issues, circulated 97 times.

35. Finley's works, including the Elsie Dinsmore series, also displayed a sharp hostility to Catholics. See Pam Hardman, "The Steward of Her Soul: *Elsie Dinsmore* and the Training of a Victorian Child," *American Studies* 29.2 (Fall 1988): 69–90; M. Sarah Smedman, "Martha Finley," in *American Writers for Children before 1900*, ed. Glenn E. Estes (Detroit: Gale Research, 1985); E. Kate Stewart, "E. P. Roe," in *Nineteenth-Century American Fiction Writers*, ed. Kent P. Ljungquist, vol. 202 of *Dictionary of Literary Biography* (Detroit: Gale Research, 1999); Scharnhorst, *Lost Life of Horatio Alger*.

36. Another Tourgée book that deals with racial issues, *Bricks without Straw*, was in the library's collection, but its circulation history is lost because of a duplicate accession number. For an example of the racism in Horatio Alger's books, see his novel *The Young Adventurer; or, Tom's Trip across the Plains* (Philadelphia: The John C. Winston Co., 1876), 126.

37. Daniel T. Rodgers, *The Work Ethic in Industrial America, 1850–1920* (Chicago: University of Chicago Press, 1979), 136; Scharnhorst, *Lost Life of Horatio Alger*, 127, 129.

38. See Stephen Pentecost's discussion of Thomas Bailey Aldrich's *Story of a Bad Boy*, which circulated 167 times. The popularity of this tongue-in-cheek story suggests that tales for boys were often read with a critical eye. Stephen Pentecost, "Topic Modeling," in "Presentation at Ball State," http://talus.artsci.wustl.edu.

39. Mavis Reimer, "Elizabeth Thomasina Meade," in *British Children's Writers, 1880–1914*, ed. L. M. Zaidman, vol. 141 of *Dictionary of Literary Biography* (Detroit: Gale Research, 1994).

40. See Johnson, "Augusta Jane Evans Wilson."

41. G. W. H. Kemper, "My Childhood and Youth in the Early Days of Indiana," *Indiana Magazine of History* 19.4 (December 1923): 309.

5. "Bread Sweet as Honey"

1. MPL minutes, January 5, 1885, 77.

2. Thomas B. Helm, *History of Delaware County, Indiana, with Illustrations and Biographical Sketches of Some of Its Prominent Men and Pioneers* (Chicago: Kingman Bros., 1881), 56.

3. G. W. H. Kemper, ed., *A Twentieth Century History of Delaware County, Indiana*, 2 vols. (Chicago: Lewis Publishing Company, 1908), 1:238.

4. Ibid., 1:245. See also Ernest J. Black, "History of Delaware County Schools," in *Twenty-Eighth Biennial Report of the State Superintendent of Public Instruction* (Fort Wayne, Ind.: Fort Wayne Printing Company, 1917), 270–74.

5. Richard Gause Boone, *A History of Education in Indiana* (New York: D. Appleton, 1892), 336. Boone was principal of Eastern State Normal College (now Eastern Michigan University) from 1893 to 1899.

6. Untitled article, *Muncie Morning News*, April 3, 1895; "Muncie Public Library," *Muncie Daily Herald*, June 23, 1897.

7. Kemper, *Twentieth Century History*, 1:237.

8. 1900 U.S. census, s.v. "Charley Streeter," Muncie. All U.S. census records cited in this chapter were accessed through Ancestry.com; unless otherwise noted, the city or township location is Delaware County, Ind. In Muncie, African American children were allowed into the predominantly white public school system. Muncie High School's first African American graduate was Adora L. Knight, in 1879; she was not enrolled as a patron of the Muncie Public Library. During a period of rapid population growth in the city, the black community of Muncie numbered 187 in 1880, 418 (3.7 percent of the total population) in 1890, and 739 in 1900. Luke Eric Lassiter et al., eds., *The Other Side of Middletown: Exploring Muncie's African American Community* (Walnut Creek, Calif.: Altamira, 2004), 53–54, 134–35. See also the National Assessment of Adult Literacy, on the website of the National Center for Education Statistics, http://nces.ed.gov; and Lawrence C. Stedman and Carl F. Kaestle, "Literacy and Reading Performance in the United States," in Kaestle et al., *Literacy in the United States: Readers and Reading since 1880* (New Haven: Yale University Press, 1991), 125.

9. Horatio Alger, *Ragged Dick and Struggling Upward*, ed. Carl Bode (New York: Penguin, 1985), 28.

10. Bode, introduction, ibid., xvii.

11. Of the twelve books for which there are no borrowing records, nine came from Marsh's Library and had probably been discarded by 1891 when the extant transaction records begin. Another book, *Bound to Rise; or, Harry Walton's Motto*, was acquired on May 27, 1875, from the Muncie druggist G. H. Andrews, who supplied the library with many of its books. It too may have been discarded before 1891. A copy of *Andy Grant's Pluck* was bought by the library on January 9, 1903, too late for the surviving borrowing records; it is listed as present in the 1905 printed catalog. For reasons unknown, only the library's sole copy of *The Errand Boy; or, How Phil Brent Won Success* (1888 edition), purchased by the board for $1.25 on July 9, 1900, failed to attract a single reader.

12. Daniel T. Rodgers, *The Work Ethic in Industrial America, 1850–1920* (Chicago: University of Chicago Press, 1979), 127–43.

13. The practice of purchasing new copies of worn-out books, if it was less expensive than having them rebound, was a change in policy initiated around the turn of the century. For example, at one of its meetings the board approved the purchase of a "list of books on which the copyright had expired, which could be purchased at less than the cost of repairs." MPL minutes, February 6, 1900, 245. For several years the library's book repairs were done by Robert P. Campbell, a Muncie-based binder.

14. The borrowing statistics for the library's first copy of *Ragged Dick* (accession no. 568) show a similar pattern, though on a much smaller scale. See chapter 4 for further discussion of the social character of Alger's readership.

15. Quoted in Joseph Rosenblum, "Young Adult Literature," in *The Continuum Encyclopedia of American Literature,* ed. Steven R. Serafin (New York: Continuum International Publishing Group, 2003), 1276.

16. Ibid., 1276.

17. On the vogue for tomboy heroines, see Christian McEwen's introduction to her anthology *Jo's Girls: Tomboy Tales of High Adventure, True Grit, and Real Life* (Boston: Beacon Press, 1997). McEwen writes that in most girls' books of this subgenre, the age of the tomboy is "a perpetual twelve" (xviii) and that "not one includes a tomboy who remains untamed into adulthood" (xvi). Her discussion gives little consideration to the tomboy propensities of the reader, but according to Sarah Wadsworth, "tomboyism, followed by its forced abandonment in the middle to late teens, was far more widespread among American girls in the nineteenth century than convention has led us to suppose." Wadsworth, *In the Company of Books: Literature and Its "Classes" in Nineteenth-Century America* (Amherst: University of Massachusetts Press, 2006), 61.

18. Martha Farquharson [Martha Finley], *Elsie Dinsmore* (New York: Dodd, Mead, 1867), 37.

19. Louisa May Alcott, *Eight Cousins; or, The Aunt-Hill* (Boston: Roberts Brothers, 1876), 198 (chap. 27).

20. Wadsworth, *In the Company of Books,* 66 and n44.

21. Clara Vostrovsky, "A Study of Children's Reading Tastes," *Pedagogical Seminary* 6.4 (December 1899): 533–34. If we are seeking an individual work that appealed to juvenile readers and balances the genders in terms of its readership, Harriet Beecher Stowe's *Uncle Tom's Cabin* best fulfills these criteria. Of the seventy-five identifiable borrowers of the library's copy, forty-one were born after 1880 and thirty-four before. Thirty-five were male, and forty were female. Thirteen males and twenty-one females can be identified as white-collar; among blue-collar readers, there were twenty-two males and sixteen females.

22. 1900 U.S. census, s.v. "Charles Moore," Muncie.

23. 1910 U.S. census, s.v. "George Peterson," Muncie.

24. 1910 and 1920 U.S. censuses, s.v. "George Peterson," Muncie; Beech Grove Cemetery Records, s.v. "George Peterson," MDC-DRL.

25. In Muncie, children could first enroll as patrons at the age of ten (and were sometimes allowed to join sooner), but according to Dee Garrison, twelve was the more common age adopted by public libraries across the nation. Garrison, *Apostles of Culture: The Public Librarian and American Society, 1876–1920* (1979; repr., Madison: University of Wisconsin Press, 2003), 207.

26. Jonathan Rose, *The Intellectual Life of the British Working Classes* (New Haven: Yale University Press, 2001), 371.

27. G. Stanley Hall, "Psychology of Childhood as Related to Reading and the Public Library," *Pedagogical Seminary* 15 (1908): 109.

28. The book was Ernst Remin's novel *Die Versaillerin,* borrowed by Foorman in November 1899, when she was twelve.

29. See, for example, *Muncie Illustrated* (Muncie: Commercial Publishing Co., 1897), 4.

30. Kemper, *Twentieth Century History,* 1:264–66, gives the later school population of Muncie as 1,419 in 1887, 2,219 in 1892, 3,635 in 1904, and 4,370 in 1906.

31. Laurie Moses Hines, "Community and Control in the Development of the Extracurriculum: Muncie Central High School, 1890–1930," in *Hoosier Schools Past and Present,* ed. William J. Reese (Bloomington: Indiana University Press, 1998), 101.

32. Robert S. Lynd and Helen Merrell Lynd, *Middletown: A Study in Modern American Culture* (1929; repr., New York: Harcourt, Brace, 1957), 181–82.

33. Advertisement in *Zetetic: The Junior Annual of the Muncie High School* (Muncie, 1894), n.p., MPL.

34. Advertisement in *Muncie of To-day: Its Commerce, Trade and Industries* (Muncie: The Muncie Times, 1895), 56.

35. Ibid., 7.

36. *Muncie, Indiana: The Natural Gas City of the West* (Muncie: Muncie Natural Gas Land Improvement Company, ca. 1899), 10.

37. "Course of Study": "Science," *Zetetic*, n.p. According to the *Muncie Daily News*, the *Zetetic* was compiled and edited by juniors who were to graduate as the Muncie High School class of 1895. The article reports the organization, under the direction of the school's English teacher, of a reading circle by what it extols as "Muncie's noblest class." "R. S. S. S. S. —Senior Class of the High School Organizes a Reading Circle," *Muncie Daily News*, September 18, 1894.

38. Diploma awarded to William Van Horne Cassady, class of 1899 (OVA.007), BSUL. He was one of thirty students to graduate that year.

39. "English," *Muncie Junior and Senior High School Annual*, 1916, n.p., MPL; "English," *XYZ Annual*, "Published by the Kappa Alpha Phi Fraternity in the Interest of Muncie High School," June 1902, n.p., MPL.

40. Boys outnumbered girls in 1868 (4–2) and 1886 (12–4); the classes with no male graduates were those of 1868 (6 girls) and 1876 (7 girls).

41. By way of comparison, the "Senior Statistics" listed in the school's student magazine for the 71 members of the class of 1913 (65 of whom graduated) include fathers' occupations: fifteen mechanics, five farmers, ten manufacturers or factory foremen, six traveling salesmen, five merchants, five contractors, four clerks, three lawyers, two in real estate, two in insurance, and one each as doctor, dentist, mail clerk, baker, railroad office, cigarmaker, tailor, barber, laborer, policeman, and horticulturist. Three were retired. *The Munsonian*, Commencement Number, 1912, n.p., MPL.

42. J. A. Son [pseudonym], "Sophomore Class Prophecy," *Zetetic*, n.p.

43. The Eva Aldstadt Mann Muncie High School book (1896–97), in the Thomas P. and Eva Mann Papers, 1896–1975 (MSS 46), box 1, folder 1, BSUL (scans available at BSU-DMR), contains a receipt (inserted at p. 91), dated February, 1, 1897, for $2.00, to cover monthly tuition in the high school. The same note lists the monthly cost of schooling in grades 1 through 4 as $1.00, and in grades 5 through 8 as $1.50. These charges may have been waived for children of poor families.

44. "Books Issued Each Month with Table of Classes" (1875–1903), MPL, scans available at BSU-DMR.

45. According to a report in the *Muncie Morning News*, in their senior year members of the class of 1896 formed a reading circle under the supervision of their English teacher, Emma Cammack. The first book they chose was *A Midsummer Night's Dream*, for which Cammack had "already written to Chicago to secure the required books." It is a reasonable assumption that books ordered for such purposes would remain the property of the school. "School Notes," *Muncie Morning News*, September 15, 1895.

46. The full tally of graduating seniors for previous years is recorded in the *Muncie High School Annual* for 1921.

47. *XYZ Annual*, June 1902, n.p.

48. Ibid.
49. Hines, "Community and Control," 100; *The Munsonian*, Commencement Number, 1912, n.p.
50. Lynd and Lynd, *Middletown*, 182–83.
51. *Muncie Junior and Senior High School Annual*, 1917, n.p.
52. Lynd and Lynd, *Middletown*, 187.
53. 1900 and 1910 U.S. censuses, s.v. "Edward Noland," Muncie.
54. Artena Chapin, *A Sketch of the Muncie Public Library* (Muncie: Privately printed, 1907), 30.
55. Joanne E. Passet, *Cultural Crusaders: Women Librarians in the American West, 1900–1917* (Albuquerque: University of New Mexico Press, 1994).
56. Chapin, *Sketch of the Muncie Public Library*, 32.
57. Ibid., 31, 33, 24. On the librarian's role in the supervision of children's reading, see Garrison, *Apostles of Culture*, 180.
58. Chapin, *Sketch of the Muncie Public Library*, 28.
59. *Library Occurent* 1 (Indianapolis, 1906–1908), 11; Chapin, *Sketch of the Muncie Public Library*, 28. The school's catalog was probably a card catalog. As far as we are aware, it has not survived.
60. All of these figures are culled from the 1905 *Catalogue of Books in the Muncie Public Library*, xii–xiii. Chapin, however, gives a figure of 19,291 as the number of books in the new library, so there is some unresolved inconsistency here. *A Sketch of the Muncie Public Library*, 22.
61. *Catalogue of Books in the Muncie Public Library*, xxii.
62. Chapin, *Sketch of the Muncie Public Library*, 23, 27–28.
63. Class dicta, *The Munsonian*, Commencement Number, 1912, n.p. The student was Ruth Sellers (Baker).

6. Reading and Reform

1. Unidentified clipping, January 28, 1895, in "Minutes, Feb. 1892–Jan. 1896," box 2, folders 2–5, Woman's Club of Muncie records and photographs (MSS 008), BSUL (hereafter cited as WCM).
2. Karen J. Blair, *The Clubwoman as Feminist: True Womanhood Redefined, 1896–1914* (New York: Holmes and Meier, 1980); Maureen A. Flanagan, *Seeing with Their Hearts: Chicago Women and the Vision of the Good City, 1871–1933* (Princeton: Princeton University Press, 2002); Daphne Spain, *How Women Saved the City* (Minneapolis: University of Minnesota Press, 2001); Robyn Muncy, *Creating a Female Dominion in American Reform, 1890–1935* (New York: Oxford University Press, 1991); Paula Baker, "The Domestication of Politics: Women and American Political Society, 1780–1920," *American Historical Review* 89.3 (June 1984): 620–47.
3. Blair, *Clubwoman as Feminist*, 57–72; Anne Ruggles Gere, *Intimate Practices: Literacy and Cultural Work in U.S. Women's Clubs, 1880–1920* (Champaign: University of Illinois Press, 1997). See also Barbara Sicherman, *Well-Read Lives: How Books Inspired a Generation of American Women* (Chapel Hill: University of North Carolina Press, 2010).
4. Gere, *Intimate Practices*; Elizabeth Long, "Aflame with Culture: Reading and Social Mission in the Nineteenth-Century White Women's Literary Club Movement," in *A History of the Book in America*, vol. 4: *Print in Motion: The Expansion of Publishing and Reading in the United States, 1880–1940*, ed. Carl F. Kaestle and Janice A. Radway

(Chapel Hill: University of North Carolina Press, 2009), 476–90; Sicherman, *Well-Read Lives.*

5. One could argue that the Woman's Club of Muncie formed an "interpretive community" because it conditioned its members to read fiction in a certain way, at least when they were reading texts tied to club-based activity. See Stanley Fish, "Interpreting the 'Variorum,'" *Critical Inquiry* 2.3 (Spring 1976): 465–85.

6. Jane Croly Cunningham, *The History of the Woman's Club Movement in America,* vol. 1 (New York: Henry G. Allen, 1898), 443.

7. "Constitution By-Laws of the Woman's Club of Muncie, Ind.," 1886, box 2, folder 2, WCM.

8. Members' names were gathered from an unidentified newspaper clipping, WCM minutes, January 28, 1895.

9. WCM minutes, April 3, 1899.

10. WCM minutes, June 12, 1899. Fannie Cohn was clearly Jewish; see "Obituary: Henry Cohn," *Wisconsin Jewish Chronicle,* August 11, 1933.

11. Croly, *History of the Woman's Club Movement,* 442–46.

12. Ibid., 94, 104.

13. WCM minutes, June 10, 1901.

14. WCM minutes, March 22, 1897.

15. WCM minutes, January 11, 1897.

16. WCM minutes, October 7 and November 28, 1898, May 6, 1899, March 4, 1901, and March 17, 1902.

17. Sixth District Woman's Suffrage Association" and "Evening Session," *Muncie Daily Times,* November 29, 1887; WCM minutes, November 14, 1887.

18. WCM minutes, June 4, 1888, October 22, 1894, and January 9, 1899.

19. Mrs. Rose Budd-Stewart, "I. U. of L. C.: Work of Constituent Clubs," undated clipping, WCM minutes, June 15, 1896.

20. Morton White, *Social Thought in America: The Revolt against Formalism* (New York: Viking, 1949).

21. WCM minutes, October 3, 1897, and January 8, 1900.

22. WCM minutes, October 19, 1896, October 17, 1898, and November 12, 1900.

23. WCM minutes, July 26, 1897, and April 4, 1898.

24. WCM minutes, April 3, 1899; Margaret McFadden, "Women and War, Women and Peace," *NWSA Journal* 15.2 (Summer 2003): ix–x.

25. WCM minutes, June 27, 1898; David C. MacWilliams, "The Novelistic Melodramas of Hall Caine: Seventy Years On," *English Literature in Transition, 1880–1920* 45.4 (Fall 2002): 426.

26. WCM minutes, October 30, 1899, 173.

27. WCM minutes, May 13, 1901.

28. Ibid.; Susan H. Lindley, "Women and the Social Gospel Novel," *Church History* 54.1 (March 1985): 56–73.

29. The library did not own a copy of *Tom Jones,* perhaps because of its lubricious reputation. Twenty-three patrons borrowed the library's copy of *Bleak House* a total of 28 times.

30. WCM minutes May 29, 1899, 279–81.

31. McRae Club program, 1898–1899 (December 8, 1898), box 2, folder 11, McRae Club Records, 1894–1990 (MSS 111), BSUL; unidentified clipping, WCM minutes, May 30, 1899.

32. Gisela Argyle, "Mrs. Humphry Ward's Fictional Experiments in the Woman Question," *Studies in English Literature, 1500–1900* 43.4 (Autumn 2003): 946–48.

33. On the effort to distinguish professional literary criticism from the interpretive practices of women's clubs, see Gere, *Intimate Practices,* 208–47.

34. WCM minutes, January 27, 1896.

35. WCM minutes, April 14, 1902.

36. WCM minutes, January 27, 1902.

37. Of all of the Woman's Club members who patronized the library, only one, Mabel Hagadorn (discussed later in this chapter), borrowed in a pattern that can be considered highly typical of the group of library users who fell within the same sex and age range. See Stephen Pentecost, "(A)typical Borrowers," in "Presentation at Ball State," http://talus.artsci.wustl.edu, part of the Reading What Middletown Read project.

38. "History of the Mary Martha Club," unidentified clipping, box 1, folder 8, Mary Martha Club records (MSS 005), BSUL; WCM minutes, December 19, 1892.

39. Blair, *Clubwoman as Feminist,* 15.

40. J. C. Croly, *Thrown on Her Own Resources; or, What Girls Can Do* (New York: Thomas Y. Crowell, 1891), 24, 5–6, 7, 24–25, 46.

41. Ibid., 78–81.

42. Ibid., 151.

43. Ibid., 7, 143–44.

44. The table does not include periodical titles, which were borrowed heavily as well, particularly the *Century Illustrated Monthly Magazine, Harper's New Monthly Magazine, Lippincott's Monthly Magazine,* and *Scribner's,* as well as two children's periodicals, *St. Nicholas* and *Harper's Young People.* The total number of loans for each of these magazines is quite large. For instance, the *Century* circulated 205 times among Woman's Club members, but that figure includes many different volumes and individual issues.

45. One club member, Kate Wilson, is not included in the data reported in the table because she was the librarian during this period and, as we have seen, she allowed a very large number of patrons to borrow using her account. Among those loans identifiably hers, no obvious pattern appears.

46. Janice Milner Lasseter, "Rebecca (Blaine) Harding Davis," in *American Women Prose Writers, 1820–1870,* ed. Amy E. Hudock and Katharine Rodier (Detroit: Gale Group, 2001), vol. 239 of *Dictionary of Literary Biography;* William Morton Payne, "Recent Fiction: 'Jerome, a Poor Man,' " *The Dial* 24.279 (February 1, 1898): 79–80, repr. in *Twentieth-Century Literary Criticism,* ed. Dennis Poupard, vol. 9 (Detroit: Gale Research, 1983).

47. "Regionalism and Local Color in Nineteenth-Century Literature," in *Nineteenth-Century Literature Criticism,* vol. 188, ed. Russell Whitaker and Kathy D. Darrow (Detroit: Gale, 2008).

48. Meri-Jane Rochelson, *A Jew in the Public Arena: The Career of Israel Zangwill* (Detroit: Wayne State University Press, 2008), 92–102. See also Lilian Falk, "*The Master:* Reclaiming Zangwill's Only *Künstlerroman,*" *English Literature in Transition, 1880–1920* 44.3 (2001): 275–96, repr. in *Twentieth-Century Literary Criticism,* ed. Linda Pavlovski, vol. 150 (Detroit: Gale, 2004).

49. Francis Marion Crawford, *The Novel: What It Is* (New York: Macmillan, 1893), 8–9, 43.

50. Ibid., 44–46; John Pilkington Jr., "F(rancis) Marion Crawford," in *American Literary*

Critics and Scholars, 1880–1900, ed. John Wilbert Rathbun and Monica M. Grecu (Detroit: Gale Research, 1988), vol. 71 of *Dictionary of Literary Biography.*

51. Robert S. Lynd and Helen Merrell Lynd, *Middletown: A Study in Modern American Culture* (1929; repr., New York: Harcourt, Brace, 1957), 296.

7. Schoolboys and Social Butterflies

1. For biographical details on McRae see *History of Grant County, Indiana: From the Earliest Time to the Present,* 2 vols. (Chicago: Brant & Fuller, 1886), 2:660–62. On Bartlett see Frank D. Haimbaugh, *History of Delaware County, Indiana,* 2 vols. (Indianapolis: Historical Publishing Company, 1924), 2:681–83.

2. Robert S. Lynd and Helen Merrell Lynd, *Middletown: A Study in Modern American Culture* (1929; repr., New York: Harcourt, Brace, 1957), 37.

3. 1910 U.S. census, s.v. "Willard A. Bartlett," Center Township; 1920 U.S. census, s.v. "Wilfred [*sic*] A. Bartlett," Muncie; 1930 U.S. census, s.v. "Willard A. Bartett [*sic*]," Muncie. All U.S. census records cited in this chapter were accessed through Ancestry. com; unless otherwise noted, the city or township location is Delaware County, Ind.

4. 1900 U.S. census, s.v. "Grant Frazier," Center Township.

5. 1910 U.S. census, s.v. "Jasper Poor," New Castle, Henry County, Ind.; "Jap Poor," Baseball-Reference.com: Minor Leagues, www.baseball-reference.com. On Poor's career see "Signed by Toledo," *Weekly Argus News* (Crawfordsville, Ind.), October 14, 1899.

6. See Clevenger's College Football Hall of Fame biography, www.footballfoundation.org. The Wikipedia article on Clevenger provides a useful overview of his entire career.

7. 1900 U.S. census, s.v. "Louis E. Bloom," Center Township; 1920 U.S. census, s.v. "Louis L. Bloom," Hot Springs, Garland County, Ark.

8. The quotation is taken from the author's preface to an early reprint of the work.

9. For more on Louis Bloom, see John Plotz, "This Book Is 119 Years Overdue: The Wondrous Database That Reveals What Americans Checked Out of the Library a Century Ago," *Slate,* November 17, 2011, www.slate.com.

10. The library owned forty-six volumes by Henty, and several of his titles, like *By Pike and Dyke,* were represented by more than one copy.

11. 1920 U.S. census, s.v. "Landess Bloom," Muncie. His first name is sometimes spelled incorrectly as "Landis" in public records and newspaper reports. His sister, Ella May, was married to John L. Miller. Their mother, Jennie, now 70, also lived with them.

12. 1900 U.S. census, s.v. "Rudolph Bloom," Muncie.

13. In the 1900 census, their surname is recorded as "Saxton."

14. Nellie M. Stouder, Nettie Wood, and John Rollin Marsh, "Brief History of the Muncie Public Library. Jan. 1 1904," in *Catalogue of Books in the Muncie Public Library,* xiii.

15. Ann C. Sparanese, "Service to the Labor Community: A Public Library Perspective," *Library Trends* 51.1 (Summer 2002): 23; Dee Garrison, *Apostles of Culture: The Public Librarian and American Society, 1876–1920* (1979; repr., Madison: University of Wisconsin Press, 2003), xiv.

16. 1880 U.S. census, s.vv. "Frederick Burmaster" and "Augusta Burmaster," Spencer, Owen County, Ind.; 1900 U.S. census, s.v. "Huston W. Burmaster," Center Township.

17. The baker was Aug. M. Maick, who (according to the U.S. census) had emigrated from Germany in 1876; 1900 U.S. census, s.v. "Aug M. Maick," Center Township. He was likely Rosa's uncle or cousin, since her mother's maiden name was Maick.

18. See Lynne Tatlock, *German Writing, American Reading: Women and the Import of Fiction, 1866–1917* (Columbus: Ohio State University Press, 2012).

19. Although not an exact contrast, Alger's *Phil, the Fiddler* and *Ragged Dick* were two of the first eight books borrowed by ten-year-old Huston Burmaster after he joined the library in 1899. It is always possible that Rosa borrowed these and similar items prior to the surviving circulation records.

20. "Miss Rosa Burmaster, Teacher Here for Fifty Years, Dies," unidentified clipping, MDC-DRL.

21. G. W. H. Kemper, ed., *A Twentieth Century History of Delaware County, Indiana*, 2 vols. (Chicago: Lewis Publishing Company, 1908), 1:485.

22. Ibid.

23. Sarah E. Igo, *The Averaged American: Surveys, Citizens, and the Making of a Mass Public* (Cambridge: Harvard University Press, 2007), 43, 50.

24. Thomas Carlyle, *On Heroes, Hero-Worship, and the Heroic in History* (1841), ed. Michael K. Goldberg, J. Joel Brattin, and Mark Engel (Berkeley: University of California Press, 1993), 140.

25. Oscar Wilde, *The Importance of Being Earnest and Other Plays*, ed. Peter Raby (Oxford: Oxford World's Classics, 1995), 282, 273 (Act 2). It should be noted that, during his tour of the United States, Wilde delivered a lecture in Indianapolis on February 22, 1882. According to an Indiana historian, "The town had been briefed beforehand on his carefully cultivated getup of long hair and smallclothes [knee-length breeches], word of which had preceded him. A British critic had remarked that Wilde, in his aesthetic costume, 'resembled nothing so much as a great, homely girl.' The audience agreed and decided to be amused." William George Sullivan, *English's Opera House: A Paper Read before the Indianapolis Literary Club, March 5, 1951* (Indianapolis: Indiana Historical Society, 1960), 365.

26. Thomas L. Ryan diaries, 4 vols. BSUL holds a photocopy of the first volume (MSS.087), covering 1886; the whereabouts of the original are unknown. The remaining three volumes, covering 1888–1890, are held by the MPL. Entry dates in this section refer to these diaries. Scans are available at BSU-DMR.

27. John W. Ryan, *A Life's Story: A Story of the Life and Character of Lida A. Ryan, 1841–1893* (Muncie: Privately printed, 1902), 45, scans available in the Middletown Women's History Collection, BSU-DMR.

28. Ned H. Griner, *Gas Boom Society* (Muncie: Minnetrista Cultural Foundation, Inc., 1991).

29. Kemper, *Twentieth Century History*, 1:268. Kemper states that only one stockholder, David H. Case, subscribed for five shares, but the minutes of the library board for May 30, 1874, 3–4, show that at least eight other citizens did the same.

30. Lynd and Lynd, *Middletown*, 233.

31. According the Lynds, "in 1890 fourteen graduated, one for every 810 persons" in the city, and "the high school enrollment was only 8 per cent. of the total school enrollment." Lynd and Lynd, *Middletown*, 183.

32. The item had not reached him by May 1, when he "sent a postcard to Conn. asking why they did not send my book." In his "Expense Account" at the end of the 1886 diary, he lists its cost as twelve cents.

33. "Burdock's Goat," in George M. Baker, *The Prize Speaker* (Boston: Lee and Shepard, 1880), Part 1, 70.

34. Lynd and Lynd, *Middletown*, 202.

35. The book may have been Angus Sinclair's *Locomotive Engine Running and Management: A Treatise on Locomotive Engines* (1888).

36. The book was probably either Philip Phillips's *The Forth Bridge in Its Various Stages of Construction* (1890) or Wilhelm Westhofen's *The Forth Bridge* (1890).

37. Jacob Piatt Dunn, *Indiana and Indianans: A History of Aboriginal and Territorial Indiana and the Century of Statehood,* 5 vols. (Chicago: American Historical Society, 1919), 5:2125.

38. T. H. Blair, *The Amateur Guide to Photography,* rev. ed. (Boston: The Blair Camera Co., 1888), iii.

39. Emily Kimbrough, *How Dear to My Heart* (New York: Dodd, Mead, 1944), 112.

40. Lynd and Lynd, *Middletown,* 483.

41. E. Dan Rottenberg, *Middletown Jews* (Bloomington: Indiana University Press, 1997), xviii–xix.

42. 1910 U.S. census, s.v. "Thomas L. Ryan," Muncie.

43. *Emerson's Delaware County Route Directory 1907–1908* (Muncie, 1907), 6.

44. *XYZ Annual,* "Published by the Kappa Alpha Phi Fraternity in the Interest of Muncie High School," June 1902, n.p., MPL.

45. Sarah A. Heinsohn Diary, photocopy (SC 444), BSUL; the whereabouts of the original are unknown. Entry dates in this section refer to this diary.

46. "Memoirs of Sarah Heinsohn Hartley," unpaginated manuscript (SC 147), BSUL.

47. Supplement, *The Oddfellow's Talisman and Literary Journal* (Indianapolis) 15.8 (August 1882): ii.

48. *A Portrait and Biographical Record of Delaware and Randolph Counties, Ind.* (Chicago: A. W. Bowen, 1894), 305.

49. "Memoirs of Sarah Heinsohn Hartley."

50. Ibid. For a contemporary account of Mme. Fredin's Eden Park School and details of its curriculum, see *History of Cincinnati and Hamilton County, Ohio: Their Past and Present,* 2 vols. (Cincinnati: S. B. Nelson, 1894), 1:134–35.

51. "Memoirs of Sarah Heinsohn Hartley."

52. A New York edition of Hugo's *Les Misérables* entered the library in 1876, a second copy was donated in 1878, and three more copies were purchased between 1889 and 1902. These were borrowed a total of 139 times during the period for which we have records. In August 1897 the library acquired Hugo's *Quatrevingt-treize* in French, which was borrowed 57 times, including at least once by a graduating senior from the Muncie High School. A copy of Dumas's *The Count of Monte Cristo,* purchased by the library in 1892, was borrowed a total of 101 times, and was supplemented by a second copy in 1902. Verne's *Underground City; or, The Child of the Cavern,* bought by the library in September 1889, was borrowed 108 times. That surpassed *A Tour of the World in Eighty Days,* checked out 43 times, and *A Journey to the Center of the Earth,* 56 times. In Muncie, Verne was the most popular French author writing for children and young adults during the 1890s. German classical authors such as Goethe, Schiller, and Heine, though represented in the library, were rarely borrowed, though a translation of *Faust* was taken out 29 times. As we noted in chapter 3, by far the most widely read nineteenth-century German author was E. Marlitt (Eugenie John), followed by Wilhelmine von Hillern, Adolf Streckfuss, Berthhold Auerbach, Ossip Schubin (Aloisia Kirschner), E. Werner, and Moritz von Reichenbach (Valeska Bethusy-Huc). The vogue for such authors in the Midwest may have owed much to the German origin or ancestry of many readers, Sarah Heinsohn included.

53. This was not the home that provided the model for the novel's seven-gabled house, which is thought to be one owned by Hawthorne's cousin, Susanna Ingersoll, in Salem, Massachusetts.

54. "Memoirs of Sarah Heinsohn Hartley."

55. On Hartley, see Kemper, *Twentieth Century History*, 2:626–29.

56. "Memoirs of Sarah Heinsohn Hartley."

57. Belatedly, the library's petty cash ledger book records a payment, "By cash on st[oc]k Julius Heinsohn," of $2 on March 2, 1876 (p. 10). This appears to represent the purchase of stock in his wife's name. 1875–1876 Muncie Public Library accounting ledger, MPL, scans available at BSU-DMR.

58. 1900 U.S. census, s.v. "Royal Tyler," Center Township.

59. Norene Hawk Diaries, MPL, scans available at BSU-DMR. Dates supplied in this section refer to these diaries.

60. 1900 U.S. census, s.v. "George Hawk," Center Township.

61. MPL minutes, February 4 and March 3, 1896, 201–2. The specific book that Winton Hawk donated, an edition of John Milton's "L'Allegro," "Il Penseroso," and "Lycidas," is unrecorded in the minutes, but can be traced through the accessions ledger. Milton was studied in the senior year at Muncie High School.

62. *Biennial Report of Fred A. Sims, Secretary of State of the State of Indiana* (Indianapolis: Wm. B. Burford, 1906), 154.

63. [William Eidson], "First Baptist Church Muncie: History," http://fbcmuncie.org.

64. Christine Pawley, *Reading on the Middle Border: The Culture of Print in Late Nineteenth Century Osage, Iowa* (Amherst: University of Massachusetts Press, 2001), 128.

65. Kemper, *Twentieth Century History*, 1:277.

66. The 1898–99 diary is in notebook 1, and the 1905 diary is in notebooks 2 and 3. All three notebooks were unknown until they were donated anonymously to the Muncie Public Library in 2009.

67. 1910 U.S. census, s.v. "Warren C. Emerson," Muncie.

68. According to David E. Nye, "Local citizens organized the Muncie Bell Telephone Exchange, securing a franchise from the city in February 1880 and starting operations the next month with forty subscribers." Nye, *Electrifying America: Social Meanings of a New Technology, 1880–1940* (Cambridge: MIT Press, 1990), 2. By the 1890s, although owning a telephone had become far more commonplace, it seems that the novelty had not worn off.

69. The library was given a copy of Stevenson's *Dr. Jekyll and Mr. Hyde* (which had made its first appearance in 1886) in 1897. It was borrowed sporadically, about twenty times in the following five years.

70. The Lynds remark that "playing cards on Sunday was tabooed by many people [during the 1920s], though less so than in 1890." According to Emily Kimbrough, even children's games such as hide-and-seek and hopscotch were proscribed on Sunday by Presbyterian families in Muncie during the early years of the twentieth century. Lynd and Lynd, *Middletown*, 281n12; Kimbrough, *How Dear to My Heart* (New York: Dodd, Mead, 1944), 173.

71. 1900 and 1910 U.S. censuses, s.v. "William F. Maggs," Center Township.

72. The inside front cover also has the initials "C.B." printed in large bold lettering. These are presumably the initials of Robert Maggs's close friend and frequently mentioned playmate, Clarence Baldwin, the son of a local grocer, who may have given him the memorandum book as a gift.

73. The extant records show a total of eighty-five patrons with a Riverside address, all but two of them joining the library after 1890. That number does not include families like the Maggses, who first registered when living in Muncie but then moved to Riverside.

74. Lynd and Lynd, *Middletown,* 339–43.

75. Ibid., 236.

76. Shane A. Hawkins, "Sound to Silence: An Investigation into the Possible Decline of Oral Reading into Silent Reading during the Nineteenth and Twentieth Centuries" (master's thesis, Ball State University, 1996), provides an excellent overview of the subject.

77. MPL minutes, April 2, 1901, 259.

78. Obituary notice for Robert Maggs, MDC-DRL.

79. Pawley, *Reading on the Middle Border,* 207–9.

80. Thomas Neely Diaries, 1867–1901 (MSS 105), and Frederick A. Putnam Diaries, 1846–1900 (MSS 2), BSUL, scans available at BSU-DMR.

Epilogue

1. "Reading: Harvard Views of Readers, Readership, and Reading History," http://ocp.hul.harvard.edu/reading/index.html; Robert Darnton, "First Steps towards a History of Reading" (1986), in *The Kiss of Lamourette: Reflections in Cultural History* (New York: Norton, 1990), 155.

2. Darnton, "First Steps towards a History of Reading," 155, 171.

3. Ibid., 158, 162.

4. Ibid., 165, 181.

5. Teresa Gerrard, "New Methods in the History of Reading: 'Answers to Correspondents' in *The Family Herald,* 1860–1900," *Publishing History* 43 (1998): 53–69.

6. Rosalind Crone, Katie Halsey, Mary Hammond, and Shafquat Towheed, "The Reading Experience Database 1450–1945 (RED)," in *The History of Reading: A Reader,* ed. Towheed, Crone, and Halsey (London: Routledge, 2011), 429.

7. Ibid. The quoted section was written by Mary Hammond.

8. The following are two examples of what can be gleaned. Searching RED (www.open.ac.uk/Arts/reading/UK) for *Huckleberry Finn,* we find that Twain's novel was one of a select group of nineteenth-century American novels that created in the mind of Mary Lakeman, the young daughter of a Cornish fisherman, "a romantic childhood vision of unlimited freedom and open space," and, many years later, caused the writer V. S. Pritchett to laugh. More promisingly, a search for *Vanity Fair* reveals (among other quotations) that for Charlotte Brontë the experience of the novel led her to claim that Thackeray "stands alone—alone in his sagacity, alone in his truth, alone in his feeling . . . , alone in his power, alone in his simplicity, alone in his self-control," whereas for her contemporary Harriet Martineau, *Vanity Fair* had shrunk in her mind to a work that "I cannot now read." By contrast, a few years later and across the world, another mid-nineteenth-century reader, J. B. Castieau, an Australian prison governor, had no compunction about rereading the novel, which he "found . . . even more enjoyable than when I read it for the first time," adding, "I really think I like the Book better even than any of those of Dickens." In the early twentieth century, RED records that *Vanity Fair* was one of two books—the other was *Les Misérables*—that first "taught . . . human sympathy" to F. W. Jowett, a Labour Party M.P. from the West Yorkshire

city of Bradford. The What Middletown Read database can give us no parallel information of the reactions of the 136 recorded patrons who borrowed *Huckleberry Finn* or the 80 who took out *Vanity Fair.*

9. For details on fields and counts in the database, see "Data Fields and Record Counts," on the Data Summaries page, www.bsu.edu/libraries/wmr/reports.php.

10. A list of the one hundred most active patrons is available on the Data Summaries page.

11. "Market Basket Analysis," in "Presentation at Ball State," http://talus.artsci.wustl.edu.

12. Robert S. Lynd and Helen Merrell Lynd, *Middletown: A Study in Modern American Culture* (1929; repr., New York: Harcourt, Brace, 1957), 23–24.

13. Quotations in this and the following paragraph are from T. F. Rose, President, and Nellie M. Stouder, Secretary, of the Board of the Muncie Public Library to Andrew Carnegie, February 14, 1907, series II.A.8.c., reel 86, Carnegie Records.

14. Unsigned letter to T. F. Rose, February 25, 1907, ibid.

15. Lynd and Lynd, *Middletown,* 237 and 526 (Table XVII). The Lynds' statement that the 1903 circulation figures were the earliest available confirms that they were unaware of the existence of records from the old Muncie Public Library, which were probably by then stashed away in the attics of the Carnegie building. For the period covered by the records in our database, fiction accounted for only 76 percent of adult and 81 percent of children's loans.

16. Ibid., 95, 99, 102.

17. Robert S. Lynd and Helen Merrell Lynd, *Middletown in Transition: A Study in Cultural Conflicts* (1937; repr., New York: Harcourt, Brace, 1965), 252–57, 570; Richard R. Lingeman, "Middletown Now," *New York Times Book Review,* February 26, 1967, 1, 22, 24, 26.

18. Lynd and Lynd, *Middletown,* vi, 230.

Appendix

1. The 1900 census is the closest available, since the 1890 manuscript was destroyed in a fire and the usual local copies were not retained that year. In a handful of cases we were able to derive some information from the 1880 census when the 1900 listing could not be found. Such instances are noted in the database in the notes field included with each record.

2. It should be noted that the register of borrowers continued to be employed until June 13, 1904, when Walter Lewis, whose patron number was 8826, was registered. But since the extant circulation records end on December 3, 1902, we included in the database only those patrons who joined the library before December 31, 1902. This means that the thirty-six patrons (numbers 6311–6347) who joined the library in the four weeks following December 3, 1902, have no transactions listed in the database. Please note as well that although the record of patron numbers indicates that there were 6,347 borrowers registered during the period from 1875 through 1902, the database includes only 6,328 because a handful of entries were illegible.

3. Alba M. Edwards, "A Social-Economic Grouping of the Gainful Workers of the United States," *Journal of the American Statistical Association* 28.184 (December 1933): 377–87. See also Alba M. Edwards, "Social-Economic Groups of the United States," *Publications of the American Statistical Associations* 15.118 (June 1917): 643–61.

Index